Fodor's

NEW ORLEANS

D0182136

Welcome to New Orleans

New Orleans is a vibrant melting pot of a city that famously inspires indulgence. This is the place to eat, drink, listen to jazz, take part in a parade, and immerse yourself in the atmosphere. Whether you come for Mardi Gras or the New Orleans Jazz and Heritage Festival, a visit to this unique destination is never the same trip twice, but always memorable. This book was produced in the middle of the COVID-19 pandemic. As you plan your upcoming travels to New Orleans, please confirm that places are still open and let us know when we need to make updates by writing to us at editors@fodors.com.

TOP REASONS TO GO

★ **Food:** Seafood, cutting-edge cuisine, and Creole and Cajun specialties.

★ **Music:** You'll hear brass bands and funk rhythms in the street and in the clubs.

★ **History:** Frenchmen, Spaniards, Africans, and others forged the city's culture.

★ **French Quarter:** Elegant streets have everything from antiques to Bourbon Street raunch.

★ **Garden District:** A stroll here takes in centuries-old oaks and historic mansions.

★ **The Vibe:** More northern Caribbean than Southern U.S., NOLA lives like no other city.

Contents

Fodor's Features

MAPS

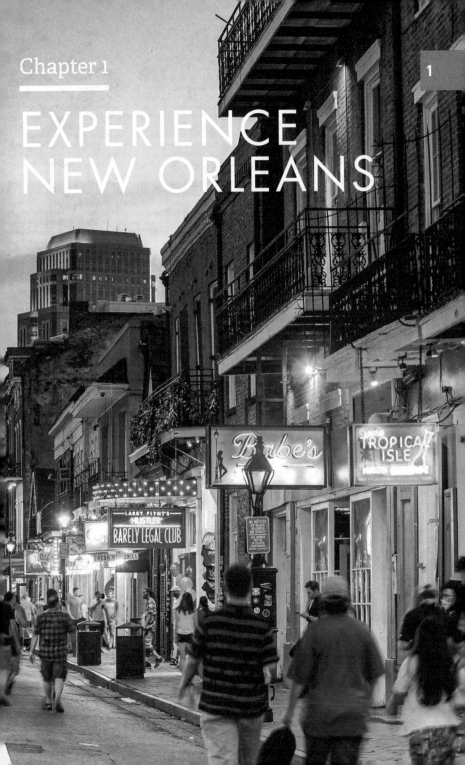

Chapter 1

EXPERIENCE
NEW ORLEANS

20 ULTIMATE EXPERIENCES

New Orleans offers terrific experiences that should be on every traveler's list. Here are Fodor's top picks for a memorable trip.

1 | Magazine Street

Spend an afternoon on a leisurely walk down this busy Garden District street, featuring the city's best collection of vintage, art, clothing, and furniture stores. *(Ch. 8)*

2 City Park

This 1,300-acre park boasts the most live oaks in the world, natural bayous, manmade lakes, gorgeous greenways, and walking paths. *(Ch. 10)*

3 Beignets at Café du Monde

Many begin a trip to New Orleans with a plate of these square donuts, best enjoyed piping hot, covered in powdered sugar, and alongside a café au lait. *(Ch. 3)*

4 Bourbon Street

The French Quarter's famed party street is equal parts grime and charm, and an essential experience for a first visit to New Orleans. *(Ch. 3)*

5 Cemetery Tours

The city's above-ground cemeteries are home to famed old city dwellers and provide a spooky setting for an afternoon stroll. *(Ch. 6, 9)*

6 Architecture in the Garden District

Nineteenth-century mansions among the mossy live oaks of St. Charles Avenue show unique architectural splendor. *(Ch. 8)*

7 Art Galleries in the Warehouse District

From the renowned Ogden Museum of Southern Art to the galleries on Julia Street, this small neighborhood is packed with contemporary and historic collections of the best art in the city. *(Ch. 7)*

8 Live Music on Frenchmen Street

Nowhere else in the city can you capture such a concentrated amount of local music and nightlife revelry as within these four blocks in the Marigny. *(Ch. 4)*

9 The St. Charles Streetcar

The oldest, most picturesque streetcar in town glides from the river bend past Audubon Park and through Uptown and the Garden District. *(Ch. 8)*

10 Nightlife in the Bywater

Some of the city's best music clubs and performance venues are on unassuming streets a few miles from the French Quarter. *(Ch. 5)*

11 Audubon Park and Zoo

Among the 100-year live oaks in this pleasant Uptown park are acres of wild animals to discover, from the exotic to the exotically local. *(Ch. 9)*

12 Jackson Square and St. Louis Cathedral

The plaza surrounding the oldest cathedral in the United States is home to lively street entertainers, palm readers, and talented local artists. *(Ch. 3)*

13 Mardi Gras

Endless parades, neighborhood parties, dazzling beads, and colorful costumes make this spring event the party of the year. *(Ch. 3)*

14 World War II Museum

The nation's official World War II museum isn't just for history buffs: expansive and diverse, this multimedia collection offers a little something for everyone. *(Ch. 7)*

15 Ghost Tours

You don't have to be a believer in ghost stories to have fun walking through the city's spookiest spots with a guide. *(Ch. 2)*

16 Occult Shops

From voodoo temples to tarot card readings, New Orleans is the perfect place to dabble in the occult. *(Ch. 3, 4, 5)*

17 French Market

A buzzing French Quarter landmark, this historical market is a great first stop for a taste of New Orleans music, culture, and choice culinary offerings. *(Ch. 3)*

18 New Orleans Cuisine

From po'boys to crawfish, decadence in the form of culinary delights is key to New Orleans culture. *(Ch. 3–10)*

19 New Orleans Jazz Festival

For two weekends every spring, this longtime popular music and culture festival draws thousands to the city's fairgrounds to see local performers and big national acts. *(Ch. 10)*

20 Swamp Tours

The wild wetlands of Louisiana are a piece of nature unique to this part of the world, with enchanting plants and wildlife. *(Ch. 11)*

{"page": 16}

WHAT'S WHERE

1 The French Quarter. The geographic and cultural heart of the city since the early 1700s, the Quarter is a vibrant commercial and residential hodge-podge of wrought-iron balconies, inviting courtyards, and, of course, rowdy Bourbon Street bars.

2 Faubourg Marigny. The Faubourg Marigny is home to restored Creole cottages and famous Frenchmen Street, lined with music clubs, restaurants, and bars.

3 The Bywater, St. Claude, and the Lower Ninth Ward. The rapidly gentrifying Bywater has a burgeoning arts scene, while St. Claude Avenue has some of the city's best live music spots. Just east, you'll find the Lower Ninth Ward, one of the neighborhoods hit hardest by Hurricane Katrina.

4 Tremé/Lafitte and the Seventh Ward. The cradle of jazz and second-line parades, Tremé remains a historical hub of African American and Creole traditions in the city.

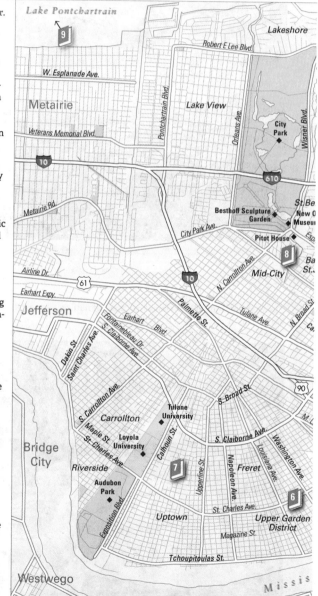

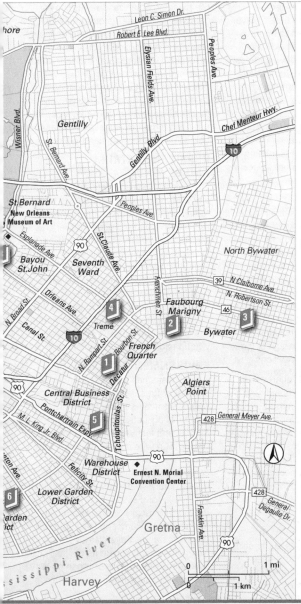

5 **The CBD and the Warehouse District.** The city's trendy urban area is undergoing a building boom; most of the newer hotels are clustered here. There also are museums, art galleries, fine restaurants, and a casino.

6 **The Garden District.** Stunning early-19th-century mansions make this a great neighborhood for walking, followed by an afternoon browsing the shops and cafés along ever-evolving Magazine Street.

7 **Uptown and Carrollton-Riverbend.** Audubon Park and the campuses of Tulane and Loyola universities anchor oak-shaded Uptown; hop on the St. Charles Avenue streetcar to survey it in period style.

8 **Mid-City and Bayou St. John.** City Park is Mid-City's playground and encompasses the New Orleans Museum of Art and the adjacent Besthoff Sculpture Garden. A stroll along Bayou St. John is a good way to see this residential neighborhood.

9 **Side Trips.** If you have time, head to Plantation Country to learn more about the South's complicated history or explore Cajun Country and its musical towns.

New Orleans Today

POLITICS

In 2017, Democrat LaToya Cantrell became the city's first black female mayor. The new leadership under Mayor Cantrell faces expectations to improve the local school system, remedy the housing crisis, keep crime low, and best prepare the city for future storms. Politics aside, New Orleans's strength has always been in the passion its residents have for the city, and local nonprofits and grassroots organizations like the Youth Empowerment Project, Green Light New Orleans, and the Tipitina's Foundation are just a few of the bright leaders in locally based change for the future.

NEW OPENINGS

It's said that history reveals itself in New Orleans through both elegance and decay. And along those lines, the city's most famous museum is using sophisticated technology to knock the dust off its retelling of the Second World War. An ambitious $370 million expansion that will eventually quadruple the museum's size is almost complete at the National WWII Museum, and now includes an on-site hotel and parking garage alongside the new exhibits and pavilions.

But the biggest recent travel news out of the Crescent City is the brand-new terminal at MSY, the city's airport, which opened in fall 2019 after a long and expensive renovation. It is modern and sleek in design, with outposts of favorite New Orleans restaurants like Angelo Brocato's and Café du Monde, frequent live jazz performances, and local shops like Dirty Coast and Fluerty Girl.

TRADITION

Red beans and rice on Monday, St. Joseph's altars, jazz funerals, a Christmas visit to Mr. Bingle in City Park—New Orleans is a destination steeped in tradition, with its unique customs carefully guarded for more than a century. Take Mardi Gras, for example: Some of the parading organizations, known as "krewes," have been around for more than 150 years, building elaborate floats annually and parading through the streets in masks. The Mardi Gras Indian tradition is shrouded in secrecy and ritual, with "tribes" of mostly African American revelers spending months constructing fanciful, Native American–influenced costumes in tribute to actual tribes that once helped escaped slaves find freedom.

HURRICANE KATRINA AND BEYOND

2020 marks 15 years since Katrina hit the city, and the areas where tourists tend to wander—downtown, the riverfront, the French Quarter, Faubourg Marigny, the Warehouse District, and the Garden District/Uptown—all show little outward sign of floodwater devastation. But predominantly residential areas like parts of east New Orleans and the Lower Ninth Ward are still recovering. As of July 2018, Census Bureau estimates indicated that the city's population was still 81% of what it had been before the storm.

ENVIRONMENTAL ISSUES

New Orleans has survived an incredible number of fires, floods, epidemics, and scandals since its founding in 1718, and new buildings, streetcar lines, restorations, and festivals still keep the city kicking. But with the ever-growing threat of climate change, the city's unique geographical position and oft-lacking infrastructure seem to leave it particularly vulnerable for disaster. Many questions remain: The repaired levees held fast against 2012's Hurricane Isaac, but will they withstand an even larger storm? Will New Orleans move past its political scandals, crime, and the ills of urban poverty? Despite the many fortune-tellers plying their trade on Jackson Square, no one knows for sure what the future holds for the Crescent City.

DIVERSITY

It sounds like a tourist-brochure cliché, but it's true: New Orleans marches to the beat of its own drum, compared with the rest of the country. It may be due in large part to geography. This port city has seen an influx of many, many cultures over the course of its history. It welcomes diversity and tolerates lifestyles that deviate from the norm—a big reason artists and other creative types have long put down roots here. And the fact that the city lies mostly below sea level lends it a certain fatalism, which may unconsciously inspire the classic New Orleans "live for today" attitude.

GENTRIFICATION

The post-Katrina rebuild in New Orleans hasn't always been respectful or positive for all the city's residents. A combination of corporate opportunists, bad policy, and a growing popularity has brought negative change to the city in the form of rising housing prices, overdevelopment in vulnerable areas, and Airbnb and short-term rentals displacing long-term residents.

But many also complain that the more things change, the more they stay the same. New Orleans seems to move at a more leisurely pace than the rest of the country, and, while it may be slowly losing some of its rougher edges and laid-back charm, good change can be slow to come as well. In response to community outcry, politicians and leaders have pledged to do things like better regulate Airbnb, improve housing and schools for everyone, and upgrade the system of pumps and levees that are supposed to protect the city from colossal flooding. The results of these promises are still to come.

AFFORDABLE HOUSING AND AIRBNB

New Orleans is in the middle of a serious affordable housing crisis. Today, tens of thousands of low-income residents can't find affordable housing and one major reason is that Hurricane Katrina severely damaged the city's housing supply, causing demand to skyrocket. Another culprit, however, is the short-term rental website Airbnb, which has become quite popular with travelers looking for a more local (and less expensive) lodging option than a hotel. But those potential earnings from Airbnb have enticed many local landlords to take their rental units off the market and make them available strictly as short-term rentals for tourists. This has the dual effect of further increasing demand for remaining units, while also pushing out families who have rented in certain neighborhoods for decades.

Landlords insist they have the right to profit off their properties just like hotels and bed-and-breakfasts do. More traditional accommodations say short-term rental units should be held to the same regulatory standards the rest of the industry must face. All the while, an increasing number of residents in the city worry how the prevalence of short-term rentals is changing the neighborhoods in which they exist. The city government has taken some steps to mitigate the negative effects of Airbnb, but there is still a long way to go. It's a complicated issue, but as a traveler, it's always important to think about how you influence the places you visit; a good rule of thumb if you like using Airbnb is to choose room-only rentals or entire apartments whose hosts live in their properties full-time and only rent out the units while traveling.

What to Eat in New Orleans

KING CAKES

Come January, ring-shaped king cakes—adapted from older French and Spanish traditions—appear at every work and social gathering across the city to celebrate the beginning of Carnival. Classic king cakes are frosted and dusted in sugary carnival colors of purple, green, and gold.

GUMBO

New Orleanians know that a gumbo is only as good as its roux, a rich base made from frying flour until it becomes deep brown and flavorful. You then add celery, bell pepper, and onion, and a variety of other ingredients like andouille sausage, chicken, crawfish, crabs, or shrimp.

BOUDIN

Louisianans love boudin, a traditional Cajun sausage usually found at roadside stands and gas stations throughout Cajun country. This well-seasoned encased sausage includes pork mixed with rice and other seasonings, and is a real crowd-pleaser.

BEIGNETS

Pillowy fried donuts usually doused in powdered sugar, beignets top the list of must-try New Orleans foods. The classic spot for anyone's first taste is under the green-and-white-striped awnings of Café du Monde—a 24-hour historic spot next to the French Market, where beignets are served piled high, next to a steaming cup of café au lait.

PO'BOYS

As legend has it, this classic New Orleans sandwich first came to be during a streetcar strike, when restaurant owners showed their support by feeding strikers French bread sandwiches stuffed with any leftovers they could find. Roast beef "debris" po' boys are still popular at quintessential outlets like Parkway and Domilise's, but the sandwich has since evolved into many other tasty renditions. Fried shrimp, oyster, or fried catfish are among the most popular.

CRAWFISH

When it comes to eating crawfish, remember to suck the heads, pinch the tails, and that it takes a little time to perfect your technique. If you come to New Orleans in springtime, you're likely to have plenty of opportunity to practice. The small, bottom-feeding crustaceans (a distant cousin to the lobster) dominate family gatherings, picnic tables, grocery stores, and casual seafood stands throughout the season. And an important note: crawfish and crayfish are the exact same thing, but "crawfish"

Crawfish

is more widely used in New Orleans.

VIETNAMESE FOOD
Vietnamese immigrants first arrived in New Orleans as refugees after the Vietnam War, forming a large community here and an essential, vibrant part of the city's cultural layout today. You'll find authentic versions of dishes like pho (noodle soup), spring rolls, and popular banh mi sandwiches in areas like the West Bank and New Orleans East (home to award-winning Duong Phuong Bakery).

BBQ SHRIMP
First things first: New Orleans–style "barbecue" shrimp isn't grilled or smothered in a tangy red sauce. Within the Crescent City, barbecue shrimp refers to fresh Gulf shrimp that is poached in a butter sauce with plenty of spices, lemon, and pepper. Pascal Manale's on Napoleon Avenue is responsible for the dish's initial popularity, but chefs like Emeril Lagasse and Paul Prudhomme seem to have perfected it.

YA-KA-MEIN
A hangover cure locals swear by, this ramen-based beef soup includes a mix of influences that somehow all work together, much like the city itself. The satisfying original version is best found at local corner stores like Manchu Food Store on Claiborne Avenue, but the most popular vendor is the Ya-Ka-Mein Lady, who serves up her family recipe at festivals and pop-ups around town.

CHAR-GRILLED OYSTERS
For this delicious cooking method, oysters on the half shell are broiled or char-grilled over a flame with plenty of butter, cheese, and garlic. There are more complicated, caloric renditions, but the classic dish—served with plenty of French bread—is the way to go.

What to Drink in New Orleans

LOCAL BEER

Where once you'd only find Abita or Dixie drafts, there are now a dozen or so hometown craft beers to sample here. You'll find the most breweries in the converted warehouses of Tchoupitoulas Street in the Garden District (Urban South Brewery is a favorite).

SAZERAC

In this classic New Orleans favorite, rye whiskey (which has replaced brandy over the years) pairs with a light rinse of Herbsaint or absinthe, Peychaud's bitters, sugar, and a lemon twist; it's considered one of America's first cocktails. Drink a Sazerac at Chart Room in the French Quarter (one of the cheapest and best you'll find) or The Sazerac Bar at the Roosevelt Hotel. You can also dive into the drink's history (with samples, of course) at Sazerac House Museum on Canal Street.

RAMOS GIN FIZZ

Made of egg whites, citrus, gin, sugar, and orange-flower water, this dessert-like cocktail was Governor Huey P. Long's drink of choice. Today, many order a gin fizz for its dramatic presentation as much as for its sweet-tart flavor. Watch the best of the best make it at The Sazerac Bar (where Huey P. liked to drink his), and at more modern watering holes like Bar Tonique.

FRENCH 75

While this champagne cocktail was invented in a New York City restaurant during World War I, the light (but boozy) drink of gin or brandy, lemon, sugar, and sparkling wine is a favorite on many old-school New Orleans cocktail menus. Enjoy one at Arnaud's French 75 or while looking over the city at Hot Tin, a Tennessee Williams–themed rooftop bar at the top of the Pontchartrain Hotel.

FROZEN DAIQUIRI

The drive-through/walk-up daiquiri is a unique experience in the area around New Orleans, where you can literally drive up to a window and order from a menu of sugary-sweet, frozen booze concoctions. In town, try the frozen libations at places like Willie's Chicken Shack, Lafitte's Blacksmith Shop, and (a fancier version) at Compère Lapin.

FROZEN ICED COFFEE

This is a favorite treat for walking around the French Quarter at almost any time of day. You'll find the best ones at Molly's at the Market and the Erin Rose, two of the most festive Irish pubs in the city, great for people-watching or gathering before a sports game.

Sazerac

HURRICANE

Much like microbreweries have replaced familiar beers like Dixie and Budweiser in the city, so has the craft cocktail scene in New Orleans diminished the likes of sugary, brightly colored beverages sold in plastic or Styrofoam. Still, the Hurricane endures as a rite of passage for tourists here, as does passing through the doors of Pat O'Brien's to get one.

VIEUX CARRÉ

The name of this cocktail translates from French to "Old Square" and is indeed the traditional name for the French Quarter, where the cocktail was first invented in the 1930s. It's a very stiff take on an Old-Fashioned, with rye, cognac, sweet vermouth, Benedictine, and bitters. Drink one at the Carousel Bar at Hotel Monteleone, one of the first places the drink was ever sold.

PIMM'S CUP

This light British cocktail is popular in New Orleans on hot summer days (of which there are plenty). While the building is nearly two centuries old itself, Napoleon House has only been serving their Pimm's Cup—a signature mix of 7-Up soda, Pimm's cucumber liquor, and lemonade— since the 1940s, but it has been the quintessential place to enjoy one in the city ever since. Another popular place to sip one is on the porch of the Columns Hotel, overlooking St. Charles Avenue in the Garden District.

CHICORY COFFEE

New Orleanians began mixing chicory with their coffee during the Civil War, when coffee shortages forced them to get creative. The practice, originally from France, developed into a traditional New Orleans flavor, and you'll find chicory (a caffeine-free root with a dark and woody taste) in some of the bean mixes at Café du Monde, Community Coffee, and French Truck Coffee locations.

What to Buy in New Orleans

LOCAL TEES

New Orleans-themed T-shirts include chic, playful options that take New Orleans symbols and scenes beyond the fleur-de-lis, featuring icons like the streetcar, sno-balls, po'boys, and shotgun houses.

BESPOKE HATS

Just off of Canal Street in the CBD, Meyer the Hatter is a family-run hat shop that has been fitting the heads of fashionable New Orleanians since 1894. There are hats for everyone here, from Stetson to Kangol, with all the accessories (and old-fashioned customer service) to go along with them.

LOCAL LITERATURE

City book shops make sure to highlight New Orleans literary legends, past and present. In the French Quarter, Faulkner House Books honors one-time resident William Faulkner with many early editions of his work, literary events, and an annual festival for his birthday.

SWAMP MEMENTOS

Take home a little piece of Louisiana's unique flora and fauna, with crafts that utilize these homegrown materials. NOLA Boards make gorgeous cutting boards out of sinker cypress wood, aka preserved logs often found in the water of Louisiana swamps. In the Garden District, Tchoup Industries makes durable bags and backpacks out of recycled rice sacks, boat sails, alligator leather, and even nutria—Louisiana swamp rat—fur. Shops throughout the French Quarter also sell alligator heads of all sizes.

ANTIQUES AND SECOND-HAND CLOTHES

Walk the span of Royal Street in the French Quarter—one of the district's most picturesque stretches—and you'll be amazed at the variety of secondhand and boutique goods for sale. The selection ranges from centuries-old European armory and chandeliers to thrift store clothing and costume jewelry. United Apparel Liquidators is a fun stop; this crowded store sells discount designer clothing to everyday fashion lovers and movie stars alike.

VOODOO ITEMS

Voodoo shops in the French Quarter function as temples, museums, and shops; potential souvenirs include talismans, dolls, and candles. You'll get an authentic experience at Esoterica Occult Goods in the French Quarter and at Island of Salvation Botanica in the Faubourg Marigny.

Nola Boards

FRAGRANCES AND TINCTURES

The blending of herbal tinctures and fragrances goes hand-in-hand with voodoo and other practices honoring the land. Bourbon French Parfums has been blending custom fragrances in the French Quarter since 1843, as has the popular Hové Parfumeur nearby (although for not quite as long). Visit present-day, community-based apothecaries for herbal tinctures and teas, like Rosalie Apothecary in Mid-City and Maypop Community Herb Shop in St. Claude.

FOOD ITEMS

You can take home Café du Monde beignet mix, Pat O'Brien's Hurricane mix, pralines, hot sauce, and so long). much more from the French Market in the French Quarter and the stores surrounding it. Simplee Gourmet, in the CBD, sells culinary tools of all sorts, along with local spice mixes and cookbooks by New Orleans chefs.

BOUTIQUE ACCESSORIES

You'll find the best local craftspeople around Magazine Street in the Garden District as well as off of Royal and Chartres streets in the French Quarter. Check out jewelry makers like long-standing Mignon Faget or the hip Porter Lyons in the French Quarter. Both stores incorporate elements of the city and environment into their pieces. While the store has since expanded to New York City, Krewe du Optics and its finely made sunglasses and everyday frames still have their flagship store on Royal Street in the French Quarter.

LOCAL ARTS AND CRAFTS

Palace Market is a festive nighttime flea market and craft shop, selling art and finely made local goods. In the Marigny and the Bywater, you're likely to find an art market pop-up at the Art Garage on St. Claude, the Music Box Village, or the New Orleans Healing Center.

The Spookiest Experiences in New Orleans

ST. LOUIS CEMETERY #1

Most ghost tours will start off St. Louis Cemetery #1, where voodoo queen Marie Laveau is buried. The cemetery is known for its beautiful and ornate aboveground gravestones as well as for a powerful supernatural energy that surrounds the final resting spot of the priestess.

CONGO SQUARE

This corner of Armstrong Park is a sacred place; it was a meeting place of slaves, the site of harvest celebrations for the Houma tribe, and where Marie Laveau would lead chants and sell talismans. Today, there is a strong spiritual energy to the space, now used for small concerts and community festivals.

THE MUSEUM OF DEATH

What makes this French Quarter museum so spooky and unique is right in the name. With serial killer artwork and exhibits on all things death-related, from the Manson family to ancient funeral traditions, this museum can be graphic, fascinating, and not for everyone.

HAUNTED HOTELS

French Quarter hotels are either very old themselves or built on ancient sites that have seen a lot over the centuries. Because of this, former guests at some historic hotels have been known to linger, and there are a handful with very haunted stories. The Bourbon Orleans Hotel, Hotel Monteleone, and Cornstalk Hotel are among those with the most frequent reports of paranormal activity.

OCCULT AND VOODOO SHOPS

Many ghost or voodoo tours will begin at the altars of a voodoo shop. The proprietors of these shops, where tourists can buy voodoo dolls and little bags of gris-gris (small talismans said to bring on spells or luck), are part of the spiritual tradition of voodoo, and the shops usually serve as museums and temples as well. You'll also find many stores that cater to witchcraft, tarot cards, fortune-telling, and vampires.

LALAURIE MANSION

One of the scariest stories in New Orleans history took place in this French Quarter mansion. 1140 Royal Street was the home of Madame LaLaurie, a sadistic slave-owner known to torture her slaves and even starve them to death. Despite being one of the most haunted and feared buildings in the city, LaLaurie Mansion remains a private residence today, but many still report ghost sightings from the windows while walking past the building.

The Bourbon Orleans Hotel

MARIE LAVEAU'S HOUSE

The voodoo priestess lived on St. Ann, just blocks from Congo Square, where she would often do business. Marie lived in an adobe house that has since been torn down (152 St. Anne Street), but many say Laveau's energy still lives on in this spot. Some practitioners still perform rituals here, and others claim to have seen the ghost of Laveau walking the streets in a turban and long white dress.

STORYVILLE

The city's official red light district until the early 1900s, Storyville has a spooky past full of mysterious deaths. Legend says there were certain ladies' houses that male customers would enter, never to return again. Most of the original buildings were razed and replaced with modern housing, but ghost tours will walk you through this historic neighborhood and fill you in on the haunting tales. May Baily's Place, the corner bar at the Dauphine Orleans Hotel, was a famous brothel during the Storyville days. Official ghost hunters have corroborated the rumor that one of its former courtesans still haunts the historic premises, known to cast mysterious shadows and rearrange liquor bottles to her liking.

LAFITTE'S BLACKSMITH SHOP

The oldest bar in New Orleans is also one of the most haunted. Home of the famous "Purple Drink," the boisterous piano bar dates back to the 1770s and is the rumored former workshop of pirate Jean Lafitte. Patrons have reported seeing the ghost of old pirate Lafitte himself.

Under-the-Radar New Orleans

BREWERIES

Breweries have popped up around town in recent years serving high-quality craft beer, as well as often hosting food trucks, lawn games, and live music. Miel Brewery & Tap Room, Urban South Brewery, and Port Orleans Brewing Co. have all joined NOLA Brewery (the city's first craft beermakers) in the converted warehouses of Garden Street.

DRAG SHOWS

It makes sense that a city known for flair, costumes, and performance would have no shortage of drag shows. During Southern Decadence—New Orleans's own Pride festival held over Labor Day weekend—you'll find a packed schedule of lively shows at gay bars throughout the city.

CROSSING LAKE PONTCHARTRAIN

A trip across Lake Pontchartrain is worth it just for the chance to cross its 23.8-mile causeway. Second only to the Jiaozhou Bay Bridge in China as the longest bridge over water in the world, the causeway is long enough to have its own police force and host a marathon, as it did for many years.

CANOEING

An alternative to the touristy and often costly airboat, canoe trips offer a quiet nature escape. Canoe and Trail Adventures leads trips through a variety of Louisiana swampland, with expert guides providing insight on swampland history, environment, and wildlife. Be prepared for alligator, turtle, and osprey sightings, among other wildlife.

INDIE THEATER
Most big-screen multiplexes are far out of city limits, and the in-town movie scene is boutique and indie. Small theaters are often architectural wonders, each with their own quirky culture, careful pick of flicks, libations, and treats.

COMEDY SHOWS
The comedy scene in New Orleans is smaller than in cities like Chicago or New York, but certainly active, and a fun alternate way to spend a night in town. The scene revolves around themed showcases and open mics.

BOWLING
Rock'n'Bowl isn't just for bowling enthusiasts: the venue features two bars, delicious burgers, a Ping-Pong table, and dance floor. The decor and general charm is reminiscent of an old dance hall or large barn, and the music shows likewise feel more like a friendly hoedown than a concert.

Fort Macomb

EASTERN NEW ORLEANS
New Orleans East has had a hard time recovering from Hurricane Katrina, and many parts are still desolate and underdeveloped. Still, the area is rich in cultural and historical elements for those seeking a deeper understanding of New Orleans and the Gulf Coast region. One such landmark is Fort Macomb, a 19th-century military fort built after the War of 1812 and occupied by both the Confederate and Union armies during the Civil War. You might recognize the moss-covered ruins more recently from the first season of HBO's *True Detective* or Beyonce's visual album *Lemonade*.

Sports in New Orleans

For a city that loves to play so much, New Orleans once wasn't considered much of a professional sports town. Season after season of disappointment had even earned their football team the local nickname "the Aints." Things changed over the last several years, after two of the city's pro teams saw unprecedented success. The victories represented a comeback—not just for the teams, but for the entire city. .

NEW ORLEANS SAINTS

The Saints went marching in to victory in Miami in 2010 when they became Super Bowl champions for the first time. Throughout that season—which opened with 13 wins in a row—New Orleans was abuzz, united in Saints spirit like never before. The Super Bowl XLIV victory parade fell just a week before Mardi Gras and drew 800,000 people. It was the largest parade crowd some locals say they've ever seen, which is truly impressive for America's party city.

Today, despite ups and downs over the last few seasons, Saints fever continues unabated. Fans are as enthusiastic as ever and celebrate in Champions Square, just outside the Mercedes-Benz Superdome, a hot spot for pre- and postgame partying. Whether you're at the Dome or watching the Saints on TV, keep an eye out for some of the Saints' most famous fans: Halo Saint, who wears a gold Transformer-esque getup; Da Pope, dressed as the pontiff himself; Whistle Monsta, in black-and-gold face paint and Saints uniform, with a giant gold whistle atop his helmet; and Voodoo Man, sporting a tux jacket, top hat, and ghostly face paint.

Where they play: Mercedes-Benz Superdome (✉ *Sugar Bowl Dr., CBD*)

Season: August–January

How to buy tickets: Individual tickets are technically not for sale (the Dome has been sold out on season tickets alone since 2006), but resale tickets aren't hard to come by. Your best bet is the NFL Ticket Exchange (⊕ *www.nfl.com*).

Famous players, past and present: Drew Brees, Rickey Jackson, Archie Manning

Past highlights: Won Super Bowl XLIV in 2010; made playoffs in 2011, 2012, and 2013

NEW ORLEANS PELICANS

The Pelicans, who from 2002 through 2012 kept the "Hornets" moniker they arrived with from Charlotte, have seen mixed results over the years. Hurricane Katrina sent the team to Oklahoma City from 2005 to 2007, but they returned to New Orleans for the 2007–08 season and made the playoffs two years in a row. Anthony Davis led the team to the playoffs in 2014 and 2018, before leaving the franchise for good. In 2019, college basketball star Zion Williamson came on board, reigniting fans' hopes for the New Orleans Pelicans.

Where they play: Smoothie King Center (✉ *1501 Dave Dixon Dr., CBD*)

Season: October–April

How to buy tickets: Contact the ticket office by phone or online (☎ *504/525-HOOP* ⊕ *www.nba.com/hornets*).

Past highlights: Making the NBA playoffs in 2008, 2009, 2011, 2014, and 2018

New Orleans with Kids

New Orleans is a grown-up town in a lot of ways, but there are lots of activities to keep the kids interested, too.

PARKS

Audubon Park. This beautiful Uptown park is the perfect place to let the kids run free for a couple of hours. At the lagoon complex, they'll find ducks and an impressive assortment of (sometimes squawky) migratory birds nesting on Bird Island. Several play structures throughout the park—the biggest is at the downtown lakeside corner of the park near St. Charles Avenue—provide places for kids to swing, slide, and climb. And a walk around the 1.8-mile paved jogging path is an ever-popular family pastime. (*Uptown*)

City Park. There's plenty to do here for the younger set, including two free playgrounds—one with swings near the Peristyle, and another for older kids, just off Marconi Drive, with more challenging things to clamber on. Storyland, a fairy-tale theme park, is open year-round, and features a number of sculptures created by Blaine Kern Studios, the maker of Mardi Gras floats. The adjacent Carousel Gardens Amusement Park has low-impact rides, a miniature train that tours the park, and a beautiful 100-year-old carousel centerpiece. City Putt offers 36 holes of mini golf. (*Mid-City*)

ANIMALS

Aquarium of the Americas. Loads of exotic sea creatures, a penguin exhibit, and an interactive area where kids can get their hands wet make the aquarium a favorite family destination. There's a fun museum shop and an IMAX theater next door. (*The French Quarter: Riverfront*) **Audubon Insectarium.** This amazing attraction features insects for everyone—from a beautiful exhibit on butterflies to gross-out fun with the "bug chef." (*The French Quarter: Riverfront*) **Audubon Zoo.** A well-designed showcase with animals from all over the world, the zoo also has a hands-on area for kids, where young volunteers show off zoo residents, and a petting area with friendly goats and other beasties. (*Uptown*)

MUSEUMS

Louisiana Children's Museum. This longtime Warehouse District museum recently moved to a large campus in City Park, giving kids even more room to learn, romp, role-play, and dabble in the arts. (*Mid-City*)

FOR KIDS OF ALL AGES

Blaine Kern's Mardi Gras World at Kern Studios. The city's most famous float-building family offers tours of their company's vast studio, where kids can try on costumes and watch the artists at work. (*Warehouse District*) **Streetcars.** You can't leave New Orleans without taking the kids for a ride on a streetcar, which you can also use to get to several of the sites listed here, including City Park (on the Canal Street line) and Audubon Park (St. Charles Avenue).

What to Watch and Read Before You Go

A STREETCAR NAMED DESIRE

No literary figure embodies mid-20th-century New Orleans quite like Tennessee Williams, who set many of his works in his adopted home city. Every spring, the city dedicates a festival to the playwright—days of music, film, and literature, culminating each year with a "Stella!" shouting contest, from this play's classic scene. Read *A Streetcar Named Desire* to prepare for your trip, or watch the film version starring Marlon Brando and Vivien Leigh. Seedy, steamy, and emotionally charged, this is a quintessential New Orleans work.

INTERVIEW WITH THE VAMPIRE

Anne Rice is great at capturing the gothic charm and gloom of New Orleans, and her 1976 breakout novel, about an antebellum vampire living in the 20th century, takes on the best of her hometown setting. Lafayette Cemetery #1, near Rice's former Garden District home, was a source of inspiration for moments in the book and the rest of her haunting, spirit-filled work. The 1994 movie version stars Brad Pitt and Tom Cruise.

WHEN THE LEVEES BROKE: A REQUIEM IN FOUR ACTS

Spike Lee's filmmaking and journalistic talent shine in this in-depth 2006 documentary about Hurricane Katrina, the factors leading up to it, and the horrific aftermath, embracing issues like classism, racism, and government incompetence (just to name a few). This film is essential viewing to understand Hurricane Katrina's myriad dimensions and the city it left behind.

AMERICAN HORROR STORY: COVEN

The third season of the anthology series *American Horror Story* from 2013 is set in New Orleans and plays on inspiration from more haunting aspects of the Crescent City. Kathy Bates especially shines as a terrifying version of the infamous Madame LaLaurie, a real-life villian whose former home is one of the most haunted spots in the city. Angela Bassett also has a role as famed voodoo queen Marie Laveau. Garden District mansions, French Quarter landmarks, bars, restaurants, and other New Orleans icons all make their way into the show.

TREME

Aside from highlighting New Orleans music and culture, what this HBO television series does best is show the diverse mix of people and experiences that made up contemporary New Orleans in the years after Hurricane Katrina. The show delivers great scenes of the city—and of eating, drinking, and playing music—but mostly broaches issues of displacement, confusion, and trauma in the difficult years following the storm.

BEYONCE'S LEMONADE VISUAL ALBUM AND "FORMATION" MUSIC VIDEO

While it's her sister Solange who calls New Orleans home full-time, Beyonce's love of the city's culture and its sounds, dances, and iconic images inspired much of her 2015 album *Lemonade*. The music video for the song "Formation" heavily features the city, including controversial images of New Orleans after a colossal flood and sound bytes from local bounce artist Big Freedia and the late rapper Messy Mya. Other shots from the *Lemonade* visual album were filmed at the ruins of Fort Macomb, east of the city on I-10.

GIRLS TRIP

This fun comedy highlights what many, many people have been coming to New Orleans to do for years: party. The 2017 film stars Regina Hall, Tiffany Haddish, Queen Latifah, and Jada Pinkett Smith as a group of friends gathering for a reunion during Essence Festival at the Hotel Monteleone. Their adventurous, often dramatic jaunts through Bourbon Street and the French Quarter will have you excited about the city's boisterous side.

THE PRINCESS AND THE FROG

Disney's first black princess made her debut in 2009 in this twisty rendition of a classic fairytale. The film also stars the animated streets of New Orleans, the bayou, and the swampland, along with plenty of Creole and Cajun food, music, and culture.

TOP CHEF: NEW ORLEANS

Location really mattered on the 11th season of *Top Chef*, when contestants met legends like Leah Chase, hauled shrimp straight from boats, and became familiar with the unique flavors that make the city great. New Orleans even inspired fan-favorite contestant Nina Compton to return to New Orleans permanently, where she now runs the acclaimed restaurants Compère Lapin and Bywater American Bistro. With specials on seafood and classic dishes, this show is a great way to get a taste of New Orleans before you go.

A CONFEDERACY OF DUNCES BY JOHN KENNEDY TOOLE

Essential reading for any visitor, John Kennedy Toole's *A Confederacy of Dunces* is a New Orleans classic. Ignatius J. Reilly, the book's bumbling protagonist, is as quirky as the city itself.

CITY OF REFUGE AND WHY NEW ORLEANS MATTERS BY TOM PIAZZA

For more contemporary fare, look for Tom Piazza's *City of Refuge*, which looks at two fictional families—one black, one white—in the aftermath of Hurricane Katrina. (His nonfiction *Why New Orleans Matters,* written right after the hurricane, is a short but moving book about what

makes the city unique and why it was so important to rebuild.)

THE YELLOW HOUSE BY SARAH M. BROOM

In 2019, Sarah Broom became the first native-born New Orleanian to win the National Book Award, and she achieved this by taking on a part of New Orleans that is seldom given enough attention. Broom grew up the youngest of twelve siblings in New Orleans East, the once-wild expanse of land that has undergone various stages of development and destruction many times over since the mid-20th century. Broom's memoir manages to be both a vulnerable personal story about her childhood and a fascinating account of a New Orleans far from the tourist areas.

UNFATHOMABLE CITY: A NEW ORLEANS ATLAS BY REBECCA SOLNIT

Author and historian Rebecca Solnit maps the city both literally and through the essays of expert local historians, geographers, musicians, activists, and more. Aside from essays, the book contains 22 pages of maps that dig in to the city's main attractions, features, and moments—and all the real stories behind them.

FIVE DAYS AT MEMORIAL: LIFE AND DEATH IN A STORM-RAVAGED HOSPITAL BY SHERI FINK

Started as a Pulitzer Prize-winning article in the *New York Times Magazine*, this book is a chilling—and informative—investigation on tragedy and things gone wrong. The work of nonfiction is based mostly on firsthand accounts of what happened at Memorial Hospital during Hurricane Katrina, when many patients and staff were trapped inside the hospital.

THE BABY DOLLS BY KIM MARIE VAZ

This is the story of the Million Dollar Baby Dolls, one of the first female Mardi Gras krewes, whose origins can be traced back to the 1910s and the working ladies of the Storyville Red Light district. Kim Marie Vaz follows the group from their inception, all the way to their post-Katrina return, and explores how they broke down the social and racial barriers surrounding Mardi Gras traditions.

WE CAST A SHADOW BY MAURICE CARLOS RUFFIN

American racism (both the nightmarishly surreal and the all-too recognizable) is at the center of this dystopian novel starring a father and son, set in an unnamed future Southern city (that just happens to look a lot like Ruffin's lifelong home of New Orleans). Full of biting satire, this is both a heavy thought-piece and an enjoyable read.

SALVAGE THE BONES BY JESMYN WARD

Tulane creative writing professor Jesmyn Ward calls coastal Mississippi home, and it's where she based her 2011 National Book Award–winning novel. Told through the perspective of a young girl, the story is a vivid and intimate portrait of a working class African American family living in the coastal area just outside of New Orleans, in the days leading up to Hurricane Katrina.

ALL THIS COULD BE YOURS BY JAMI ATTENBERG

Attenberg sets this energetic and funny family drama in her adopted home of New Orleans, where a complicated cast of family members gather after the death of their patriarch. The characters are well drawn and entertaining, and the New Orleans backdrop adds extra personality and richness to the novel.

Chapter 2

TRAVEL SMART
NEW ORLEANS

Updated by
Matt Haines

POPULATION:
391,006

LANGUAGE:
English

$ CURRENCY:
U.S. Dollar

AREA CODE:
504

⚠ EMERGENCIES:
911

🚗 DRIVING:
On the right side of the road

⚡ ELECTRICITY:
120-240 v/60 cycles; plugs have two or three rectangular prongs

🕙 TIME:
1 hour behind New York

🌐 WEB RESOURCES:
www.nola.com
www.neworleans.com
nola.verylocal.com
www.offbeat.com

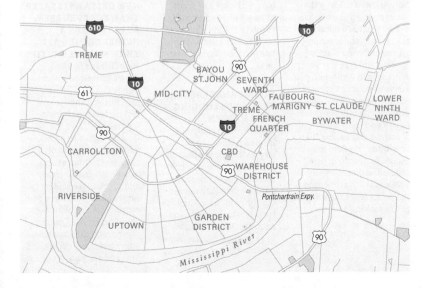

What You Need to Know Before You Go to New Orleans

As one of America's most popular cities, New Orleans can be overwhelming for a first-time visitor. Here are some key tips to help you navigate your trip, whether it's your first time visiting or your twentieth.

YES, YOU CAN DRINK OUTSIDE, BUT DON'T OVERDO IT.

New Orleans is one of just a few magical places in America where buying alcoholic drinks at a bar or liquor store and then drinking them on the streets is perfectly legal. You'll find many a bar offering to-go cups and chances are high you'll never be the only person drinking on any given street on any given night. Leniency doesn't mean free-for-all, though. For one, you're not technically allowed to leave the bar carrying a glass bottle. Before you head outside, ask the bartender for an aforementioned plastic "go cup" and transfer your drink into it. And when you arrive at your next destination, bringing an outside drink inside is at the discretion of your new host. And of course, don't allow this newfound freedom to be an excuse to overdo it; being drunk and disorderly in public is still a crime, and the police will take action if you're making a scene.

IT GETS VERY HOT IN SUMMER.

There's no question that May through September here is hot and humid— "double 100" days (100°F and nearly 100% humidity) aren't uncommon. But if you visit during sticky July and August, you'll find lower hotel prices and plenty of tables at top restaurants. Perhaps the best time to visit the city is early spring. Days are pleasant, except for seasonal cloudbursts, and nights are cool. The azaleas are in full bloom, the apricot scent of sweet olive trees wafts through the evening air, and the city bustles from one outdoor festival to the next

HURRICANE SEASON IS REAL AND FLOODING DOES HAPPEN.

June through November is known throughout the city as "Hurricane Season." The summer months bring more frequent rainstorms, and on average 10 named storms (which also includes tropical storms) form in the Atlantic Ocean this time of year, but—despite some notable exceptions—most don't find their way to New Orleans. It's never a bad idea to keep your eye on the weather before your trip, however. The formation of severe storms can usually be tracked days ahead of making landfall.

And be aware that with heavy rainfall can come street flooding. Areas closest to the river like the French Quarter, the Marigny, and the Bywater are above sea level and not typically as prone to flooding, while neighborhoods like Mid-City and Tremé can be much more problematic. Plan ahead if heavy rains are predicted during your trip, so you're not trapped in a flood zone during a storm. These floods aren't serious, per se, as most businesses are quite used to them and local pumping stations do their jobs quickly, but having to trudge back to your hotel in knee-deep waters is never a fun experience.

NEW ORLEANS IS SAFER THAN IT'S EVER BEEN, BUT STILL HAS A HIGHER CRIME RATE THAN MANY U.S. CITIES.

New Orleans has long drawn unwelcome attention for its high crime rate, but you should still feel perfectly safe visiting the city. The New Orleans Police Department regularly patrols the French Quarter and other high-traffic areas, and tourists are seldom the target of major crimes. Still, common sense is invaluable. The French Quarter is generally safe, but pay attention to your surroundings and your possessions (especially expensive cameras, smartphones, and dangling shoulder bags). Use special caution in the areas near Rampart Street and below St. Philip Street at night, and be alert on all quiet Quarter side streets. The CBD and Warehouse District are safe, but take a cab at night if there aren't many other pedestrians around. Be alert and exercise caution walking around in the Bywater or the lower part of Faubourg Marigny at night, and call a taxi or ride-share service late at night or when the distance is too great to walk; this is even more important if you've been drinking.

IF YOU'RE COMING HERE FOR A MAJOR FESTIVAL, PLAN FAR AHEAD.

Spontaneity can be valuable when exploring a new place, but if you're coming to New Orleans during a major holiday or a big event like Mardi Gras, Essence Fest, Jazz Fest, or Voodoo Fest, arriving without a plan could leave you stranded. Hundreds of thousands of tourists arrive in the city during these times, and it's impossible not to feel their presence when standing in line for your festival ticket, trying to book a hotel, or making a reservation at popular restaurants. Your best bet is to plan ahead. Accommodations can be especially challenging, booking up many months (or even a year) in advance. Cost will probably be higher no matter when you book, but most of what you find last minute will likely be astronomical.

Finally, Mardi Gras in New Orleans is a holiday on the same level as Christmas or Thanksgiving in other parts of the country. That means not every restaurant or tourist attraction will keep normal hours. Do your research and make a plan so you don't find yourself hungry and frustrated, wondering which of your must-eats will even be open.

EXPECT TO WALK, BIKE, OR TAKE TAXIS/SHARED RIDE SERVICES A LOT.

Unless you're planning a road trip outside of the city, you don't really need a car to get around here. The public transit system here isn't great or particularly helpful for getting around the city as a tourist, but when traveling between the CBD, French Quarter, and Marigny, your feet should do the trick. There are also large swaths of Uptown, the Garden District, and the Bywater that can be best appreciated by walking. If the temperature's too hot or the distance is too great, shared ride services like Lyft and Uber are easily accessible options. Another option is to use the city's bike share system called Blue Bikes. Download the app and you'll have inexpensive access to hundreds of bicycles in most sections of the city.

IF VISITING PLANTATIONS ON A DAY TRIP, BE RESPECTFUL OF THE REAL HISTORY.

Some of the city's most popular day trips are visits to one of the many plantation homes located just outside New Orleans. Visits to these homes have long been undertaken under the lens of appreciating the beautiful architecture, ornate grounds, and rich history of the owners, but more and more tours are being taken with a focus on the enslaved people who spent their lives there. It's true that many visitors, and indeed many of the plantations themselves, are still uncomfortable with this dark aspect of American history, and some tours still often gloss over slavery in favor of lessons on the plantations' architecure or the other historical contributions of slave-holders. Only one plantation in the region, Whitney Plantation, has been turned into a museum devoted to the history of American slavery. Visits to plantations still remain important as it's essential to understand every part of American history, but respect is key when planning a visit to one. More and more African Americans are visiting plantations to pay respect to their ancestors, and it's important for visitors to hold space for these experiences, understand that these plantations are much more than just pretty buildings, and to seek out tours that will teach the true history of the homes and the region at large.

Getting Here and Around

New Orleans fills an 8-mile stretch between the Mississippi River and Lake Pontchartrain. Downtown includes the French Quarter, the Central Business District (CBD), the Warehouse District, Tremé, and the Faubourg Marigny. Uptown includes the Garden District, Audubon Park, and Tulane and Loyola universities, as well as the Carrollton and Riverbend neighborhoods. The Bywater neighborhood is downriver (or east) of the Marigny, and Mid-City is north of Tremé.

It's best to know your location relative to the following thoroughfares: Canal Street (runs from the river toward the lake), St. Charles Avenue (runs uptown from Canal), Interstate 10 (runs west to the airport, east to Slidell), and LA Highway 90 (takes you across the river to the West Bank). Coming from the airport, to get to the CBD, exit Interstate 10 at Poydras Street near the Louisiana Superdome. For the French Quarter, look for the Vieux Carré exit. If approaching from the east on Interstate 10, take the Canal Street exit for the CBD or the Orleans Avenue exit for the French Quarter.

Canal Street divides the city roughly into the uptown and downtown sections (though the CBD and Warehouse District, considered part of downtown, actually lie just upriver from Canal). Keeping a visual on the Superdome is the surest way to know where the CBD is; the French Quarter lies just to the southeast of it over Canal Street.

Streets that start in the French Quarter and cross over Canal Street change names as they go upriver. For example, Decatur Street becomes Magazine Street and Royal Street becomes St. Charles Avenue. Addresses begin at 100 on either side of Canal Street, and begin at 400 in the French Quarter at the river.

✈ Air Travel

Flying time is 3 hours from New York, 2 hours 30 minutes from Chicago, 1 hour 40 minutes from Dallas, and 4 hours from Los Angeles. Book flights early for popular times such as Mardi Gras and Jazz Fest.

AIRPORTS

The major gateway to New Orleans is Louis Armstrong New Orleans International Airport (MSY), 15 miles west of the city in Kenner; a new terminal opened there in 2019 with improved local food options and other amenities. There's an airport exit off Interstate 10. Plan for about 30–45 minutes travel time from downtown New Orleans to the airport (longer at rush hour). An alternative route is Airline Drive, which will take you directly to the airport from Tulane Avenue or the Earhart Expressway. Be prepared for stoplights and possible congestion.

GROUND TRANSPORTATION

Check to see if your hotel offers shuttle service to and from the airport. If not, shuttle-bus service between the airport and locations uptown and downtown (including hotels) is available through Airport Shuttle New Orleans, the official ground transportation of Louis Armstrong International Airport. You can purchase one-way or round trip tickets online or at the Airport Shuttle ticket booths throughout the Level 1 Baggage Claim area. To return to the airport, call 24 hours ahead of your scheduled departure. The cost one-way to the CBD is $24 per person ($44 round trip), and the journey takes about 40 minutes.

The Regional Transit Authority of New Orleans and Jefferson Transit (JeT) of Jefferson Parish each offer buses to and from the airport daily. The RTA's Airport Express offers eight daily departures to downtown. The last leaves at 7 pm from the outer curb outside the Level 3 Ticket Lobby. The trip down Airline Drive to Elk Place and Canal Street, just outside the French Quarter, takes about 45 minutes. Heading to the airport, the last bus leaves downtown at 5:45 pm. Fare is $1.50.

JeT's express bus, $2, has approximately 18 departures per day and takes about 75 minutes to follow Airline Drive into the city with stops in Mid-City and downtown. From the airport, catch the E1 Veterans Airport Downtown line from the outer curb outside the Level 3 Ticket Lobby. Airport-bound buses leave every 40–60 minutes from the corner of Canal and Magazine streets downtown, and at major intersections along Canal Street in Mid-City. The last bus leaves Canal and Magazine at 8:37 pm on weekdays, 9:12 pm on Saturdays and holidays, and 9:24 pm on Sundays.

A cab ride to or from the airport and most points in the city costs $36 for up to two passengers. For groups of three or more, the rate is $15 per person. Pickup is in a dedicated taxi loading zone on the Arrival Curb outside of Level 1 Baggage Claim. There may be an additional charge for extra baggage.

Uber and Lyft also offer transportation from the airport for approximately $33. After reserving your ride on the app, meet your pick-up on Level 1 outside of the Baggage Claim between Doors 9 and 11.

🚲 Bicycle Travel

Biking is a good option for getting around New Orleans, especially when traveling to the Marigny and Bywater, Uptown, or Mid-City.

The city's bike share system, Blue Bikes, allows locals and visitors to use a mobile app to rent a bicycle in most New Orleans neighborhoods. After a one-time $5 set-up fee, rides cost 10¢ per minute and allow riders to drop-off their borrowed bike at any fixed structure near their destination. Download the app and a map will show you where the nearest bicycle is to you.

⛵ Boat Travel
BY FERRY

The $2 ferry ride across the river to Algiers is an experience in itself, affording great views of the river and the New Orleans skyline, as well as the heady feeling of being on one of the largest and most powerful rivers in the world. Pedestrians enter near Spanish Plaza and the Riverwalk shopping area and board the Canal Street Ferry from above. Bicycles board from below on the left of the terminal; cars are no longer allowed on the ferry. The trip to Algiers takes about 5 minutes. Ferries leave on the quarter-hour and three-quarter-hour from the east bank (Canal Street), and on the hour and half-hour from the West Bank (Algiers Point). Ferries run from 6 am to 9:45 pm on Monday through Thursday, from 6 am to 11:45 pm on Friday, from 10:30 am to 11:45 pm on Saturday, and from 10:30 am to 9:45 pm on Sunday. Be sure to check return times with the attendants if you are crossing in the evening—it's no fun to be stranded on the other side. There are wheelchair-accessible restrooms on the ferry.

CRUISES

Large cruise lines like Carnival, Norwegian, American Queen Steamboat Company, and American Cruise Lines depart from New Orleans up the Mississippi River or into the Gulf of Mexico and

Getting Here and Around

beyond. Royal Caribbean International and Disney Cruise Line both added cruises from the city in early 2020.

For more information, visit the Port of New Orleans website at ⊕ *www.portnola.com* or call ☎ *504/528–3318*.

Ticket/Pass	Price
Single Fare	$1.25
One-day Jazzy Pass	$3
Three-day Jazzy Pass	$9
Five-day Jazzy Pass	$15
Thirty-one-day Jazzy Pass	$55

🚌 Bus and Streetcar Travel

GETTING AROUND BY BUS AND STREETCAR

Within New Orleans, the Regional Transit Authority (RTA) operates a public bus and streetcar (locals will mock you if you call it a "trolley") system with interconnecting lines throughout the city. The buses are generally clean and on time, and run regularly from about 6 am to about 9 pm, later on some routes. Smoking, eating, and drinking are prohibited on RTA vehicles. Buses are wheelchair accessible, as are the Canal Street, Riverfront, and Loyola Avenue streetcar lines; the St. Charles Avenue streetcars are not.

ROUTES

The Riverfront streetcar covers a 2-mile route along the Mississippi River, connecting major sights from the end of the French Quarter (Esplanade Avenue) to the New Orleans Convention Center (Julia Street). Eight stops en route include the French Market, Jackson Brewery, the Aquarium of the Americas, Canal Place, the Fulton Street entertainment area, the Riverwalk, Woldenberg Park, and the Hilton Hotel. This streetcar operates 24 hours a day, with cars arriving every 20 minutes during peak hours.

The historic St. Charles Avenue streetcar line runs along St. Charles from Common Street to the Riverbend at Carrollton Avenue roughly every 10 minutes for most of the day. From Riverbend, this line continues along Carrollton Avenue, ending at South Claiborne Avenue.

Streetcar service on St. Charles Avenue runs 24 hours a day, though cars arrive every 30–40 minutes in the middle of the night.

A third streetcar line runs along Canal Street from the river near Harrah's Casino to either City Park or to the cemeteries. A streetcar leaves Harrah's Casino approximately every 8 minutes, although you should make sure you get on the car marked for your correct destination. Streetcars leave from City Park roughly every 15–20 minutes. Going from Harrah's Casino to the cemeteries, it passes every 16 minutes. As it gets closer to City Park, it passes every 30 minutes. The Canal Street line operates 24 hours a day, but runs much less frequently after 2 am and doesn't run all the way to the cemeteries or City Park at that time.

The newest streetcar line runs along Loyola Avenue, with stops in the CBD and along the French Quarter, then heads eastward into the Faubourg Marigny and Bywater. It departs from the Union Passenger Terminal every 20 minutes between 6:10 am and 11:30 pm.

COSTS

Bus and streetcar fare is $1.25 exact change plus 25¢ for transfers. Unlimited passes, valid on both buses and streetcars, cost $3 for 1 day, $9 for 3 days, $15 for 5 days, and $55 for 31 days. The daily passes are available from streetcar and bus operators; 3-day and 31-day passes are available at many local hotels and at most Walgreens. Passes can also be purchased online.

Car Travel

CAR RENTALS

If you plan to stick to the highly touristed areas of New Orleans, you may want to keep it simple and use taxis, ride-share services, streetcars, and the airport shuttle. However, if you plan to travel beyond the French Quarter and the Garden District, renting a car is a good idea.

If you decide to rent a car, rates in New Orleans begin at around $45 per day ($250 per week) for an economy car with air-conditioning, automatic transmission, and unlimited mileage. Prices do not include local tax on car rentals, or other surcharges, which can add another 15%–20% to your cost. All major agencies, including Avis, Budget, Hertz, Enterprise, and National Car Rental, have outlets in New Orleans.

GASOLINE

Gas stations are not plentiful within the city of New Orleans. The downtown area is particularly short on stations; head for Rampart Street if you need gas while downtown. If you're in Uptown, you'll find stations along Carrollton Avenue.

PARKING

Meter maids and tow trucks are plentiful everywhere, especially in the French Quarter. Avoid spaces at unmarked corners: less than 15 feet between your car and the corner will result in a ticket. Watch for temporary "no parking" signs, which pop up along parade routes and during film shoots. The SP+ Parking and Premium Parking websites can help you find lots and garages around town.

ROAD CONDITIONS

Surface roads in New Orleans are generally bumpy, and potholes are common, thanks to the city's swampy, shifting terrain and extensive live-oak roots. Along St. Charles Avenue, use caution when crossing over the neutral ground (median); drivers must yield to streetcars and pedestrians along this route. Afternoon rush hour affects New Orleans daily, and backups on Interstate 10 can start as early as 3 pm.

Taxi Travel

Cabs are metered at $3.50 base fare (up to two passengers, plus $1 for each additional passenger), then $2 per mile and 25¢ for every 40 seconds stuck waiting in traffic. If you're trying to hail a cab in New Orleans, try Decatur Street, Canal Street, or major hotels in the Quarter or the CBD. Otherwise, call a cab.

During Mardi Gras it can be extremely difficult to get a cab or ride-share; plan an alternate way to get home, such as using a Blue Bike (or enjoy the party until public transportation starts up again in the morning).

Train Travel

Three major Amtrak lines travel to and from New Orleans Union Passenger Terminal, which is also home to a beautiful 2,166-square-foot mural showing 400 years of New Orleans history that wraps around the interior of the station. The *Crescent*, operating daily, runs to and from New York and Washington, D.C., via Atlanta. Also daily, the *City of New Orleans* runs to and from Chicago via Memphis. Running three times weekly, the *Sunset Limited* runs to and from Los Angeles via Tucson and Houston.

Essentials

Dining

New Orleanians are obsessed with food. Over lunch they're likely talking about dinner. Ask where to get the best gumbo, and you'll spark a heated debate among city natives. Everyone, no matter what neighborhood they're from or what they do for a living, wants a plate of red beans and rice on Monday, has a favorite spot for a roast beef po'boy, and holds strong opinions about the proper flavor for a shaved ice sno-ball.

The menus of restaurants in New Orleans reflect the many cultures that have contributed to this always-simmering culinary gumbo pot over the last three centuries. It's easy to find French, African, Spanish, German, Italian, and Caribbean influences—and increasingly Asian and Latin American as well. The speckled trout amandine at Antoine's could have been on the menu when the French Creole institution opened in 1840. Across the Mississippi River on the West Bank, Tan Dinh serves fragrant bowls of pho that remind New Orleans's large Vietnamese population of the home they left in the 1970s. And at Compère Lapin, Chef Nina Compton brings expert French and Italian fine-dining traditions to the down-home flavors of her St. Lucia childhood, as well as those of her new home in the Gulf South.

For years New Orleans paid little attention to food trends from the East and West Coasts. Recently, however, the city has taken more notice of the "latest things." In Orleans Parish you'll now find gastropubs, gourmet burgers, and numerous small-plate specialists. In a town where people track crawfish season as closely as football season, no one has to preach the virtues of eating seasonally. New Orleans is still one of the most exciting places to eat in America. There's no danger that will change.

RESERVATIONS

Most restaurants in New Orleans accept reservations, and many popular places are booked quickly, especially on weekend nights and around festivals. Reservations are always a good idea. Reserving several weeks ahead is not too far in advance for trips during Mardi Gras, French Quarter Fest, Jazz Fest, and other special events.

WHAT TO WEAR

Unless otherwise noted, restaurants listed in this book allow casual dress. Reviews mention dress only when men are required to wear a jacket or tie. In a luxury restaurant or in one of the old-line, conservative Creole places, dress appropriately; there are quite a few places in town that won't allow guests wearing shorts or sneakers.

PRICES

Meals in the city's more upscale restaurants cost about what you'd expect to pay in other U.S. cities. Bargains are found in the more casual restaurants, where a simple lunch or dinner can frequently be had for less than $25. However, even the more expensive restaurants offer fixed-price menus of three or four courses for substantially less than what an à la carte meal costs. Serving sizes are more than generous—some would say unmanageable for the average eater—so many diners order two appetizers rather than a starter and a main course, which can make ordering dessert more practical. Some restaurants offer small- or large-plate options. Restaurant prices in the reviews are the average cost of a main course at dinner or, if dinner is not served, at lunch.

What it Costs			
$	$$	$$$	$$$$
RESTAURANTS			
under $15	$15–$22	$23–$30	over $30

🛏 Lodging

Before you decide where to stay in New Orleans, put some thought into what you want to do during your visit. Are you interested in history and architecture? Do you want to be where the party is? Are you in town primarily to eat—and to eat well? Do you need to be close to the business district and convention center? New Orleans is a fairly compact town, but if you stay Uptown, you'll need to travel a bit to reach the Quarter. Although most hotels favored by visitors are in the French Quarter, Central Business District (CBD), or Warehouse District, there are also great options farther afield.

· The French Quarter is a destination unto itself. With fascinating architecture, vibrant nightlife, chic shopping, and incredible restaurants, you could spend several days without leaving its confines.

Hotels in the CBD, many of them chains, cater to business travelers as well as tourists; most are larger than those in the French Quarter and have more amenities. Many of the Warehouse District's hotels actually occupy facilities once used to store cotton or other goods. In most cases, thoughtful renovations have kept the original purpose as a design motif, making for an interesting architectural style.

Just across Esplanade Avenue on the north and east of the Quarter is the Faubourg Marigny. Originally a Creole plantation and one of the first "suburbs" of New Orleans, it remains a residential area today, with a bustling nightlife and restaurant scene—most famously along Frenchmen Street.

To the west, upriver of the city's center, the Garden District and Uptown neighborhoods offer streets lined by the spreading boughs of live oaks, excellent stores, interesting architecture, and more outstanding dining and music venues. You'll find several newer, boutique hotels in the Garden District around St. Charles Avenue.

RESERVATIONS

Book your room as far in advance as possible—up to a year ahead for Mardi Gras, Jazz Fest, or other special events.

SERVICES

Most hotels have private baths, central heating, air-conditioning, and private phones. More and more major hotels have added Wi-Fi or in-room broadband Internet service, though some chains continue to charge for in-room Wi-Fi. Smaller hotels and bed-and-breakfasts may not have all of these amenities; ask before you book your room.

Hotels that do not have pools may have agreements with nearby health clubs and the like to allow guests to use their facilities for a nominal fee.

Most hotels have parking available, but this can run you as much as $45 a day. Valet parking is usually available at the major hotels. If you park on the street, keep in mind that New Orleans meter attendants are relentless, and ticketing is prevalent for illegally parked vehicles. The minimum fine for a parking ticket is $20.

Essentials

PRICES

The lodgings we list are the most desirable in each price category, but rates are subject to change. Look for special offers and discounted rates around the holidays and during the heat of summer. Be aware that the cost of lodging may be higher in October (considered peak convention season) and during the July 4 weekend (due to the annual Essence Music Festival). Rates are also high at the end of April and beginning of May during Jazz Fest, but peak during Mardi Gras, when major hotels often will require a three- or four-night minimum stay. Hotel prices are the lowest cost of a standard double room in high season.

What it Costs			
$	$$	$$$	$$$$
HOTELS			
under $125	$125–$224	$225–$350	over $350

🍸 Nightlife

There are many iconic images that come to mind when people think of New Orleans nightlife, including the neon glitz of Bourbon Street and the lone jazzman playing his horn beneath an old French Quarter gas lamp. But this is only the start of what New Orleans nightlife is all about. Whether you're looking for the simple pleasures of a perfectly constructed cocktail with a balcony view or something more adventurous, you've come to the right place.

No American town places such a premium on pleasure as New Orleans. From swank hotel lounges and refined jazz halls to sweaty dance clubs and raucous Bourbon Street bars, this city is serious about frivolity—and famous for it. Partying is more than an occasional indulgence in this city—it's a lifestyle. The bars and clubs that pulse with music are the city's lifeblood and are found in every neighborhood. Like stars with their own gravity, they draw people through their doors to belly up to their bars or head feet-first onto their dance floors. Blues, jazz, funk, R&B, rock, roots, Cajun, and zydeco—there are many kinds of music and nightlife experiences to be had in New Orleans. On any day or night of the year, the city is brimming with musical possibilities.

The French Quarter and Faubourg Marigny are the easiest places to find great music and nightspots. The venues are numerous and all within easy walking distance of one another. In the nearby Warehouse District, New Orleans institutions like Howlin' Wolf, Mulate's, and Circle Bar have been joined by scores of new bars, clubs, and restaurants. Moving upriver through the Garden District and Uptown, you'll find some of the most famous music spots in the city, such as Tipitina's and Maple Leaf. Bywater, Mid-City, and Tremé are residential neighborhoods with fewer commercial strips, but they too have their crown jewels, like Vaughan's, Bullet's, and Rock'n'Bowl.

HOURS

Bars tend to open in the early afternoon and stay open well into the morning hours. Live music usually begins around 6 pm in a handful of clubs that host early sets, but things really get going between 9 and 11 pm. Bear in mind that many venues operate on "New Orleans time," meaning that if a show is advertised to start at 10 pm, it might kick off closer to 11.

If you're a night owl, plenty of clubs have late-night sets, some not starting until 1 am.

Where Should I Stay?

Neighborhood	Vibe	Pros	Cons
The French Quarter	The tourist-driven main event is action-packed but still charming. Lodging runs from small inns to luxury hotels.	Lots of visitor attractions and nationally acclaimed restaurants. Everything is within walking distance of your hotel.	Crowded, high-traffic area. If you're sound-sensitive, request a room that does not face a main street, or find a hotel away from Bourbon Street.
Faubourg Marigny/ Bywater	Residential area just to the east of the French Quarter with a bohemian feel and fast-growing nightlife scene.	Balanced residential–commercial community. Close to French Quarter nightlife, yet has an eclectic nightlife scene of its own. The area is a more peaceful alternative to the Quarter.	Can be confusing to navigate for newcomers.
CBD and Warehouse District	The Warehouse District is one of New Orleans's arts districts. It's a great area for visitors who want to stay in luxurious high-rise hotels or smaller boutique properties.	Good retail and restaurants, and some of the best galleries and museums in the city. Within walking distance of the French Quarter.	Crowded; traffic can be a problem.
Garden District/ Uptown	Residential, upscale, and fashionable, this neighborhood is a slower-paced alternative to staying downtown.	Beautiful and right on the historic St. Charles Avenue streetcar line. Traffic here is not as heavy as downtown. Excellent shopping opportunities on Magazine Street.	Farther from the French Quarter and tourist attractions; must drive or take public transportation.
Mid-City	This is primarily an urban–residential area, with few lodging options.	Many local businesses and mid-price owner-operated restaurants. Home to City Park, one of the largest urban parks in the country.	More challenging for tourists to navigate—some distance from downtown tourist attractions. You may want to use a bike, car, or ride share as public transportation in the area is not always convenient.

2

Travel Smart New Orleans ESSENTIALS

Essentials

WHAT TO WEAR

Dress codes are as rare as snow in this city. On any given night in the French Quarter—and especially during the Carnival season—you'll see everything from tuxedos to tutus, T-shirts to fairy wings, and everything in between. Wear whatever is easiest to dance in.

COVER CHARGE VS DRINK MINIMUMS

Many bars on Bourbon Street entice visitors by presenting bands with no cover charge. They make their money by imposing a one- or two-drink minimum, with draft beer costing $5 to $8 apiece. In general, prices for beer, wine, and cocktails range from $4 to $9, unless you land in a good neighborhood dive bar, and then the prices can drop by as much as half. Music clubs generally charge a flat cover of between $5 and $20, with the high-end prices usually reserved for nationally touring artists, holidays, and special occasions.

TIPPING THE BAND

Bring cash to live-music clubs; many bands play for tips alone. Expect the hat (or the bucket, or the old coffee can, or the empty goldfish bowl) to be passed around once per set.

🎭 Performing Arts

For a relatively small city, New Orleans has a remarkably vibrant and varied performing-arts community. While there are many traditional performance venues around town, one of the most exciting movements in recent years is the fringe theater action along St. Claude Avenue, in the Bywater neighborhood. The annual Infringe Fest brings pop-up performances in November, but there are also permanent venues in the area hosting performances all year round.

A great source for concert and event information is **WWOZ,** the jazz and heritage community radio station, which broadcasts worldwide over the Internet at 🌐 *www.wwoz.org.* Local musicians, music historians, and personalities make up the all-volunteer corps of DJs, and they broadcast live 24/7 out of the French Quarter.

For more detailed event listings, check out *Gambit Weekly* (🌐 *www.bestofneworleans.com*), the alternative weekly available free in many bars, cafés, and stores. *The Times-Picayune / The New Orleans Advocate* (🌐 *www.nola.com*), the city's main newspaper, publishes a dedicated entertainment section. The monthly *OffBeat* (🌐 *www.offbeat.com*) magazine has in-depth coverage of local music and venues and is available at many hotels, stores, and restaurants. **Very Local New Orleans** (🌐 *nola.verylocal.com*) releases weekly content on its website covering the city's food, drink, sports, history, and entertainment scenes.

👜 Shopping

The Crescent City's shopping is as eclectic as its music, food, and culture. In local boutiques and specialty stores, you'll find everything from rare antiques to novelty T-shirts, artwork, jewelry, fashion, and foods that represent the city's varied flavors. Up and down the Garden District's Magazine Street and throughout the French Quarter, you'll spot old-world influences intersecting with modern trends, making it easy for even the most discerning shopper to find something new to treasure.

New Orleanians have a deep love for their city and its culture. For shoppers, this translates into pride-centric merchandise, including jewelry and clothing bearing city emblems, such as the fleur-de-lis—the stylized iris design associated with New Orleans since its early days—Mardi Gras masks, black-and-gold Saints symbols, and humorous statements about political issues and local personalities. Residents strongly support local entrepreneurs, and there are many homegrown stores selling locally made goods.

Make sure to pay attention to some of the city's artwork. Posters designed around Jazz Fest and other special events, for example, often become collector's items. In the thriving arts districts, you'll find contemporary works by local artists alongside renowned names in the art world. The sounds of New Orleans—Dixieland, contemporary jazz, rhythm and blues, Cajun, zydeco, rap, hip-hop, and the unique bounce beat—are available in music stores such as Louisiana Music Factory and Peaches Records, and at live-music venues including Preservation Hall, Snug Harbor, and House of Blues. Bookstores stock a plethora of local books on photography, history, cooking, and folklore. Clothing stores focus on items that wear well in New Orleans's often intense heat and humidity, with styles ranging from the latest runway fashions to vintage frocks and styles by local designers.

The Crescent City's main shopping areas are the French Quarter, with narrow, picturesque streets lined with antiques shops, art galleries, and gift, fashion, and home decor stores (Royal Street is a good place to start); the CBD and the Warehouse District, best known for contemporary art galleries and cultural museums; and Magazine Street, the city's 6-mile boutique strip filled with designer clothing, accessories, locally made jewelry, antiques shops, art galleries, and specialty stores. Magazine Street stretches from the CBD to the Uptown area. Nearby, the Carrollton-Riverbend neighborhood is another hot spot for finding women's clothing, jewelry, and bookstores.

OPENING HOURS

Unlike big malls and chain stores, most of the independent boutiques tend to keep bankers' hours, from about 10 am to 5 or 6 pm, so plan your shopping excursions accordingly. Some stores are open seven days a week, but most of Magazine Street and the French Quarter's smaller shops are closed on Sunday. Some stores are open on weekends, but closed Monday. It's best to check websites or call ahead if you're aiming to visit a certain location.

FINDING UNIQUE GIFTS

Some of the Crescent City's best souvenirs are the edible kind. For pralines, head to the French Quarter to either **Aunt Sally's** (✉ *810 Decatur St.*), where a box of six starts around $15, or to **Laura's Candies** (✉ *331 Chartres St.*). After your visit to **Café du Monde** (✉ *800 Decatur St.,*), dust the powdered sugar off your shirt and grab a box of beignet mix ($3.59) to pack in your suitcase. **Bittersweet Confections** (✉ *725 Magazine St., CBD*) sells artisanal chocolates with New Orleans flavors, such as bananas foster and crème brûlée.

To re-create the city's Creole flavor in your own kitchen, be sure to pick up a few cookbooks. In recent years, some of the city's top chefs have produced beautiful books with cooking tips, travelogues, and memories of home, as well as lots of recipes. Don't miss Chef Donald Link's

Essentials

first book, *Real Cajun,* which won the James Beard Award, and his more recent *Down South,* both packed with gorgeous photography and mouthwatering recipes. Iconic restaurants like **Brennan's, Galatoire's,** and **Tujague's** publish their own cookbooks of century-old favorites. And fans of Chef Susan Spicer's Bayona and Mondo restaurants will want to look for her *Crescent City Cooking.* Many of the city's bookstores will also carry a hearty variety of local favorites.

For wearable souvenirs with a Crescent City sense of humor, head to **Dirty Coast** (⊠ *5631 Magazine St. and 713 Royal St.*) and **Fleurty Girl** (⊠ *617 Chartres St. and 3137 Magazine St.*) These locally owned boutiques offer T-shirts and other clothing with New Orleans–theme slogans and snazzy graphics.

For souvenirs that go beyond the typical, visit the gift shops inside New Orleans's many museums and cultural institutions. The stores, which help support these organizations' missions, are typically open to shoppers without paying museum admission. The gift shop within the **New Orleans Museum of Art** (⊠ *1 Collins C. Diboll Circle, Mid-City*), for example, has a wealth of books on art, photography, and Louisiana cooking, as well as scarves, puzzles, and locally made crafts, such as jewelry by New Orleans designer Mignon Faget. The **Ogden Museum of Southern Art** (⊠ *925 Camp St., Warehouse District*) includes the beautifully curated Center for Southern Craft and Design store, where you'll find ceramics, glasswork, jewelry, and books on and by Southern artists. The store at the **Historic New Orleans Collection's** (⊠ *520 Royal St., French Quarter*) gift shop is the place to find such items as a reproduction of a 1916 Louisiana railroad map or a *NOVA* documentary DVD on Hurricane Katrina,

as well as many other maps, prints, photos, and publications on Louisiana history. The **Aquarium of the Americas** (⊠ *1 Canal St., French Quarter*), the **Audubon Insectarium** (⊠ *423 Canal St., French Quarter*) and the **Audubon Zoo** (⊠ *6500 Magazine St., Uptown*), all part of the Audubon Nature Institute, have gift shops stocked with colorful, quirky, educational, and fun items for children and adults.

🌐 LGBTQ Travel

New Orleans has a large LGBTQ population throughout the metropolitan area. The most gay-friendly neighborhoods are the French Quarter and the Faubourg Marigny, located just outside the Quarter.

The website ⊕ *frenchquarter.com* has an LGBTQ section including an interactive map of entertainment locations and an events calendar.

Throughout the year there are a number of gay festivals. The biggest is Southern Decadence, held Labor Day weekend. The city also has gay-friendly guesthouses and B&Bs, particularly along Esplanade Avenue.

Ambush (⊕ *www.ambushmag.com*), a local newspaper published every other week, provides a list of current events in addition to news and reviews. You can find this publication at many gay bars.

💲 Tipping

A standard restaurant tip is 20%; if you truly enjoyed your meal and want to reward good service, then consider more. If you use the services of the concierge, a tip of $5 to $10 is appropriate, with an additional gratuity for special services or favors. Always keep a few dollar bills on hand—they'll come in handy for tipping bellhops, doormen, and valet parking attendants, and for rewarding the many fine street musicians who entertain day and night.

◎ Visitor Information

For general information and brochures, contact city and state tourism bureaus. The New Orleans Convention & Visitors Bureau's website is a comprehensive resource for trip planning, hotel and tour booking, and shopping in the city; you can also download brochures, coupons, walking tours, and event schedules, as well as find links to other helpful websites. The Louisiana Office of Tourism offers the same with a statewide focus.

ONLINE RESOURCES

The Louisiana Department of Culture, Recreation and Tourism's website gives a general overview of tourism in Louisiana.

New Orleans Online provides basic trip planning and travel tools. The city's official site has updates on local issues and government affairs.

The website of the *Gambit* weekly newspaper does a good job of representing varying perspectives on life in the city, with a comprehensive events calendar.

The French Quarter website gives great links to event, lodging, and parking information, as well as an interactive French Quarter map. And for that something extra, Experience New Orleans has links to a blog, podcast, and fun video tours, in addition to the standard tourist sites. Very Local New Orleans connects its readers to the people, events, food, culture, and entertainment that makes the city special. Visitors can use the website to see what's going on around town, as well

as to gain in-depth information on what makes those events so interesting and important to the city.

For general information about events, hotels, and restaurants, check the official New Orleans travel site, ⊕ *www. neworleans.com*. For Louisiana music coverage (plus other entertainment news), *OffBeat* magazine's website is a good bet, as is the radio station WWOZ, which streams online and maintains a music calendar. Everything you need to know about the New Orleans Jazz & Heritage Festival can be found at its website. A site devoted entirely to Mardi Gras, Mardi Gras New Orleans, includes histories, parade schedules, and other specific Mardi Gras information.

For arts happenings around town, the Arts Council of New Orleans website has a calendar of art, music, dance, film, theater, literature, and culinary events in the city. The site also includes an artist directory and other resources.

A Good Gallery Walk in the Warehouse District

Julia Street in the Warehouse District is a major center of New Orleans's contemporary arts scene, and for art enthusiasts a day on (and just off) Julia is a requirement.

The street is lined with galleries, specialty shops, and modern apartment buildings, and the greatest concentration of them stretches from South Peters Street to Camp Street.

Start your walk on Camp and St. Joseph streets. Whet your appetite inside the airy, contemporary, stone-and-glass-walled **Ogden Museum of Southern Art** (⌧ *925 Camp St.* ☎ *504/539–9650*), which houses the largest collection of Southern art anywhere. Across the street, the multidisciplinary **Contemporary Arts Center** (⌧ *900 Camp St.* ☎ *504/528–3805*) hosts performances, concerts, and lectures, and runs stimulating and eclectic exhibitions by local and foreign artists. Pop in if there's an exhibition, and then continue on your way down Camp to Julia Street. Turn left on Julia to see five gallery and studio spaces in the single block between this corner and St. Charles Avenue.

At Camp and Julia streets you'll find **Gallery 600 Julia** (⌧ *600 Julia St.* ☎ *504/895–7375*), in the first of the Thirteen Sisters addresses that make up the historic Julia Street Row. Gallery 600 shows a mix of contemporary and historical paintings depicting Louisiana scenery and life, from wetlands wildlife to New Orleans cityscapes.

A longtime champion of the visual arts scene in New Orleans, **Arthur Roger** maintains a world-class gallery (⌧ *432–434 Julia St.* ☎ *504/522–1999*) that occupies two adjacent Julia Street addresses behind gleaming glass-walled facades.

A Good Gallery Walk in the Warehouse District

WHERE TO START:
Camp Street at the Ogden Museum of Southern Art

DISTANCE:
About a half mile

TIMING:
Several hours to all day, depending on how much time you have and how much you want to see

WHERE TO STOP:
Julia and Commerce streets

BEST TIME TO GO:
First Saturday of every month, when Art Walks are hosted by Warehouse District galleries from 6 to 9 pm. Two Saturdays not to be missed if you happen to be in town are Jammin' on Julia in May and Whitney White Linen Night in August—both wildly popular, all-out art-themed block parties enjoyed by enthusiastic crowds.

WORST TIME TO GO:
Sunday, when nearly all galleries are closed

GOOD IN THE HOOD:
Charcuterie and Southern cuisine are showcased at Cochon. Next door, Cochon Butcher is more casual, with sandwiches and small plates. Rye & Pie Pizza Bar serves its creative pizzas in a pleasant street-facing courtyard.

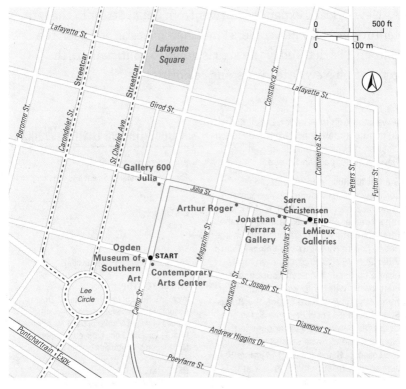

The gallery is a leader in representing prominent local artists and works from around the globe, and is an influential presence in the national art scene.

In the next block you'll find contemporary work with a political edge and a public conscience at **Jonathan Ferrara Gallery** (✉ 400a Julia St. ☎ 504/522–5471).

Next door, the lofty whitewashed brick-and-glass space inside **Søren Christensen** (✉ 400 Julia St. ☎ 504/569–9501) provides a gorgeous backdrop for always-excellent exhibitions, largely featuring contemporary painting but sometimes photography and sculpture.

Keep heading toward the river to **LeMieux Galleries** (✉ 332 Julia St. ☎ 504/522–5988), where contemporary Southern artists are the stars; drawings, paintings, photography, and sculpture from throughout the region are showcased here.

A Good Garden District Walk

As New Orleans expanded upriver from Canal Street in the 19th century, wealthy newcomers built their majestic homes in the Garden District. Today the area is home to politicians, fifth-generation New Orleanians, and celebrities.

A walk through the Garden District, just a 20-minute streetcar ride from the French Quarter, provides a unique look at life in New Orleans, past and present.

Start at **the Rink,** a small shopping complex at the Washington Avenue and Prytania Street intersection, a block from the streetcar stop. Walk east on Prytania (the main artery of the district) to the corner of Fourth Street to see **Colonel Short's Villa** (✉ 1448 Fourth St.), known for its ornate cornstalk fence and supposedly built for his wife, who was homesick for Kentucky. Toward Third Street, the **Briggs-Staub House** (✉ 2605 Prytania St.) is one of the few Gothic Revival houses in the city. No expense was spared in building the **Lonsdale House** (✉ 2521 Prytania St.) across the street, which was a Catholic chapel for more than 70 years. The **Maddox House** (✉ 2507 Prytania St.) next door is an example of the five-bay Greek Revival expansion. Across Prytania at the corner of Second is the **Women's Guild of the New Orleans Opera Association House** (✉ 2504 Prytania St.), with its distinctive octagonal turret; it's now a catering hall for weddings and social events. At First and Prytania streets are the regal **Bradish-Johnson House** (✉ 2343 Prytania St.), now a private girls' school, and the relatively modest, raised **Toby-Westfeldt House** (✉ 2340 Prytania St.), an example of a Creole colonial home.

Turn right and walk down First Street. Built in 1869, **Morris-Israel House** (✉ 1331 First St.), on the corner of Coliseum, and

A Good Garden District Walk

A Good Garden District Walk

WHERE TO START:
The Rink on Prytania Street and Washington Avenue

DISTANCE:
1 mile

TIMING:
45 minutes (without stops inside)

WHERE TO STOP:
Women's Guild of the New Orleans Opera Association House for interior tours on Monday (closed Memorial Day to Labor Day) from 11 am until 3 pm; Lafayette Cemetery No. 1, open to visitors daily until 2:30 pm

BEST TIME TO GO:
Mornings, especially in spring and fall; Monday for the Women's Guild tours

WORST TIME TO GO:
Midday, especially in summer; major holidays when the cemetery is closed

GOOD IN THE HOOD:
Stein's Deli, District Donuts, Tracey's Irish Channel Bar, Coquette bistro and wine bar, Commander's Palace

Carroll-Crawford House (✉ 1315 First St.) next door (where Toys in the Attic was filmed), are decorated with "iron lace," exemplifying the era's romantic Italianate style. Across Chestnut Street, **Brevard House** (✉ 1239 First St.), also known as

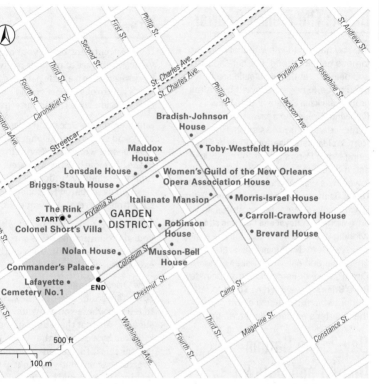

Rosegate for the ornate cast-iron gate that extends the length of the block, used to be the home of author Anne Rice.

Walk back up First Street toward Coliseum, which takes you past some of the most beautiful and historic homes in the South. The **Italianate Mansion** at 2425 Coliseum Street is the home of actor John Goodman. Across the street from each other at Coliseum and Third streets are the white-columned **Robinson House** (✉ *1413 Third St.*), thought to be the first house in New Orleans with indoor plumbing, and the intricate iron-balconied **Musson-Bell House** (✉ *1415 Third St.*) built by Edgar Degas's uncle. The

white-columned **Nolan House,** at 2707 Coliseum, is where Benjamin Button was raised in the film *The Curious Case of Benjamin Button*. Next door, one of New Orleans's most famous restaurants, **Commander's Palace** (✉ *1403 Washington Ave.*), is a great stop for lunch. Across Washington Avenue is the white-walled **Lafayette Cemetery No. 1,** arguably the most beautiful cemetery in the city.

Great Itineraries

Day 1: The French Quarter

Start by getting to know the city's most famous neighborhood. The café au lait and beignets at **Café du Monde** are a good place to begin, followed by a stroll around **Jackson Square** and **St. Louis Cathedral.** Cross the seawall and take in the views of the Mississippi River from **Woldenberg Riverfront Park.** Wander along North Peters Street to the shops and market stalls in the **French Market,** followed by a walk in the mostly residential **Lower Quarter** and **Faubourg Marigny.** After lunch, explore the antiques stores and art galleries on **Royal and Chartres streets,** winding it all up with a cocktail in a shady courtyard—try **Napoleon House,** an atmospheric bar and café that makes a mean Pimm's Cup, or French Quarter mainstay **Pat O'Brien's.** Save **Bourbon Street** for after dinner (which you should eat at one of the Quarter's esteemed restaurants).

Day 2: The Garden District and Uptown

The **St. Charles Avenue streetcar** rumbles past some of the South's most prized real estate; relax in one of the antique wooden seats and admire the scenery on the way to leafy **Audubon Park.** In the park you can follow the paved footpath to the **Audubon Zoo,** keeping an eye out for the zoo's white tiger and rare white alligators. Board an inbound **Magazine Street** bus near the zoo entrance and take it a couple of blocks past Louisiana Avenue, where a number of restaurants, some with sidewalk tables, are clustered. Continue along Magazine to Washington Avenue and head left through the **Garden District.** Prytania Street, just past **Lafayette Cemetery No. 1** (Anne Rice fans,

take note), is a good axis from which to explore the neighborhood's elegant side streets. Catch a downtown-bound streetcar on St. Charles, or wrap up the afternoon shopping and dining on Magazine Street.

Tips

If you're venturing out in your own vehicle, be aware of massive repaving projects; with a little patience, you'll get through some gnarly construction-zone traffic patterns.

Summer in New Orleans arrives early and sticks around longer than most people would like. If visiting in the hot months, stay hydrated, limit your midday outdoor activities, and be prepared for sudden, sometimes torrential downpours.

Bring a sweater or light jacket with you: air-conditioning in restaurants and other destinations can be excessive.

New Orleanians are friendly, but odd offers from people on the street to tell you where you got your shoes—"You 'got them on your feet," followed by a demand that you pay for this information—or other overtures from chatty, dubious-looking types should be ignored. Trust your intuition.

Before you book your trip, visit ⊕ *www.neworleans.com,* click "Trip Planning Tools" at the bottom, and download "deals and coupons" for lodging, dining, attractions, tours, and shopping discounts. The site is owned by the New Orleans Tourism Marketing Corporation and is a great source for event information.

Day 3: Art, History, and Culture

Dedicate one day to a deeper exploration of the city's cultural attractions. Art lovers shouldn't miss the **Warehouse District,** where a pair of fine museums—the **Ogden Museum of Southern Art** and the **Contemporary Arts Center**—anchor a vibrant strip of contemporary art galleries, most of which feature local artists. History buffs will want to check out the **National World War II Museum,** also in the Warehouse District, and the **Historic New Orleans Collection** in the French Quarter, which hosts changing exhibits in a beautifully restored town home. The **Louisiana State Museum Cabildo** was the former seat of Spanish colonial power in New Orleans and is now a museum that guides visitors through the history of the land that is now Louisiana.

Day 4: Remembering Katrina

It may strike some as macabre, but touring neighborhoods devastated by Katrina's floodwater has become a ritual for many visitors, much the same as pilgrimages to Lower Manhattan's Ground Zero. You can opt for a guided bus tour, which takes you to **Lakeview** and the infamous **17th Street Canal levee breach;** some companies also travel to the **Lower Ninth Ward** and **Chalmette.** After a somber tour of Hurricane Katrina's destruction, take heart by looking to the many signs of renewal and rebirth. **City Park,** which sustained extensive wind and flood damage, still holds its stately botanical gardens; nearby stands the venerable **New Orleans Museum of Art** and the adjacent **Sydney and Walda Besthoff Sculpture Garden.** Wind down from the day with dinner and live music downtown at one of the clubs on **Frenchmen Street,** in the Faubourg Marigny neighborhood, where the city's inexhaustible spirit parties on.

Day 5: Head Out of Town

Consider a day trip out of town to explore **Cajun Country,** take a guided **swamp tour,** or take a somber and educational visit to one of the region's plantation homes. Although swamp tours may sound hokey, they're actually a good way to see south Louisiana's cypress-studded wetlands (and get up close and personal with the alligators and other critters that live there). Continue the nautical theme in the evening with a ride to **Algiers Point** aboard the Canal Street Ferry for lovely sunset views of the New Orleans skyline. Of the many antebellum mansions between New Orleans and Baton Rouge, the best to visit is **Whitney Plantation,** the only plantation that has honored its horrific legacy by becoming a museum fully dedicated to the history of slavery.

Best Tours in New Orleans

If you're new to New Orleans, a tour can be a great way to familiarize yourself with your general surroundings or to dig deeper on the specific topics that most interest you. Whether you want to know more about the local cocktail scene or you just want to get an overview of this special place by foot, by bus, or by boat, the Crescent City has plenty of tour guides ready to show you something new.

Bus Tours

Gray Line. This well-regarded tour company leads excursions by bus, boat, or foot. See the French Quarter, learn about the history of cocktails, explore the region's swamps, and much more—there are dozens of options depending on your interests. Gray Line also gives visitors the opportunity to customize their experience by combining tours, as well as offering seasonal excursions. Tours are as short as 2 hours and 15 minutes. ☒ 400 Toulouse St. ☎ 504/569–1401 ⊕ www.graylineneworleans.com ✉ From $44.

New Orleans Tours. If you're coming to town on a work function or with a larger group, New Orleans Tours can help satisfy your transportation needs. Their motorcoaches range in capacity from 25 to 56 passengers, and will work with your group to organize airport transportation, tour planning, tour guides, and sightseeing packages. ☎ 504/592–1991 ⊕ www.notours.com.

Tours by Isabelle. For a smaller group experience, join Isabelle on intimate tours throughout the city, to the region's plantation homes, or even on an airboat through the swamps. Tours by Isabelle arrange pick-up and drop-off at accommodations around the city or anywhere in the French Quarter, and the company's small van allows access to places where larger buses can't visit. City tours teach a little about the effects of Hurricane Katrina and are generally four hours long. Guests can customize by combining experiences. ☎ 504/398–0365 ⊕ www.toursbyisabelle.com ✉ From $90.

Food and Drink Tours

Destination Kitchen. This local tour company offers several different food tours, cocktail tours, and food **and** cocktail tours. They focus on different sections of the city and include plenty of opportunities to eat and drink. The French Quarter Cocktail & Foodie Tour, for example, is three-and-a-half hours long and offers five drinks and six tastes of New Orleans favorites for $125. Book tickets via their website. ☎ 855/353–6634 ⊕ www.destination-kitchen.com ✉ From $125.

Drink & Learn: The Cocktail Tour. Culinary historian and Louisiana native Elizabeth Pearce leads a deeply informative two-hour walking tour dedicated to the city's cocktail culture. The $55 ticket includes four drinks. ☒ French Quarter ☎ 504/578–8280 ⊕ www.drinkandlearn.com ✉ From $55.

New Orleans Original Cocktail Tour. This Gray Line walking tour leads you through the saloons and wine cellars of the French Quarter. Admission includes one complimentary cocktail and there are frequent stops to purchase additional libations along the route, guaranteeing you'll get firsthand experience of the city's best drinks. The two-and-a-half-hour tours depart daily at 3 and 4 pm from the Lighthouse ticket office at Toulouse Street and the Mississippi River. ☒ French Quarter ☎ 504/569–1401 ⊕ www.graylineneworleans.com/cocktail-tour.html ✉ From $32.

New Orleans Brewery Tours. This brewery tour van will pick you up (and drop you off later) wherever you're staying. During the three-hour tour, you'll visit three great local breweries and learn a little bit about brewing and the history of beer in New Orleans. ☎ *504/494–0424* ⊕ *www. neworleansbrewerytour.com* ✉ *From $69 per person.*

Riverboat Cruises

New Orleans Paddle Wheels. This company has a Mississippi River cruise aboard the *Creole Queen*. Highlighting the port and French Quarter, the cruise has a pair of two-hour history-focused tours to the nearby Chalmette Battlefield, the site of the Battle of New Orleans. The evening session features a live jazz band. Cruises start at $36 with upgrades like lunch, dinner, and bottomless mimosas available. ✉ *1 Poydras St.* ☎ *504/529–4567* ⊕ *www.creolequeen.com* ✉ *From $36.*

New Orleans Steamboat Company. The New Orleans Steamboat Company offers narrated two-hour riverboat cruises up and down the Mississippi, complete with a jazz band, on the authentic paddle wheeler, the *Steamboat Natchez*. Ticket sales and departures for the *Natchez* are at the Toulouse Street Wharf behind Jackson Brewery. Options include a dinner cruise, a Sunday brunch cruise, or a daytime harbor option. ✉ *400 Toulouse St., French Quarter* ☎ *504/586–8777, 800/365–2628* ⊕ *www.steamboat-natchez.com* ✉ *From $36.*

Special-Interest Tours

New Orleans School of Cooking. At the New Orleans School of Cooking, guests have two options: sit back, watch, and learn from skilled and entertaining chefs preparing Creole and Cajun classics; or jump in for a hands-on culinary adventure of your own. Either way, your taste buds will be busy, because eating is part of both experiences. Check the website for the day's menu and to reserve your spot (they sell out in advance). Demo classes start at $30, while the hands-on classes start at $145. ✉ *524 St. Louis St.* ☎ *504/525–2665* ⊕ *www.neworleansschoolofcooking.com* ✉ *From $30.*

Save Our Cemeteries. The city's Catholic history and unique geology have combined to create cemeteries unlike any other in America. Why do New Orleanians bury their dead above ground? Find out this (and much more) on one of several tours offered by Save Our Cemeteries. The most popular excursion is the tour of St. Louis Cemetery No. 1, which takes you into one of New Orleans's "Cities of the Dead" that is only accessible with a tour guide. Reserve your spot online. ☎ *504/525–3377* ⊕ *www.saveourcemeteries.org* ✉ *From $25.*

Swamp Tours

Dr. Wagner's Honey Island Swamp Tours. One of the least-altered river swamps in the country, taking a small boat tour into the 250-square-mile Honey Island Swamp is a special experience. You'll see Spanish moss hanging from cypress trees emerging from pristine swamps, and you'll learn about the indigenous people and pirates who called this area home from your expert guide. A two-hour tour starts at $25. Round-trip transportation to and from your hotel is offered for an additional charge. ✉ *41490 Crawford Landing Rd.* ☎ *985/641–1769* ⊕ *www. honeyislandswamp.com* ✉ *From $25.*

Jean Lafitte Swamp and Airboat Tours. Memorable swamp and airboat tours are

Best Tours in New Orleans

possible just 25 miles outside of New Orleans. Four swamp tours meander through the protected Jean Lafitte National Park and Preserve's Barataria Preserve each day, starting at $29. The company also offers four thrilling airboat tours that buzz through some of the State's bayous, starting at $65. Tours are approximately 1 hour and 45 minutes, with round-trip hotel transportation possible for an additional cost. An authentic Cajun lunch is another optional add-on for swamp tour guests. ☎ 504/689–4186 ⊕ www.jeanlafitteswamptour.com ✉ From $29.

Walking Tours

Friends of the Cabildo. A nonprofit that supports the Louisiana State Museum, Friends of the Cabildo offer twice-daily (10:30 am and 1:30 pm), two-hour walking tours through the historic French Quarter. Conducted by licensed guides, tours begin at the 1850 House Museum Store (*523 St. Ann St.*) and focus on New Orleans's history, architecture, and folklore. ⊠ 523 St. Ann St., French Quarter ☎ 504/523–3939 ⊕ www.friendsofthecabildo.org ✉ $22.

Haunted History Tours. New Orleans is infamously one of America's most haunted cities. If you want to learn more about that history, consider booking with Haunted History Tours. Depending on the tour you choose, your guide will connect you to the city's relationship with voodoo, vampires, and cemeteries in the French Quarter or Garden District, or take you to some of the city's most haunted sites (including pubs). There's also a bus option if you're tired of walking. ⊠ 723 St. Peter St., French Quarter ☎ 504/861–2727 ⊕ www.hauntedhistorytours.com ✉ From $25.

Historic New Orleans Tours. With Historic New Orleans Tours, you'll find excursions covering the history and architecture of the Garden District, cocktails, the city's music scene, JFK assassination conspiracy theories, the Crescent City's haunted past, the French Quarter, local literary history, and more. Tours last for about two hours and can be booked online. ☎ 504/947–2120 ⊕ www.tourneworleans.com ✉ From $25.

Jean Lafitte National Historical Park and Preserve French Quarter Visitor Center. Hour-long walking tours along the Mississippi River levee, with a discussion on the interaction between the river and the city, are given Tuesdays through Saturdays at 9:30 am by park rangers . Tickets are available at the Jean Lafitte Park's French Quarter Visitor Center starting at 9 am on the morning of the tour. Tours about the indigenous people of the region are also occasionally available. Check website for details. Tickets are free, but tour size is limited. ⊠ 419 Decatur St., French Quarter ☎ 504/589–3882 ⊕ www.nps.gov/jela/french-quarter-site.htm ✉ Free.

New Orleans Spirit Tours. If you're interested in the haunted history of New Orleans, this might be the tour company for you. Whether you're looking for tales of ghosts and graveyards, information about voodoo, a haunted pub crawl, or a traditional walk through the Garden District, New Orleans Spirit Tours has something for nearly everyone. Tours start at $25 and usually last about two hours. ⊠ 723 St. Peter St. ☎ 504/314–0806 ⊕ www.neworleansspirittours.com ✉ From $25.

On the Calendar

Winter

Christmas New Orleans Style. Throughout the month of December, Canal Street sparkles with the season's decorations, and historic homes across the city put on their holiday best. St. Louis Cathedral opens its doors for free weekly concerts, and thousands of carolers gather in Jackson Square to raise their voices by candlelight. You'll find specials at hotels, as well as holiday *reveillon* menus at restaurants. Celebration in the Oaks lights up City Park, and bonfires are set on the Mississippi River's levee from New Orleans into Cajun Country—a Cajun tradition illuminating the way for Papa Noel. ✉ *New Orleans* ⊕ *holiday. neworleans.com.*

Mardi Gras. The biggest event on the city's cultural calendar is also the oldest—it's been around for more than a century. Parades roll almost nightly for the last few weeks of the Carnival season, which starts on Twelfth Night and culminates on Mardi Gras (or Fat Tuesday), the last blow-out party before Lent begins on Ash Wednesday. The big day itself is a city holiday, with the streets taken over by costumed revelers, floats, marching bands, and throngs of partiers. Plastic beads are the currency of the day. Every year, Mardi Gras falls on a different date, but it's always in either February or March. ✉ *New Orleans* ⊕ *www.mardigras.com.*

New Year's Eve. Join the crowd for live music on Jackson Square, and help count down to the new year with the drop of a giant fleur-de-lis on the riverfront near Jax Brewery. A barrage of fireworks lights up the Mississippi as clocks strike midnight. ✉ *French Quarter* ⊕ *www.neworleans. com.*

Spring

Easter Parades. Three fun parades hit the streets of the French Quarter on Easter Sunday: one led by local entertainer Chris Owens, another dedicated to the late socialite Germaine Wells, and the last an incredible gay parade that takes the festive bonnet tradition to a whole new level. ✉ *French Quarter* ⊕ *www.neworleans. com/events/holidays-seasonal/easter.*

French Quarter Festival. With stages set up throughout the Quarter and on the river at Woldenberg Park, the focus here is on free local entertainment—and, of course, food. A lot of locals consider this April festival the best in the city. ✉ *French Quarter* ☎ *504/522–5730* ⊕ *www.fqfi. org.*

New Orleans Jazz & Heritage Festival. Topnotch local, national, and international musical talent takes to several stages the last weekend of April and first weekend of May. The repertoire covers much more than just jazz, with big-name rock and pop stars in the mix as well as dozens of lectures, quality arts and crafts booths, and awesome food to boot. Next to Mardi Gras, Jazz Fest is the city's biggest draw; book your hotel as far in advance as possible. ✉ *1751 Gentilly Blvd, Gentilly* ⊕ *www.nojazzfest.com.*

New Orleans Wine & Food Experience. Winemakers and oenophiles from all over the world converge for five days of seminars, tastings, and fine food each May. The Royal Street Stroll, when shops and galleries host pourings and chefs set up tables on the street, is especially lively. ✉ *New Orleans* ⊕ *www.nowfe.com.*

St. Patrick's Day and St. Joseph's Day. A couple of big parades roll on the weekend closest to March 17: one starts at Molly's at the Market and winds

On the Calendar

through the French Quarter; the other, in Uptown, goes down Magazine Street and turns the area around Irish Channel neighborhood bars Parasol's and Tracey's into one big, green block party. Two days later (March 19) the town celebrates St. Joseph's Day with home-cooked food and goodie bags filled with cookies and lucky fava beans. Check the NOLA tourism website for announcements of altars that you can visit. ⊠ *New Orleans* ⊕ *www.stpatricksdayneworleans.com.*

Tennessee Williams & New Orleans Literary Festival. The annual March multi-day tribute to the *Streetcar Named Desire* playwright draws well-known and aspiring writers, lecturers, and a handful of Williams's acquaintances, along with music and theater, both classic and original. It closes with contestants re-enacting Stanley Kowalski's big "Stella-a-a!" moment. ⊠ *New Orleans* ☎ *504/581–1144* ⊕ *www.tennesseewilliams.net.*

Summer

Essence Music Festival. Held around Independence Day, this three-day festival brings in more than a half-million visitors and draws top names in R&B, pop, and hip-hop to the Mercedes-Benz Superdome. The event also includes talks by prominent African American figures and empowerment seminars. ⊠ *Mercedes-Benz Superdome, 1500 Sugar Bowl Dr.* ⊕ *www.essence.com/festival.*

New Orleans Wine and Food Experience. Serious wine drinkers line up for this four-day celebration of Bacchus over Memorial Day weekend. Popular events include a series of vintner dinners at local restaurants, a wine-fueled stroll through the shops of Royal Street, and the two-day Grand Tasting, where nearly 75 restaurants serve food and 1,000 different wines are poured. ⊠ *New Orleans* ☎ *504/934–1474* ⊕ *www.nowfe.com.*

Satchmo SummerFest. The August weekend-long tribute to the late, great Louis Armstrong honors Satchmo with jazz performances staged throughout the Quarter, seminars and discussions with Armstrong scholars, a Satchmo Club Strut down Frenchmen Street, and the Louis Armstrong Birthday Party. ⊠ *French Quarter* ⊕ *www.satchmosummerfest. org.*

Southern Decadence. On Labor Day weekend, hundreds of drag-queens-for-a-day parade through the Quarter. What began as a small party among friends has evolved into one of the South's biggest gay celebrations. The parade rolls—and as the day wears on, staggers—along on Sunday, but Decadence parties and events start Thursday evening. ⊠ *New Orleans* ⊕ *www.southerndecadence.net.*

Tales of the Cocktail. Each July, the annual Tales of the Cocktail, billed as "the most spirited event of the summer," brings thousands of experts and enthusiasts together for an internationally acclaimed, five-day celebration dedicated to the artistry and science of making drinks. In addition to enjoying some of "the best cocktails ever made," attendees participate in dinners, demonstrations, tastings, competitions, seminars, book signings, tours, and parties. ⊠ *New Orleans* ☎ *504/948–0511* ⊕ *www.talesofthecocktail.com.*

Fall

Art for Art's Sake. Art lovers and people-watchers alike pack Warehouse District and Magazine Street galleries in early October for the annual Saturday-evening kickoff to the visual arts season. What's on the walls usually takes a back seat to the party scene. ✉ *Warehouse Arts District and Uptown* ⊕ *www.cacno.org.*

New Orleans Film Festival. Cinephiles can get their fix during this juried festival in October, which brings an influx of indie and film culture to town and commandeers screens at venues throughout the city. The Film Society, which presents the annual festival, also hosts screenings year-round, a French film fest, themed film series, and a gala. ✉ *New Orleans* ☎ *504/309–6633* ⊕ *www.neworleansfilmsociety.org.*

Voodoo Music + Arts Experience. Part music festival, part giant interactive art exhibition, and part Halloween bash, Voodoo Experience is a festival that's held the last weekend of October. It attracts eclectic young masses with its mix of edgy national acts, local bands, and art installations in various media. ✉ *City Park* ⊕ *www.voodoofestival.com.*

Contacts

✈ Air Travel

AIRPORTS Louis Armstrong New Orleans International Airport. (*MSY*). ⊠ 1 Terminal Dr., Kenner ☎ 504/464–0831 ⊕ www. flymsy.com.

GROUND TRANSPORTATION Airport Shuttle New Orleans. ⊠ 4220 Howard Ave. ☎ 504/522–3500, 866/596–2699 ⊕ www. airportshuttleneworleans. com. **Jefferson Transit.** ☎ 504/248–3900 ⊕ www. jeffersontransit.org/route/ e1-veterans.

🚲 Bicycle Travel

Bicycle Michael's. ⊠ 622 Frenchmen St., Faubourg Marigny ☎ 504/945–9505 ⊕ www.bicyclemi-chaels.com. **Blue Bikes.** ☎ 504/608–0603 ⊕ www. bluebikesnola.com. **Fat Tire Tours.** ⊠ 214 Decatur St., across from House of Blues, French Quarter ☎ 504/619–4162, 877/734–8687 ⊕ www. fattiretours.com/ new-orleans.

⛴ Boat Travel

Canal Street Ferry. ⊠ Bottom of Canal St., at Convention Center Blvd. ☎ 504/309–9789 ⊕ www.norta.com/ Maps-Schedules/ New-Orleans-Ferry.

🚌 Bus and Streetcar Travel

RTA. ☎ 504/248–3900 ⊕ www.norta.com.

🚗 Car Travel

GARAGES Premium Parking . ☎ 844/236–2011 ⊕ premi-umparking.com. **Parking. com.** ☎ 504/525–5476 ⊕ www.parking.com/ new-orleans.

🚕 Taxi Travel

United Cabs. ☎ 504/522–9771 ⊕ www.unitedcabs. com. **Veterans.** ☎ 504/367–6767. **White Fleet-Elks Elite Cab Co.** ☎ 504/822–3800.

🚆 Train Travel

Amtrak. ☎ 800/872–7245 ⊕ www.amtrak.com. **Union Passenger Terminal.** ⊠ 1001 Loyola Ave. ☎ 504/299–1880.

📍 Visitor Information

CONTACTS Louisiana Office of Tourism. ☎ 800/677–4082 ⊕ www. louisianatravel.com. **New Orleans & Company.** ⊠ 2020 St. Charles Ave. ☎ 800/672–6124, 504/566–5011 ⊕ www. neworleans.com.

ALL ABOUT LOUISIANA The Louisiana Department of Culture, Recreation and Tourism. ⊕ www.crt.state. la.us.

ALL ABOUT NEW ORLEANS City of New Orleans. ⊕ www.nola.gov. **Experience New Orleans.** ⊕ www.experiencene-worleans.com. **Frenchquarter.com.** ⊕ www.french-quarter.com. **Very Local New Orleans.** ⊕ nola.very-local.com. **NewOrleans. com.** ☎ 800/672–6124 ⊕ www.neworleans.com.

MUSIC, FESTIVALS, AND EVENTS Arts Council of New Orleans. ⊕ www. artsneworleans.org. **Mardi Gras New Orleans.** ⊕ www. mardigrasneworleans. com. **New Orleans Jazz & Heritage Festival.** ☎ 504/558–6100 ⊕ www. nojazzfest.com. **OffBeat Magazine.** ☎ 504/944–4300 ⊕ www.offbeat.com. **WWOZ.** ☎ 504/568–1239 ⊕ www.wwoz.org.

PERIODICALS Gambit. ☎ 504/486–5900 ⊕ www. bestofneworleans.com. **The Times-Picayune / The New Orleans Advocate.** ⊠ 840 St. Charles Ave. ☎ 504/636–7400 ⊕ www. nola.com.

Chapter 3

THE FRENCH QUARTER

Updated by
Cameron Quincy Todd

⊙ Sights   🅥 Restaurants   🛏 Hotels   🛍 Shopping   🍸 Nightlife
★★★★★   ★★★★★   ★★★★★   ★★★★★   ★★★★★

NEIGHBORHOOD SNAPSHOT

TOP REASONS TO GO

Jackson Square. Mule-drawn carriage tours, artists selling their wares, and quirky street performers and musicians converge on Jackson Square, with the historic St. Louis Cathedral as a backdrop.

Shopping. The French Market and the random stores and warehouses that surround it are great for finding inexpensive souvenirs.

Drinking. From rowdy Bourbon Street to fancy hotel bars, you'll never go thirsty here. Savor your cocktail in a beautiful courtyard, or ask for a "go cup."

Gallery-hopping on Royal Street. Fine antiques, upscale boutiques, and artwork abound on this classy thoroughfare.

Live music. The French Quarter has some great music venues, including Preservation Hall, the Palm Court Jazz Cafe, Fritzel's European Jazz Pub, and One-Eyed Jack's.

GETTING AROUND

French Quarter streets are laid out in a grid pattern. Locals describe locations based on the proximity to the river or the lake and to uptown or downtown. Thus, "It's on the downtown, lakeside corner" indicates that a destination in the Quarter is on the northeast corner. Locals also refer to the number block that a site is on (as in "the 500 block of Royal Street"). Numbers across the top of the map are applicable to all streets parallel to North Rampart Street. Streets perpendicular to North Rampart start at 500 at Decatur Street and progress north in increments of 100.

MAKING THE MOST OF YOUR TIME

Many visitors never leave the French Quarter, which is the center of New Orleans. Daytime offers history buffs, antiques lovers, shoppers, and foodies a feast of delights while the Quarter lights up with fine and casual dining, live music, and infamous **Bourbon Street** debauchery at night.

QUICK BITES

■ **Café du Monde.** Open around the clock for late-night treats, Café du Monde has been serving up café au lait and beignets for more than a century. If the open-air café is crowded, go around back to the take-out window and enjoy your treats on the Mississippi riverfront. ✉ *800 Decatur St., French Quarter* ☎ *504/525–4544* ⊕ *www. cafedumonde.com* ▭ *No credit cards.*

■ **Napoleon House Bar and Café.** Here the house specialty Pimm's Cup can be enjoyed in the lush courtyard or in the cool interior, along with bites like pulled-duck po'boys. The residence was built in 1797 and was purportedly chosen as Napoléon's would-be New World residence in an escape plan hatched for the exiled emperor. ✉ *500 Chartres St., French Quarter* ☎ *504/524–9752* ⊕ *www. napoleonhouse.com.*

■ **Verti Marte Deli.** Pick up a sandwich or a hot lunch to-go from this distinctly New Orleans take on a deli, open 24 hours, and a prime refueling point for the late-night bar crawl. If you're really hungry, try the All That Jazz po'boy (ham, turkey, shrimp, and two cheeses with grilled mushrooms and tomatoes). ✉ *1201 Royal St., French Quarter* ☎ *504/525–4767* ▭ *No credit cards.*

Even locals love to get lost in the history and romance of the French Quarter, the city's oldest neighborhood. As you stroll through narrow side streets flanked by historic architecture, you'll marvel at the neighborhood's ability to endure. Keep walking, slowly, and take the time to look up at fabled wrought-iron balcony railings or peer down cobblestone corridors for a glimpse of secret courtyard gardens.

The French Quarter will not run out of ways to entertain you. The Vieux Carré, French for "Old Square," is technically the entire French Quarter, but you'll notice a divide at Decatur Street, as things start to feel more modern toward the river, and chain stores and restaurants pop up. The historic part of the French Quarter is where you can slip down a quiet street, gaze up at a row of balconies, and forget for a moment that you are living in the 21st century. During the day, the French Quarter offers several different faces to its visitors. The streets running parallel to the river all bear distinct personas: Decatur Street is a strip of tourist shops, hotels, restaurants, and bars uptown from Jackson Square; downtown from the square, it becomes a hangout for hipsters and leather-clad regulars drawn to shadowy bars, vintage clothing boutiques, funky antiques emporiums, and novelty stores. Modern development along the river side of Decatur Street can make this strip feel like a suburban corridor, but some of the best of old New Orleans is still here, like the massive Mississippi River, Café du Monde, and the French Market.

Chartres Street remains a relatively calm stretch of inviting shops and eateries. Royal Street is, perhaps aptly, the address of sophisticated antiques shops, glittering jewelry stores, and many of the Quarter's finest residences. Bourbon Street claims the strip bars, sex shops, extravagant cocktails, and flashy music clubs filmmakers love to feature. Dauphine and Burgundy streets are more residential, with just a few restaurants and bars offering retreats for locals.

After dark you'll find fine dining and easy-going eateries aplenty and music pouring from the doorways of bars as freely as the drinks flowing inside (and outside—plastic "go cups" for your cocktails are standard at the exit of every bar and club since consuming alcohol on public streets is legal in New Orleans). On any ordinary evening a stroll through the French Quarter is a moving concert.

Strains of traditional jazz, blues, classic rock 'n' roll, and electronic dance beats all flow from the various bars and nightclubs, while street musicians add their unique sounds to the mix.

For all its evening-time adult entertainment, the French Quarter by day is quite kid-friendly. Children adore eating beignets, watching ships sail across the Mississippi, walking through the tunnel-shaped Caribbean fish tank at the Aquarium of the Americas, munching crunchy treats made out of bugs at the Audubon Insectarium, and savoring the same delicious po'boy sandwiches and fried seafood that their parents enjoy.

French Quarter Below Royal Street

⊙ Sights

★ A Gallery for Fine Photography

MUSEUM | The rare books and photography here include works from local artists like Josephine Sacabo and Richard Sexton; luminaries such as E. J. Bellocq, Ansel Adams, and Henri Cartier-Bresson; and contemporary giants, including Annie Leibovitz, Walker Evans, Helmut Newton, and Herman Leonard. ✉ *241 Chartres St., French Quarter* ☎ *504/568–1313* ⊕ *www. agallery.com* ⊗ *Closed Tues. and Wed.*

★ Audubon Aquarium of the Americas

ZOO | FAMILY | This giant aquatic showplace perched on the Mississippi riverfront has four major exhibit areas: the Amazon Rain Forest, the Mississippi River, the Gulf of Mexico, and the Great Maya Reef gallery, all of which have fish and animals native to their respective environments. The aquarium's spectacular design allows you to feel like you're part of these watery worlds by providing close-up encounters with the inhabitants. One special treat is Parakeet Pointe, where you can spend time amid

hundreds of parakeets and feed them by hand. A gift shop and café are on the premises. Woldenberg Riverfront Park, which surrounds the aquarium, is a tranquil spot with a view of the Mississippi. Your aquarium tickets include a movie at the **Entergy Giant Screen Theater** ($29.95), but the best deal is the Audubon Experience, which includes the aquarium, theater, **Audubon Insectarium**, and **Audubon Zoo** for $49.95 (tickets are good for 30 days). ■ TIP→ **Save $2 by booking your ticket online ($27.95).** ✉ *1 Canal St., French Quarter* ☎ *504/861–2537, 800/774–7394* ⊕ *www.audubonnatureinstitute.org* 🎫 *$29.95* ⊗ *Closed Mon.*

Audubon Butterfly Garden and Insectarium

ZOO | FAMILY | Shrink down to ant size and experience "Life Underground," explore the world's insect myth and lore, venture into a Louisiana swamp, and marvel at the hundreds of delicate denizens of the Japanese butterfly garden. Then tour the termite galleries and other sections devoted to the havoc insects wreak, so you can sample Cajun-fried crickets and other insect cuisine without a twinge of

---

Chess Champions ⊙

Frances Parkinson Keyes's historical novel *The Chess Players* is based on the life of Paul Morphy, a New Orleanian considered to be one of the greatest modern chess masters. The Beauregard-Keyes House was originally built for Morphy's grandfather. If you're interested in challenging a living chess master, stop by Jude Acers's sidewalk table outside the Gazebo Café on Decatur Street. A two-time world-record holder for simultaneous games, Acers is at his table most days and takes on any challenger for a small fee.

guilt. ✉ *423 Canal St., French Quarter*
☎ *800/774–7394* ⊕ *www.auduboninstitute.org* ☑ *$24.95 ($2 off online)*
⊙ *Closed Mon.*

Beauregard-Keyes House and Garden Museum

MUSEUM | This stately 19th-century mansion was briefly home to Confederate general and Louisiana native P.G.T. Beauregard, but a longer-term resident was the novelist Frances Parkinson Keyes, who found the place in a sad state when she arrived in the 1940s. Keyes restored the home—today filled with period furnishings—and her studio at the back of the large courtyard remains intact, complete with family photos, original manuscripts, and her doll, fan, and teapot collections. Keyes wrote 40 novels there, all in longhand, among them local favorite *Dinner at Antoine's.* Even if you don't have time for a tour, take a peek at the beautiful walled garden through the gates at the corner of Chartres and Ursulines streets. Landscaped in the same sun pattern as Jackson Square, it blooms year-round. ✉ *1113 Chartres St., French Quarter* ☎ *504/523–7257* ⊕ *www. bkhouse.org* ☑ *$10* ⊙ *Closed Sun.*

The Cabildo

BUILDING | Dating from 1799, this Spanish colonial building is named for the Spanish council—or *cabildo*—that met here. The transfer of Louisiana to the United States was finalized in 1803 in the front room on the second floor overlooking the square. The Cabildo later served as city hall and then state supreme court. Three floors of multicultural exhibits recount 300 years of Louisiana history—particularly from the colonial period through Reconstruction—with countless artifacts, including the death mask of Napoléon Bonaparte. In 1988 the building suffered terrible damage from a four-alarm fire. Most of the historic pieces inside were saved, but the top floor (which had been added in the 1840s), the roof, and the cupola had to be replaced. The Cabildo

is almost a twin to the **Presbytère** on the other side of the cathedral. ■TIP→ **Both sites—as well as the Old U.S. Mint and the 1850 House—are part of the Louisiana State Museum system. Buy tickets to two or more state museums and receive a 20% discount.** ✉ *Jackson Sq., 701 Chartres St., French Quarter* ☎ *504/568–6968* ⊕ *www.louisianastatemuseum.org* ☑ *$10* ⊙ *Closed Mon.*

Canal Street

NEIGHBORHOOD | At 170 feet wide, Canal Street is often called the widest street (as opposed to avenue or boulevard) in the United States, and it's certainly one of the liveliest—particularly during Carnival parades. It was once slated for conversion into a canal linking the Mississippi River to Lake Pontchartrain; plans changed, but the name remains. In the early 1800s, after the Louisiana Purchase, the French Creoles residing in the French Quarter segregated themselves from the Americans who settled upriver. What is now Canal Street—specifically the central median running down Canal Street—was neutral ground between them. Today, animosities between these two groups are history, but the term "neutral ground" has survived as the name for all medians throughout the city.

Some of the grand buildings that once lined Canal Street remain, many of them former department stores that now serve as hotels, restaurants, or souvenir shops. The Werlein Building (No. 605), once a multilevel music store, is now the **Palace Café** restaurant. The former home of Maison Blanche (No. 921), once the most elegant of downtown department stores, is now a **Ritz-Carlton hotel**. One building still serving its original purpose is **Adler's** (No. 722), the city's most elite jewelry and gift store. For the most part, these buildings have been faithfully restored, so you can still appreciate the grandeur that once reigned on this fabled strip. ✉ *French Quarter* ⊕ *www.neworleans. com/plan/streets/canal-street.*

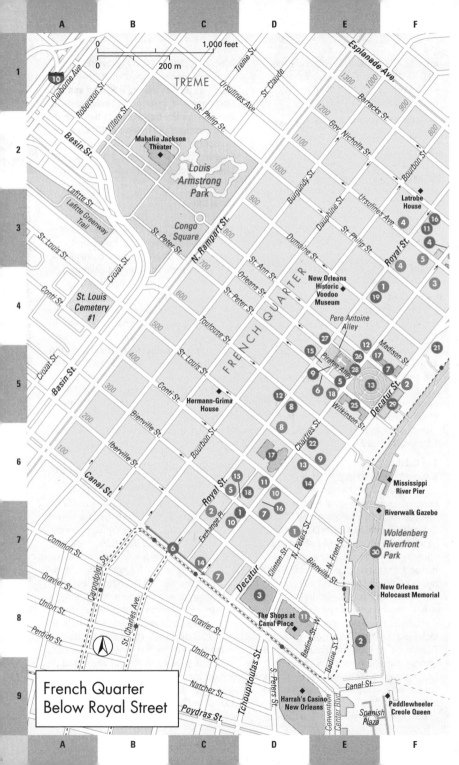

French Quarter
Below Royal Street

Sights ▼

1 A Gallery For Fine Photography....... **D7**
2 Audubon Aquarium of the Americas.......... **E8**
3 Audubon Butterfly Garden and Insectarium.............. **D8**
4 Beauregard-Keyes House and Garden Museum **F3**
5 The Cabildo................ **E5**
6 Canal Street.............. **C7**
7 1850 House **F5**
8 Elliott Gallery **D5**
9 Faulkner House **E5**
10 French Market **H3**
11 Gallier House............. **F3**
12 Historic New Orleans Collection **D5**
13 Jackson Square **E5**
14 Jean Lafitte National Park Visitor Center............ **D6**
15 LaBranche Houses...... **E5**
16 LaLaurie Mansion **F3**
17 Louisiana Supreme Court Building........... **D6**
18 Michalopoulos Galleries **D6**
19 Miltenberger Houses..... **E4**
20 Mississippi River........ **H5**
21 New Orleans Jazz National Historical Park **F5**
22 New Orleans Pharmacy Museum **E6**
23 Old Ursuline Convent... **G4**
24 Old U.S. Mint **H3**
25 Pontalba Buildings **E5**
26 The Presbytère........... **E5**
27 Rodrigue Studio.......... **E4**
28 St. Louis Cathedral **E5**
29 Washington Artillery Park **F5**
30 Woldenberg Riverfront Park **E7**

Restaurants ▼

1 Café Amelie **F4**
2 Café Du Monde **F5**
3 Central Grocery.......... **G4**
4 Croissant d'Or Patisserie **F3**
5 Green Goddess **C6**
6 Gumbo Shop **E5**
7 Irene's Cuisine **D7**
8 The Italian Barrel **G3**
9 Johnny's Po-boys........ **E6**
10 Justine **C7**
11 Kingfish **D6**
12 Muriel's Jackson Square **E5**
13 Nola **D6**
14 Palace Café **C7**
15 Pelican Club.............. **D6**
16 SoBou..................... **D7**
17 Stanley.................... **E5**
18 Sylvain **E5**

Hotels ▼

1 Bienville House Hotel...................... **D7**
2 Hotel Monteleone **C7**
3 Hotel Provincial.......... **F4**
4 Hotel Royal **F3**
5 Hotel Villa Convento..... **F3**
6 Le Richelieu in the French Quarter.......... **G3**
7 New Orleans Marriott Hotel **C7**
8 Omni Royal Orleans Hotel............ **D6**
9 Soniat House............ **G3**
10 W Hotel New Orleans French Quarter.......... **D6**
11 The Westin New Orleans Canal Place.............. **D8**

1850 House

HOUSE | This well-preserved town house and courtyard provide rare public access beyond the storefronts to the interior of the exclusive **Pontalba Buildings.** The rooms are furnished in the style of the mid-19th century, when the buildings were designed as upscale residences and retail spaces. Notice the ornate iron-work on the balconies of the apartments; the original owner, Baroness Micaela Pontalba, popularized cast (or molded) iron with these buildings, and it eventually replaced much of the old handwrought ironwork in the French Quarter. The initials for her families, *A* and *P* (Almonester and Pontalba), are worked into the design. A gift shop and bookstore run by the Friends of the Cabildo is downstairs. The Friends also offer informative two-hour walking tours of the French Quarter ($22) from this location Tuesday through Sunday at 10:30 am and 1:30 pm that include admission to the house. ⊠ *523 St. Ann St., French Quarter* ☎ *504/524–3918* ⊕ *www.louisianastatemuseum.org/museums/1850-house* ⊠ *$5* ⊗ *Closed Mon.*

Elliott Gallery

MUSEUM | Pioneers of modern and contemporary art are represented, with a large selection of prints and paintings by Marc Chagall, Picasso, and others. ⊠ *540 Royal St., French Quarter* ☎ *504/523–3554* ⊕ *www.elliottgallery.com.*

Faulkner House

HOUSE | The young novelist William Faulkner lived and wrote his first book, *Soldiers' Pay,* here in the 1920s. He later returned to his native Oxford, Mississippi, where his explorations of Southern consciousness earned him the Nobel Prize for literature. The house is not open for tours, but the ground-floor apartment Faulkner inhabited is now a bookstore, **Faulkner House Books,** which specializes in local and Southern writers. The house is also home to the **Pirate's Alley Faulkner Society** literary group, which hosts an annual literary festival celebrating the writer's birthday. ⊠ *624 Pirate's Alley, French Quarter* ☎ *504/524–2940* ⊕ *www.faulknersociety.org.*

★ French Market

MARKET | The sounds, colors, and smells here are alluring: ships' horns on the river, street performers, pralines, muffulettas, sugarcane, and Creole tomatoes. Originally a Native American trading post and later a bustling open-air market under the French and Spanish, the French Market historically began at the present-day Café du Monde and stretched along Decatur and North Peters streets all the way to the downtown edge of the Quarter. Today, the market's graceful arcades have been mostly enclosed and filled with shops, trinket stands, and eateries, and the farmers' market has been pushed several blocks downriver, under sheds built in the 1930s as part of a Works Progress Administration project. **Latrobe Park,** a small recreational area at the uptown end of the French Market, honors Benjamin Latrobe, designer of the city's first waterworks. An evocative modern fountain marks the spot where Latrobe's steam-powered pumps once stood. Sunken seating, fountains, and greenery make this a lovely place to relax with a drink from one of the nearby kiosks. ⊠ *Decatur St., French Quarter* ⊕ *www.frenchmarket.org.*

Gallier House

HOUSE | Irish-born James Gallier Jr. was one of the city's most famous 19th-century architects; he died in 1866, when a hurricane sank the paddle-steamer on which he was a passenger. This house, where he lived with his family, was built in 1857 and contains an excellent collection of early Victorian furnishings. During the holiday season, the entire house is filled with Christmas decorations. ⊠ *1132 Royal St., French Quarter* ☎ *504/525–5661* ⊕ *www.hgghh.org* ⊠ *$15, combination ticket with Hermann-Grima House $25* ⊗ *Closed Wed.*

Historic Jackson Square is lorded over by the stunning St. Louis Cathedral.

Historic New Orleans Collection

MUSEUM | This private archive and exhibit complex, with thousands of historic photos, documents, portraits, and books, is one of the finest research centers in the South. It occupies the 19th-century town house of General Kemper Williams and the 1792 Merieult House. Changing exhibits focus on various aspects of local history. Architecture, history, and house tours are offered several times daily, and a museum shop sells books, prints, and gifts. The Williams Research Center addition, at 410 Chartres Street, hosts additional free exhibits. ✉ *533 Royal St., French Quarter* ☎ *504/523–4662* ⊕ *www. hnoc.org* ✉ *Free, tours $5.*

★ Jackson Square

PLAZA | **FAMILY** | Surrounded by historic buildings and atmospheric street life, this beautifully landscaped park is the heart of the French Quarter. **St. Louis Cathedral** sits at the top of the square, while the **Cabildo** and **Presbytère,** two Spanish colonial buildings, flank the church. The

handsome brick apartments on each side of the square are the **Pontalba Buildings.** During the day, dozens of artists hang their paintings on the park fence and set up outdoor studios where they work on canvases or offer to draw portraits of passersby. Musicians, mimes, tarot-card readers, and magicians perform on the flagstone pedestrian mall, many of them day and night.

A **statue of Andrew Jackson,** victorious leader in the Battle of New Orleans in the War of 1812, commands the center of the square; the park was renamed for him in the 1850s. The words carved in the base on the cathedral side of the statue ("The Union must and shall be preserved") are a lasting reminder of the Federal troops who occupied New Orleans during the Civil War and who inscribed them. ✉ *701 Decatur St., French Quarter* ⊕ *www.experiencene- worleans.com.*

Jean Lafitte National Park Visitor Center

INFO CENTER | Visitors who want to explore the areas around New Orleans should stop here first. The office supervises and provides information on the Jean Lafitte National Park Barataria Preserve, a beautiful wetland area across the river from New Orleans, and the Chalmette Battlefield, where the Battle of New Orleans was fought in the War of 1812. Each year in January, near the anniversary of the battle, a reenactment is staged at the Chalmette site. This visitor center has free visual and audio exhibits on the customs of various communities throughout the state, as well as information-rich riverfront tours called "history strolls," offered Tuesday through Saturday. The hour-long tour leaves at 9:30 am; tickets are handed out individually (you must be present to get a ticket) beginning at 9 am, for that day's tour only. Arrive at least 15 minutes before tour time to be sure of a spot. You'll need a car to visit the preserve or the battlefield. ⊠ *419 Decatur St., French Quarter* ☎ *504/589–2636* ⊕ *www.nps.gov/jela* ☾ *Closed Sun. and Mon.*

LaBranche Houses

HOUSE | This complex of lovely town houses, built in the 1830s by sugar planter Jean Baptiste LaBranche, fills the half block between Pirate's Alley and Royal and St. Peter streets behind the Cabildo. The house on the corner of Royal and St. Peter streets, with its elaborate, rounded cast-iron balconies, is among the most frequently photographed residences in the French Quarter. ⊠ *700 Royal St., French Quarter.*

LaLaurie Mansion

HOUSE | Locals (or at least local tour guides) say this is the most haunted house in a generally haunted neighborhood. Most blame the spooks on Madame LaLaurie, a wealthy but torture-loving 19th-century socialite who fell out with society when, during a fire, neighbors who rushed into the house found mutilated slaves in one of the apartments. Madame LaLaurie fled town that night, but there have been stories of hauntings ever since. The home is a private residence, not open to the public. Actor Nicolas Cage bought the property in 2007; two years later, the house sold at a foreclosure auction. The house and Madame LaLaurie herself have gained infamy in recent years thanks to the television show *American Horror Story: Coven*, which features them both extensively. ⊠ *1140 Royal St., French Quarter.*

Louisiana Supreme Court Building

GOVERNMENT BUILDING | The imposing building that takes up the whole block of Royal Street between St. Louis and Conti streets is the Old New Orleans Court, erected in 1908. Later, it became the office of the Wildlife and Fisheries agency. After years of vacancy and neglect, the magnificent edifice was restored and reopened in 2004 and is now the elegant home of the Louisiana Supreme Court. The public can visit the courthouse but must pass through security and cannot take photos inside. ⊠ *400 Royal St., French Quarter* ⊕ *www.lasc.org* ☾ *Closed weekends.*

Mardi Gras

FESTIVAL | Mardi Gras (French for "Fat Tuesday") is the final day of Carnival, a Christian holiday season that begins on the Twelfth Night of Christmas (January 6) and comes crashing to a halt on Ash Wednesday, the first day of Lent. Though Mardi Gras is merely one day within the season, the term is used interchangeably with Carnival, especially as the season builds toward the big day. As sometimes befalls the Christmas holiday, the religious associations of Carnival serve mainly as a pretext for weeks of indulgence. Likewise, Carnival claims elaborate traditions of food, drink, and music, as well as a blend of public celebrations (parades) and more exclusive festivities, which take the form of lavish private balls.

On Mardi Gras, many New Orleanians don costumes, face paint, and masks, and then take to the streets for the last hurrah before Lent. It's an official city holiday, with just about everyone but the police and bartenders taking the day off. People roam the streets, drink Bloody Marys for breakfast and switch to beer in the afternoon, and admire one another's finery. Ragtag bands ramble about with horns and drums, Mardi Gras anthems pour from stereos, and king cakes (ring-shaped cakes topped with purple, green, and gold sugar) are everywhere. Weeks of parades are capped by Zulu, Rex, and the "trucks" parades that roll from Uptown to downtown with large floats carrying riders who throw plastic beads and trinkets (called "throws") to onlookers.

Don't be smug: If you visit, you'll be caught up in the revelry of America's largest street party. After a few moments of astonished gaping, you'll yell for throws, too, draping layers of beads around your neck, sipping from a plastic "go cup" as you prance along the street, dancing with the marching bands, and having a grand old time.

Michalopoulos Galleries

MUSEUM | One of New Orleans's most beloved artists, James Michalopoulos exhibits his expressionistic visions of New Orleans architecture in this small gallery. Michalopoulos's palette-knife technique of applying thick waves of paint invariably evokes van Gogh—but his vision of New Orleans, where no line is truly straight and every building appears to have a soul, is uniquely his own. His work has become a prized adornment of many a New Orleanian's walls. Michalopoulos was commissioned to create the official poster of the New Orleans Jazz and Heritage Festival in 1998, 2001, 2003, 2006, 2009, and 2013, bringing a new perspective to some of New Orleans's greatest musicians like Mahalia Jackson, Louis Armstrong, Dr. John, Fats Domino, and Aaron Neville. ✉ 617 Bienville St., French Quarter ☎ 504/558–0505 ⊕ www.michalopoulos.com.

Miltenberger Houses

HOUSE | The widow Amélie Miltenberger built this row of three picturesque brick town houses in the 1830s for her three sons. Her daughter Alice Heine became famous for wedding Prince Albert of Monaco. Although the marriage ended childless and in divorce, Princess Alice was a sensation in New Orleans. ✉ 900, 906, and 910 Royal St., French Quarter.

Mississippi River

BODY OF WATER | When facing the river with the French Quarter at your back, you will see, to your right, the **Crescent City Connection,** a twin-span bridge between downtown New Orleans and the West Bank, and a ferry that crosses the river every 30 minutes. The river flows to the left downstream for another 100 miles until it merges with the Gulf of Mexico. **Woldenberg Riverfront Park** and **Spanish Plaza** are prime territory for watching everyday life along the Mississippi: steamboats carrying tour groups, tugboats pushing enormous barges, and oceangoing ships. Directly across the river from the Quarter are the ferry landing and a dry dock for ship repair. ✉ French Quarter.

New Orleans Jazz National Historical Park

ARTS VENUE | FAMILY | In 1987 the U.S. Congress declared jazz a "national American treasure," and shortly thereafter the New Orleans Jazz National Historical Park was created to educate people about the art form and to preserve its history. The park hosts free performances and educational events in two locations around the French Quarter: the Visitor Center and the **Old U.S. Mint,** which also houses the state's jazz collection. Some of the park's rangers are also working musicians; don't miss the chance to catch their lively and informative demonstrations exploring the full range of Louisiana's musical heritage. ⊠ *Visitor Center, 916 N. Peters St., French Quarter* ☎ *504/589–4841* ⊕ *www.nps.gov/jazz* ☜ *Free* ☉ *No performances Sun. or Mon.*

★ New Orleans Pharmacy Museum

MUSEUM | To tour this musty shop is to step back into 19th-century medicine—the window display alone, with its enormous leech jar and other antiquated paraphernalia, is fascinating. This building was the apothecary shop and residence of Louis J. Dufilho Jr., America's first licensed pharmacist, in the 1820s. His botanical and herbal gardens are still cultivated in the pretty back courtyard (complete with a postcard-worthy fountain). Watch for free 19th-century seasonal health tips posted in the front window. ⊠ *514 Chartres St., French Quarter* ☎ *504/565–8027* ⊕ *www.pharmacymuseum.org* ☜ *$5* ☉ *Closed Sun. and Mon.*

Old Ursuline Convent

RELIGIOUS SITE | The Ursulines were the first of many orders of religious women who came to New Orleans and founded schools, orphanages, and asylums, and ministered to the needs of the poor. The original tract of land for a convent, school, and gardens covered several French Quarter blocks. The current structure, which replaced the original convent, was completed in 1752 and is now the oldest French-colonial building in the Mississippi Valley, having survived the disastrous 18th-century fires that destroyed the rest of the Quarter. **St. Mary's Church,** adjoining the convent, was added in 1845. Now an archive for the archdiocese, the convent was used by the Ursulines for 90 years. The Ursuline Academy, a girls' school founded in 1727, is now Uptown on State Street, where a newer convent and chapel were built. The academy is the oldest girls' school in the country. The Old Ursuline Convent is open to the public for self-guided tours Monday through Saturday. ⊠ *1110 Chartres St., French Quarter* ☎ *504/525–9585* ⊕ *www.oldursulineconventmuseum.com* ☜ *$8* ☉ *Closed Sun.*

★ Old U.S. Mint

MUSEUM | Minting began in 1838 in this ambitious Ionic structure, a project of President Andrew Jackson's. The New Orleans mint was to provide currency for the South and the West, which it did until Louisiana seceded from the Union in 1861. Both the short-lived Republic of Louisiana and the Confederacy minted coins here. When Confederate supplies ran out, the building served as a barracks—and then a prison—for Confederate soldiers. The production of U.S. coins recommenced only in 1879; it stopped again, for good, in 1909. After years of neglect, the federal government handed the Old Mint over to Louisiana in 1966. The state now uses the building for exhibitions of the Louisiana State Museum collection, and the New Orleans Jazz National Historical Park has events here. After repairs from damage by Hurricane Katrina, the museum reopened to the public in 2007.

The first-floor exhibit recounts the history of the mint. The principal draw, however, is the second floor, dedicated to items from the **New Orleans Jazz Collection**. At the end of the exhibit, displayed in its own room like the Crown Jewels, you'll find Louis Armstrong's first cornet.

The **Louisiana Historical Center,** which holds the French and Spanish Louisiana archives, is open to researchers by appointment. At the foot of Esplanade Avenue, notice the memorial to the French rebels against early Spanish rule. The rebel leaders were executed on this spot and gave nearby Frenchmen Street its name. ⊠ *400 Esplanade Ave., French Quarter* ☎ *504/568–6993* ⊕ *louisianastatemuseum.org* ☜ *$9* ☉ *Closed Mon.*

Continued on page 85

DID YOU KNOW?

Years ago, yelling "Hey, mister! Throw me somethin', mister!" probably would have gotten you beads made of Czechoslovakian glass in traditional purple, green, and yellow. Although beads come in more colors these days, they're generally plastic and made in China.

MARDI GRAS TIME IN NEW ORLEANS

Odds are, most of what you know about Mardi Gras is wrong. The bare breasts of Bourbon Street have nothing to do with the real experience—a party steeped in tradition that New Orleanians throw (and pay for) themselves. They generously invite the rest of the world to join in the fun, so hold on to your fairy wings, your tutus, and your beads; things are about to get crazy!

Mardi Gras (French for "Fat Tuesday") is actually the final day of Carnival, a Christian holiday season that begins on the Twelfth Night of Christmas (January 6) and comes crashing to a halt on Ash Wednesday, the first day of Lent. The elite celebrate with private balls, while the rest of the city takes to the streets for weeks of parades and mischief. Don't be shy—after a few moments of astonished gaping, and maybe some Hurricane cocktails, you too will be bebopping to the marching bands, yelling for throws, and draped in garlands of beads.

On Mardi Gras day, New Orleanians don costumes and masks, drink Bloody Marys for breakfast and roam the streets until dark. It's an official city holiday, with just about everyone but the police and bartenders taking the day off. Two of Carnival's most important parades, Zulu and Rex, roll that day before noon, smaller walking krewes meander through the side streets, tribes of Mardi Gras Indians emerge in Tremé, and silent bands of skeletons mysteriously appear. For one day, an entire city becomes a surreal, flamboyant party.

(top) Masked revelers get in the Mardi Gras spirit

MARDI GRAS HISTORY

"The Carnival at New Orleans," a wood engraving drawn by John Durkin and published in Harper's Weekly, March 1885.

On February 24, 1857, a group of men dressed like demons paraded through the streets of New Orleans in a torch-lighted cavalcade. They called themselves the **Mistick Krewe of Comus,** after the Greek god of revelry. It was the start of modern Mardi Gras.

Based on European traditions, these men formed a secret society and sent 3,000 invitations to a ball held at New Orleans's Gaiety Theater. Many years later, when a 1991 City Council ordinance—later ruled unconstitutional—required all krewes to reveal their members to obtain a parade permit, Comus stopped parading. Its annual ball, however, remains one of the city's most exclusive.

Through the years, other groups of men organized Carnival krewes, each with its own character. In 1872, 40 businessmen founded the School of Design, whose ruler would be dubbed **Rex.** The krewe still parades on Mardi Gras morning and holds its lavish ball Mardi Gras night. Rex and his queen are considered the monarchs of the entire Carnival celebration, and their identities are kept secret until Lundi Gras morning.

For many decades, these "old-line" krewes were strictly segregated, so other parts of society started their own

clubs. The **Zulu Social Aid and Pleasure Club** was organized in 1909 by working-class black men, and they started parading in 1915. Zulu was one of the first krewes to integrate, and today members spanning the racial and economic spectrums parade down St. Charles Avenue on Mardi Gras day, preceding Rex.

Parade standards changed in 1969, when a group of businessmen founded the **Krewe of Bacchus,** named after the god of wine. The sassy group stunned the city with a stupendous show featuring lavish floats that dwarfed the old-line parades. The king was Danny Kaye, not a homegrown humanitarian, as was custom, but a famous entertainer. And you didn't have to be socially prominent—or white—to join the after-party, which they called a rendezvous, not a ball.

The arrival of Bacchus ushered in an era of new krewes with open memberships, including satiric krewes such as **Tucks** and **Muses**, that put on many of today's most popular parades.

PEOPLE STILL TALK ABOUT...

1972: Major parades rolled one last time through the French Quarter's narrow streets.

2000: The 19th century Krewe of Proteus returned after a seven-year hiatus.

2006: Despite the 2005 devastation of Katrina, New Orleanians insisted on holding a smaller (but no less enthusiastic) Mardi Gras.

2010: Saints quarterback Drew Brees reigned as king of Bacchus, tossing Nerf footballs to the crowds a week after winning the Super Bowl.

EXPERIENCE MARDI GRAS

Don't forget your costume! Mardi Gras spectators are often the wackiest.

Carnival parades begin in earnest two weekends before Mardi Gras day, with krewes rolling day and night on the final weekend. Almost all krewes each year select **a different theme**, ranging from the whimsical to hard-edged satire. Off-color jokes and political incorrectness are part and parcel of the subversiveness that characterizes Carnival. Throws will sometimes reflect a parade's theme, which is one reason why locals dive for the cups, doubloons, and other plastic trinkets. The floats and high school marching bands make up the bulk of the parades, with the odd walking club, dance troupe, or convertible car tossed into the mix.

Night parades also have the **flambeaux**, torch-bearing dancers who historically lighted the way for the parades. These days they provide little more than nostalgia and some fancy stepping to the bands, but they still earn tips for their efforts.

There are no day parades Monday, but **Lundi Gras**, literally "Fat Monday," has become a major event downtown by the riverfront. Rex and the Zulu King each arrive by boat to greet their subjects and each other. Zulu also hosts free concerts throughout the day. On Mardi Gras day, nearly every corner of New Orleans sees something marvelous, including walking clubs that follow unannounced routes and Mardi Gras Indians who wage mock battles to prove who's the prettiest. Mardi Gras and the Carnival season end with the arrival of Ash Wednesday.

FOR EARLY BIRDS

While most revelers arrive in New Orleans the Friday before Mardi Gras, many major parades actually start earlier in the week. They follow the traditional route down St. Charles Avenue to Canal Street. Note: times might change

Wednesday: Krew of Druids, 6:30 pm; Krewe of Nyx, 7 pm

Thursday: Knights of Babylon, 5:45 pm; Knights of Chaos, 6:30 pm; Krew of Muses, 6:30 pm

MARDI GRAS PARADE SCHEDULE: NOTEABLE KREWES

KREWES (EST.)	Rolls	Participants	Claim to fame	Watch for	Prize throws
Hermes (1937)	Friday 6 pm	Local businessmen	Oldest continuous night parade	Large line-up of marching bands	Lighted medallion beads
Le Krewe d'Etat (1996)	Friday 6:30 pm	Sardonic lawyers and well-heeled elites	Led by a dictator instead of a king	The Dictator's "Banana Wagon" pulled by mules	"D'Etat Gazette" with drawings of every float
Morpheus (2000)	Friday 7 pm	Lovers of traditional parades	Youngest parading krewe in New Orleans	Old-school floats and generous throws	Plush moons
Iris (1917)	Saturday 11 am	Upper crust ladies	Oldest all-female krewe	Flirtatious ladies throwing silk flowers	Ceramic beads
Tucks (1969)	Saturday 12 pm	Exuberant and irreverent young men and women	Took name from defunct Friar Tucks bar	Tongue-in-cheek themes	Plastic plungers and stuffed Friar Tucks dolls
Endymion (1966)	Saturday 4:15 pm	Partiers from around the country	Largest Mardi Gras parade; follows a unique route through Mid-City	Massive, spectacular floats and celebrity riders	Plush Endymion mascots
Okeanos (1949)	Sunday 11 am	Civic-minded business leaders	Queen selected by lottery	Trailer carrying a traditional jazz band	Frisbees
Mid-City (1934)	Sunday 11:45 am	Men from Mid-City	First krewe to have "animated" floats	Floats decorated in colored tinfoil	Bags of potato chips
Thoth (1947)	Sunday 12 pm	Guys with a charitable bent	Unique route passes retirement homes and Children's Hospital	Lavishing throws on children	Thoth baseballs
Bacchus (1968)	Sunday 5:15 pm	Devotees of the god of wine	First "superkrewe"	The Bacchagator and King Kong floats	Wine colored "king" doubloons
Proteus (1882)	Monday 5:15 pm	Members of the city's oldest families	Second-oldest krewe	Beautiful floats built on 19th century wagons	Plush seahorses
Orpheus (1993)	Monday 6 pm	Musicians and music lovers of any gender	Founded by singer Harry Connick Jr.	Latest parade technology, including confetti blowers	Stuffed Leviathan with flashing eyes
Zulu (1916)	Tuesday 8 am	Predominantly African American	Oldest African American Mardi Gras parade	Faces painted in black and white	Hand-painted coconuts
Rex (1872)	Tuesday 10 am	The most elite men in New Orleans society	King of Carnival	Crossing St. Charles to toast Rex mansion	Traditional Rex beads

WHERE TO WATCH THE PARADES

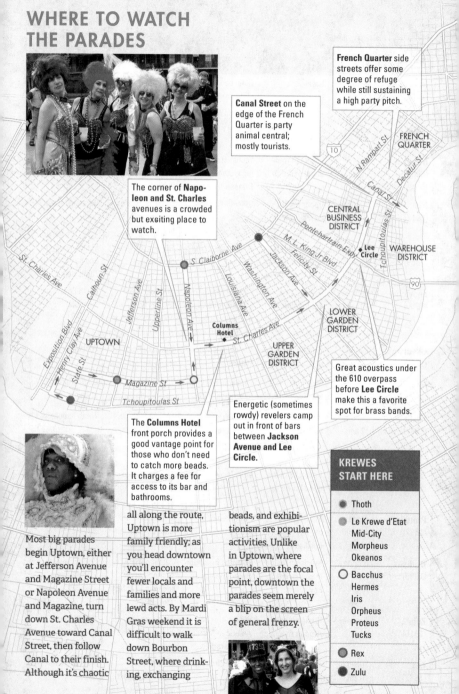

French Quarter side streets offer some degree of refuge while still sustaining a high party pitch.

Canal Street on the edge of the French Quarter is party animal central; mostly tourists.

The corner of **Napoleon and St. Charles** avenues is a crowded but exciting place to watch.

Great acoustics under the 610 overpass before **Lee Circle** make this a favorite spot for brass bands.

Energetic (sometimes rowdy) revelers camp out in front of bars between **Jackson Avenue and Lee Circle.**

The **Columns Hotel** front porch provides a good vantage point for those who don't need to catch more beads. It charges a fee for access to its bar and bathrooms.

Most big parades begin Uptown, either at Jefferson Avenue and Magazine Street or Napoleon Avenue and Magazine, turn down St. Charles Avenue toward Canal Street, then follow Canal to their finish. Although it's chaotic all along the route, Uptown is more family friendly; as you head downtown you'll encounter fewer locals and families and more lewd acts. By Mardi Gras weekend it is difficult to walk down Bourbon Street, where drinking, exchanging beads, and exhibitionism are popular activities. Unlike in Uptown, where parades are the focal point, downtown the parades seem merely a blip on the screen of general frenzy.

KREWES START HERE

- ● Thoth
- ● Le Krewe d'Etat
  Mid-City
  Morpheus
  Okeanos
- ○ Bacchus
  Hermes
  Iris
  Orpheus
  Proteus
  Tucks
- ● Rex
- ● Zulu

MARDI GRAS TRADITIONS

Royalty

Indian   Dancer

New Orleans's many Carnival traditions often collide on Mardi Gras. Here are some of the characters you're bound to meet.

Mardi Gras Royalty. Each krewe selects monarchs to preside over its parade and ball. In old-line krewes, members choose the king, who is often a prominent local philanthropist and businessman. Super krewes like Bacchus and Endymion pick celebrity kings or grand marshals. Some krewes elect a queen; others have a more elaborate process. To become the reigning woman of the Twelfth Night Revelers, a debutante must find a golden bean in a faux king cake.

Mardi Gras Indians. The African American Mardi Gras Indians began their rituals in the late 19th century in response to being excluded from white Mardi Gras festivities. On Fat Tuesday morning—dressed in intricately beaded and feathered "suits" that often take all year to create—the tribes chant songs and square off in mock battles to decide whose Big Chief is the prettiest. You'll find the Uptown tribes across St. Charles Avenue from the Garden District between Jackson and Washington avenues. Downtown tribes generally meander through Tremé on Ursulines Street.

Dancers. First it was troupes of suburban middle-school girls that entertained between parade floats. Later, grown women thought this looked fun and created groups like the Pussyfooters and Camel Toe Lady Steppers. Despite the risqué names, many members are lawyers, professors, and other professionals; all members practice choreographed routines for months. In 2010, the 610 Stompers, the first all-male troupe, took to the streets in tight blue gym shorts and red satin jackets. Their motto was "Ordinary Men, Extraordinary Moves."

MARDI GRAS SAFETY

■ Use common sense; don't bring excess cash, valuables, or tempting jewelry.

■ Establish a meeting spot where your family or group will convene at preset times throughout the day.

■ Do not throw anything at the floats or bands, a ticketable and truly hazardous act.

■ You will probably get away with flashing in the French Quarter, but elsewhere you might get ticketed.

■ Be aware that cell phone photos and videos shot on Bourbon Street can wind up on the Internet; think twice before you flash for beads.

■ Each year accidents occur when children (or adults) venture too near the wheels of floats. If you have kids with you, pick a spot some way back from the parade.

MARDI GRAS YEAR-ROUND

A sculptor working on a float at Blaine Kern's Mardi Gras World.

BACKSTREET CULTURAL MUSEUM
This small museum in Tremé chronicles New Orleans's street culture, including the Mardi Gras Indians. Elaborate costumes are on display.

BLAINE KERN'S MARDI GRAS WORLD
Tour the workshop of one of the most prominent Carnival float builders. Floats from previous parades are on display in the warehouse.

GERMAINE WELLS MARDI GRAS MUSEUM
This free Mardi Gras museum is full of photos, masks, and more than two dozen mid-20th-century ball gowns, most worn by Germaine Wells, daughter of the restaurant's founder and queen of more than twenty-two Mardi Gras balls.

THE PRESBYTERE
Part of the Louisiana State Museum, this historic building on Jackson Square hosts a permanent Mardi Gras exhibit on the second floor.

MARDI GRAS RESOURCES

■ **Arthur Hardy's Mardi Gras Guide** (⊕ www.mardigrasguide.com).

■ **MardiGras.com** (⊕ www.mardigras.com).

■ **New Orleans Convention and Visitors Bureau** (⊕ www.neworleanscvb.com).

MARDI GRAS LINGO

King cake: An oval cake decorated with purple, green, and gold sugar and glaze, eaten from January 6—"Twelfth Night"—until Mardi Gras. A plastic baby is hidden inside, and by tradition whoever gets it must host the next year's Mardi Gras party.

Krewe: A term used by Carnival organizations to describe themselves, as in Krewe of Iris.

Lundi Gras: French for "Fat Monday," the day before Mardi Gras.

Mardi Gras: "Fat Tuesday" in French; the day before Ash Wednesday and the culmination of the festivities surrounding Carnival season.

Purple, green, and gold: The traditional colors of Mardi Gras (purple represents justice, green faith, and gold power), chosen by the first Rex in 1872.

Throw: Anything tossed off a float, such as beads, plastic cups, doubloons (fake metal coins), or stuffed animals.

"Throw me somethin', mister": Phrase shouted at float riders to get their attention so they will throw you beads.

Pontalba Buildings

HOUSE | Baroness Micaela Pontalba built this twin set of town houses, one on each side of Jackson Square, around 1850; they are known for their ornate cast-iron balcony railings. Baroness Pontalba's father was Don Almonester, who sponsored the rebuilding of the St. Louis Cathedral in 1788. The strong-willed Miss Almonester also helped fund the landscaping of the square and the erection of the Andrew Jackson statue at its center. The Pontalba Buildings are publicly owned; the side to the right of the cathedral, on St. Ann Street, is owned by the state, and the other side, on St. Peter Street, by the city. On the state-owned side is the **1850 House,** and at 540-B St. Peter Street on the city-owned side is a plaque marking the apartment of Sherwood Anderson, writer and mentor to William Faulkner. ⊠ *French Quarter.*

★ The Presbytère

MUSEUM | One of the twin Spanish colonial buildings flanking the St. Louis Cathedral, this one, on the right, was built on the site of the priests' residence, or *presbytère.* It served as a courthouse under the Spanish and later under the Americans. It is now a museum showcasing a spectacular collection of Mardi Gras memorabilia. Displays highlight both the little-known and popular traditions associated with New Orleans's most famous festival. "Living with Hurricanes: Katrina and Beyond" is a $7.5-million exhibition exploring the history, science, and powerful human drama of one of nature's most destructive forces. The building's cupola, destroyed by a hurricane in 1915, was restored to match the one atop its twin, the Cabildo. Allow at least an hour to see the exhibits. ⊠ *751 Chartres St., on Jackson Sq., French Quarter* ☎ *504/568–6968* ⊕ *www.louisianastatemuseum.org* 🏷 *$7* ⊙ *Closed Mon.*

Rodrigue Studio

MUSEUM | Cajun artist George Rodrigue began his career as a painter with moody yet stirring portraits of rural Cajun life, but he gained popular renown in 1984 when he started painting blue dogs, inspired by the spirit of his deceased pet, Tiffany. Since then, the blue dog can be found in thousands of manifestations in various settings in the cult artist's paintings. Rodrigue died in late 2013, and his principal gallery, a space rather eerily lined almost entirely with paintings of the blue dog, is now managed by his family as a gallery and event space. ⊠ *730 Royal St., French Quarter* ☎ *504/581–4244* ⊕ *www. georgerodrigue.com.*

★ St. Louis Cathedral

RELIGIOUS SITE | The oldest active Catholic cathedral in the United States, this beautiful church and basilica at the heart of the Old City is named for the 13th-century French king who led two crusades. The current building, which replaced two structures destroyed by fire, dates from 1794 (although it was remodeled and enlarged in 1851). The austere interior is brightened by murals covering the ceiling and stained-glass windows along the first floor. Pope John Paul II held a prayer service for clergy here during his New Orleans visit in 1987; to honor the occasion, the pedestrian mall in front of the cathedral was renamed Place Jean Paul Deux. Of special interest is his portrait in a Jackson Square setting, which hangs on the cathedral's inner side wall. Docents often give free tours. You can also pick up a brochure ($1) for a self-guided tour. Books about the cathedral are available in the gift shop. A mass occurs daily at 11:30 am. ■**TIP**→ **Nearly every evening in December there's a free concert at the cathedral, in addition to a free concert series throughout the year.**

The statue of the Sacred Heart of Jesus dominates **St. Anthony's Garden,** which extends behind the cathedral to Royal

Street. The garden is also the site of a monument to 30 crew members of a French ship, who died in a yellow fever epidemic in 1857. The garden has been redesigned by famed French landscape architect Louis Benech, who also redesigned the Tuileries gardens in Paris. ✉ *615 Père Antoine Alley, French Quarter* ☎ *504/525–9585* 🌐 *www.stlouiscathedral.org* 🎟 *Free.*

Washington Artillery Park

MILITARY SITE | This raised concrete area on the river side of Decatur Street, directly across from Jackson Square, is a great spot to photograph the square or the barges and paddle wheelers on the Mississippi. The cannon mounted in the center and pointing toward the river is a model 1861 Parrot Rifle used in the Civil War. This monument honors the local 141st Field Artillery of the Louisiana National Guard that saw action from the Civil War through World War II. Marble tablets at the base give the history of the group, represented today by the Washington Artillery Association. ✉ *Decatur St., between St. Peter and St. Ann Sts., French Quarter* 🌐 *www.washingtonartillery.com.*

Woldenberg Riverfront Park

NATIONAL/STATE PARK | This 16-acre stretch of green from Canal Street to Esplanade Avenue overlooks the Mississippi River as it curves around New Orleans, inspiring the "Crescent City" moniker. The wooden promenade section in front of Jackson Square is called the **Moon Walk,** named for Mayor Moon Landrieu (father of recent mayor Mitch Landrieu), under whose administration in the 1970s the riverfront beyond the flood wall was reopened to public view. Today, the French Quarter Festival's main stages are erected here every April. It's a great place for a rest (or a muffuletta sandwich or café au lait and beignet picnic) after touring the Quarter, and you'll often be serenaded by musicians and amused by street performers. The park is also home to art pieces including the modest **Holocaust Memorial,** with its spiral walkway clad in Jerusalem stone. At the center of the spiral are nine sculptural panels by Jewish artist Yaacov Agam. A statue of local businessman Malcolm Woldenberg, the park's benefactor, is located near *Ocean Song;* local artist John T. Scott's large kinetic sculpture's wind-powered movements are intended to evoke the patterns of New Orleans music. ✉ *French Quarter* 🌐 *www.auduboninstitute.org/aquarium/exhibits-and-attractions/woldenberg-park.*

🍴 Restaurants

In the city's oldest neighborhood, grand restaurants that opened before the Civil War sit around the corner from contemporary, cutting-edge destinations. The Quarter, as locals call it, is a living neighborhood, and though it's packed with tourists, you'll certainly bump into residents grabbing a cup of coffee or tucking into a po'boy for lunch.

Café Amelie

$$$ | **AMERICAN** | There's no shortage of charming courtyards in the French Quarter, but the candlelit, ivy-covered stone carriageway at Café Amelie is one of the most romantic places to get a gourmet meal. The Louisiana-inspired entrées feature hearty portions of lamb steak, pork chops, and fresh seafood. **Known for:** creative cocktails; romantic setting; reservations needed far in advance. [$] *Average main: $27* ✉ *912 Royal St., French Quarter* ☎ *504/412–8965* 🌐 *www.cafeamelie.com* 🕒 *Closed Mon.*

★ Café du Monde

$ | **CAFÉ** | **FAMILY** | No visit to New Orleans is complete without a chicory-laced café au lait paired with the addictive, sugar-dusted beignets at this venerable institution. The tables under the green-and-white-stripe awning are jammed with

Micaela Pontalba

Every life has its little dramas, but how many of us can claim a life dramatic enough to inspire an opera? The Baroness Micaela Almonester de Pontalba numbers among that rarefied group, albeit posthumously. In 2003, on the 200th anniversary of the Louisiana Purchase, the New Orleans Opera Association commissioned an opera based on Pontalba, whose legacy you can easily see in the Pontalba Buildings, the elegant brick apartments lining Jackson Square.

Micaela Almonester was the daughter of the wealthy Spanish entrepreneur and developer Don Andres Almonester, who was instrumental in the creation of the Cabildo and Presbytère on Jackson Square. Don Almonester died while Micaela was still young, but not before passing on to his daughter a passion for building and urban design. The rest of her life would become a tale of international scope.

At the time of the Louisiana Purchase, in 1803, New Orleans was in a state of cultural upheaval. Following a period under Spanish rule during the late 18th century, the French had reacquired the colony—and merrily sold it to the Americans. The already complex blend of French and Spanish societies was further complicated by the anticipated imposition of American laws and mores, so foreign to the population of New Orleans. Micaela Almonester was right in the middle of the confusion: daughter of Spanish gentry, she fell in love and married a Frenchman, who took her to Paris with his family to avoid coming under American rule in New Orleans.

The Pontalbas' marriage was particularly unhappy, and Micaela's relationship to her in-laws was poisoned by mistrust over family property. Control of her New Orleans inheritance became part of an increasingly bitter feud that resulted in separation from her husband and, at its dramatic pinnacle, her attempted murder by her father-in-law. After the old baron inflicted four gunshot wounds on his daughter-in-law, he committed suicide, believing he had protected his son and his property. But Micaela, now Baroness de Pontalba following the old baron's death, survived her wounds. Within two years she had recovered enough to conceive the plan for the buildings that bear her name, but a long series of delays, including a bitter divorce, halted the project. Micaela finally returned to New Orleans in the 1840s in order to direct construction of the elegant apartments that would complete the square her father had been instrumental in developing. The Pontalba Buildings, designed by James Gallier in the French style favored by Micaela, were dedicated in 1851 to great fanfare.

locals and tourists at almost every hour, for very good reason. **Known for:** world's most famous beignets; local landmark status; long waits and 24-hour service. [$] *Average main: $3* ✉ *800 Decatur St., French Quarter* ☎ *504/525–4544* 🌐 *www.cafedumonde.com.*

Central Grocery

$ | DELI | FAMILY | This old-fashioned grocery store creates authentic muffulettas, a gastronomic gift from the city's Italian immigrants. Made by filling nearly 10-inch round loaves of seeded bread with ham, salami, provolone and Emmentaler cheeses, and olive salad, the muffuletta is nearly as popular locally as the po'boy. (Central Grocery also sells a vegetarian version.) The sandwiches are available in wholes and halves (they're huge—unless you're starving, you'll do fine with a half). **Known for:** the city's best (and biggest) muffulettas; lively setting; early closing at 5 pm. $ *Average main: $8* ⊠ *923 Decatur St., French Quarter* ☎ *504/523–1620* ⊕ *www.centralgrocery.com* ⊙ *No dinner.*

Croissant d'Or Patisserie

$ | CAFÉ | In a quiet corner of the French Quarter, you'll have to look for the quaint Croissant d'Or Patisserie. Once you've found it, you'll understand why locals and visitors return to this colorful pastry shop for excellent and authentic French croissants, pies, tarts, and custards, as well as an imaginative selection of soups, salads, and sandwiches (don't miss the hot croissant sandwiches with creamy béchamel sauce). **Known for:** croissaint sandwiches; authentic French pastries; king cake during Mardi Gras. $ *Average main: $5* ⊠ *617 Ursulines St., French Quarter* ☎ *504/524–4663* ⊙ *Closed Tues. No dinner.*

Green Goddess

$ | ECLECTIC | At this cozy (read: small) restaurant in the heart of the French Quarter, diners are wowed by the inventive and globally inspired cuisine, though the service is a bit eclectic, too. Menus change regularly, but may feature apple cheddar French toast and beet burrata kale salad for lunch, or a bacon sundae with pecan-praline ice cream for dessert. **Known for:** tasty French toast and sandwiches; outside dining in nice weather; vegetarian options. $ *Average main: $15* ⊠ *307 Exchange Pl., French Quarter* ☎ *504/301–3347* ⊕ *www.greengoddessrestaurant.com* ⊙ *Closed Mon. and Tues.*

Gumbo Shop

$ | CREOLE | FAMILY | Even given a few modern touches—like the vegetarian gumbo offered daily—this place evokes

a sense of old New Orleans. The menu is chock-full of regional culinary anchors: jambalaya, shrimp Creole, rémoulade sauce, red beans and rice, bread pudding, and seafood and chicken-and-sausage gumbos, all heavily flavored with tradition but easy on the wallet. **Known for:** classic Creole food; cheap prices; shabby-chic decor. $ *Average main: $14* ⊠ *630 St. Peter St., French Quarter* ☎ *504/525–1486* ⊕ *www.gumboshop.com.*

Irene's Cuisine

$$ | ITALIAN | FAMILY | The walls here are festooned with enough snapshots, garlic braids, and crockery for at least two more restaurants, but it all just adds to the charm of this cozy Italian-Creole eatery. From Irene DiPietro's kitchen come succulent roast chicken brushed with olive oil, rosemary, and garlic; delicious, velvety soups; and fresh shrimp, aggressively seasoned and grilled before they join linguine glistening with herbed olive oil. **Known for:** piano bar on-site; local vibe; long waits for a table. $ *Average main: $20* ⊠ *529 Bienville St., French Quarter* ☎ *504/529–8811* ⊙ *Closed Sun. No lunch.*

The Italian Barrel

$$$ | ITALIAN | Here Verona-born chef Samantha Castagnetti turns out sumptuous, authentic northern Italian pasta dishes, like fusilli with peas, shallots, and Italian prosciutto in an elegant white cream sauce, alongside meaty mains, such as veal osso buco over decadent polenta. This is the kind of place that turns first dates into lifelong affairs; you'll feel like you're dining at nonna's house. **Known for:** hearty pasta; affordable wine list; good people-watching. $ *Average main: $25* ⊠ *1240 Decatur St., French Quarter* ☎ *504/569–0198* ⊕ *www.theitalianbarrel.com.*

Johnny's Po-boys

$ | DELI | FAMILY | Strangely enough, good po'boys are hard to find in the French

The King Cake

New Orleans is known for lots of local flavor, from pralines and po'boys to beignets and chicory coffee. But for a true taste of Mardi Gras, you can't beat a king cake.

The origins of the king cake go back to early-12th-century Europe, when a similar type of cake was baked to represent the arrival of the biblical Three Kings on the 12th day after Christmas. It is thought that French immigrants passed along the tradition to the residents of New Orleans in the late 19th century. Many years and iterations later, the king cake lives on, and starting on the Epiphany (January 6, the first day of Mardi Gras) through Fat Tuesday (the day before

Ash Wednesday), no party is complete without a king cake at hand.

Traditional king cakes are a ring-shape, cinnamon-flavored brioche with purple, gold, and green icing for the colors of Mardi Gras. Nowadays king cakes come in a variety of flavors and fillings, like cream cheese, almond, praline, or chocolate. A small plastic toy baby, said to represent Baby Jesus, is hidden inside the cake. It's tradition that whoever gets the slice with the hidden baby must host the next Mardi Gras party or buy the king cake for the next celebration.

You can find them all around the area in special bakeries and local grocery stores.

Quarter, but Johnny's, established in 1950, compensates for that scarcity with a cornucopia of overstuffed options, even though quality can be inconsistent and the prices somewhat inflated for tourists. Inside the soft-crust French bread come the classic fillings, including lean boiled ham, well-done roast beef in garlicky gravy, and crisply fried oysters or shrimp. **Known for:** classic po'boys; lots of tourists; early closing at 4:30 pm. $ *Average main: $8* ⊠ *511 St. Louis St., French Quarter* ☎ *504/524–8129* ⊘ *No dinner.*

Justine

$$$$ | **BISTRO** | Celebrated local chef Justin Devillier (of Le Petite Grocery fame) brings an entirely new concept to the French Quarter with Justine. With a nightly DJ, boisterous brunches, and loads of neon and Instagrammable spaces, the emphasis here is more on a festive experience than the food itself (though the Parisian bistro menu has its strong points). Justine herself, a marble statue and the restaurant's patron saint,

gazes over the zinc bar top imported from Paris, and Ellen Macomber's dual mural-collages of Paris and New Orleans make the back room dazzle. **Known for:** boozy brunches; chic aesthetic; French bistro classics. $ *Average main: $34* ⊠ *225 Chartres St., French Quarter* ☎ *504/218–8533* ⊕ *www.justinenola.com* ⊘ *No lunch Mon.*

Kingfish

$$ | **CREOLE** | Named after former Louisiana Governor Huey P. Long, who went by the nickname "Kingfish," this stylish French Quarter restaurant pays homage to the Jazz Age, with its pressed-tin ceilings and suspendered bartenders (the excellent craft cocktail list was written by local legend Chris McMillian). **Known for:** snazzy cocktails; small plates of modern Southern cuisine; jazz-friendly atmosphere. $ *Average main: $22* ⊠ *337 Chartres St., French Quarter* ☎ *504/598–5005* ⊕ *www.kingfishneworleans.com.*

Muriel's Jackson Square

$$$ | CREOLE | Among Jackson Square's many dining spots, Muriel's is easily the most ambitious, in both atmosphere and menu. In the large downstairs rooms, architectural knickknacks and artwork evoke the city's colorful past, while diners indulge in hearty updates of old Creole favorites. **Known for:** entertaining setting in the middle of French Quarter action; inventive Creole flavors; Sunday brunch with live jazz. $ *Average main: $26 ⊠ 801 Chartres St., French Quarter ☎ 504/568–1885 ⊕ www.muriels.com.*

★ Nola

$$$ | CREOLE | Fans of Emeril Lagasse will want to grab a seat at the food bar overlooking the open kitchen at his French Quarter restaurant. Freewheeling appetizers are among the big attractions—the stand-out being "Mama's stuffed chicken wings" with peanut dipping sauce—while entrées, such as the garlic-crusted drum, are filling but delicious. **Known for:** stuffed chicken wings and buttermilk fried chicken; decadent desserts; modern decor. $ *Average main: $28 ⊠ 534 St. Louis St., French Quarter ☎ 504/522–6652 ⊕ www.emerilsrestaurants.com.*

Palace Café

$$$ | CREOLE | FAMILY | Occupying what used to be New Orleans's oldest music store, this Dickie Brennan stalwart is a convivial spot to try some of the more imaginative contemporary Creole dishes, such as andouille-crusted fish, crabmeat cheesecake, and pepper-crusted duck breast with foie gras. Desserts, especially the white-chocolate bread pudding and the homemade ice creams, are luscious. **Known for:** classic Sunday jazz brunch; excellent happy hour; Parisian-style sidewalk seating. $ *Average main: $27 ⊠ 605 Canal St., French Quarter ☎ 504/523–1661 ⊕ www.palacecafe.com.*

Pelican Club

$$$$ | ECLECTIC | Sassy New York flourishes permeate the menu of chef Richard Hughes's smartly decorated, eminently comfortable restaurant in the heart of the French Quarter, but there's still evidence of Hughes's Louisiana origins. The Maine lobster with shrimp and diver scallops is decadent, while the rack of lamb with rosemary-pesto crust is almost a spiritual experience. **Known for:** well-heeled locals; Gulf fish dishes; old-school menu. $ *Average main: $32 ⊠ 312 Exchange Pl., French Quarter ☎ 504/523–1504 ⊕ www.pelicanclub.com ⊗ No lunch.*

SoBou

$$ | CREOLE | This sleek venture (whose name is short for "South of Bourbon Street") from the Commander's Palace team puts cocktails, beer, and wine front and center. The menu includes Louisiana-style snacks, such as grilled alligator sausage or cracklings with pimento-cheese fondue, and the cocktails are a mix of pre-Prohibition classics and crowd-pleasing originals. **Known for:** delicious fish tacos; Louisiana classics with a Latin flair; self-service wine machines. $ *Average main: $15 ⊠ W Hotel French Quarter, 310 Chartres St., French Quarter ☎ 504/552–4095 ⊕ www.sobounola.com.*

Stanley

$ | CREOLE | FAMILY | Chefs across America are ditching the white tablecloths and applying fine-dining flair to burgers, bar food, and comfort fare, and here chef Scott Boswell attempts this with the food of Louisiana. Though some grumble about paying a premium for what is, at heart, New Orleans neighborhood fare, this crisply decorated café sits on a coveted corner of Jackson Square—and that view is priceless. **Known for:** eggs Benedict with a Cajun twist; prime real estate; spicy oyster po'boys. $ *Average main: $13 ⊠ 547 St. Ann St., French Quarter ☎ 504/587–0093 ⊕ www.stanleyrestaurant.com ⊟ No credit cards.*

Sylvain

$$ | AMERICAN | Enjoy the best of contemporary food in an antique setting, at this sleek gastropub within an 18th-century carriage house. Sylvain celebrates

the new and old with an elegant but light touch (look, for example at the "Champagne and fries" starter: a bottle of the finest brut accompanies a plate of hand-cut fries for $90). **Known for:** romantic setting; fried chicken sandwich; popular Sylvain Burger. [$] *Average main: $21* ✉ *625 Chartres St., French Quarter* ☎ *504/265–8123* 🌐 *www.sylvainnola.com* 🕑 *No lunch Mon.–Thurs.*

Hotels

Bienville House Hotel
$$ | **HOTEL** | Some of the antiques-filled rooms open to gorgeous sundecks, while others have balconies overlooking the courtyard's saltwater pool. **Pros:** close to the Canal Street streetcars and Jackson Square; complimentary breakfast and good bar on-site; affordable for the location. **Cons:** noise can be a problem at night; standard rooms are on the small side; no fitness center. [$] *Rooms from: $154* ✉ *320 Decatur St., French Quarter* ☎ *504/529–2345* 🌐 *www.bienvillehouse.com* 🛏 *83 rooms* 🍴 *Free breakfast.*

★ **Hotel Monteleone**
$$ | **HOTEL** | One of the grand old hotels of New Orleans, the Hotel Monteleone dates to 1886 and oozes sophistication, romance, and history. **Pros:** great location in the French Quarter; Royal Street shopping; fabulous and famous carousel bar. **Cons:** the lobby and entrance can get crowded; attracts big parties; rooms on the small side. [$] *Rooms from: $249* ✉ *214 Royal St., French Quarter* ☎ *504/523–3341, 800/535–9595* 🌐 *www.hotelmonteleone.com* 🛏 *655 rooms* 🍴 *No meals.*

Hotel Provincial
$$ | **HOTEL** | This memorably authentic inn feels nicely secluded yet close to the action. **Pros:** quaint atmosphere; quiet surroundings (in a residential section of the French Quarter); free Wi-Fi. **Cons:** suites are pricey; mixed service; reports of paranormal activity. [$] *Rooms from: $212* ✉ *1024 Chartres St., French Quarter* ☎ *504/581–4995, 800/535–7922* 🌐 *www.hotelprovincial.com* 🛏 *99 rooms* 🍴 *Free breakfast.*

Hotel Royal
$ | **HOTEL** | Think of a cool big-city boutique hotel, mix in some authentic New Orleans elegance and a good location, and you've got Hotel Royal. **Pros:** central location; complimentary breakfast and pralines upon arrival; free Wi-Fi. **Cons:** rooms are small and limited; no elevator and steps to reach upper floors; housekeeping inconsistent. [$] *Rooms from: $119* ✉ *1006 Royal St., French Quarter* ☎ *504/524–3900, 800/776–3901* 🌐 *www.hotelroyalneworleans.com* 🛏 *43 rooms* 🍴 *No meals.*

Hotel Villa Convento
$$ | **HOTEL** | This intimate, four-story 1833 Creole town house is located on a quiet street close to the Old Ursuline Convent, yet just blocks from the Quarter's tourist attractions, shopping, and restaurants. **Pros:** located in the quieter residential section of the French Quarter; true New Orleans flavor; free Wi-Fi in all rooms. **Cons:** rooms on the small side; no restaurant on-site; no pool or fitness center. [$] *Rooms from: $165* ✉ *616 Ursulines Ave., French Quarter* ☎ *504/522–1793* 🌐 *www.villaconvento.com* 🛏 *25 rooms* 🍴 *No meals* ☞ *No children under 10.*

Le Richelieu in the French Quarter
$$ | **HOTEL** | Guests appreciate the personal friendliness of this old-fashioned, budget-friendly hotel, as well as nice touches such as the outdoor saltwater pool—all at a moderate rate in a great location. **Pros:** good value; affordable on-site parking; close to the Old Ursuline Convent and the French Market. **Cons:** café open only for breakfast and lunch; bathrooms are small and dated; rooms need updating. [$] *Rooms from: $180* ✉ *1234 Chartres St., French Quarter* ☎ *504/529–2492, 800/535–9653* 🌐 *www.lerichelieuhotel.com* 🛏 *87 rooms* 🍴 *No meals.*

New Orleans Marriott Hotel

$$$ | HOTEL | FAMILY | This centrally located 41-story skyscraper boasts fabulous views of the Quarter, downtown, and the Mississippi River. **Pros:** centrally located; stunning city and river views; can be a good deal during busy season. **Cons:** typical chain hotel; lacks charm; charge for Wi-Fi in the rooms (access is free from the lobby). $ *Rooms from: $239* ✉ *555 Canal St., French Quarter* ☎ *504/581–1000, 800/228–9290* ⊕ *www.neworleansmarriott.com* ⇄ *1,329 rooms* ❚❍❙ *No meals.*

Omni Royal Orleans Hotel

$$ | HOTEL | One of the more elegant options in the French Quarter, this large white-marble landmark is a replica of the grand 1800s St. Louis Hotel, with columns, gilt mirrors, and magnificent chandeliers: traditional elegance in a central location. **Pros:** old-world grandeur; central location; beautiful common areas. **Cons:** can be crowded in the lobby and pool areas; daily charge for Wi-Fi; smaller rooms. $ *Rooms from: $225* ✉ *621 St. Louis St., French Quarter* ☎ *504/529–5333, 800/843–6664* ⊕ *www.omnihotels.com* ⇄ *371 rooms* ❚❍❙ *No meals.*

★ Soniat House

$$$ | B&B/INN | Many frequent New Orleans visitors consider these meticulously restored town houses from the 1830s to be the city's finest hotel, with elegant rooms where stunning artwork—including some pieces on loan from the New Orleans Museum of Art—complements polished hardwood floors, Oriental rugs, and American and European antiques. **Pros:** very refined; expert service; timeless elegance. **Cons:** breakfast is delicious, but costs extra; several rooms are accessible by steps only; limited amenities. $ *Rooms from: $245* ✉ *1133 Chartres St., French Quarter* ☎ *504/522–0570, 800/544–8808* ⊕ *www.soniathouse.com* ⇄ *29 rooms* ❚❍❙ *No meals.*

New Orleans Coffee 🍴

Local coffee brands like Community, French Market, Luzianne, and Café du Monde add up to 30% chicory to their coffee, which gives it a bitter quality that some people like (it also served to stretch out coffee supplies during past shortages). Chicory is caffeine-free and reportedly helps control blood sugar, reduce cholesterol, and boost bone-mineral density, and may be good for your liver.

W Hotel New Orleans French Quarter

$$$ | HOTEL | The many perks here include one of the best locations in the Quarter, rooms designed with funky jazz and tarot-card themes, and balconies that overlook either the courtyard or Chartres Street. **Pros:** beautiful courtyard and pool; excellent service with 24-hour concierges; lively contemporary decor with a New Orleans flavor. **Cons:** small driveway area can get crowded with valet activity; lines at check-in and check-out; cleanliness inconsistent. $ *Rooms from: $299* ✉ *316 Chartres St., French Quarter* ☎ *504/581–1200, 888/627–8260* ⊕ *www.wfrenchquarter.com* ⇄ *102 rooms* ❚❍❙ *No meals.*

The Westin New Orleans Canal Place

$$$ | HOTEL | Views from this large convention hotel are enviable: two-story arched lobby windows overlook the French Quarter, and guest rooms tower over the great bend in the Mississippi River. **Pros:** luxurious rooms and suites; fabulous views of the Mississippi River and the French Quarter; close to shopping. **Cons:** hotel has a chain feel; groups can overwhelm common spaces; daily charge for Internet access. $ *Rooms from: $232* ✉ *100 Iberville St., French Quarter*

☎ 504/566–7006, 800/996–3426 ⊕ www.starwoodhotels.com/westin ⊋ 478 rooms ☯ No meals.

☯ Nightlife

The French Quarter, with its Spanish architecture and narrow, French-named streets, is the hub of the Crescent City and remains the beating heart of New Orleans's nightlife. Live music comes at you from all directions—from bars, clubs, concert halls, restaurants, and even from the streets themselves—and many of the neighborhood's restaurants, shops, cafés, and galleries stay open late to accommodate the night crowd. Although mostly fueled by tourists, the French Quarter remains the city's premiere nightlife destination because of its diversity and convenience.

BARS AND LOUNGES

★ Cane and Table

BARS/PUBS | With its elegant, understated Caribbean decor, dim lighting, and low volumes, this rum house is a refreshing relief from the general chaos of the neighborhood. The friendly barkeeps love making "ProtoTiki Cocktails" (specialty rum drinks with modern twists), but there's a sophisticated list of Spanish wines to choose from as well. The space offers a large marble bar, charming courtyard out back, and small tables for intimate dining. Come for the cocktails and atmosphere, but don't miss out on the food: the menu combines Caribbean and Southern culinary traditions, and the dishes are inventive and intensely flavorful. ⊠ 1113 Decatur St., French Quarter ☎ 504/581–1112 ⊕ www.caneandtable-nola.com.

★ Carousel Bar

BARS/PUBS | A favorite New Orleans drinking destination since 1949, the revolving bar has served the likes of Tennessee Williams, Truman Capote, and Ernest Hemingway. If the famed carousel bar is too crowded, there's a second (stationary) bar and a stage that hosts free shows by local musicians Wednesday through Saturday. ⊠ Hotel Monteleone, 214 Royal St., French Quarter ☎ 504/523–3341 ⊕ www.hotelmonteleone.com.

Chart Room

BARS/PUBS | Unpretentious even by New Orleans standards, this little dive not far from Canal Street draws a good number of locals from the Quarter and beyond for inexpensive drinks and wide-open doorways that offer table seating just off the sidewalk. Note that it's cash-only. ⊠ 300 Chartres St., French Quarter ☎ 504/522–1708.

Kerry Irish Pub

BARS/PUBS | This well-worn favorite has a pool table, a jukebox stocked with the Pogues and Flogging Molly, and, of course, Guinness on draft. A small stage at the back hosts Irish musicians, singer-songwriters, and R&B or jazz musicians nightly with no cover charge. It's one of the last venues for Irish music in the Quarter. ⊠ 331 Decatur St., French Quarter ☎ 504/527–5954.

Molly's at the Market

BARS/PUBS | Grab a perch almost any time of day at one of the best-known and most popular bars along the far stretch of Decatur Street, where you'll find perfect pints of Guinness, generously poured cocktails, and gregarious bartenders. From a window seat, you can watch the crowds of shop-goers, sightseers, and all-day revelers. Everyone from politicians to punk rockers eventually drifts through these doors. ⊠ 1107 Decatur St., French Quarter ☎ 504/525–5169 ⊕ www.mollysatthemarket.net.

★ Napoleon House Bar and Café

BARS/PUBS | It's a living shrine to what may be called the semiofficial New Orleans school of decor: faded grandeur. Chipped wall paint, diffused light, and a tiny courtyard with a trickling fountain and lush banana trees create a timeless escapist mood. The house specialty is a Pimm's Cup (here they top Pimm's No. 1 with lemonade and 7-Up). This vintage restaurant and watering hole has long been popular with writers, artists, and other free spirits, although today most customers are tourists. But even locals who don't venture often into the French Quarter will make an exception for Napoleon House. ⊠ *500 Chartres St., French Quarter* ☎ *504/524–9752* ⊕ *www. napoleonhouse.com.*

🎭 Performing Arts

Le Petit Théâtre du Vieux Carré

THEATER | Since 1916, Le Petit Théâtre has entertained the French Quarter with plays, musicals, and variety shows. The oldest continuously running community theater in the United States occupies a historic building in the Quarter. The community-based group were originally housed in one of the Pontalba apartments on Jackson Square, but they quickly outgrew that space and moved to this building in 1922. The flagstone patio with its fountain is postcard-perfect. Renovations have resulted in many improvements to the theater itself, and also made room for Tableau, a restaurant featuring contemporary Creole fare by local restaurateur Dickie Brennan. The theater presents children's entertainment in addition to its usual calendar of classics, musicals, and dramas, often with local themes. Events in the Tennessee Williams Festival take place here in March. ⊠ *616 St. Peter St., French Quarter* ☎ *504/522–2081* ⊕ *www.lepetitthea-tre.com.*

🛍 Shopping

Browsing through the French Quarter is as much a cultural experience as a shopping excursion. Royal Street, known for its antiques stores, is great for a stroll and some window-shopping. Along

Shopping Tours 🛍

Local art-and-antiques shopping consultant **Macon Riddle** (☎ *504/899–3027* ⊕ *www.neworleansantiquing.com*) conducts half- and full-day personalized shopping expeditions by appointment. She can sometimes gain access to antiques warehouses not normally open to the public.

both Royal and Chartres streets, you'll find clusters of high-end art galleries displaying traditional, contemporary, and New Orleans–centric works. Many stores sell decorative Carnival masks that range from simple feather-and-ceramic styles that go for about $10 apiece to handcrafted, locally made varieties that carry much heftier price tags. Jewelry stores feature estate and antique jewelry alongside contemporary creations. Souvenir shops are around every corner, especially as you approach the heavily trafficked areas near the river. If your energy lags, plenty of cafés, coffee shops, candy stores, and bistros are there to provide a boost.

SHOPPING CENTERS AND MARKETS

Jax Brewery

SHOPPING CENTERS/MALLS | A historic factory building that once produced Jax beer now holds a mall filled with local shops and a few national chain stores, like Chico's, along with a food court and balcony overlooking the Mississippi River. Shops carry souvenirs, clothing, books, artwork, and more, with an emphasis on New Orleans–themed items. The mall is open daily. On hot summer days, it's an air-conditioned refuge. ⊠ *600 Decatur St., French Quarter* ☎ *504/566–7245* ⊕ *www. thejaxbrewery.com.*

The Shops at Canal Place

STORE/MALL | At the foot of Canal Street, this mall offers high-end shopping at department stores, chains, and a few local boutiques. The **Westin New Orleans at Canal Place** tops the complex; its dining rooms and lobby have fantastic river views. ⊠ *333 Canal St., French Quarter* ☎ *504/522–9200* ⊕ *www.theshopsatcanalplace.com.*

ANTIQUES AND COLLECTIBLES

★ M.S. Rau

ANTIQUES/COLLECTIBLES | Antiques lovers may want to set aside several hours to marvel at the extensive collection here. Rare pieces, such as furniture from royal families, join 18th- and 19th-century French, American, and English antiques, sterling silver, statuary, fine art, and jewelry in this 30,000-square-foot store, which opened in 1912. ⊠ *630 Royal St., French Quarter* ☎ *504/523–5660, 888/557–2406* ⊕ *www.rauantiques.com.*

Secondline Arts and Antiques

ANTIQUES/COLLECTIBLES | This 8,000-square-foot retail wonderland is filled with interesting antiques, light fixtures, salvaged items, and art. The store's selection of salvaged elements, mostly from old New Orleans houses, and art from emerging local artists, allows shoppers to take home a unique piece of the city. A night market stays open in the courtyard until 10 pm weekdays and midnight on weekends. ⊠ *1209 Decatur St., French Quarter* ☎ *504/875–1924* ⊕ *www.secondlinenola.com.*

ARTWORK

Artist's Market

ART GALLERIES | This co-op of regional artists showcases a wide variety of works, including handmade masks, photography focusing on New Orleans personalities and scenery, ceramics, blown glass, paintings, wrought-iron architectural accents, turned-wood bowls and vases, prints, jewelry, beads, and more. ⊠ *1228 Decatur St., French Quarter* ☎ *504/561–0046* ⊕ *www.artistsmarket-nola.com.*

Kurt E. Schon, Ltd.

ART GALLERIES | In a hushed art-museum atmosphere, this gallery, with its well-educated staff, showcases high-end European paintings from the 18th and 19th centuries. Visits are by appointment only. ⊠ *510 St. Louis St., French Quarter* ☎ *504/524–5462* ⊕ *www.kurteschonltd.com.*

BEAUTY

★ Hové Parfumeur, Ltd.

PERFUME/COSMETICS | A must for perfume lovers, this store has been creating fragrances since 1931. Scented oils, soaps, sachets, and potpourri have been made on-site for four generations and are sold all over the world. There are dozens of fragrances for men and women, as well as bath salts, anti-aging treatments, massage and body oils, antique shaving and dressing-table accessories, and new and antique perfume bottles. ⊠ *434 Chartres St., French Quarter* ☎ *504/525–7827* ⊕ *www.hoveparfumeur.com.*

BOOKS

★ Faulkner House Books

BOOKS/STATIONERY | Named for William Faulkner, who rented a room here in 1925, this bookstore is designated a National Literary Landmark. It specializes in first editions and rare and out-of-print books—mostly by Southern authors—but also carries new titles. The store keeps thousands of additional books at an off-site warehouse and hosts an annual *Happy Birthday, Mr. Faulkner!* Festival that salutes Faulkner and new Southern writers. ⊠ *624 Pirate's Alley, French Quarter* ☎ *504/524–2940* ⊕ *www.faulknerhouse.net.*

CLOTHING

★ Fleurty Girl

CLOTHING | Owned by the ebullient Lauren Thom, Fleurty Girl—its name is a play on "fleur-de-lis"—is the place to go for New Orleans apparel, home decor, and gifts. The store is known for its T-shirts displaying the humorous catchphrases and iconography of local culture and New Orleans Saints pride. There's affordable jewelry, children's books, colorful rain boots, Carnival-themed gear, and fleurs-de-lis in every imaginable form. There's also a location in the Garden District, at 3117 Magazine Street. ⊠ *617 Chartres St., French Quarter* ☎ *504/304–5529* ⊕ *www.fleurtygirl.net.*

Perlis Clothing French Quarter

CLOTHING | A smaller version of the locally owned Perlis boutique on Magazine Street, this shop features such items as polo shirts and neckties with crawfish logos, as well as everything from Hawaiian shirts to boxer shorts printed with images of Tabasco products and New Orleans themes. ⊠ *Jax Brewery, 600 Decatur St., Suite 104, French Quarter* ☎ *504/523–6681* ⊕ *www.perlis.com.*

United Apparel Liquidators

CLOTHING | Label-loving locals as well as celebrities in town shooting movies are known to shop at this designer clothing liquidator. The tiny boutique is busting with deeply discounted apparel, shoes, and accessories by major designers, such as Marni, Balenciaga, Michael Kors, Phillip Lim, and Prada. Contemporary lines, such as Serfontaine Denim, Steven Alan, Yigal Azrouel, and Alexander Wang, have also been spotted on the racks. The stylish, friendly, and eminently helpful sales staff has created a loyal cult of frequent shoppers. ⊠ *518 Chartres St., French Quarter* ☎ *504/301–4437* ⊕ *www.shopual.com.*

Violet's

CLOTHING | Girly girls rule at this boutique, which caters to the softer side of feminine dress, featuring skirts, sexy blouses, handbags, jewelry, and accessories, with styles ranging from contemporary to retro romantic. ⊠ *808 Chartres St., French Quarter* ☎ *504/569–0088.*

New Orleans Writers 🛍

Literary legends like Tennessee Williams, William Faulkner, Truman Capote, and Anne Rice called New Orleans home for at least part of their lives, and a number of other writers still work in and write about the city. Because of this literary heritage, bookstores give local authors optimum shelf space.

FOOD

★ Aunt Sally's Praline Shop

FOOD/CANDY | Satisfy your sweet tooth with an array of pralines, made while you watch. The traditional version is concocted from cane sugar spiked with pecans, but other flavors include chocolate, café au lait, and even bananas Foster. You can also buy hot sauce, prepackaged muffuletta mix, and Bourbon Street glaze, as well as art and books about New Orleans, zydeco CDs, and logo cups and aprons. ⊠ *French Market, 810 Decatur St., French Quarter* ☎ *504/524–3373, 800/642–7257* ⊕ *www.auntsallys.com.*

Evans Creole Candy Factory

FOOD/CANDY | The aroma of candy cooking will draw you into this sweets shop, established in 1900. You'll find a variety of pralines, pecan logs, and New Orleans's own Cuccia Chocolates, as well as coffee and gift baskets. ⊠ *848 Decatur St., French Quarter* ☎ *504/522–7111, 800/637–6675.*

Laura's Candies

FOOD/CANDY | In the candy-making business since 1913, this shop sells sweet pralines as well as chocolate specialties—including its signature Mississippi mud, made with milk or dark chocolate laced with caramel. ⊠ *331 Chartres St., French Quarter*

If you're in town for Mardi Gras, buy a mask at one of the city's many costume shops.

☎ *504/525–3880, 800/992–9699* ⊕ *www.laurascandies.com.*

New Orleans School of Cooking and Louisiana General Store

FOOD/CANDY | Learn how to make a roux and other Louisiana cooking techniques at this school that's inside a renovated 1800s molasses warehouse. Lessons are seasoned with history and tales of the state's famous cuisine. The general store stocks all kinds of regional spices, condiments, sauces, snacks, gift baskets, and cookbooks. ⊠ *524 St. Louis St., French Quarter* ☎ *504/525–2665, 800/237–4841* ⊕ *www.neworleansschoolofcooking.com.*

Tabasco Country Store

FOOD/CANDY | Named for the famous Louisiana-produced hot sauce, this store also offers spices, cookbooks, New Orleans–themed clothing and aprons, kitchen accoutrements, ties, posters, pewter items, and more. ⊠ *537 St. Ann St., French Quarter* ☎ *504/539–7900* ⊕ *www.nolacajunstore.com.*

JEWELRY AND ACCESSORIES

★ Fifi Mahony's

JEWELRY/ACCESSORIES | Anyone with a passion for playing dress-up and a flair for the dramatic will love this place filled with custom wigs, wild accessories, makeup, and hair products. The shop provides essential resources for Mardi Gras and Halloween costumes as well as ample creative advice. ⊠ *934 Royal St., French Quarter* ☎ *504/525–4343* ⊕ *www.fifimahonys.com.*

NOLA Couture

JEWELRY/ACCESSORIES | Preppy motifs and New Orleans pride are the twin hallmarks of this line of locally designed accessories. You'll find belts, neckties, pet leashes, wallets, hats, headbands, bags, glassware, and totes emblazoned with tiny Crescent City symbols—fleurs-de-lis, sno-balls, pelicans, hurricane swirls, streetcars—all in repeat patterns. There is also a location Uptown, at 3308 Magazine Street. ⊠ *Jackson Sq., 528 St. Peter St., French Quarter* ☎ *504/875–3522* ⊕ *www.nolacouture.com.*

Porter Lyons

JEWELRY/ACCESSORIES | The cuff bracelets, pendants, and other fine jewelry at this chic, minimalist boutique have a distinctly funky yet simplistic style. The store also carries scents, candles, and other small gifts. ✉ *631 Toulouse St., French Quarter* ☎ *504/518–4945* ⊕ *www.porterlyons. com.*

Quarter Smith

JEWELRY/ACCESSORIES | Gemologist and gold- and silversmith Ken Bowers designs contemporary jewelry in gold, silver, and platinum and carries a selection of antique pieces. ✉ *535 St. Louis St., French Quarter* ☎ *504/524–9731* ⊕ *www. quartersmith.com.*

Sterling Silvia

JEWELRY/ACCESSORIES | Silvia and Juan Asturias operate this business near the French Market, where Silvia's fleur-de-lis and flower-inspired designs share space with other silver jewelry from Chile, Mexico, Indonesia, Russia, Thailand, and elsewhere. There are also coral pieces, gift items, ceramic dolls, and more. ✉ *41 French Market Pl., French Quarter* ☎ *504/299–9225* ⊕ *www.sterlingsilvia. com.*

MARDI GRAS MASKS

Maskarade

LOCAL SPECIALTIES | A large selection of Mardi Gras masks range from locally made funky crafts to handmade Venetian creations, as well as custom designs and a large selection of affordable masks under $50. ✉ *630 St. Ann St., French Quarter* ☎ *504/568–1018* ⊕ *www.the-maskstore.com.*

NOVELTIES AND GIFTS

Esoterica Occult Goods

GIFTS/SOUVENIRS | Calling itself "the one-stop shop for all your occult needs," this store is a great place to pick up potions, gris-gris bags, jewelry, spell kits, incense, and altar and ritual items as well as books on magic and the occult arts. Tarot readings are also available.

✉ *541 Dumaine St., French Quarter* ☎ *504/581–7711, 866/581–7711* ⊕ *www. onewitch.com.*

Forever New Orleans

GIFTS/SOUVENIRS | It's all about the Crescent City in this small shop filled with New Orleans–themed items, including glassware adorned with pewter fleurs-de-lis, affordable jewelry that boasts local icons, stationery, tiles, clocks, ceramics, framed crosses, charms, bottle stoppers, frames, candles, cookbooks, and more. This is a great place to pick up upscale souvenirs and gifts. ✉ *700 Royal St., French Quarter* ☎ *504/586–3536* ⊕ *www. shopforeverneworleans.com.*

Idea Factory

GIFTS/SOUVENIRS | At this fun little shop, wood becomes art at the hands of craftspeople who carve functional clocks, clipboards, and jewelry boxes, as well as whimsical whirligigs, hand-carved board games, puzzles, kaleidoscopes, and toys, proving that not all playthings need to be plugged in. ✉ *924 Royal St., French Quarter* ☎ *504/524–5195, 800/524–4332* ⊕ *www.ideafactoryneworleans.com.*

Nadine Blake

BOOKS/STATIONERY | New Orleans native Nadine Blake worked in interior design in New York before moving home and setting up shop. Her delightful store reflects her varied travels and eclectic interests with quirky gifts, gorgeous design books, handmade note cards, vintage furniture, and a slew of cool whatnots. ✉ *1036 Royal St., French Quarter* ☎ *504/529–4913* ⊕ *www.nadineblake.com.*

OMG!

GIFTS/SOUVENIRS | Freshly poured, handmade candles make great gifts here, and come in locally specific scents like Spanish Moss, Beignet, and Magnolia. There are paintings, photographs, and jewelry by local artists for sale too as well as vintage religious pieces. ✉ *542 St. Peter St., French Quarter* ☎ *504/522–8443* ⊕ *www. omg-nola.com.*

Mardi Gras Shopping

The best way to experience the joys of Carnival is to go in costume. To assemble the perfect get-up, start at the top, with a custom-made wig from Fifi Mahony's on Royal Street in the French Quarter. Feel free to turn to the store's expert staff for all manner of advice, from how to properly apply glitter eye shadow and false eyelashes to how to pull off Lady Gaga's platinum bow-tied hairdo. For the rest of your outfit, stroll down to the French Market, where you can find cheap sunglasses, feather boas, and all sorts of other accessories, or continue to the **Artist's Market**, where there are masks you'll want to keep long after Mardi Gras has faded into Lent. For a one-stop costume experience, travel to Magazine Street and **Funky Monkey** for costumes, stockings, wigs, and accessories, or the **Encore Shop**, where you can choose from affordable ball gowns, suits, and more. Mardi Gras is all about having fun. So dress the part, enjoy the sardonic humor of the Carnival krewes, and have a ball.

Rendezvous Inc.

GIFTS/SOUVENIRS | A throwback to the days of Southern belles, this shop on Jackson Square has linens and lace, ranging from christening outfits for babies to table runners, napkins, women's handkerchiefs, and more. It also offers a charming array of antiques and reproductions, such as perfume bottles, tea sets, fleurs-de-lis, and crosses. ⊠ *Jackson Sq., 522 St. Peter St., French Quarter* ☎ *504/522–0225* ⊕ *www.rendezvouslinens.com.*

Santa's Quarters

GIFTS/SOUVENIRS | It's Christmas year-round at this shop, which displays a diverse range of traditional and novelty ornaments and decorations, Santa Clauses of all kinds, and a host of Louisiana-themed holiday items. ⊠ *1025 Decatur St., French Quarter* ☎ *504/581–5820* ⊕ *www.santasquarters.com.*

What's New

GIFTS/SOUVENIRS | Everything in this store carries a New Orleans theme, making it a great place to buy souvenirs people will actually want to keep, including fleur-de-lis–covered flasks, decorative pillows, nightlights with shades made from photographs of city scenes, glassware, ceramics, jewelry, and other works by local artists. ⊠ *French Market, 824 Decatur St., French Quarter* ☎ *504/586–2095* ⊕ *www.whatsnew-nola.com.*

TOYS

Little Toy Shop

TOYS | FAMILY | For more than 50 years, this has been the stop for a mix of New Orleans souvenirs, miniature die-cast metal cars (from the Model T to the Hummer), character lunchboxes, puppets, plastic animals, and collectible Madame Alexander dolls. There is a second location in the French Quarter at 513 St. Ann Street. ⊠ *900 Decatur St., French Quarter* ☎ *504/522–6588* ⊕ *www. littletoyshopnola.com.*

French Quarter Above Royal Street

◉ Sights

Angela King Gallery

MUSEUM | Gallery owner Angela King renovated an 1850s jewelry store into a modern gallery that exhibits oil paintings, prints, and metal and cast-glass

When to Go

Save Bourbon Street for after dinner at one of the Quarter's esteemed restaurants; like anything that's lived hard and been around a long time, Bourbon Street is much more attractive in low light.

sculptures from about 25 contemporary artists. ⊠ *241 Royal St., French Quarter* ☎ *504/524–8211* ⊕ *www.angelakinggallery.com.*

Bourbon Street

NEIGHBORHOOD | Ignore your better judgment and take a stroll down Bourbon Street past the bars, restaurants, music clubs, adult stores, and novelty shops that have given this strip its reputation as the playground of the South. The bars of Bourbon Street were among the first businesses of the city to reopen after Katrina; catering to off-duty relief workers, they provided their own form of relief. Today, the spirit of unbridled revelry here is as alive as ever. The noise, raucous crowds, and bawdy sights are not family fare, however; if you go with children, do so before sundown. St. Ann Street marks the beginning of a short strip of gay bars, some of which figure in the long history of LGBTQ culture in New Orleans. Although Bourbon Street is usually well patrolled, it is wise to stay alert to your surroundings. The street is blocked to create a pedestrian mall at night; crowds often get shoulder-to-shoulder, especially during major sports events, on New Year's Eve, and during Mardi Gras. ⊠ *French Quarter.*

Gauche House

HOUSE | The cherubs featured in the effusive ironwork on this distinctive house stops people in the street. Built in 1856, this mansion and its service buildings were once the estate of businessman John Gauche, who lived there until 1882. Although the privately owned house is not open to the public, its exterior still merits a visit to snap a few photos. ⊠ *704 Esplanade Ave., French Quarter.*

Germaine Wells Mardi Gras Museum

MUSEUM | During a 31-year period (1937–68), Germaine Cazenave Wells, daughter of Arnaud's restaurant founder Arnaud Cazenave, was queen of Carnival balls a record 22 times for 17 different krewes (organizations). Many of her ball gowns—in addition to costumes worn by other family members, photographs, krewe invitations, and jewelry—are on display in this dim, quirky museum above Arnaud's restaurant. ⊠ *Arnaud's restaurant, 813 Bienville St., 2nd fl. (enter through restaurant), French Quarter* ☎ *504/523–5433* ⊕ *www.arnaudsrestaurant.com/mardi-gras-museum* 🆓 *Free.*

Harouni Gallery

MUSEUM | David Harouni, a favorite local artist, offers his take on neo-Expressionism in his paintings of faces, figures, and streetscapes, created in this gallery-studio space. ⊠ *933 Royal St., French Quarter* ☎ *504/299–4393* ⊕ *www.harouni.com.*

Hermann-Grima House

HOUSE | Noted architect William Brand built this Georgian-style house in 1831, and it's one of the largest and best-preserved examples of American architecture in the Vieux Carré. Cooking demonstrations on the open hearth of the Creole kitchen are held most Thursdays from November through April. You'll want to check out the gift shop, which has many local crafts and books. ⊠ *820 St. Louis St., French Quarter* ☎ *504/274–0750* ⊕ *www.hgghh.org* 🆓 *$15, combination ticket with Gallier House $25* ⊙ *Closed Wed.*

Latrobe House

HOUSE | Architect Benjamin Henry Latrobe, who designed the U.S. Capitol, built this modest house with Arsene Latour in 1814. Its smooth lines and porticoes started a passion for Greek Revival architecture in Louisiana, as later evinced in many plantation houses upriver as well as in a significant number of buildings in New Orleans. Latrobe would die in New Orleans six years later from yellow fever. This house, believed to be the earliest example of Greek Revival in the city, is not open to the public. ⊠ *721 Governor Nicholls St., French Quarter.*

New Orleans Historic Voodoo Museum
MUSEUM | This homegrown museum may turn skeptics into believers. Voodoo isn't just something marketed to visitors; it lingers on in the lives of many New Orleanians, who still light candles for good luck or rely on a potion to find love. The large collection of artifacts on display here include portraits by and of voodoo legends, African artifacts believed to have influenced the development of the religion, and lots of gris-gris (African and Caribbean amulets). The gift shop sells customized gris-gris, potions, and hand-crafted voodoo dolls. A psychic reader is on duty to divine your future. ✉ *724 Dumaine St., French Quarter* ☎ *504/680–0128* 🌐 *www.voodoomuseum.com* 🎟 *$8.*

Orleans Ballroom
HISTORIC SITE | In the early 1800s, the wooden-rail balcony extending over Orleans Street was linked to a ballroom where free women of color met their French suitors—as Madame John of "Madame John's Legacy" is said to have done. The quadroons (technically, people whose racial makeup was one-quarter African) who met here were young, unmarried women of legendary beauty. A gentleman would select a favorite and, with her mother's approval, buy her a house and support her as his mistress. The sons of these unions, which were generally maintained in addition to legal marriages with French women, were often sent to France to be educated. This practice, known as *plaçage,* was unique to New Orleans at the time. The ballroom later became part of a convent and school for the Sisters of the Holy Family, a religious order founded in New Orleans in 1842 by the daughter of a quadroon to educate and care for African American women. The ballroom itself is not open to visitors, but a view of the balcony from across the street is enough to set the historical stage. ✉ *Bourbon Orleans Hotel, 717 Orleans St., 2nd fl., French Quarter.*

Talk of the Town

Although it's just two blocks away from Bourbon Street in the French Quarter, Burgundy Street is not pronounced like the wine (New Orleanians say "bur-GUN-dee" instead). And if you trot out your high-school French to ask for directions to Chartres Street, a bemused local will probably ask if you mean "CHAW-tuhs." Farther uptown, the streets named for the muses offer more challenges: Calliope ("CAL-ee-ope") and Melpomene ("MELL-pa-meen").

Restaurants

Acme Oyster House
$$ | **SEAFOOD** | **FAMILY** | A rough-edge classic in every way, this no-frills eatery is a prime source for briny, chilled Gulf oysters; legendary shrimp, oyster, and roast-beef po'boys; and tender, expertly seasoned red beans and rice. Even locals can't resist, although most opt for the less crowded, if less charming, suburban branches (there's one in Metairie). **Known for:** some of the best and freshest oysters in the French Quarter; long lines; local specialties. [$] *Average main: $15* ✉ *724 Iberville St., French Quarter* ☎ *504/522–5973* 🌐 *www.acmeoyster.com.*

Antoine's
$$$$ | **CREOLE** | Though some people believe Antoine's heyday passed before the turn of the 20th century, others wouldn't leave New Orleans without at least one order of the original oysters Rockefeller—baked oysters topped with a parsley-based sauce and bread crumbs. Other notables on the bilingual menu include *pommes de terre soufflées*

(fried potato puffs), *poisson amadine* or *meuniere* (fish prepared in toasted almond or brown butter-and-lemon sauce), and baked Alaska. **Known for:** old-school charm; historic oysters Rockefeller; slightly stuffy atmosphere (dress up or sit at the adjoining Hermes Bar). [$] *Average main: $36* ✉ *713 St. Louis St., French Quarter* ☎ *504/581–4422* 🌐 *www.antoines.com* 🕒 *No dinner Sun.*

★ Arnaud's

$$$$ | CREOLE | In the main dining room of this grande dame of classic Creole restaurants, ornate etched glass reflects light from charming old chandeliers while the late founder, Arnaud Cazenave, gazes from an oil portrait. The ambitious menu includes classic dishes as well as more contemporary ones, including vegetarian options. **Known for:** on-site Mardi Gras museum; char-grilled oyster specialties and classic cocktails; jackets requested in the main dining room. [$] *Average main: $35* ✉ *813 Bienville St., French Quarter* ☎ *504/523–5433* 🌐 *www.arnaudsrestaurant.com* 🕒 *No lunch Mon.–Sat.*

★ Bayona

$$$ | MODERN AMERICAN | "New World" is the label Louisiana native Susan Spicer applies to her cooking style, the delicious hallmarks of which include goat cheese croutons with mushrooms in madeira cream, a Bayona specialty, and delightfully flavorful vegetable soups, like Caribbean pumpkin or cream of garlic. The imaginative dishes on the constantly changing menu are served in an early-19th-century Creole cottage that glows with flower arrangements, elegant photographs, and trompe-l'oeil murals of Mediterranean landscapes. **Known for:** famous smoked duck sandwich; global flavors from a stellar chef; homemade ice cream. [$] *Average main: $30* ✉ *430 Dauphine St., French Quarter* ☎ *504/525–4455* 🌐 *www.bayona.com* 🕒 *Closed Sun. No lunch Mon. and Tues.*

Bourbon House

$$$ | CREOLE | On one of the French Quarter's busiest corners is Dickie Brennan's biggest and flashiest restaurant yet (he also owns Palace Café and Dickie Brennan's Steakhouse), and it's a solid hit with seafood aficionados and—you guessed it—bourbon lovers (there are five flights to choose from and a vast selection of 90 American whiskeys to boot). The raw bar is prime real estate, with its sterling oysters on the half shell, chilled seafood platters, and antique, decorative oyster plates, but the elegant main dining room is more appropriate for digging into the Creole catalog—charbroiled oysters, boiled shrimp, and Gulf fish "on the half shell" with lump crab meat. **Known for:** bourbon-milk punch; classy raw bar; diverse bourbon flights. [$] *Average main: $26* ✉ *144 Bourbon St., French Quarter* ☎ *504/522–0111* 🌐 *www.bourbonhouse.com.*

Brennan's

$$$$ | CREOLE | This luxuriously appointed restaurant, located in a gorgeous, salmon-pink, circa-1795 building, serves lavish breakfasts, served by pink-bow-tied waiters, that include "eye openers" like Caribbean milk punch to start the day, alongside hearty but elegantly prepared dishes such as eggs sardou with crispy artichokes and accoutrements such as coffee-cured bacon and house-made English muffins. Don't miss sumptuous desserts, like the flaming bananas Foster, which was reportedly created here. **Known for:** tourist-heavy atmosphere; Creole brunch; legendary bananas Foster. [$] *Average main: $35* ✉ *417 Royal St., French Quarter* ☎ *504/525–9711* 🌐 *www.brennansneworleans.com.*

Broussard's

$$$ | CREOLE | If local restaurants were judged solely by the beauty of their courtyards, Broussard's would certainly be a standout, but the food here is also outstanding. Expect dishes like crispy shrimp toast with pickled okra slaw;

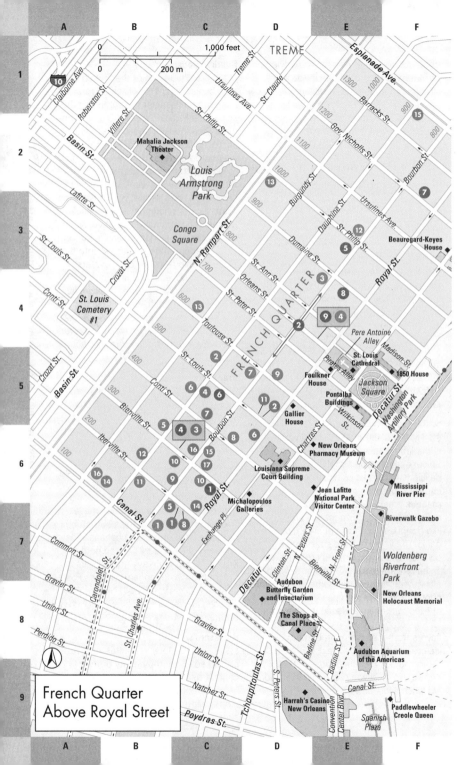

French Quarter
Above Royal Street

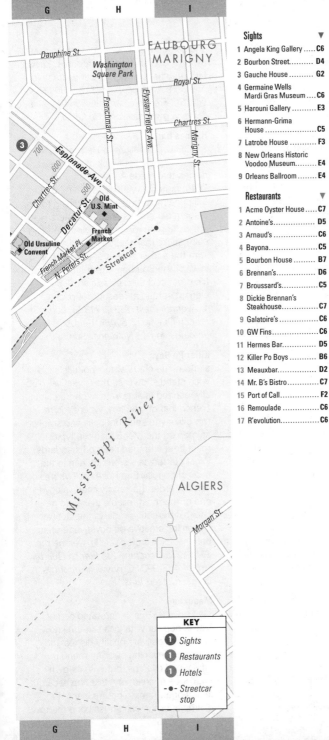

Sights ▼

1 Angela King Gallery **C6**
2 Bourbon Street.......... **D4**
3 Gauche House **G2**
4 Germaine Wells Mardi Gras Museum **C6**
5 Harouni Gallery **E3**
6 Hermann-Grima House **C5**
7 Latrobe House **F3**
8 New Orleans Historic Voodoo Museum......... **E4**
9 Orleans Ballroom **E4**

Restaurants ▼

1 Acme Oyster House **C7**
2 Antoine's................. **D5**
3 Arnaud's **C6**
4 Bayona.................... **C5**
5 Bourbon House **B7**
6 Brennan's................ **D6**
7 Broussard's.............. **C5**
8 Dickie Brennan's Steakhouse.............. **C7**
9 Galatoire's **C6**
10 GW Fins................... **C6**
11 Hermes Bar............. **D5**
12 Killer Po Boys **B6**
13 Meauxbar................ **D2**
14 Mr. B's Bistro............. **C7**
15 Port of Call................ **F2**
16 Remoulade **C6**
17 R'evolution................ **C6**

Hotels ▼

1 Astor Crowne Plaza **B7**
2 Audubon Cottages....... **C5**
3 Bon Maison Guest House.............. **E4**
4 Bourbon Orleans Hotel...................... **E4**
5 Chateau LeMoyne...... **B5**
6 Dauphine Orleans **C5**
7 Four Points by Sheraton French Quarter.......... **D5**
8 Hotel Le Marais.......... **C6**
9 Hotel Maison de Ville... **D5**
10 Hotel Mazarin **C6**
11 Hyatt French Quarter... **B6**
12 Lafitte Guest House **E3**
13 The Maison Dupuy **C4**
14 Ritz-Carlton New Orleans **B6**
15 Royal Sonesta New Orleans **C6**
16 The Saint Hotel.......... **A6**

KEY

❶ Sights

❶ Restaurants

❶ Hotels

-•- Streetcar stop

Creole crab croquettes; and broiled redfish with a rosemary-and-mustard crust. **Known for:** charming courtyard; Sunday jazz brunch; excellent broiled redfish. [$] *Average main: $30* ✉ *819 Conti St., French Quarter* ☎ *504/581–3866* 🌐 *www.broussards.com* ⏲ *No lunch Tues.–Thurs.*

Dickie Brennan's Steakhouse

$$$$ | **STEAKHOUSE** | "Straightforward steaks with a New Orleans touch" are the words to live by at this clubby shrine to red meat, the creation of a younger member of the Brennan family of restaurateurs, who also runs Palace Café and the Bourbon House. Start with stellar martinis in the dark cherrywood-paneled lounge, then head back to the cavernous dining room to dig into classic cuts of top-quality beef and seafood. **Known for:** elegant atmosphere; steak with light seasoning and a brush of Creole-seasoned butte; Creole-inspired sides. [$] *Average main: $36* ✉ *716 Iberville St., French Quarter* ☎ *504/522–2467* 🌐 *www.dickiebrennanssteakhouse.com* ⏲ *No lunch Sun.–Thurs.*

★ Galatoire's

$$$ | **CREOLE** | With many of its recipes dating to 1905, Galatoire's epitomizes the old-style French Creole bistro. Fried oysters and bacon en brochette are worth every calorie, and the brick-red rémoulade sauce sets a high standard. **Known for:** amazing rémoulade sauce; formal dress required (no shorts or T-shirts); old-school vibes. [$] *Average main: $30* ✉ *209 Bourbon St., French Quarter* ☎ *504/525–2021* 🌐 *www.galatoires.com* ⏲ *Closed Mon.* 👔 *Jacket required.*

GW Fins

$$$ | **SEAFOOD** | If you're looking for seafood, you won't be disappointed with GW Fins, which impresses with quality and variety—the bounty of fish species from around the world is among the menu's lures. Chef Tenney Flynn's menu changes daily, depending on what's fresh, but typical dishes have included luscious lobster dumplings, Hawaiian big-eye tuna, and sautéed rainbow trout with spinach, oysters, and shiitake mushrooms. **Known for:** fresh fish; modern setting; creative menu. [$] *Average main: $27* ✉ *808 Bienville St., French Quarter* ☎ *504/581–3467* 🌐 *www.gwfins.com* ⏲ *No lunch.*

Hermes Bar

$ | **CREOLE** | The allure of Hermes Bar is that you'll have your pick of the classic dishes that made Antoine's (founded in 1840) famous, without committing to a full-price meal in its austere dining room. Elegant bar snacks such as oysters Rockefeller, shrimp rémoulade, and fried eggplant sticks make just as grand a meal, with the added benefit of a front-row view of the Bourbon Street crowd. **Known for:** great cocktails; classic small bites; elegant setting at reasonable prices. [$] *Average main: $13* ✉ *713 St. Louis St., French Quarter* ☎ *504/581–4422* 🌐 *www.antoines.com* ⏲ *No dinner Sun.*

Killer Po Boys

$ | **DELI** | The chefs at this no-frills sandwich stand showcase their creative, globally inspired talents within the traditional French loaf of a po'boy, where you're more likely to see pork belly and smoked salmon on the menu than the typical roast beef and fried seafood standards. What started as a small kitchen in the back of popular Erin Rose bar (where you can still order the sandwiches) is now one of the most reliable places to get a cheap, interesting meal in the Quarter. **Known for:** creative po'boys; vegetarian options; local craft beer. [$] *Average main: $11* ✉ *219 Dauphine St., French Quarter* ☎ *504/462–2731* 🌐 *www.killerpoboys.com* ⏲ *Closed Tues.*

Meauxbar

$$$ | **FRENCH** | This understated corner bistro, popular with locals-in-the-know, constantly delivers quality dishes and a pleasant evening out. The menu is influenced by Paris, but with its own flourishes of creativity: take the escargot in sun-dried tomato beurre blanc, for example, or the can't-miss bone marrow

with grilled bread. **Known for:** fantastic bone marrow; creative cocktails; good date spot. [$] *Average main: $27* ✉ *942 N. Rampart St., French Quarter* ☎ *504/569–9979* 🌐 *www.meauxbar.com* ⏲ *No lunch Mon.–Fri.*

Mr. B's Bistro

$$$ | CREOLE | FAMILY | Those who wonder if there really is a New Orleans restaurant that can properly cater to both tourists and locals need look no farther than Mr. B's. Using as many Louisiana ingredients as possible, the chef offers a hearty braised Louisiana rabbit, an irresistible honey-ginger-glazed pork chop, and one of the best barbecue shrimp dishes in the city. **Known for:** upscale yet accessible Louisiana classics; Sunday jazz brunch; hot buttered pecan pie for dessert. [$] *Average main: $28* ✉ *201 Royal St., French Quarter* ☎ *504/523–2078* 🌐 *www.mrbsbistro.com.*

Port of Call

$ | AMERICAN | FAMILY | Every night, no matter the weather, people wait for more than an hour outside Port of Call for fist-thick burgers made from freshly ground beef, served with always-fluffy baked potatoes (there are no fries here). For the classic Port of Call experience, drink a Neptune's Monsoon (their mind-bending house grog) while you wait, and order your potato "loaded" (with mushrooms, cheddar cheese, sour cream, butter, chives, and bacon bits). **Known for:** rowdy locals; long waits; perhaps the best burger in New Orleans. [$] *Average main: $14* ✉ *838 Esplanade Ave., French Quarter* ☎ *504/523–0120* 🌐 *www.portofcallnola.com.*

Remoulade

$ | CREOLE | FAMILY | Operated by the owners of the posh Arnaud's, Remoulade is more laid-back and less pricey but serves the same Caesar salad and pecan pie, as well as a few of the signature starters: shrimp Arnaud in rémoulade sauce, baked oysters, turtle soup, and shrimp bisque. "Tasters," or sampler plates of three dishes like gumbo, crawfish pie, and jambalaya, are a steal at $17.50. The marble-counter oyster bar and mahogany cocktail bar date to the 1870s; a dozen oysters shucked here, paired with a cold beer, can easily turn into two dozen, maybe three. **Known for:** oyster bar from the 1870s; classic cocktails; old-time New Orleans environment with a family-friendly ambience. [$] *Average main: $13* ✉ *309 Bourbon St., French Quarter* ☎ *504/523–0377* 🌐 *www.remoulade.com.*

R'evolution

$$$$ | CREOLE | Superstars rarely start over when they're on top—but celebrity chef Rick Tramonto, best known for his avant-garde creations at Chicago's Tru, headed south when he needed a new challenge. Tramonto hooked up with Louisiana culinary renaissance man John Folse and the two set about remaking the state's creations, combining Folse's deep knowledge of Cajun and Creole food with Tramonto's modern techniques and impeccably high standards. **Known for:** quail three ways; caviar towers; rare wines. [$] *Average main: $33* ✉ *Royal Sonesta Hotel, 777 Bienville St., French Quarter* ☎ *504/553–2277* 🌐 *www.revolutionnola.com* ⏲ *No lunch Mon.–Thurs. and Sat.*

Hotels

Astor Crowne Plaza

$$ | HOTEL | A great location within walking distance of nearly everything in the Quarter comes with a rooftop pool, spectacular views, and a great in-house restaurant. **Pros:** convenient location; large rooms; big fitness center and outdoor pool. **Cons:** Bourbon Street right next door is too close for some; fees for various Wi-Fi plans; room decor uninspired. [$] *Rooms from: $206* ✉ *739 Canal St., French Quarter* ☎ *504/962–0500, 877/408–9661* 🌐 *www.astorneworleans.com* 🛏 *743 rooms* 🍴 *No meals.*

Haunted Hotels

In New Orleans, reminders of human mortality are never far from view. The city's graves have traditionally been built aboveground, both in keeping with Catholic and French custom and because New Orleans is mostly at or below sea level. Today, walled cemeteries are common tourist destinations. As a port city, New Orleans has always been a boisterous place, where pirates, prostitutes, gamblers, and characters of all stripes could find a comfortable home. The city's reputation as a home for voodoo is well founded; it is the birthplace of legendary voodoo priestess Marie Laveau. Not surprisingly, many of the city's hotels are purportedly home to restless spirits. Guests at the **Dauphine Orleans** (✉ *415 Dauphine St., French Quarter*) report seeing a dancing woman in the courtyard and the spirit of a patron roaming the grounds, a reminder of the days when there was a brothel here. The grandfather clock in the lobby of the **Hotel Monteleone** (✉ *214 Royal St., French Quarter*) is said to be haunted by the ghost of its maker, and in the Garden District's **Columns Hotel** (✉ *3811 St. Charles Ave., Uptown*), a former owner—who died in 1898—is occasionally still seen by guests. Hurricane Katrina was only the most recent catastrophe to befall New Orleans; yellow fever was a scourge on the city in the 18th and 19th centuries. The **Lafitte Guest House** (✉ *1003 Bourbon St., French Quarter*) is only one hotel in which victims of the disease are said to linger. Of course you can't talk about the haunted hotels of New Orleans without mentioning the **Bourbon Orleans Hotel** (✉ *717 Orleans, French Quarter*). Once a ballroom, and later a convent, the storied building is said to house apparitions of former tenants, like the Confederate soldier roaming the sixth and seventh floors and the dancer seen swaying underneath the crystal chandelier in the hotel's ballroom. There are a number of tour operators that cater to those with an interest in the supernatural, but if you stay at the right hotel, you may not need their services.

Audubon Cottages

$$$$ | **B&B/INN** | Seven one- and two-bedroom cottages in the heart of the French Quarter make up this luxury retreat, affording a wonderful sense of privacy. **Pros:** lovely pool with outdoor lounge and cabanas; private butler service; use of the fitness center at the nearby Dauphine Orleans Hotel. **Cons:** limits two to four guests per cottage; some courtyards are shared; breakfast just okay. [$] *Rooms from: $400* ✉ *509 Dauphine St., French Quarter* ☎ *504/586–1516* 🌐 *www.auduboncottages.com* 🛏 *7 cottages* 🍴 *Free breakfast.*

Bon Maison Guest House

$$$ | **B&B/INN** | This spot proves it's possible to find quiet, homey accommodation on Bourbon Street. **Pros:** on the less touristy end of the Quarter's main drag, but within walking distance of attractions and lots of restaurants; free Wi-Fi; warm welcome from hosts. **Cons:** can be difficult to reserve; minimum three-night stay most of the time; no parking or breakfast. [$] *Rooms from: $260* ✉ *835 Bourbon St., French Quarter* ☎ *504/561–8498* 🌐 *www.bonmaison.com* 🛏 *4 rooms* 🍴 *No meals.*

Bourbon Orleans Hotel

$$ | **HOTEL** | This hotel's location is about as central as it gets, though the beautiful

courtyard and pool provide welcome sanctuary from the loud, 24-hour Bourbon Street action just outside the door. **Pros:** welcome cocktail and complimentary coffee and tea in the lobby; nice fitness center; live entertainment in the on-site bar. **Cons:** lobby level is often crowded; street-facing rooms can be noisy; historic location shows some wear and tear. [$] *Rooms from: $218* ✉ *717 Orleans St., French Quarter* ☎ *504/523–2222* 🌐 *www.bourbonorleans.com* 🛏 *246 rooms* 🍴 *No meals.*

Chateau LeMoyne

$$ | **HOTEL** | Just one block off Bourbon Street, this branch of the Holiday Inn chain is pleasantly distinctive, with spacious rooms occupying a historic 19th-century New Orleans landmark, designed in part by famous architect James Gallier. **Pros:** great location; large, heated saltwater swimming pool; affordable rates. **Cons:** some bathrooms are small; restaurant serves only breakfast; old plumbing. [$] *Rooms from: $179* ✉ *301 Dauphine St., French Quarter* ☎ *504/581–1303, 800/465–4329* 🌐 *www.hi-chateau.com* 🛏 *171 rooms* 🍴 *No meals.*

Dauphine Orleans

$$ | **HOTEL** | A great location—within easy walking distance of the action but removed enough to make this a secluded respite—comes with lots of charm. **Pros:** French Quarter architecture; saltwater pool; complimentary breakfast, in-room coffee, and bottled water. **Cons:** some rooms require climbing stairs; outdated decor; small lobby. [$] *Rooms from: $174* ✉ *415 Dauphine St., French Quarter* ☎ *504/586–1800, 800/521–7111* 🌐 *www.dauphineorleans.com* 🛏 *110 rooms* 🍴 *Free breakfast.*

Four Points By Sheraton French Quarter

$$$ | **HOTEL** | With a heart-of-the-party Bourbon Street location, the most coveted of the well-kept rooms here (especially during Mardi Gras) are the ones with balconies overlooking the street. **Pros:** ideal for those who want to be in the center of the French Quarter action; free Wi-Fi; great courtyard. **Cons:** the high-traffic location means the party outside your front door never ends; no mini-fridges in rooms; pricey breakfast. [$] *Rooms from: $243* ✉ *541 Bourbon St., French Quarter* ☎ *504/524–7611, 866/716–8133* 🌐 *www.fourpointsfrenchquarter.com* 🛏 *186 rooms* 🍴 *No meals.*

Hotel Le Marais

$$ | **HOTEL** | This contemporary outpost in the heart of the historic French Quarter has trendy furnishings and a blacklighted lobby that combines urban chic with a voguish New Orleans vibe. **Pros:** modern furnishings; free in-room Wi-Fi; double-paned windows ensure quiet rooms despite location. **Cons:** not for those who want a traditional-looking hotel; no in-hotel restaurant; busy surroundings. [$] *Rooms from: $159* ✉ *717 Conti St., French Quarter* ☎ *504/525–2300* 🌐 *www.hotellemarais.com* 🛏 *66 rooms* 🍴 *Free breakfast.*

Hotel Maison de Ville

$$$ | **HOTEL** | A collection of historic town houses and "bachelor quarters" make up this charming hotel with a delightfully secluded vibe amid the excitement of the French Quarter. **Pros:** lots of local history; unique rooms; free Wi-Fi. **Cons:** slightly worn decor; no on-site restaurant; setting too quirky for some. [$] *Rooms from: $315* ✉ *727 Toulouse St., French Quarter* ☎ *504/324–4888* 🌐 *www.maisondeville.com* 🛏 *16 rooms* 🍴 *Free breakfast.*

★ **Hotel Mazarin**

$$ | **HOTEL** | An enviable French Quarter location combines with loads of charm, including a picture-perfect courtyard with a fountain and guest rooms featuring black-marble floors. **Pros:** great location; excellent guest services; free welcome cocktail in the 21st Amendment, an on-site, Prohibition-theme bar. **Cons:** rooms facing the street can be noisy;

no tubs; no pool. $ *Rooms from:
$217 ✉ 730 Bienville St., Downtown
☎ 504/581–7300, 800/535–9111 ⊕ www.
hotelmazarin.com ⇆ 105 rooms* ❙◎❙ *Free
breakfast.*

Hyatt French Quarter

$$$ | HOTEL | Airy public spaces, land-
scaped courtyards, an attractive pool
area, and some of the largest guest
rooms in the Quarter create a sense of
luxury here. **Pros:** right on the edge of the
Quarter but set back from the hubbub
of Bourbon Street; outdoor pool and
poolside bar; 24-hour fitness center. **Cons:**
slight chain-hotel feeling; very noisy at
check-in and check-out times; pricey for
what it is. $ *Rooms from: $269 ✉ 800
Iberville St., French Quarter ☎ 504/586–
0800, 800/766–3782 ⊕ frenchquarter.
hyatt.com ⇆ 254 rooms* ❙◎❙ *No meals.*

Lafitte Guest House

$$$ | B&B/INN | In this four-story, 1849
French-style manor house, each room
has different details, from marble fire-
places to four-poster beds. **Pros:** loads
of historic-mansion charm; "mansion
rooms" with balconies are spectacular;
updated furnishings. **Cons:** located on
a high-traffic corner of Bourbon Street;
needs some repairs; doesn't have the
amenities of a big hotel. $ *Rooms from:
$259 ✉ 1003 Bourbon St., French Quarter
☎ 504/581–2678, 800/331–7971 ⊕ www.
lafitteguesthouse.com ⇆ 14 rooms*
❙◎❙ *Free breakfast.*

The Maison Dupuy

$$$ | HOTEL | Seven restored 19th-cen-
tury town houses just two blocks from
Bourbon Street surround one of the
Quarter's prettiest courtyards. **Pros:** quiet
yet still close to French Quarter action;
free Wi-Fi in guest rooms; great pool and
courtyard. **Cons:** lobby can be cramped
at check-in; rooms could use updating;
crowded during high season. $ *Rooms
from: $239 ✉ 1001 Toulouse St., French
Quarter ☎ 504/586–8000, 800/535–9177
⊕ www.maisondupuy.com ⇆ 200 rooms*
❙◎❙ *No meals.*

Mardi Gras Views ◉

One of the best spots for viewing
Mardi Gras madness in the French
Quarter is the balcony at the **Royal
Sonesta Hotel.** To keep revelers
from climbing up from the street
below, the staff grease the support
poles with petroleum jelly. The
media turn out in droves, and the
hotel turns the event into a party.
Festivities start at 10 am the Friday
before Mardi Gras.

★ Ritz-Carlton New Orleans

$$$$ | HOTEL | One of the city's most regal
hotels sits on Canal Street, with luxurious
rooms and suites occupying what was
once the Maison Blanche department
store. **Pros:** possibly the best spa in New
Orleans and excellent New Orleans fare
at M Bistro; central location; afternoon
tea here is one of the most civilized tra-
ditions in the city. **Cons:** sometimes feels
like a chain; rates are among the highest
in town; Internet speed inconsistent.
$ *Rooms from: $399 ✉ 921 Canal St.,
French Quarter ☎ 504/524–1331 ⊕ www.
ritzcarlton.com ⇆ 565 rooms* ❙◎❙ *No
meals.*

★ Royal Sonesta New Orleans

$$$ | HOTEL | Adding a touch of class to
its Bourbon Street environs, this French
Quarter favorite is soothing from the
moment you step into the marbled lobby,
where lush plants enhance a cool, serene
atmosphere. **Pros:** excellent restaurant
and bars; bustling, cavernous lobby; great
balcony views of the Quarter. **Cons:** con-
sistently high occupancy can lead to slow
elevator service; rooms facing Bourbon
Street are noisy; limited fitness room.
$ *Rooms from: $299 ✉ 300 Bourbon St.,
French Quarter ☎ 504/586–0300 ⊕ www.
sonesta.com/royalneworleans ⇆ 517
rooms* ❙◎❙ *No meals.*

The Saint Hotel

$$$ | HOTEL | In the 1909 beaux-arts Audubon Building, up-to-the-minute decor really pops in a lobby glittering with chandeliers, atmospheric Carnival photos, and acres of sheer tulle curtains. **Pros:** on the Canal Street streetcar line and parade route; a few blocks from French Quarter action; marble baths. **Cons:** may be too edgy and stark for some guests; lacks traditional New Orleans ambience and charm; on busy street. $ *Rooms from: $229* ✉ *931 Canal St., French Quarter* ☎ *504/522–5400* ⊕ *www.thesainthotel-neworleans.com* ⌕ *171 rooms* ⦿ *No meals.*

ⓨ Nightlife

BARS AND LOUNGES

Bar Tonique

BARS/PUBS | An eclectic spot on North Rampart Street, this brick-walled room with private nooks and intimate corner booths looks like a cross between a dive and a lounge on the Riviera. The book-length drinks menu, with everything from pre-Prohibition classics to modern creations, practically recounts the history of the cocktail. The talented staff can turn out any of those offerings with aplomb. ✉ *820 N. Rampart St., French Quarter* ☎ *504/324–6045* ⊕ *www.bartonique. com.*

Bombay Club

BARS/PUBS | A rather swanky lounge for the French Quarter, with leather chairs and dark paneling, covers cocktail history with an encyclopedic menu that starts with drinks from the mid-19th century, and boasts the largest selection of martinis in town. Tucked away from the street in the Prince Conti Hotel, it also hosts piano players and jazz combos nightly. ✉ *Prince Conti Hotel, 830 Conti St., French Quarter* ☎ *504/577–2237* ⊕ *www. bombayclubneworleans.com.*

⭐ Cat's Meow

BARS/PUBS | Before you see it, you'll hear this Bourbon Street landmark, New Orleans's most popular karaoke bar. Given an ideal corner location, the bar's tall doors and windows open onto two streets, luring undergrads, conventioneers, and bachelorette parties to hit the dance floor and grab the mic. High-energy MCs and DJs keep the night spinning along, but get on the sign-up sheet early if you want a chance at French Quarter fame. ✉ *701 Bourbon St., French Quarter* ☎ *504/523–2788* ⊕ *www.catskaraoke. com.*

Cosimo's

BARS/PUBS | Few tourists make their way to this hip neighborhood hangout, in a far corner of the Lower Quarter. A short flight of stairs leads to a darts and billiards room. Quirky wagon wheel–shape ceiling fans, ample windows, and a friendly vibe make it a low-key place to wind down. Food options include pizzas, burgers, and Cosimo's famous fried green beans. ✉ *1201 Burgundy St., French Quarter* ☎ *504/522–9428.*

⭐ French 75

BARS/PUBS | This is a must-visit for any who love to submerge themselves in old-time elegance. Adjoining Arnaud's, the classic New Orleans Creole restaurant, this dark-wood bar is complete with leather-backed chairs and imposing columns. The bartenders work magic with their encyclopedic knowledge of cocktails and arsenal of ingredients. Be sure to venture upstairs to the free Germaine Wells Mardi Gras Museum, a slightly bizarre showcase for memorabilia and ball gowns worn by the original owner's daughter. ✉ *813 Bienville St., French Quarter* ☎ *504/523–5433* ⊕ *www. arnaudsrestaurant.com/french-75.*

⭐ Lafitte's Blacksmith Shop

BARS/PUBS | Perhaps the most photographed building in the Quarter after St. Louis Cathedral, this 18th-century blacksmith shop was once a front for the eponymous pirate's less legitimate business ventures—or so says local legend. Today, it's an atmospheric piano bar with a rustic, candlelit interior and a small outdoor patio shaded by banana trees. Despite the addition of a few flat-screen TVs, a drink here just after sundown, under the soft glow of candles, lets you slip back in time for an hour or so. It's also known as the oldest bar in New Orleans as well as one of the most haunted. ⊠ *941 Bourbon St., French Quarter* ☎ *504/593–9761* ⊕ *www. lafittesblacksmithshop.com.*

Longway Tavern

BARS/PUBS | Like its sister restaurant Sylvain, this cozy tavern converts a historic French Quarter location into a stylish hang-out where old-world charm pairs with a creative cocktail menu and good ole fashioned beer-and-shot combos. Come for the cocktails, but stay for the snacks, which are just as exciting; caviar, charred vegetables, crab claws, and housemade aiolis elevate a classic pub menu into something else entirely. ⊠ *719 Toulouse St., French Quarter* ☎ *504/962– 9696* ⊕ *www.longwaytavern.com.*

Old Absinthe House

BARS/PUBS | In its 200-year history, this low-key oasis with its famous marble absinthe fountain has served guests including Oscar Wilde, Mark Twain, Franklin Roosevelt, and Frank Sinatra. It's now mostly frequented by tourists and casual local characters who appreciate a good brewski or cocktail to go. Thousands of business cards stapled to the wall serve as interesting wallpaper. Walk through the courtyard next door to find Belle Epoque, a speakeasy-style lounge and sophisticated extension of Old Absinthe House. ⊠ *240 Bourbon St., French Quarter* ☎ *504/523–3181* ⊕ *www.ruebourbon. com/old-absinthe-house.*

Pat O'Brien's

BARS/PUBS | Sure, it's touristy, but there are reasons Pat O's has been a must-stop on the New Orleans drinking trail since Prohibition. Friendly staff, an easy camaraderie among patrons, and a signature drink—the pink, fruity, and extremely potent Hurricane, which comes with a souvenir glass—all make this French Quarter stalwart a pleasant afternoon diversion. There's plenty of room to spread out, from the elegant side bar and piano bar that flank the carriageway entrance to the lush (and in winter, heated) patio. Expect a line on weekend nights, and if you don't want your glass, return it for the deposit. ⊠ *718 St. Peter St., French Quarter* ☎ *504/525–4823* ⊕ *www.patobriens.com.*

Patrick's Bar Vin

BARS/PUBS | Dapper Patrick Van Hoorebeek holds court at his wine bar in a clubby atmosphere of dark wood and red upholstery. Wines by the glass are the specialty, but there's also an excellent selection of cocktails and beers, including Van Hoorebeek's own Belgian brew. Major oenophiles can rent personal wine lockers. Only a few steps from Bourbon Street, Bar Vin feels like another world. It opens at noon on Friday to catch the lunch crowd. ⊠ *730 Bienville St., French Quarter* ☎ *504/200–3180* ⊕ *www.patricksbarvin.com.*

LGBTQ BARS AND CLUBS

Bourbon Pub

BARS/PUBS | It's impossible to miss this 24-hour video bar at the corner of St. Ann and Bourbon streets, especially in early evenings, when the doors are open and the dance crowd spills into the street. There's usually a cover charge on Friday and Saturday nights after 10 pm; Sunday afternoon is devoted to vintage videos by assorted gay icons. ⊠ *801 Bourbon St., French Quarter* ☎ *504/529–2107* ⊕ *www. bourbonpub.com.*

Café Lafitte in Exile

BARS/PUBS | This Bourbon Street stalwart attracts a somewhat older and very casual group of gay men. The second floor has a pool table, pinball machine, and wraparound balcony with a bird's-eye view of the lively street scene below. Sunday afternoon, when the oldies spin and the paper-napkin confetti flies, is especially popular. ⊠ 901 Bourbon St., French Quarter ☎ 504/522–8397 ⊕ www. lafittes.com.

Corner Pocket

BARS/PUBS | Filmmaker John Waters reportedly counts the Pocket as a New Orleans favorite, and with skinny, tattooed strippers on the bar and an inebriated drag queen emcee, it's easy to see why. Sleazy fun on a good night, but keep your wits about you. ⊠ 940 St. Louis St., French Quarter ☎ 504/568–9829 ⊕ www.cornerpocket.net.

The Golden Lantern

BARS/PUBS | The Lower Quarter has become a lot more upscale since this neighborhood gay haunt's heyday, but (the officially named) Tubby's Golden Lantern soldiers on. The bartender's whim determines the music, the drinks are strong, and happy hour runs from noon to 8 pm Monday and Tuesday, and from 8 am to 8 pm every other day. The bar is best known as ground zero for the annual Southern Decadence drag parade, when a crowd gathers out front for the kick-off. It's cash-only. ⊠ 1239 Royal St., French Quarter ☎ 504/529–2860.

Good Friends

BARS/PUBS | With its tasteful decor and reasonable volume level, this is a slightly more upscale, sedate alternative to the blasting disco bars down the street. The Queen's Head Pub on the second floor, open weekends, has darts, a wraparound balcony, and respectable martinis. Brush up on your show tunes at the popular Sunday afternoon piano sing-along. ⊠ 740 Dauphine St., French Quarter ☎ 504/566–7191 ⊕ www.goodfriendsbar.com.

Napoleon's Itch

BARS/PUBS | The only gay bar in New Orleans that's also attached to a large hotel, this narrow space is in the heart of St.-Ann-and-Bourbon gay central; it's a must-visit during the annual Southern Decadence festival. The comfy sofas and handsome bartenders are a plus, and the crowd tends to be a bit dressier than at similar venues. ⊠ Bourbon Orleans Hotel, 734 Bourbon St., French Quarter ☎ 504/237–4144.

Oz

DANCE CLUBS | A spacious dance club that mainly attracts young gay men also draws straight men and women, largely because of the scarcity of good dance floors in the French Quarter. It's open around the clock and tends to peak very late. ⊠ 800 Bourbon St., French Quarter ☎ 504/593–9491 ⊕ www.ozneworleans. com.

Parade Disco

DANCE CLUBS | High-energy disco is the rule at this dance club above the Bourbon Pub. If it gets to be too much, a quieter back bar and a balcony offer respite. The crowd is mostly male and young, but women are welcome. ⊠ 801 Bourbon St., above Bourbon Pub, French Quarter ☎ 504/529–2107 ⊕ www.bourbonpub. com.

Rawhide

BARS/PUBS | As the name indicates, this is a rowdy—and sexually charged—leather-and-Levi's gay bar. It's two blocks from Bourbon Street and is open around the clock. ⊠ 740 Burgundy St., French Quarter ☎ 504/525–8106 ⊕ www.rawhide2010.com.

Antiques shops are one of New Orleans's specialties.

🛍 Shopping

ANTIQUES AND COLLECTIBLES

Brass Monkey

ANTIQUES/COLLECTIBLES | This small, charming shop specializes in Limoges boxes with design motifs ranging from small red beans—a favorite food in New Orleans—to baby carriages. It also has antique walking sticks, Venetian glass, and English Staffordshire porcelain. ⊠ *407 Royal St., French Quarter* 🕾 *504/561–0688.*

French Antique Shop

ANTIQUES/COLLECTIBLES | One of the largest collections of European crystal and bronze chandeliers in the country glitters over gilded mirrors, 18th- and 19th-century hand-carved marble mantels, French and Continental furniture, porcelain, and objets d'art in this shop, which originally opened in 1947 and is run by the second and third generations of its founding family. ⊠ *225 Royal St., French Quarter* 🕾 *504/524–9861* ⊕ *www.gofrenchantiques.com.*

Harris Antiques

ANTIQUES/COLLECTIBLES | Locals and visitors alike are drawn to this shop for its two floors of 19th-century paintings, 18th- and 19th-century French and English furniture, large mirrors, bronze sculptures, and chandeliers. ⊠ *233 Royal St., French Quarter* 🕾 *504/523–1605* ⊕ *www.harrisantiques.com.*

James H. Cohen & Sons Inc.

ANTIQUES/COLLECTIBLES | Pick up a piece of history in this shop, opened in 1898, which sells many one-of-a-kind antique firearms, swords, and currency, including coins from as early as 319 BC. There are also obsolete bank notes, jewelry made from rare coins, and collectibles such as antique opera glasses. ⊠ *437 Royal St., French Quarter* 🕾 *504/522–3305* ⊕ *www.cohenantiques.com.*

Keil's Antiques

ANTIQUES/COLLECTIBLES | Leave yourself plenty of time to browse the three floors of 18th- and 19th-century French and English furniture, chandeliers, estate jewelry, art, statuary, and other furnishings.

The shop, run by the fourth generation of the family that founded it in 1899, is a favorite stop for interior designers. ✉ *325 Royal St., French Quarter* ☎ *504/522–4552* ⊕ *www.keilsantiques.com.*

Moss Antiques

ANTIQUES/COLLECTIBLES | This store specializes in French and English antiques from the early 19th century, including jewelry, wooden boxes, furniture, porcelain oyster plates, sculpture, objets d'art, walking sticks, and silver services. ✉ *411 Royal St., French Quarter* ☎ *504/522–3981* ⊕ *www.mossantiques.com.*

Royal Antiques

ANTIQUES/COLLECTIBLES | French, English, and Continental antique furniture and Biedermeier pieces can be found alongside chandeliers, sconces, trumeau mirrors, accessories, and estate jewelry in this shop, which was founded in 1899. ✉ *309 Royal St., French Quarter* ☎ *504/524–7033* ⊕ *www.royalantiques. com.*

Vintage 329

ANTIQUES/COLLECTIBLES | An essential stop for memorabilia collectors, Vintage 329 carries items autographed by celebrities, such as a framed photo signed by Gene Autry, a music sheet autographed by Fred Astaire and Ginger Rogers, and a guitar signed by the Allman Brothers. There are also concert posters, costume jewelry, and signed first edition books. New items arrive every week. ✉ *329 Royal St., French Quarter* ☎ *504/525–2262.*

ARTWORK

Great Artists' Collective

ART GALLERIES | More than 50 regional artists display their works in this double-shotgun house in the middle of the French Quarter. You'll find paintings, metalwork mirrors, a vast array of earrings, blown glass, ceramics, wood sculptures, handmade clothing, hats, ironwork, masks, and vignettes in oyster shells. ✉ *815 Royal St., French Quarter*

New Orleans Scents 🛍

Take home the scents of New Orleans with soaps, sprays, candles, and perfumes in sweet olive or vetiver. The latter was a staple in proper Creole households, where it was used to keep moths away from fabrics and add a pleasant scent to bed linens and clothing stored in armoires. The oil extracted from the roots of this grass is popular with aromatherapy enthusiasts, who claim the scent relieves stress and increases energy.

☎ *504/525–8190* ⊕ *www.greatartistscollective.com.*

BEAUTY

Bourbon French Parfums

PERFUME/COSMETICS | Opened in 1843, this old world–style shop offers about three dozen fragrances for men and women, including a 200-year-old formula for men's cologne. It will custom-blend perfumes for individuals based on assessments of body chemistry, personality, and scent preferences. The shop also sells perfume bottles and toiletries. ✉ *805 Royal St., French Quarter* ☎ *504/522–4480* ⊕ *www. neworleansperfume.com.*

BOOKS

Dauphine Street Books

BOOKS/STATIONERY | New and used books focus on local history, the arts, modern fiction, and out-of-print works, including a fine selection of antiquarian books and obscure titles. ✉ *410 Dauphine St., French Quarter* ☎ *504/529–2333.*

CLOTHING

★ Trashy Diva Boutique

CLOTHING | New Orleans–based designer Candice Gwinn puts a retro-romantic spin on the women's fashions she creates. Inspired by styles from the 1940s to the 1950s, the Trashy Diva line includes dresses, blouses, skirts, coats, jewelry, and upscale shoes with vintage flair and modern fit. The Trashy Diva lingerie shop, located at 712 Royal Street, features corsets and romantic evening wear. An expansive Trashy Diva shoe, clothing, and lingerie boutique is also located in the 2000 block of Magazine Street. ✉ *537 Royal St., French Quarter* ☎ *504/522–4233* ⊕ *www.trashydiva.com.*

JEWELRY AND ACCESSORIES

Currents Fine Jewelry

JEWELRY/ACCESSORIES | Owners Terry and Sylvia Weidert create a variety of chic, art deco–inspired designs in 14- and 18-karat gold and platinum. ✉ *627 Royal St., French Quarter* ☎ *504/522–6099.*

Goorin Brothers

JEWELRY/ACCESSORIES | From fedoras to flat caps, you'll find hats of every style and shape at this national chain with a local sensibility, including straw toppers perfect for strolling the streets of the French Quarter. Another branch, at 2127 Magazine Street, offers custom millinery for those looking for a personal fit. ✉ *709 Royal St., French Quarter* ☎ *504/523–4287* ⊕ *www.goorin.com.*

Krewe du Optic

JEWELRY/ACCESSORIES | Luxury sun and optical frames crafted by local designer Stirling Barrett have been featured by celebrities and beauty magazines and garnered enough national attention to open an outpost in Manhattan's Soho. This flagship store features custom fittings, a sunroom, courtyard, and espresso bar. ✉ *809 Royal St., French Quarter* ☎ *504/407–2925* ⊕ *www.krewe.com.*

MARDI GRAS MASKS

Mask Gallery

LOCAL SPECIALTIES | Artist Dalili fabricates his intricate but wearable masks out of leather at a workstation in the front of the store. There also are masks made by other local artists, as well as Venetian and feather versions, pewter sculptures, jewelry, and figurines. ✉ *841 Royal St., French Quarter* ☎ *504/523–6664* ⊕ *www. neworleansmask.com.*

Chapter 4

FAUBOURG MARIGNY

Updated by Cameron
Quincy Todd

⊙ Sights	🍴 Restaurants	🛏 Hotels	🛍 Shopping	🍸 Nightlife
★★☆☆☆	★★★★☆	★★☆☆☆	★★☆☆☆	★★★★☆

NEIGHBORHOOD SNAPSHOT

TOP REASONS TO GO

Frenchmen Street. This bustling strip of bars, clubs, restaurants, cafés, and shops is the heart of the Marigny. At night this is *the* place to hear live music and watch eccentric street artists.

Marigny architecture. In 1974 the entire Marigny neighborhood was added to the National Register of Historic Places; 35 years later it was awarded the distinguished "Great Places in America" designation by the American Planning Association.

The performing arts. Some of the best music and art performances take place in the Marigny, from cabaret shows, DJ sets, and small shadowbox seatings on St. Claude Avenue to opera and orchestra at the gorgeous Marigny Opera House.

Dining. The Marigny is a hotbed for new and exciting restaurants in New Orleans.

GETTING HERE AND AROUND

The Marigny borders the French Quarter to the east, and is within easy walking distance. The bus and streetcar will also land you in or close to it. Biking is a great way to get around the French Quarter and the Marigny.

The **No. 5 Marigny/Bywater bus** runs along the south edge (river side) of the French Quarter, out to the far edge of Bywater. The **No. 88 St. Claude/ Jackson Barracks bus** runs along the north edge (lake side) of the French Quarter all the way into the Lower Ninth Ward. The ride from the French Quarter takes about 15 minutes. The Rampart–St. Claude streetcar line runs from the French Quarter (at Canal Street) down St. Claude Avenue into the Marigny.

MAKING THE MOST OF YOUR TIME

Frenchmen Street and the "Marigny Triangle" are within easy reach of the Quarter, whereas businesses on St. Claude Avenue in the Marigny require a longer walk or a cab ride in the evening. During the day, spend some time exploring the area's galleries, parks, cafés, and vintage stores. At night, Frenchmen Street is the best place in the city for live music.

QUICK BITES

■ **Nola Mia Gelato.** This is a charming little stop on the way down St. Claude Avenue. The friendly owner will fix you a cappuccino (or hot-pressed panini), while you decide over dozens of flavors of freshly made gelato. ⊠ *2230 St. Claude Ave., Faubourg Marigny* ☏ *504/249–5009* ⊕ *www. nolamiagelato.com.*

■ **Shank Charcuterie.** This hip butcher shop specializes in all things meat, with plenty to enjoy inside or take to go. Along with quality cuts of meat (and beer and wine), there's boudin, charcuterie boards, tasty sandwiches, and rotisserie items. ⊠ *2352 St. Claude Ave., Faubourg Marigny* ☏ *504/218–5281* ⊕ *www. shankcharcuterie.com* ⊘ *Closed Mon.*

The Faubourg Marigny (pronounced "FOE-berg MAR-ah-nee," though mainly referred to as simply "the Marigny") is made up of two distinct sections. The Marigny Triangle is the trendy area, with the Frenchmen Street commercial district on the border of the French Quarter. Its mazelike streets are lined with beautiful cottages, Creole plantation homes, and charming guesthouses.

You'll have no problem finding great restaurants, bars, music clubs, and hip shops. The Marigny Rectangle begins on the other side of Elysian Fields Avenue.

The Marigny was one of the earliest neighborhoods in the city. It was formed in 1805 when the young Bernard Xavier Philippe de Marigny de Mandeville embarked on what is now practically an American pastime: creating subdivisions. With architectural styles ranging from classic Creole cottages to Victorian mansions, the streets are mainly peaceful and the residents often bohemian—similar to the French Quarter 30 years ago.

◉ Sights

★ Frenchmen Street
NEIGHBORHOOD | The three-block stretch closest to the French Quarter is where it's at—complete with cafés, bars, and music clubs. The true magic happens come nightfall, when live music spills from the doorways of clubs and crowds gather for street performers, but it's still a great daytime destination, too. ⊠ *Frenchmen St. between Decatur and Dauphine Sts., Faubourg Marigny.*

New Orleans Center for Creative Arts
(*NOCCA*)
COLLEGE | Many of New Orleans's most talented musicians, artists, actors, and writers have passed through this high school arts program on their way to fame, including Harry Connick Jr., Trombone Shorty, the Marsalis brothers, Donald Harrison, Terence Blanchard, Anthony Mackie, and Wendell Pierce. More than just a beautiful campus built along the Marigny's industrial riverfront area, NOCCA hosts a year-round schedule of celebrated performances, exhibitions, and other public events. ⊠ *2800 Chartres St., Faubourg Marigny* ☎ *504/940–2787* ⊕ *www.nocca.com.*

New Orleans Healing Center
LOCAL INTEREST | This is a great place to get in touch with the spiritual side of New Orleans. It's the product of an

innovative collaboration of more than a dozen of New Orleans's most progressive (and intriguing) organizations. Visitors can check out everything from the Wild Lotus Yoga Studio to the New Orleans Food Co-Op, from the Café Istanbul Performance Hall to the Island of Salvation Botanica, the famous voodoo shop run by the internationally renowned priestess Sallie Ann Glassman. ✉ *2372 St. Claude Ave., Faubourg Marigny* ☎ *504/940–1130* 🌐 *www.neworleanshealingcenter.org.*

Plessy vs. Ferguson Site

MEMORIAL | The inciting incident leading to the landmark 1896 "separate but equal" Supreme Court case took place at the train tracks between the Bywater and the Marigny, when a man named Homer Plessy boarded an all-whites train as an act of planned civil disobedience. A historical marker at the spot commemorates Plessy's bravery in paving the way for later civil rights action. Keith Plessy and Phoebe Ferguson, modern day descendants of Homer Plessy and Judge Ferguson (who voted against Plessy in the case), unveiled the plaque in 2009 and today run the Plessy & Ferguson Foundation, dedicated to civil rights education and history. ✉ *700 Homer Plessy Way, Faubourg Marigny* 🌐 *www.plessyandferguson.org.*

🍴 Restaurants

The carefully preserved and colorfully painted cottages and shotgun houses of the Faubourg Marigny are home to artists, hipsters, and gay couples. You'll find cool cafés, interesting international options, and neighborhood hangouts with cheap eats. Most travelers make a beeline for Frenchmen Street, a three-block stretch of live-music clubs and bars known as "Bourbon Street for locals."

Adolfo's

$$ | **ITALIAN** | Rustic and charming, this cramped dining room lords over Frenchmen Street and serves big plates of classic Italian-American cuisine with a Creole twist. Decadent seafood sauces are especially pleasing for garlic lovers. **Known for:** cash-only policy; no reservations so be prepared to wait; lively and fun atmosphere. [$] *Average main: $20* ✉ *611 Frenchmen St., Faubourg Marigny* ☎ *504/948–3800* 🕒 *No lunch* 💳 *No credit cards.*

Frenchmen Street Personalities

Street life on Frenchmen can be as entertaining as anything going on inside the clubs and bars. Artists and brass bands gather on corners and in doorways on most weekends and turn intersections and sidewalks into impromptu, open-air galleries, boutiques, and dance parties. A poet selling custom love sonnets typed up on a vintage typewriter and a shopping cart–turned–mechanical bull with built-in music and smoke machine are just some of the rarities you'll encounter on an average night.

Bao & Noodle

$ | **CHINESE** | Hand-pulled noodles and fluffy steamed bao are the specialties at this local favorite. Sichuan and Cantonese dishes pack the occasional punch (the Mixed Sauce noodles are pleasantly mouth-numbing), and everything is full of flavor. **Known for:** spicy dan dan noodles with pork; steamed bun appetizers; family-style dining. [$] *Average main: $13* ✉ *2266 St. Claude Ave., Faubourg Marigny* ☎ *504/272–0004* 🌐 *www.baoandnoodle.com* 🕒 *Closed Sun. and Mon.*

An artist works on a Mardi Gras mural that feels right at home in the colorful Marigny neighborhood.

Elysian Bar

$ | **AMERICAN** | The team behind popular Bywater wine garden Bacchanal opened this chic bar and restaurant at the Hotel Peter and Paul, where you'll find dizzying walls of chartreuse and ochre, a generous apertivo hour, and a cavernous back bar that seems carved out of a fairy tale. Large plates like the chicken confit and grilled Gulf shrimp are perfect for sharing with a date, but plant-based small plates, like whipped ricotta with preserved mushrooms, are particularly satisfying. **Known for:** romantic interiors; apertivo hour; above-and-beyond bar snacks. $ *Average main: $15* ✉ *Hotel Peter and Paul, 2317 Burgundy St., Faubourg Marigny* ☎ *504/356–6769* ⊕ *www.hotelpeterandpaul.com/libations.*

Em Trai Sandwich Co.

$ | **VIETNAMESE** | This casual counter-service eatery is a good place to fuel up while exploring the Marigny and next-door Bywater. Traditional Vietnamese dishes like banh mi sandwiches, pho, and spring rolls meet the American South with additions like BBQ pulled pork and smoked brisket or wonton chips with crab dip. **Known for:** Bang Bang shrimp; excellent pho and spring rolls with a Southern twist; local craft beer. $ *Average main: $13* ✉ *New Orleans Healing Center, 2372 St. Claude Ave., Faubourg Marigny* ☎ *504/302–7772* ⊗ *Closed Sun.*

Kebab

$ | **MIDDLE EASTERN** | The gyro sandwich with a side of Belgian fries (and indulgent housemade aioli) here is a satisfying meal for those looking to make a late night at the St. Claude Avenue clubs and bars that surround this casual hipster establishment. Vegetarians and vegans will be pleased by the selection of falafel, hummus, and other plant-based choices as well. **Known for:** great fries; plenty of vegetarian options; one of the city's best gyros. $ *Average main: $13* ✉ *2315 St. Claude Ave., Faubourg Marigny* ☎ *504/383–4328* ⊕ *www.kebabnola.com* ⊗ *Closed Tues.*

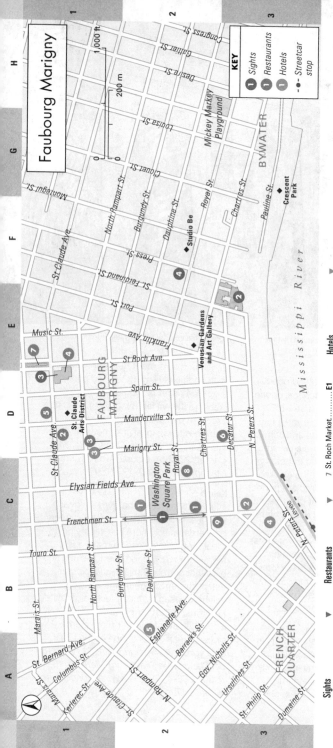

Faubourg Marigny

KEY

- **1** Sights
- **1** Restaurants
- **1** Hotels
- ●━● Streetcar stop

Mississippi River

FAUBOURG MARIGNY

BYWATER

FRENCH QUARTER

Crescent Park

Washington Square Park

Mickey Mackey Playground

St. Claude Arts District

● Studio Be

● Venusian Gardens and Art Gallery

Sights ►

1 Frenchmen Street..........**C2**
2 New Orleans Center for Creative Arts..........**E3**
3 New Orleans Healing Center..........**D1**
4 Plessy vs. Ferguson Site..........**F2**

Restaurants ►

1 Adolfo's..........**C2**
2 Bao & Noodle..........**D1**
3 Elysian Bar..........**D1**
4 Em Trai Sandwich Co...**D1**
5 Kebab..........**D1**
6 Paladar 511..........**D3**
7 St. Roch Market..........**E1**
8 Sukho Thai..........**C2**
9 Three Muses..........**C3**

Hotels ►

1 Claiborne Mansion..........**C2**
2 The Frenchmen Hotel..........**C3**
3 Hotel Peter and Paul....**D1**
4 Lions Inn..........**C3**
5 Melrose Mansion..........**B2**

Paladar 511
$$ | **ITALIAN** | This airy, industrial space has two equally enjoyable identities, depending on the time of day. Weekend brunches are bustling and lively and heavily feature their popular boozy brunch drinks and the to-die-for lemon ricotta pancakes while at night, things are more subdued under the chandelier and pendant lamps when the open kitchen serves up housemade pastas and pizza. **Known for:** wood-fired pizza; lemon ricotta pancakes; Italian farm-to-table comfort food. [$] *Average main: $19* ✉ *511 Marigny St., Faubourg Marigny* ☎ *504/509–6782* 🌐 *www.paladar511.com* 🕓 *Closed Tues. No lunch weekdays.*

St. Roch Market
$$ | **ECLECTIC** | This revamped food hall offers visitors a (slightly overpriced) chance to sample from a wide array of flavors. Vendors offer casual local favorites as well as global cuisine, from Haiti to Burma; there's also a chic little oyster bar, bottles of wine and specialty foodstuffs to take home, and a full bar with a generous happy hour. **Known for:** unique global fare; something for everyone; local oysters. [$] *Average main: $15* ✉ *2381 St. Claude Ave., Faubourg Marigny* ☎ *504/267–0388* 🌐 *www.strochmarket.com.*

Sukho Thai
$$ | **THAI** | Certainly the most extensive Thai restaurant in the area, Sukho Thai fits into its artsy neighborhood with servers wearing all black and a hip, art-gallery approach to decorating. You can't go wrong with any of the curries, but the fried whole fish with three spicy chili sauces is a showstopper. **Known for:** authentic curries and fried whole fish; affordable lunch specials; Thai-inspired cocktails. [$] *Average main: $18* ✉ *2200 Royal St., Faubourg Marigny* ☎ *504/948–9309* 🌐 *www.sukhothai-nola.com* 🕓 *Closed Mon.*

Three Muses
$$ | **ECLECTIC** | The most eclectic mix of music, food, and people can be found on Frenchmen Street, and Three Muses captures everything that makes this vibrant stretch of the Faubourg Marigny worth seeking out. The small-plates menu spans the globe, with charcuterie, cheese plates, and standout delicacies like the Korean-style steak bulgogi. **Known for:** live music; romantic ambience; small space so call ahead. [$] *Average main: $15* ✉ *536 Frenchmen St., Faubourg Marigny* ☎ *504/252–4801* 🌐 *www.3musesnola.com* 🕓 *No lunch.*

Hotels

Claiborne Mansion
$ | **B&B/INN** | One of the most beautiful places to stay in Faubourg Marigny, the Claiborne Mansion has enormous rooms with high ceilings, canopy beds, polished hardwood floors, and rich fabrics. **Pros:** big rooms; within walking distance of several great restaurants and jazz clubs; free Wi-Fi. **Cons:** limited on-site parking; all the quirks and character of a B&B; noisy nightlife-friendly surroundings. [$] *Rooms from: $125* ✉ *2111 Dauphine St., Faubourg Marigny* ☎ *504/301–1027* 🌐 *www.claibornemansion.com* 🛏 *7 rooms* 🍴 *Free breakfast.*

The Frenchmen Hotel
$$ | **HOTEL** | A casual choice for those who want to be near the action (and don't mind hearing it all night), rooms and amenities here are minimal, but the rooftop terrace and pool in the inner courtyard add extra appeal. **Pros:** good pool area; one of the only options to stay right on Frenchmen Street; some rooms are quieter. **Cons:** parking is difficult; area can be loud and overwhelming; old world charm, but could use some upgrades. [$] *Rooms from: $211* ✉ *417 Frenchmen St., Faubourg Marigny* ☎ *504/945–5453* 🌐 *www.frenchmenhotel.com* 🛏 *27 rooms* 🍴 *Free breakfast.*

★ Hotel Peter and Paul

$$ | HOTEL | A longtime neighborhood resident teamed with a boutique hotel group to renovate this former church and rectory, creating a one-of-a-kind hotel, supremely rooted in place. **Pros:** gorgeous architecture and decor create a fully unique experience; great restaurant and bar; free parking lot. **Cons:** limited shared common areas; most rooms are small; lacks some amenities of a chain hotel. $ *Rooms from: $229* ⌧ *2317 Burgundy St., Faubourg Marigny* ☎ *504/356–5200* ⊕ *www.hotelpeterandpaul.com* ⇨ *71 rooms* ¶○¶ *No meals.*

Lions Inn

$$ | B&B/INN | Old South room decor adds to the traditional ambience of this bed-and-breakfast, while a swimming pool and hot tub in the private garden offer a welcome escape. **Pros:** private courtyard; lovely neighborhood feel; free Wi-Fi. **Cons:** a 10-minute walk to the Quarter or Frenchmen Street means you may want to take a cab at night; street parking only. $ *Rooms from: $139* ⌧ *2517 Chartres St., Faubourg Marigny* ☎ *504/945–2339* ⊕ *www.lionsinn.com* ⇨ *10 rooms* ¶○¶ *Free breakfast.*

Melrose Mansion

$$ | B&B/INN | Just steps from the French Quarter, this renovated Victorian mansion turns on the grandeur with antique furnishings, hardwood floors, cathedral ceilings, and large chandeliers—and lots of luxurious, modern conveniences. **Pros:** private and luxurious, with lots of pampering; complimentary wine and cheese nightly; breakfast included. **Cons:** one night's stay is charged prior to arrival (special-event policies vary); guest should use caution when walking around at night; weekends fill up fast with weddings. $ *Rooms from: $199* ⌧ *937 Esplanade Ave., Faubourg Marigny* ☎ *504/944–2255, 800/650–3323* ⊕ *www.melrosemansion.com* ⇨ *21 rooms* ¶○¶ *Free breakfast.*

▼ Nightlife

Frenchmen Street in the Marigny is the hottest music strip in town, and is also known for its food and street life. Much of Frenchmen's activity is within a three-block area (between Decatur and Dauphine streets), where fun-seekers crawl bars and people-watch on the sidewalk. Some clubs along this strip charge a $5–$10 cover for music, but many charge nothing at all. Along St. Claude Avenue a diverse cluster of bars and clubs offers everything from brass-band jams to death metal to experimental, avant-garde indie rock.

BARS AND LOUNGES

AllWays Lounge & Theatre

MUSIC CLUBS | This lounge-theater combo has become one of the centerpieces of the local indie, avant-garde, and art scenes. Evoking 1930s Berlin, the lounge has a black-and-red color scheme and frayed-at-the-edges art deco aesthetic. Musicians, burlesque dancers, clowns, artists, and jacks-of-all-trades take to the stage here most nights of the week. Meanwhile, in the back of the house, the 100-seat AllWays Theatre hosts weekend plays and other performances. ⌧ *2240 St. Claude Ave., Faubourg Marigny* ☎ *504/321–5606* ⊕ *www.theallwayslounge.net.*

Brieux Carré

BREWPUBS/BEER GARDENS | This pint-sized, colorful microbrewery is making a name for itself as having some of the best local beer in the area. There are around nine beers on tap at any given time, often exotic varieties with locally inspired names. A large beer garden and outdoor patio in the back is the brewery's best feature. ⌧ *2115 Decatur St., Faubourg Marigny* ☎ *504/304–4242* ⊕ *www.brieuxcarre.com.*

LGBTQ Scene in New Orleans

New Orleans has a laissez-faire attitude about many things, and that includes sexual orientation. The city has one of the oldest and most vibrant gay, lesbian, and transgender communities in the nation, which is just part of the reason that New Orleans has long been a popular destination for gay travelers. Another key factor is partying. The LGBTQ community is famous for their megacelebrations around holidays like Mardi Gras and Southern Decadence (held Labor Day weekend). Social clubs, often organized around bars or other gay-owned business sponsors, join forces to throw parades, costume balls, and themed parties. The street party at Bourbon and St. Anne streets in the French Quarter is always a popular event. This intersection tends to be a main hub of the gay social scene, with **Bourbon Pub** and **Oz** perched on each side of the street, pumping out music from the discotheque-style dance floors. Great crowds also turn out for Halloween and for Easter, when a gay Easter parade rolls through the Quarter. The city celebrates Gay Pride in October, but it actually tends to be a fairly low-key affair compared to these other more lavish parties. It's probably because gay pride is evident here 365 days a year.

Most of the social scene is focused in the French Quarter, but the Faubourg Marigny and Bywater have some great gay bars, restaurants, and other destinations.

Stop in **FAB-Faubourg Marigny Art and Books** (⌧ 600 Frenchmen St.), one of the oldest (and funkiest) gay bookstores in the nation, and pick up a copy of *Ambush Magazine*, the alternative biweekly. Or visit ⊕ www.gayneworleans.com, another great resource.

4

Faubourg Marigny

Buffa's

BARS/PUBS | This simple neighborhood spot has been popular for live music and festive vibes since 1939. The burgers are famous in their own right, as are the Bloody Marys and other to-go drinks. There is live music in Buffa's backroom each night (keep an eye out for Walter "Wolfman" Washington's sets), and a fun traditional jazz brunch on Sundays. ⌧ 1001 Esplanade Ave., Faubourg Marigny ☎ 949–0038 ⊕ www.buffasrestaurant.com.

Checkpoint Charlie's

MUSIC CLUBS | This bustling corner bar draws young locals who shoot pool and listen to blues and rock, whether live or from the jukebox—24 hours a day, seven days a week. Weekends often feature hard rock, punk, and metal bands. There's also a paperback library, a menu of bar grub, and even a fully functioning laundromat. ⌧ 501 Esplanade Ave., Faubourg Marigny ☎ 504/281–4847.

Mag's 940

BARS/PUBS | This friendly gay bar hosts special events ranging from country western line-dance lessons to burlesque and drag shows. There's a big-screen TV for games and a large selection of vodkas and top-shelf bourbons. It proclaims itself "the cleanest bar in New Orleans." The owner also runs a small guesthouse above the bar. ⌧ 940 Elysian Fields Ave., Faubourg Marigny ☎ 504/948–1888 ⊕ www.mags940guesthouse.com.

The Maison

DANCE CLUBS | This historic building—with a sprawling three-story floor plan, interior balconies, and a terrific kitchen, plus multiple bars, stages, and dance floors—has become one of Frenchmen Street's most popular destinations. Live music every night of the week (normally with no cover) make it inviting, and the managers skillfully weave local and touring DJs into their lineup of parties and events. ✉ *508 Frenchmen St., Faubourg Marigny* ☎ *504/371–5543* ⊕ *www.maisonfrenchmen.com.*

Mimi's

BARS/PUBS | A popular local hangout, this two-story nightspot perches on the corner of Franklin and Royal streets with a wraparound balcony and big windows that stay open most evenings. Downstairs is a bar with table seating, couches, and a pool table, while upstairs is home to a tapas-style kitchen and dance floor. Due to permit issues, live music is intermittent, but entertainment and local personalities are big here every night. ✉ *2601 Royal St., Faubourg Marigny* ☎ *504/872–9868* ⊕ *mimismarigny.com.*

Phoenix

BARS/PUBS | This lounge bills itself as a "Leather/Levi Neighborhood Alternative Bar," and that's a pretty apt description. The downstairs bar is a popular Marigny nightspot, with a calendar of special events and themed parties, including the International Mr. Leather Contest. The upstairs bar, called The Eagle, is notorious for its "anything goes" atmosphere. ✉ *941 Elysian Fields Ave., Faubourg Marigny* ☎ *504/945–9264* ⊕ *www.phoenixbarnola.com.*

R Bar

BARS/PUBS | Behind the tinted windows of this corner bar, find a red-vinyl-clad hipster hangout and stylish social hub with a throwback ambience. In addition to crawfish boils on Friday afternoons (in season), the place runs offbeat

Whistling "Dixie"

👁

One popular theory for the origin of the term "Dixie" points back to the Citizens Bank of New Orleans, which issued bilingual $10 banknotes bearing the French word "*dix*" (meaning "ten") on the reverse. The notes thus became known as "dixies," and the term eventually became synonymous first with Louisiana, and then with the entire South. Historians are still debating this etymology—but it's a good story nonetheless.

specials—on Monday night, for example, 10 bucks gets you a shot and a haircut—and it's prime real estate on costume holidays like Mardi Gras and Halloween. ✉ *Royal St. Inn, 1431 Royal St., Faubourg Marigny* ☎ *504/948–7499* ⊕ *www.royalstreetinn.com.*

LIVE MUSIC

Blue Nile

MUSIC CLUBS | Soul Rebels, Kermit Ruffins and the BBQ Swingers, and Corey Henry & The Tremé Funktet are among the talented local acts that regularly grace the stage at this long-standing, bare-bones music club. You're likely to catch a free act during the week; on weekends, tickets range from $15–$20 and can be purchased at the door or online in advance for most shows. Price is higher than some of the other clubs, but performance quality is consistent as it's a true Frenchmen Street institution. ✉ *532 Frenchmen St., Faubourg Marigny* ☎ *504/766–6193* ⊕ *www.bluenilelive.com.*

Snug Harbor

MUSIC CLUBS | This intimate club with a sometimes-steep cover charge is one of the city's best rooms to soak up modern jazz. It is the home base of such esteemed talent as vocalist Charmaine Neville, who plays every Monday, and pianist-patriarch Ellis Marsalis (father of Wynton and Branford). The dining room serves good local food but is best known for its burgers. ⊠ *626 Frenchmen St., Faubourg Marigny* ☎ *504/949–0696* ⊕ *www.snugjazz.com.*

★ The Spotted Cat

MUSIC CLUBS | Jazz, old-time, and swing bands perform nightly at this rustic club right in the thick of the Frenchmen Street action. Sets start at 2 pm and the music continues until at least midnight. Drinks cost a little more at this cash-only destination, but there's never a cover charge and the entertainment is great—from the popular bands to the cadres of young, rock-step swing dancers. ⊠ *623 Frenchmen St., Faubourg Marigny* ⊕ *www.spottedcatmusicclub.com.*

Performing Arts

Marigny Opera House

ARTS CENTERS | An elegant, whitewashed building on a quiet residential street, this "Church of the Arts" has been hosting the Marigny Opera Ballet since 2014. Besides highly coveted private events and weddings, the House also hosts New Orleans Opera Association productions, other plays, and mostly classical music. ⊠ *725 St. Ferdinand St., Bywater* ☎ *504/948–9998* ⊕ *www.marignyoperahouse.org.*

 Shopping

A mostly residential neighborhood with a vibrant nightlife scene, the Marigny is filled with restaurants and bars on or around Frenchmen Street and the St. Claude Avenue Arts District. A scattering of shops and outdoor vendors stay open late into the evening, perfect for a quick browse as you explore the neighborhood's music scene.

ANTIQUES AND COLLECTIBLES

Byrdie's Pottery

CERAMICS/GLASSWARE | A pottery studio on a busy corner, there is always a nice array of unique vases, planters, bowls, and mugs for sale here. Check the website for workshops, events, and open hours, which can be a little sporadic (Saturdays are a good bet). ⊠ *2402A St. Claude Ave., Faubourg Marigny* ⊕ *www.byrdiespottery.org.*

Island of Salvation Botanica

SPECIALTY STORES | Owned by voodoo priestess Sallie Ann Glassman and located inside the New Orleans Healing Center, this mystical shop specializes in voodoo religious supplies (candles, herbs, tinctures, books, incense), as well as Haitian and world art. Glassman also offers crystal-ball readings by appointment, while other staff members do psychic visions and tarot card readings. ⊠ *New Orleans Healing Center, 2372 St. Claude Ave., Suite 100, Faubourg Marigny* ☎ *504/948–9961* ⊕ *www.islandofsalvationbotanica.com.*

Palace Market

OUTDOOR/FLEA/GREEN MARKETS | A revival of Frenchmen Street's longtime arts market, local crafters gather here each evening to sell their wares, ranging from jewelry and ornaments to paintings and sculptures. It's a pleasant place to wander in between music shows and people-watching. The market opens at 7 pm nightly, and stays open until around midnight. ⊠ *619 Frenchmen St., Faubourg Marigny* ☎ *504/249–9003* ⊕ *www.palacemarketnola.com.*

MUSIC

Louisiana Music Factory

MUSIC STORES | A favorite resource for New Orleans and regional music—new and old—the Louisiana Music Factory has records, tapes, CDs, DVDs, sheet music, and books, as well as listening stations, music-oriented T-shirts, original art, and a stage that hosts frequent live concerts. ✉ *421 Frenchmen St., Faubourg Marigny* ☎ *504/586–1094* ⊕ *www.louisianamusic-factory.com.*

WINE

Faubourg Wines

WINE/SPIRITS | This charming shop is packed with both fine and affordable wines, as well as select gourmet ciders and beers. For a $2 corkage fee, imbibers can enjoy purchases at a curtained window alcove or sidewalk bistro table. The shop provides glasses, and sells fresh bread and cheese selections from Bellegarde Bakery and St. James Cheese Co. Free wine tastings are usually held on Wednesdays from 6 to 8 pm. ✉ *2805 St. Claude Ave., Faubourg Marigny* ☎ *504/342–2217* ⊕ *www.faubourgwines.com.*

Chapter 5

THE BYWATER, ST. CLAUDE, AND THE LOWER NINTH WARD

Updated by
Cameron Quincy Todd

◉ **Sights**	🍴 **Restaurants**	🛏 **Hotels**	🛍 **Shopping**	🍸 **Nightlife**
★★★☆☆	★★★★☆	★☆☆☆☆	★★★☆☆	★★★★☆

NEIGHBORHOOD SNAPSHOT

TOP EXPERIENCES

■ **The Bywater arts scene.** This constantly gentrifying neighborhood is an enclave of artists, musicians, and creative outliers, and you'll see it in everything from the decorated cars and funky boutiques to the intricate street art on warehouses and buildings.

■ **Entertaining brunches.** Drag-themed spectacles, lively Cajun dancing, praline-coated bacon, Bloody Marys, boutique coffee, and homebaked sweet treats are among the delicious brunch options in the Bywater.

■ **The community history of the Lower Ninth Ward.** Small, community-run museums paint a picture of cultural and historical significance within this neighborhood hit hard by Hurricane Katrina.

GETTING HERE

The Bywater is located downriver (east) of the French Quarter, about a 30-minute walk. You'll spend most of your time here near the river, on streets like Burgundy and Royal and along busy St. Claude Avenue in St. Claude, a popular city throughway that becomes Rampart Street closer to downtown. The No. 88 St. Claude/Jackson Barracks bus runs along the north edge (lake side) of the French Quarter all the way into the Lower Ninth Ward. Hop on the bus or the Rampart–St. Claude streetcar to access shops and restaurants along St. Claude Avenue, and walk down to the rest of Bywater from there. Uber and Lyft are easily available in this area.

PLANNING YOUR TIME

The Bywater is pleasant during the day, when it's fun to walk through its more picturesque, residential sections near the river, and the bars along St. Claude Avenue are great at night. It's best to avoid the more desolate areas north of St. Claude Avenue and around Poland Avenue late at night or when walking alone. The Lower Ninth Ward is mostly residential and still quite desolate in some pockets, but there are a few sights that make it worthwhile to spend a couple hours here.

QUICK BITES

■ **Bywater Bakery.** This is everything you could want from a neighborhood coffee shop: delicious coffee, premium baked goods, and hearty sandwiches and comfort food for a quick breakfast or lunch. The pies are great around the holidays, as are the king cakes during Carnival season. ⊠ 3624 Dauphine St., Bywater ☎ 504/336–3336 ⊕ www.bywaterbakery.com ☉ Closed Wed. No dinner.

■ **Frady's One Stop Food Store.** Both a convenience store and a lunch counter, this friendly neighborhood institution is the perfect place to stop for a cold drink and a delicious carry-out po'boy. ⊠ 3231 Dauphine St., Bywater ☎ 504/949–9688 ☉ Closed Sun. No dinner.

■ **Satsuma Café.** Drop into this lively bohemian hang-out for a healthy breakfast, a midday repast, or a restorative glass of juiced fruits and vegetables. ⊠ 3218 Dauphine St., Bywater ☎ 504/304–5962 ⊕ www.satsumacafe.com ☉ No dinner.

A once crumbling but beautiful old neighborhood east of the train tracks at Press Street, the Bywater has become a magnet for hip newcomers seeking to make "authentic" New Orleans their home.

The Bywater and St. Claude

The Mississippi River runs the length of the Bywater's boundary, and the bars and coffee shops scattered around the neighborhood's gritty and shiny parts alike combine elements of its working-class roots with the more recent hipster influx to make for a lively and distinctly local experience. It doesn't have the head-turning array of sights you'll find in the French Quarter, but a visit to the Bywater gives you a feel for New Orleans as it lives day to day, in a colorful, overgrown, slightly sleepy cityscape reminiscent of island communities and tinged with a sense of perpetual decay. Northwest of the Bywayer (away from the river) is St. Claude, another section of the Upper Ninth Ward that often gets grouped together with the Bywater. The commercial and cultural heart of this neighborhood is St. Claude Avenue, a busy city throughway that's also home to art and dance studios, small shops and restaurants, and avant-garde entertainment venues.

 Sights

Christopher Porché-West Galerie
MUSEUM | Legendary independent photographer Christopher Porché-West operates out of this working studio and exhibit space. The atmosphere depends on the current focus and vigor of Porché-West's activities: sometimes it is more work-oriented, sometimes more formally organized around exhibits of his work or that of other artists. The gallery occupies an old pharmacy storefront at the hub of a hip block boasting restaurants, boutiques, and a yoga studio. Whenever the artist happens to be in, the gallery is open. You can also make an appointment by calling (he's almost always nearby). ⊠ *3201 Burgundy St., Bywater* ☎ *504/947–3880* ⊕ *www.porche-west. com.*

Crescent Park
CITY PARK | The newest park in New Orleans stretches along the Mississippi riverfront and provides for spectacular views of the New Orleans skyline, Algiers, and the mighty Mississippi itself. The best place to enter the park is at Mazant Street in the Bywater, where you can explore the park's promenades, green spaces, and repurposed wharves, and walk the 1.4-mile path along the water. Plans are in the works to extend the park through the Marigny and beyond. ⊠ *Mazant St. at Chartres St., Bywater* ⊕ *www.nola.gov/city/ crescent-park.*

Dr. Bob
MUSEUM | A small compound of artists' and furniture-makers' studios includes

Crescent Park has many charming spaces for bikers and walks to stop, including this arched bridge entryway.

the headquarters of this beloved local folk artist, whose easily recognizable work can be found hanging across New Orleans. "Be Nice or Leave," "Be Gay and Stay," "Shalom, Ya'll," and "Shut Up and Fish" are just a few of his popular themes. Dr. Bob's shop is chock-full of original furniture, colorful signs, and unidentifiable objects of artistic fancy. Prices start as low as $30 for a small "Be Nice," and most pieces are in the $200–$500 range. The sign outside advertises the open hours as "9 am–'til"—best to call ahead. ⌧ *3027 Chartres St., Bywater* ☎ *504/945–2225* ⊕ *www.drbobart.net.*

Music Box Village

ARTS VENUE | A whimsical creation of repurposed urban wasteland, this artist-built sculpture garden features an interactive landscape of music-making structures and houses. The space hosts musical acts, performances, and workshops. Most weekend days when there isn't an event, the space is open for the public to explore and play (check the website calendar for "Open Hours"

before visiting). ⌧ *4557 N. Rampart St., Bywater* ⊕ *www.musicboxvillage.com* ✉ *Suggested $12 donation.*

St. Claude Arts District

NEIGHBORHOOD | The Bywater neighborhood is home to dozens of alternative art spaces, many of which have banded together under the loose umbrella of the St. Claude Arts District (SCAD). From old candle factories to people's living rooms, this burgeoning scene—centered around St. Claude Avenue and nearby streets—produces some of the most intriguing and innovative work in the city, with several major artists and arts organizations. In addition to galleries, several independent theater spaces have sprung up as well, offering venues for live performances, magic and burlesque shows, fringe theater, and more. The second Saturday of each month is opening night, when galleries and venues host new shows and parties. ⌧ *Bywater* ⊕ *www. artsdistrictstclaude.com.*

Studio Be

MUSEUM | Artist Brandan "BMike" Odums's larger-than-life graffiti murals and installations fill this 35,000-square-foot warehouse in an industrial nook of the Bywater, easy to spot thanks to its bright front exterior and giant mural of a young African American girl shrugging her arms up towards the sky. Work here excites and awakens viewers, with its themes on social justice, African American history, racial violence, and other contemporary issues in New Orleans and beyond. Check Brandan's website for more projects around town. ✉ *2941 Royal St., Bywater* ☎ *504/330–6231* 🌐 *www.bmike.com* 🎟 *$10* 🕒 *Closed Sun.–Tues.*

🍴 Restaurants

Minutes from the French Quarter but still relatively untouched by tourists, edgy Bywater has recently seen an influx of new residents, new restaurants, and new vitality.

Bywater American Bistro

$$$ | **AMERICAN** | The latest project from chef Nina Compton, *Top Chef*contestant and owner of popular Compère Lapin in the Warehouse District, is a real neighborhood place, a friendly yet refined bistro where friends can get together to enjoy a good meal. The atmosphere here is upscale and dinner is on the pricey side, but there is a warm and homey quality to the experience. **Known for:** pasta and curries; tasty shared plates; house-bottled negronis. [$] *Average main: $24* ✉ *2900 Chartres St., Bywater* ☎ *504/605–3827* 🌐 *www.bywateramericanbistro.com* 🕒 *Closed Mon. and Tues. No lunch weekdays.*

Capulet

$ | **AMERICAN** | This lofted space has great vegetarian options and hearty sandwiches that skew creative; think a BLT with kimchi and thick-slab bacon or smoked cauliflower, broccoli falafel, and braised beef with Bloody Mary seasoning. Cocktails are equally unique, utilizing shrubs, fresh juices, and kombucha. **Known for:** creative cocktails; great vegetarian options; industrial chic. [$] *Average main: $11* ✉ *3014 Dauphine St., Bywater* ☎ *504/507–0691* 🌐 *www.capuletbywater.com* 🕒 *Closed weekends. No dinner.*

★ **Elizabeth's**

$ | **SOUTHERN** | "Real food, done real good" is the motto at hipster-haven Elizabeth's, where the vinyl-print tablecloths look just like grandma's and breakfast really is the most important meal of the day. The menu offers everything from po'boys to a stellar seared duck, but the highlight is the buzzy weekend brunch served from 8 am to 2:30 pm that includes "lost bread" (also known as French toast), "redneck eggs" (fried green tomatoes with poached eggs and hollandaise), and a traditional country breakfast with a smoked pork chop (there's also bottomless mimosas, if you want to start the party early). **Known for:** one of the city's best brunch experiences; famous praline bacon; no breakfast or brunch reservations accepted so expect a wait. [$] *Average main: $15* ✉ *601 Gallier St., Bywater* ☎ *504/944–9272* 🌐 *www.elizabethsrestaurantnola.com* 🕒 *No dinner weekends.*

Galaxie

$ | **MEXICAN** | Inside this gas station–turned–taco shop, meats are spit-roasted and masa is crafted by hand. The casual, open-air space serves counter-service tacos and snacks inspired by Oaxaca and Mexico City, but much of the focus is on the large bar, where seasoned local talents craft rum, mezcal, and tequila-based concoctions. **Known for:** al pastor tacos; handmade tortillas; fantastic margaritas. [$] *Average main: $12* ✉ *3060 St. Claude Ave., Bywater* ☎ *504/827–1443* 🕒 *Closed Mon. No lunch.*

Jack Dempsey's

$$ | **SEAFOOD** | As the Bywater dining scene has largely shifted towards the new, trendy, and exploratory, this

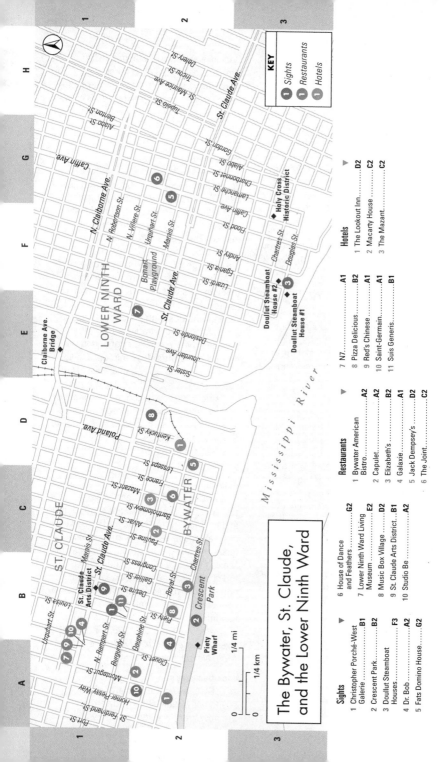

The Bywater, St. Claude, and the Lower Ninth Ward

Sights ▶

1 Christopher Porché-West Galerie G2
2 Crescent Park B2
3 Doullut Steamboat Houses F3
4 Dr. Bob A2
5 Fats Domino House G2
6 House of Dance and Feathers G2
7 Lower Ninth Ward Living Museum E2
8 Music Box Village D2
9 St. Claude Arts District B1
10 Studio Be A2

Restaurants ▶

1 Bywater American Bistro A2
2 Capulet A2
3 Elizabeth's B2
4 Galaxie A1
5 Jack Dempsey's D2
6 The Joint C2
7 N7 .... A1
8 Pizza Delicious B2
9 Red's Chinese A1
10 Saint-Germain A1
11 Suis Generis B1

Hotels ▶

1 The Lookout Inn D2
2 Macarty House C2
3 The Mazant C2

KEY
1 Sights
1 Restaurants
1 Hotels

historical location on Poland Avenue has stood its ground, remaining one of the only classic New Orleans dinner joints in the area. Expect large portions of fried and boiled seafood favorites, like catfish, redfish, oysters, and shrimp, as well as po'boys, stuffed flounder, and surf-and-turf plates. **Known for:** local seafood; family-style portions; no-frills atmosphere. [$] *Average main: $23* ✉ *738 Poland Ave., St. Claude* ☎ *504/943–9914* 🌐 *www.jackdempseys.net* 🕒 *Closed Sun. and Mon. No dinner Tues.*

The Joint

$ | SOUTHERN | FAMILY | You can't miss this bright, yellow-striped building, but it's the smell of the meat—pork shoulder, pork ribs, beef brisket, and chicken—cooking in the custom-made smoker that will draw you in. In a town not really known for great barbecue, the Joint is an exception, which is why it draws hungry patrons from far and wide. **Known for:** perhaps the best ribs in the city; peanut butter pie for dessert; local beers. [$] *Average main: $12* ✉ *701 Mazant St., Bywater* ☎ *504/949–3232* 🌐 *www.alwayssmokin.com* 🕒 *Closed Sun.*

★ **N7**

$$ | TAPAS | It might seem unlikely that a restaurant specializing in canned fish would be one of the most romantic places to dine in New Orleans, but N7 is just that. Once you find this hidden gem, tucked behind a barely marked large wooden fence on a quiet street off of St. Claude Avenue, the adorable, candlelit courtyard and Parisian bistro interior will whisk you away to a dreamy European evening. **Known for:** habanero-smoked oysters; French wine list; romantic date nights. [$] *Average main: $18* ✉ *1117 Montegut St., Bywater* 🌐 *www.n7nola.com* 🕒 *Closed Sun. No lunch.*

Pizza Delicious

$ | PIZZA | Hipsters, lifelong Bywater residents, and locals far across town all take great pride in "Pizza D" as one of the only (and best) places to get authentic New York–style pizza in New Orleans. A tall can of PBR and a slice of cheese will satisfy most, but delve into the specialty pies, pastas, and surprisingly pleasing salads for the full experience. **Known for:** New York–style slices; hipster clientele and dive bar ambience; long lines on weekends. [$] *Average main: $15* ✉ *617 Piety St., Bywater* ☎ *504/676–8482* 🌐 *www.pizzadelicious.com* 🕒 *Closed Mon.*

Red's Chinese

$ | ASIAN FUSION | The funky, Mission Chinese–style Asian fusion served here pairs well with late night dancing and drinking on St. Claude Avenue. Expect flavor bombs like the sweet-and-spicy fried chicken, kung pao pastrami, and creamy crawfish wontons, hipster attitudes and service, and a fun meal different from the New Orleans norm. **Known for:** hipster vibes; fried chicken; crawfish wontons. [$] *Average main: $13* ✉ *3048 St. Claude Ave., St. Claude* ☎ *504/304–6030* 🌐 *www.redschinese.com.*

Saint-Germain

$$$$ | FRENCH FUSION | The seasonal five-course menu changes constantly at this romantic Parisian-style bistro, which is quickly becoming one of the finest dining experiences in New Orleans. Optional wine pairings and a lovely courtyard add to the romance of this special, date-night spot. **Known for:** tasting menu and wine pairings; romantic setting; reservations for dinner a must. [$] *Average main: $65* ✉ *3054 St. Claude Ave., St. Claude* ☎ *504/218–8729* 🌐 *www.saintgermainnola.com* 🕒 *Closed Wed. No lunch.*

Suis Generis

$$ | INTERNATIONAL | Devotees of this unassuming neighborhood spot wait with bated breath on Friday afternoons, when a new menu is posted online (and outside the restaurant) showcasing the offerings for that week. The space is intimate and funky, and the food is the same, where ingredients from local farms inspire risottos, curries, housemade ice creams, slow-roasts, and marinades and spices from around the globe. **Known for:** exciting menus of seasonal ingredients; favorite for locals; Thursday Taco Nights. [$] *Average main: $18* ✉ *3219 Burgundy St., Bywater* ☎ *504/309–7850* 🌐 *www.suisgeneris.com* 🕒 *Closed Mon. and Tues. No lunch weekdays.*

Hotels

There are a fair number of Airbnbs and short-term rentals in the Bywater, enough to draw the ire of many residents with legitimate complaints about the city's affordable housing crisis. The few hotel choices available give a homey and often quirky B&B experience that fits with the neighborhood's charm.

The Lookout Inn

$ | **B&B/INN** | Suites at this laid-back inn are surprisingly spacious, and the cozy backyard comes with a hot tub, pool, and outdoor bar. **Pros:** great neighborhood; plenty of space; charming backyard with pool and grill. **Cons:** more of a rental house than a hotel; no breakfast; residential area can be too quiet for some. [$] *Rooms from: $99* ✉ *833 Poland Ave., Bywater* ☎ *504/947–8188* 🌐 *www.lookoutneworleans.com* 🔑 *4 rooms* 🍴 *No meals.*

Macarty House

$ | **RENTAL** | Formerly a bed and breakfast, this house now rents to large groups and comes with a saltwater pool, private baths in each room, and plenty of private space and amenities. **Pros:** great pool, courtyard, and outdoor bar; friendly owners who make you feel at home; charming interiors. **Cons:** must book entire house (no individual rooms); some noise travels from room to room; strict cancellation policy. [$] *Rooms from: $75* ✉ *3820 Burgundy St., Bywater* ☎ *504/267–1564* 🌐 *www.macartyhouse.com* 🔑 *8 rooms* 🍴 *No meals.*

The Mazant

$$ | **B&B/INN** | An 1880s Greek Revival mansion, the Mazant offers a historic stay steps from the best of the Bywater, complete with breakfast and the option to book single rooms or rent the entire house. **Pros:** free breakfast; great shared living room and outdoor spaces; charming, spacious setting. **Cons:** shared house setting not for everyone; not all rooms have private bathrooms; books up far in advance. [$] *Rooms from: $150* ✉ *906 Mazant St., Bywater* ☎ *504/517–3193* 🌐 *www.mazant.com* 🔑 *8 rooms* 🍴 *Free breakfast.*

Nightlife

Perhaps the edgiest local scene in New Orleans can be found in Bywater, home to a dozen low-key bars. Past the corner of Royal and Franklin streets a smattering of watering holes cater to a varied crowd. As an added incentive to explore this neighborhood, local idol Kermit Ruffins (of *Treme* fame) plays in Bywater and the Seventh Ward some nights.

BARS AND LOUNGES

★ Bacchanal Fine Wine & Spirits

BARS/PUBS | In the far reaches of the Bywater, Bacchanal is part wineshop, part bar, part music club—and 100% neighborhood hangout. Enter the old building first, then beyond the wine racks you'll find a courtyard with seating and a spacious bar upstairs that serves beer and liquor. You can have a bottle uncorked on the premises or order by the glass. The kitchen supplies gourmet cheese plates and small, tasty dishes that go well with the wine selections—osso buco, mussels, and confit chicken leg are among the best. Local bands play seven nights a week. ✉ *600 Poland Ave., Bywater* ☎ *504/948–9111* 🌐 *www.bacchanalwine.com.*

BJ's Lounge

BARS/PUBS | This gritty corner bar is a beloved neighborhood joint. Most weekends it hosts music, like Little Freddie King, who blows the top off the place. ⊠ *4301 Burgundy St., Bywater* ☎ *504/945–9256* ⌕ *Cash only.*

Country Club New Orleans

BARS/PUBS | A mixed crowd enjoys an elegant retreat from the hustle and bustle of the city in this handsome 19th-century Bywater mansion. The interior restaurant, bar, and parlor rooms have a trippy Palm Springs vibe, with plenty of glitter and neon. The outdoor pool and deck bar hidden away behind lush vegetation and high walls is especially popular with the gay crowd. Pool access requires a small fee, and towels and lockers are available. ⊠ *634 Louisa St., Bywater* ☎ *504/945–0742* ⊕ *www.thecountryclubneworleans. com.*

The Domino

WINE BARS—NIGHTLIFE | Billing itself as a wine bar for everyone, there's as much Carlo Rossi on the menu here as there is pinot noir. From the same owner of the well-loved Twelve Mile Limit bar in Mid-City, you'll find a similar refined dive atmosphere, with checker-board table tops, a generous happy hour, and wide horseshoe bar. Picnic tables out front let you people-watch on St. Claude while sipping your wine spritzer, and there's a food pop-up most nights of the week. ⊠ *3044 St. Claude Ave., St. Claude* ☎ *504/354–8737.*

Markey's Bar

BARS/PUBS | The embodiment of a blue-collar New Orleans neighborhood bar, Markey's also draws more than a few hipsters from the Bywater and other neighborhoods. During baseball season, games are broadcast via satellite. The drinks are cheap and the pool table is free. ⊠ *640 Louisa St., Bywater* ☎ *504/943–0785.*

Parleaux Beer Lab

BREWPUBS/BEER GARDENS | At the first microbrewery in the Bywater, you can spend your time discussing hops and

malts with other enthusiasts, or just relax in the large backyard while enjoying the best of local food truck fare. The community-oriented space often hosts special events like fundraisers, multicourse dinners, and outdoor yoga classes. ⊠ *634 Lessups St., Bywater* ☎ *504/702–8433* ⊕ *www.parleauxbeerlab.com.*

MUSIC CLUBS

Vaughan's

MUSIC CLUBS | Legendary Thursday night live music sets (served up with free red beans and rice late in the evening) are the big draw at this ramshackle place in the Bywater's farthest reaches. At other times, the place is an exceptionally friendly neighborhood dive. ⊠ *800 Lesseps St., at Dauphine St., Bywater* ☎ *504/947–5562.*

🎭 Performing Arts

Tigermen Den

DANCE | FAMILY | Every second Sunday from 11 am to 3 pm, this quaint venue hosts a family-friendly Cajun brunch, a traditional "fais do-do," where a rowdy pack of tourists and locals crowd into the rustic space for live Cajun music. There's plenty of alcoholic beverages, coffee, and delicious food, usually provided by a local vendor like Bywater Bakery. Don't worry, beginner's dance lessons each brunch will have you Cajun two-steppin' in no time. The charge is usually $10 at the door on Sundays; other times, check the website for cultural events and concerts that take place here. ⊠ *3113 Royal St., Bywater* ☎ *504/230–0131* ⊕ *www.thetigermenden.com.*

🛍 Shopping

The few stores in this mostly residential neighborhood reflect the area's bohemian spirit, selling unique and locally made products.

ANTIQUES AND COLLECTIBLES
Bargain Center

ANTIQUES/COLLECTIBLES | Inside this funky muraled storefront on a busy Bywater corner, you'll find thrifted art, clothing, furniture, and knickknacks ranging from junk to vintage treasures, as well as some local arts and crafts. ⊠ *3200 Dauphine St., Bywater* ☏ *504/948–0007.*

Euclid Records

SPECIALTY STORES | Old-school music lovers flock to this colorful storefront that carries a curated selection of standards, rare finds, and new releases. Friendly staff will ship your vinyl home for a small fee. There's a variety of genres, and the local artists' section is especially well-stocked. ⊠ *3301 Chartres St., Bywater* ☏ *504/947–4348* ⊕ *www.euclidnola.com.*

NOVELTIES AND GIFTS
Anchor & Arrow Dry Goods Co.

CLOTHING | This Bywater storefront is a fun, friendly stop for vintage dresses, Hawaiian shirts, Western wear, boots, household goods, and musical instruments. ⊠ *3528 Dauphine St., Bywater* ☏ *504/302–7273* ⊕ *www.anchor-arrow-dry-goods-co.business.site.*

Maypop Community Herb Shop

PERFUME/COSMETICS | Specializing in herbs, tinctures, essential oils, and natural medicines, this cozy little shop also sells scents and other natural body products, usually made by local small crafters. The community-oriented space offers health consultations and workshops too; check the website for more information. ⊠ *2701 St. Claude Ave., St. Claude* ☏ *504/304–5067* ⊕ *www.maypopherbshop.com.*

Spomenik Supply

HOUSEHOLD ITEMS/FURNITURE | This funky furniture store stocks unique vintage and thrifted pieces from a few different eras and styles, as well as candles, art, trendy home goods, oddities, and gifts. ⊠ *1237 Poland Ave., St. Claude* ☏ *504/264–2265.*

Pride in Bloom ◉

The fleur-de-lis, historically an emblem of French royalty, has long been a symbol of New Orleans. Since Hurricane Katrina, however, locals have elevated the fleur-de-lis into a symbol of pride and recovery. You can find creative examples all over the city, worked into jewelry, artwork, candles, glassware, T-shirts, and even tattoos.

The Lower Ninth Ward

The Lower Ninth Ward has long been a cultural touchstone for New Orleans, producing some of the most venerable artists and colorful traditions the city has to offer. But the neighborhood became a touchstone for the whole nation—indeed, the world—for the tragedy of Hurricane Katrina, as no neighborhood in the city endured as much destruction or suffering as this low-lying residential stretch, which fell victim to the failed levees.

Nowadays the neighborhood is a changed place. Signs of the deluge persist—empty lots where houses were literally swept off their foundations, boarded-up buildings with overgrown weeds and an eerie quiet—but signs of life and renewed vigor show too. A slow but steady reconstruction effort led by hard-hit locals is reclaiming the landscape one lot at a time. Groups like Habitat for Humanity and Global Green have also embarked on innovative and environmentally sustainable rebuilding projects in and around the neighborhood, such as the New Orleans Musicians' Village and the Holy Cross Project.

At the House of Dance and Feathers, visitors can learn about the fascinating history and legends of Mardi Gras Indian culture.

 Sights

Doullut Steamboat Houses

HOUSE | In 1905, Paul Doullut was inspired to build a home that resembled the great steamboats of the Mississippi, where he spent his time as a riverboat captain. In 1913, he built a similar home for his son, down the street at 503 Egania. Towering over the Mighty Mississippi and the rest of the neighborhood with wraparound verandas fitted with guardrails and high-perched widow's walks, these houses are architectural oddities specific to their environment. Because the first floors are constructed of ceramic tile, the Doullut houses are uniquely equipped to withstand flooding, and both survived Hurricane Katrina with little damage. Today these are private residences that can only be toured from the outside. ✉ *400 Egania St. and 503 Egania St., Lower Ninth Ward.*

Fats Domino House

HOUSE | When music legend Fats Domino passed away in 2017, a city-wide second-line parade culminated at his former home in the Lower Ninth Ward: a black-and-yellow shotgun house emblazoned with the letters "F D", a bright reminder of the artist's dedication to the neighborhood. Blocks from where he was raised, Domino built this two-house compound in 1960, at the height of his musical career, and kept it as his homebase throughout decades on tour. While he spent his later years across the river in Harvey, Louisiana, it was in this house where Fats endured Katrina, and was later rescued by the Coast Guard (and visited by President G. W. Bush) after losing almost everything he owned. ✉ *1208 Caffin Ave., Lower Ninth Ward.*

House of Dance and Feathers

MUSEUM | One of the most fascinating and heartwarming locations in the Lower Ninth Ward has to be the House of Dance and Feathers, a tiny backyard museum, which is a labor of love for community character Ronald Lewis, a retired streetcar conductor. Formed almost by accident—after his wife threw his extensive collection of Mardi Gras Indian and second-line paraphernalia out of the house and into the yard—this small glass-paneled building contains a trove of Mardi Gras Indian lore and local legend. Intricately beaded panels from Indian costumes, huge fans and plumes of feathers dangling from the rafters, and photographs cover almost every available inch of wall space. Lewis, who among many other things can list "president of the Big Nine Social and Pleasure Club" and "former Council Chief of the Choctaw Hunters" on his résumé, is a qualified and dedicated historian whose vision and work have become a rallying point for a hardscrabble neighborhood. Call before visiting to make sure he's around (he usually is). ✉ *1317 Tupelo St., Lower Ninth Ward* ☎ *504/957–2678* ⊕ *www.houseofdanceandfeathers.org* ⊠ *Free* ☉ *By appointment only.*

★ Lower Ninth Ward Living Museum

MUSEUM | To get a better sense of the Lower Ninth Ward's extensive history, visit this small, community-run museum with particular focus on the before and after of Hurricane Katrina. It celebrates the neighborhood's past, present, and future through oral histories and various exhibits, and is free to the public (cash donations are welcomed). ✉ *1235 Deslonde St., Lower Ninth Ward* ☎ *504/220–3652* ⊕ *www.l9livingmuseum.org* ⊠ *Free; donations welcome* ☉ *Closed Mon.*

Chapter 6

TREMÉ/LAFITTE AND THE SEVENTH WARD

Updated by
Cameron Quincy Todd

◉ Sights	🍴 Restaurants	🛏 Hotels	🛍 Shopping	🍸 Nightlife
★★☆☆☆	★★★★☆	★★☆☆☆	★★☆☆☆	★★★☆☆

NEIGHBORHOOD SNAPSHOT

TOP EXPERIENCES

■ **The birthplace of jazz.** Tremé is a crucible of New Orleans musical tradition. Visit the site of Congo Square (now in Louis Armstrong Park) where jazz was born, or drop by the Backstreet Cultural Museum.

■ **African American History in Tremé.** Community-run museums, shops, and restaurants in Tremé celebrate the neighborhood's long and vibrant past as the oldest African American neighborhood in the country.

■ **Local living in the Seventh Ward.** From great coffeeshops to award-winning theater, the Seventh Ward is a large and pleasant residential neighborhood that will have you loving the laid-back side of New Orleans.

GETTING HERE

Tremé sits just above the French Quarter, and can be accessed by foot or public transportation via the No. 47/48 Canal streetcar and several buses. The Lafitte Greenway, a paved pedestrian and bicycle through-way surrounded by greenery, runs through Tremé starting at Basin Street by Armstrong Park, through the Seventh Ward (Broad Street) all the way to City Park. In the Seventh Ward, buses on Broad Street and Esplanade Avenue (No. 91 and 94) will connect you to the neighborhood's more commercial areas.

PLANNING YOUR TIME

The museums and best restaurants in Tremé are concentrated to a few central areas, and music clubs are usually close to the French Quarter and around Claiborne Avenue. Tremé is generally safe these days, but still, use good judgement. Like many parts of the city, poorly lit streets and occasional crime will have you wanting to take a cab late at night. The Seventh Ward is a sprawling, mostly residential area, and most shops, restaurants, and cafés are concentrated in the area around Bayou Road, Broad Street, and Esplanade Avenue. Unless attending a show at the Southern Rep, plan to visit the Seventh Ward during the day. There's not much to do at night, and many restaurants and cafés close on the early side.

QUICK BITES

■ **Buttermilk Drop Bakery.** This well-loved bakery is known for its glazed buttermilk doughnut holes, but also makes king cakes and other baked goods. ✉ 1781 N. Dorgenois St., Seventh Ward ⊕ www.buttermilkdrop.com Ⓜ No. 102/105, 51/52 Bus St. Bernard Ave. at N. Dorgenois St.

■ **Pagoda Café.** Third-wave coffee and breakfast tacos come with great neighborhood people-watching at this mostly outdoor café. ✉ 1430 N. Dorgenois St., Seventh Ward ⊕ www.facebook.com/pagodacafenola Ⓜ No. 91 Bus Esplanade Ave. at N. Rocheblave St.

■ **Wing Snack.** This tiny take-out joint is always lively, especially during Carnival and on Saints game days. It serves up over a dozen flavors of wings and hearty New Orleans casual fast food that won't disappoint. ✉ 759 N. Claiborne Ave., Tremé ⊕ www.wingsnackexpress.com Ⓜ No. 47/48 Streetcar Canal at N. Claiborne.

Just across Rampart Street from the French Quarter is Tremé (pronounced "truh-MAY"), one of the oldest neighborhoods in the city, perhaps in the country. The rows of cottages, churches, and corner stores belie the raucous historical and musical legacy of this area, originally built and populated largely by free people of color.

This is the birthplace of jazz, after all, not to mention the site of the old Congo Square gathering place for African and Caribbean slaves, and the location of the fabled Storyville red-light district. Through its many incarnations it has remained true to its heritage as one of the oldest African American neighborhoods in the nation. Tremé continues to be one of the great driving forces behind the musical culture of New Orleans.

The Seventh Ward is a traditionally Creole neighborhood, settled largely by French-speaking free people of color as early as 1720. In later centuries, factors like the construction of Interstate 10 through this neighborhood did damage to its peace and prosperity. Today, you'll find small, community-oriented businesses scattered among residential blocks. The great craftsmanship of the neighborhood's early inhabitants is evident in the architecture of the houses.

◉ Sights

Backstreet Cultural Museum
MUSEUM | Local photographer and self-made historian Sylvester Francis is an enthusiastic guide through this rich collection of Mardi Gras Indian costumes and other musical artifacts tied to the street traditions of New Orleans. The museum hosts traveling and featured exhibits in addition to its permanent collection. Sylvester is also an excellent source for current musical goings-on in Tremé and throughout town. ✉ 1116 Henriette Delille St., Tremé ☎ 504/657–6700, 504/606–4809 ⊕ www.backstreetmuseum.org 🖀 $10 ⊗ Closed Sun.

Benachi House & Gardens
HOUSE | This Greek Revival mansion was built in 1859 for the Greek consul in New Orleans and was a significant part of the city's original expansion into this neighborhood. Directly across from the Degas House, this intersection forms something of a historical hub. The house earned the nickname "Rendezvous des Chasseurs" (meeting place of hunters) during the 19th century, when much of this area was still undeveloped swampland. The

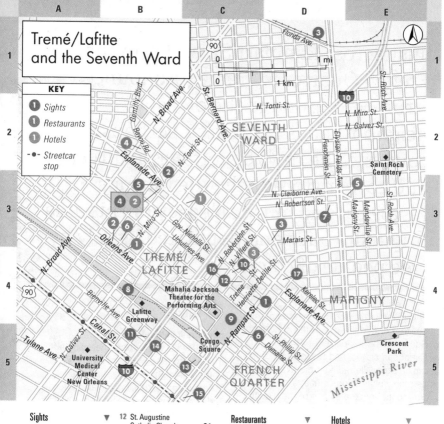

Tremé/Lafitte and the Seventh Ward

KEY
- 1 Sights
- 1 Restaurants
- 1 Hotels
- -•- Streetcar stop

gorgeous house and gardens are now primarily a private event space and a popular setting for New Orleans weddings. ⊠ *2257 Bayou Rd., at N. Tonti St., Bayou St. John* ☎ *800/308–7040* ⊕ *www. benachihouse.com.*

Celebration Distillation

WINERY/DISTILLERY | Founded in 1995, this craft distillery is the oldest maker of rum (Old New Orleans Rum, to be exact) in the continental United States. Tours ($15) start with a cocktail and end with a tasting of four different rums. Complimentary transportation from the French Quarter is available during the week—make reservations in advance. ⊠ *2815 Frenchmen St., Seventh Ward* ☎ *504/945–9400* ⊕ *www.celebrationdistillation.com.*

Edgar Degas House Museum, Courtyard, and Inn

HOUSE | The Impressionist Edgar Degas, whose Creole mother and grandmother were born in New Orleans, stayed with his cousins in this house during an 1872 visit to New Orleans, producing 18 paintings and four drawings while here. "This is a new style of painting," Degas wrote in one of the five known letters he sent from New Orleans, explaining that the breakthrough he experienced here led to "better art." Today, this house museum and bed-and-breakfast offers public tours, given by Degas's great-grandnieces, which include the screening of an award-winning film on Degas's family and their sojourn in New Orleans, plus a walk through the historic neighborhood focusing on details from the artist's letters. In 2019, the site was designated as a French monument by the French ambassador to the United States. Feel free to drop by for a look if you're in the vicinity, but check the website or call ahead for event dates or to make an appointment for a full tour. ⊠ *2306 Esplanade Ave., Bayou St. John* ☎ *504/821–5009* ⊕ *www. degashouse.com* ⊠ *$29 for guided tour.*

Free People of Color Museum

MUSEUM | Long before the Civil War, free people of color lived alongside enslaved African Americans in New Orleans, making up the largest population of free blacks in the South and becoming an important part of the city's cultural identity. Founded by the McKenna Family (descendants of the original free people of color and who also run the African American Art Museum in Central City), this museum provides a well-informed narrative into a crucial area of New Orleans history. Visits are by guided tour only, which must be scheduled in advance. ⊠ *2336 Esplanade Ave., Seventh Ward* ☎ *504/323–5074* ⊕ *www. lemuseedefpc.com* ⊠ *$15* ⊗ *Closed Mon. and Tues. By appointment only.*

J&M Music Shop

HISTORIC SITE | Although the patrons of the laundromat that now occupies this space probably don't pay the historical provenance much heed, this is one of the most significant musical landmarks in New Orleans. A plaque on this 1835 building marks it as the former site of the recording studio that launched the rock 'n' roll careers of such greats as Fats Domino, Jerry Lee Lewis, Little Richard, and Ray Charles. Owned by Cosimo Matassa, the studio operated from 1945 to 1955. ⊠ *840 N. Rampart St., Tremé.*

Jelly Roll Morton House

HOUSE | Jazz enthusiasts would do well to follow Frenchmen Street beyond the borders of the Marigny to pay homage to Jelly Roll Morton at the pianist and composer's modest former home, now a private residence with nary a plaque to suggest its importance. The current residents, however, have put a photo of the musician in the window. Morton was a "Creole of color" (free African American of mixed race), a clear distinction in those days—Morton himself always described his roots as "French." The neighborhood has declined some since Morton's days,

You'll find many unique Creole cottages in Tremé, like this one across the street from the Backstreet Cultural Museum.

so plan to take a car or taxi at night. ⊠ *1443 Frenchmen St., Seventh Ward.*

Lafitte Greenway

TRAIL | In the corridor that was once a historic canal vital to the city's transportation system, today this 2.6-mile bike and walking path connects the city from Armstrong Park to City Park. Along the way are greenspaces, community gardens, basketball courts, and playgrounds. The path is lit at night, but is still safest to explore during the day. The trail begins at Basin Street, in the northwest corner of Armstrong Park. ⊠ *Basin St. at Armstrong Park, Tremé* ⊕ *www.lafitte-greenway.org.*

Louis Armstrong Park

CITY PARK | With its huge, lighted gateway and its paths meandering through 32 acres of grassy knolls, lagoons, and historic landmarks, Louis Armstrong Park is a fitting tribute to the famed jazz musician's legacy. Elizabeth Catlett's famous statue of Louis Armstrong is joined by other artistic landmarks, such as the bust of Sidney Bechet, and the park now houses the New Orleans Jazz National Historical Park.

Inside the park and to the left is **Congo Square,** marked by an inlaid-stone space, where slaves in the 18th and early 19th centuries gathered on Sunday, the only time they were permitted to play their music openly. The weekly meetings held here have been immortalized in the travelogues of visitors, leaving invaluable insight into the earliest stages of free musical practices by Africans and African Americans. Neighborhood musicians still congregate here at times for percussion jams, and it is difficult not to think of the musical spirit of ancestors hovering over them. Marie Laveau, the greatly feared and respected voodoo queen of antebellum New Orleans, had her home a block away on St. Ann Street and is reported to have held rituals here regularly.

HBO's *Treme*

The Tremé neighborhood has always held a special place in the hearts of musicians and musical historians for its role in the development of jazz and other African American musical traditions, but it wasn't until more recently that the neighborhood captured the imagination of a much wider audience, thanks to the HBO series *Treme*. In the wake of Hurricane Katrina, the award-winning team of David Simon and Eric Overmyer (*The Wire*) decided to turn their lens on the Crescent City. They found the ornate and deeply rooted traditions of working-class Tremé to be the perfect focal point for the larger story of recovery and perseverance in New Orleans. *Treme*, the fourth and final season of which was completed in 2013, is widely regarded as one of the best and most accurate representations of New Orleans ever captured on film—no small feat for anyone trying to render the intricacies of the social, cultural, musical, and political dynamics of this city.

The producers employed a small army of local writers, fact-checkers, and historians to help ensure that the script and scene work were as accurate and realistic as possible. The casting team used locals whenever possible, and the location scouts and set producers went to remarkable lengths to ensure the authenticity of sets, props, and costumes.

The show cast a spotlight on many of New Orleans's underground spots. Suddenly, crowds of music lovers showed up to catch Kermit Ruffins performing at Bullet's Sports Bar (⊠ *2441 AP Tureaud Ave.*), a bar that has long been a staple of Tremé nightlife. Local institutions like Bywater nightclub Vaughan's (⊠ *4229 Dauphine St.*), the Mid-City café Angelo Brocato's (⊠ *214 N. Carrollton Ave.*), and the French Quarter restaurant Bayona (⊠ *430 Dauphine St.*) were also featured.

Treme proved to be a galvanizing creative force in the city of New Orleans, bringing people together to celebrate their own world and traditions. More than that, it's a recognition, a rendering, and a celebration of the perseverance and unique temperament of this city and its denizens in the face of an unprecedented national tragedy—and that has a healing quality all its own.

Behind Congo Square is a large gray building, the **Morris F.X. Jeff Municipal Auditorium;** to the right, behind the auditorium, is the beautifully renovated **Mahalia Jackson Center for the Performing Arts,** which is home to the New Orleans Opera and the New Orleans Ballet and hosts an excellent year-round calendar of events—everything from readings to rock concerts. The St. Philip Street side of the park houses the **Jazz National Historical Park,** anchored by **Perseverance Hall,** the oldest Masonic temple in the state. However, be aware that the park is often nearly deserted, and bordered by some rough stretches of neighborhood; it's patrolled by a security detail, but be very careful when wandering and don't visit after dark. ⊠ *N. Rampart St. between St. Philip and St. Peter Sts., Tremé.*

Louis Armstrong Park is home to historic Congo Square.

New Orleans African American Museum

MUSEUM | Set in a historic villa surrounded by a lovely small park and gardens, this terrific museum offers a year-round calendar of events and exhibits that highlight African and African-diaspora art and artists. The building itself is a prime example of the West Indies–style French colonial architecture that used to fill much of the French Quarter. The house was built in 1829 by Simon Meilleur, a prosperous brick maker; the main house was constructed with Meilleur's bricks, and the brick patio behind it bears imprints identifying the original manufacturer. While the larger museum is currently undergoing a massive renovation, there are several exhibits set up across the street, at 1417 Governor Nicholls Street. The museum holds events and programming in the villa's gardens as well. ⊠ *1417-1418 Governor Nicholls St., Tremé* ☎ *504/566–1136* ⊕ *www.noaam. org* ✉ *$20* ⊘ *Closed Mon.–Wed.*

St. Augustine Catholic Church

RELIGIOUS SITE | Ursuline nuns donated the land for this church in 1841 and upon its completion in 1842, St. Augustine's became an integrated place of worship; slaves were relegated to the side pews, but free blacks claimed just as much right to enter pews as whites did. The architect, J.N.B. de Pouilly, attended the École des Beaux-Arts in Paris and was known for his idiosyncratic style, which borrowed freely from a variety of traditions and resisted classification. Some of the ornamentation in his original drawings was eliminated when money ran out, but effusive pink-and-gold paint inside brightens the austere structure. The church grounds now also house the Tomb of the Unknown Slave, a monument dedicated in 2004 to the slaves buried in unmarked graves in the church grounds and surrounding areas. Following Hurricane Katrina, the Archdiocese of New Orleans planned to close seven churches in the city, including

St. Augustine. Public outcry, the church's historical significance, and parishioners' dedication saved the parish, and its 10 am Sunday gospel-jazz services continue although fundraising efforts are still needed to mend the serious wear on the building. Tours are available by appointment. ⊠ *1210 Governor Nicholls St., Tremé* ☎ *504/525–5934* ⊕ *www. staugchurch.org.*

★ **St. Louis Cemetery No. 1**
CEMETERY | The oldest and most famous of New Orleans's cities of the dead, founded in the late 1700s, is just one block from the French Quarter. Stately rows of crypts are home to many of the city's most legendary figures, including Homer Plessy of the *Plessy v. Ferguson* 1896 U.S. Supreme Court decision establishing the "Jim Crow" laws ("separate but equal"), and voodoo queen Marie Laveau, whose grave is still a popular pilgrimage among the spiritual, the superstitious, and the curious. Visitors are required to be part of a tour group in order to enter the cemetery, so join one of the many groups that come through each day. The nonprofit group Save Our Cemeteries gives guided tours daily leaving from the Basin Street Station Visitors Center at 501 Basin Street. ⊠ *499 Basin St., bounded by Basin, Conti, Tremé, and St. Louis Sts., Tremé* 🖾 *Save Our Cemeteries tours $25.*

St. Louis Cemetery No. 2
CEMETERY | Established in 1823, St. Louis No. 2 includes the tombs of a number of notable local musicians, including Danny Barker and Ernie K-Doe. Also entombed here are Dominique You, a notorious pirate, and Andre Cailloux, African American hero of the American Civil War. Located on Claiborne Avenue, four blocks beyond St. Louis Cemetery No. 1, it is in a more dangerous area of town so it's best to visit the cemetery with a tour group like Save Our Cemeteries. ⊠ *N.*

Claiborne Ave. between Iberville and St. Louis Sts., Tremé ⊕ *www.saveourcemeteries.org.*

Seven-Three Distilling Co.
WINERY/DISTILLERY | Come to sample spirits named for, and inspired by, the city, like Bywater Bourbon, Irish Channel Whiskey, and the popular St. Roch Vodka. Tours include stories on the history of distilling in New Orleans and run for about 45 minutes. Visitors can book a tour and tasting online ($15) or take a seat at the cocktail bar and sample the liquors used in the bartender's tasty concoctions. You'll want to take a bottle or two home with you. ⊠ *301 North Claiborne Ave., Tremé* ☎ *504/265–8545* ⊕ *www.seventhreedistilling.com.*

Storyville
NEIGHBORHOOD | The busy red-light district that lasted in New Orleans from 1897 to 1917 has since been destroyed, and in its place stand federal housing projects still partially under renovation. Known as Storyvillle, (named after the neighborhood's creator Sidney Story), the area's splendid Victorian homes served as brothels and provided a venue for the raw sounds of ragtime and early jazz—an extremely young Louis Armstrong cut his teeth in some of the clubs here. The world's first electrically lighted saloon, Tom Anderson's House of Diamonds, was at the corner of Basin and Bienville streets, and the whole area has been the subject of many novels, songs, and films. In 1917, after several incidents involving naval officers, the government ordered the district shut down. Some buildings were razed almost overnight, but it would be years before federal funding would be available for the housing project in the 1930s. Only three structures from the Storyville era remain, all former saloons: **Lulu White's Saloon** (*237 Basin St.*), **Joe Victor's Saloon** (*St. Louis and Villere Sts.*), and **"My Place" Saloon** (*1214 Bienville*

St. Louis Cemetery No. 1 is the most famous of the city's aboveground cemeteries.

St.). Currently, a historical marker on the "neutral ground" (median) of Basin Street is the only visible connection to Alderman Sidney Story's experiment in legalized prostitution. The area is also a popular stop on many ghost tours. ⊠ *Basin St., next to St. Louis Cemetery No. 1, Tremé.*

Tremé's Petit Jazz Museum
MUSEUM | This small, home-grown museum is among many spots in Tremé where you'll get a chance to really dig into fascinating local history. Owner and enthusiastic jazz historian Al Jackson will lead you through his one-room, colorful collection of art, photographs, and memorabilia, providing insight on the origins of jazz and its place in the neighborhood. Located a block from the New Orleans African American Museum (and four blocks from the Backstreet Cultural Museum), the location makes it easy to visit a couple Tremé museums in the same afternoon. ⊠ *1500 Governor Nicholls St., Tremé* ☎ *504/715–0332* ⊕ *www.tremespetitjazzmuseum.com* ⊠ *$10* ⊘ *Closed Sun.*

Voodoo Spiritual Temple
LOCAL INTEREST | Priestess Miriam Chamani shares her traditional West African spiritual practices here, offering a more authentic experience than many of the tourist shops in the French Quarter. The priestess sells her own line of essential oils and voodoo dolls, as well as jewelry, sachets, incense, and books on voodoo, and is available to book for consultations and healings. Voodoo walking tours, like the New Orleans Spirit Tour (www.neworleansspirittours.com), will often take visitors here. ⊠ *1428 N. Rampart St., Tremé* ☎ *504/943–9795* ⊕ *www.voodoospiritualtemple.org.*

🍴 Restaurants

Beloved Tremé and Seventh Ward restaurants are often family-run, with a focus on down-home favorites like fried chicken.

Dooky Chase

$$ | CREOLE | This famous spot has hosted multiple presidents, musicians, actors, and literary figures, and you can soak in the history just by viewing the numerous pictures and articles from over the decades that cover the wall. Come for the lunch buffet during the week for a chance to sample the famous fried chicken, red beans, and other soulful staples. **Known for:** famous weekday lunch buffet; local history; simple and comforting menu of Southern classics. $ *Average main: $20* ✉ *2301 Orleans Ave., Seventh Ward* ☎ *504/821–0600* ⊕ *www.dookychaserestaurant.com* ⊗ *Closed Sat.–Mon. No dinner Tues.–Thurs.*

Gabrielle Restaurant

$$$ | CAJUN | Despite its white tablecloths and refined menu, this small, family-run bistro has a wonderful neighborhood feel to it. The Cajun-Creole kitchen originally opened in 1992 and after a brief closing due to Hurricane Katrina, its elevated Cajun fare and friendly service has quickly made its way back into the heart of local diners. **Known for:** duck and rabbit dishes; BBQ shrimp pie; slightly more upscale menu than other eateries in the neighborhood. $ *Average main: $29* ✉ *2441 Orleans Ave., Tremé* ☎ *504/603–2344* ⊕ *www.gabriellerestaurant.com* ⊗ *Closed Sun. and Mon. No lunch weekdays.*

The Green Room Kukhnya

$ | EASTERN EUROPEAN | What started in the back kitchen of a St. Claude Avenue bar has expanded to its own spot, with an Eastern European influence that can be seen in both the food and drink menus. The atmosphere is divey, but the food is surprisingly delicious; pierogi, cabbage rolls, and sweet and savory blini are served alongside reubens and burgers. **Known for:** Eastern European dishes like pierogi; vegetarian options; rare imported beers. $ *Average main: $12* ✉ *1300 St. Bernard Ave., Faubourg Marigny* ☎ *504/766–1613* ⊕ *www.greenroomnola.com* ⊗ *Closed Tues. No lunch.*

McHardy's Chicken & Fixin'

$ | SOUTHERN | This carry-out-only spot closes early (7 or 8 pm daily), but it's a great place to pick up a large order of fried chicken and sides for a party or group. The chicken is some of the best in the area, and the mac and cheese is also excellent. **Known for:** fried chicken; tasty sides; perfect addition to a picnic. $ *Average main: $10* ✉ *1458 N. Broad St., Seventh Ward* ☎ *504/949–0000.*

Melba's

$ | SOUTHERN | Along with po'boys, you can find just about every type of grilled, fried, and gravied specialty famous in New Orleans here, served with plenty of sides, 24 hours a day. Not everything is the best you'll taste while in town, but the food is cheap and fresh at any hour. **Known for:** late-night snacks; great po'boys; cheap eats. $ *Average main: $10* ✉ *1525 Elysian Fields Ave., Seventh Ward* ☎ *504/267–7765* ⊕ *www.melbas.com.*

Willie Mae's Scotch House

$ | SOUTHERN | There's little argument among true New Orleans locals about where to get the best fried chicken in the city: the answer is Willie Mae's. The popularity of this bare-bones soul food restaurant often means long lines around the corner (and a slightly higher price tag) so it's best to go early for lunch, and during the week. **Known for:** the city's best fried chicken; long lines; excellent soul food sides like mac and cheese. $ *Average main: $15* ✉ *2401 St. Ann St., Tremé* ☎ *504/822–9503* ⊕ *www.williemaesnola.com* ⊗ *Closed Sun.*

Continued on page 160

by Alison Fensterstock
and Jennifer Odell

Above and opposite, French Quarter jazz clubs, Maison Bourbon and Preservation Jazz Hall.

NEW ORLEANS NOISE

The late local R&B star Ernie K-Doe once said, "I'm not sure, but I think all music comes from New Orleans." He wasn't far off. The Crescent City has crafted American music for hundreds of years—from Jelly Roll Morton's Storyville jazz piano to the siren sound of Louis Armstrong's genre-defining trumpet; from Little Richard's first French Quarter rock 'n'roll recording session to Lil Wayne's hip-hop domination.

Right, New Orleans' musical legend, Louis Armstrong.

THE SOUNDS OF THE BIG EASY

JAZZ

The roots of New Orleans jazz reach back to the 17th century, when slaves sang traditional songs in Congo Square. As their African and Caribbean polyrhythms blended with European styles, new sounds were born.

In the Storyville red-light district in 1895, cornetist Buddy Bolden played what is considered to be the first jazz. It was a march-meets-syncopation sound that drew from the city's numerous fraternal and societal brass marching bands, from ragtime, and from blues.

Pianist Jelly Roll Morton, who also got his start playing in Storyville's bordellos, helped transition ragtime into jazz with his more flamboyant playing style. In 1915 he published the first jazz composition, "Jelly Roll Morton Blues."

But it was the cornet and trumpet players of the day who really sounded off. Joe "King" Oliver, Louis Armstrong's mentor, changed his cornet's sound by holding a plunger over the bell. Sidney Bechet revolutionized soloing with his radical fingering. Louis Armstrong made jazz a phenomenon with his skill, improvisational style, and showmanship. These men were the originators of New Orleans Dixieland, which rapidly spread across the nation and was itself transformed—here and elsewhere—through the decades.

Today, young New Orleans musicians benefit from the work of contemporary jazz players and educators like pianist Ellis Marsalis. His students have included Terence Blanchard, Donald Harrison, Jr., and Nicholas Payton, as well as his own talented sons: Wynton (trumpet), Branford (sax), Delfeayo (trombone), and Ellis III (drums).

LISTEN TO: King Oliver, Louis Armstrong, Sidney Bechet, Jelly Roll Morton, Kid Ory, Donald Harrison, Jr., Nicholas Payton, Trombone Shorty, Christian Scott.
GO TO: Preservation Hall and Palm Court Jazz Café (traditional; French Quarter). Snug Harbor and the Blue Nile (contemporary; Faubourg Marigny).
EXPERIENCE IT: during ranger-led talks and walks at the Jazz National Historic Park (www.nps.gov/jazz).

Far left, clockwise from left, jazz at Bourbon Street, Jelly Roll Morton, Louis Armstrong. Below right, Zydeco accordionist. Left, Soul Rebel Brass Band.

BRASS BANDS

To lay down those 2/4 and 4/4 rhythms, traditional New Orleans Dixieland was greatly influenced by the format of the city's brass bands: trumpet or coronet for melody; clarinet for countermelody and harmony; trombone to emphasize the chord-change notes; banjo (later replaced by guitar); tuba (later, the piano); and drums.

In the 1970s and '80s, young brass bands like Rebirth and Dirty Dozen updated the traditional rollicking drum-and-horn street parade sound with funk and hip-hop. Now they're the elder statesmen of a thriving scene.

LISTEN TO: Hot 8, Stooges, Rebirth, Soul Rebels.
GO SEE: Rebirth at the Maple Leaf (Tues., Uptown); Soul Rebels at Le Bon Temps Roulé (most Thurs., Uptown).
EXPERIENCE IT: at the Backstreet Cultural Museum (www.backstreetmuseum.org), with artifacts from the Mardi Gras Indian, brass band, and second-line traditions.

CAJUN AND ZYDECO

Most purveyors of plaintive French-language balladry and squeeze-box and fiddle-driven dancehall rhythms play a few hours outside of the city. But some bands, like the Grammy-nominated Lost Bayou Ramblers, do make their way into *la ville*. The same is true of zydeco, accordion and washboard-driven music that evolved from the rural black-Creole sounds and urban R&B.

LISTEN TO: Cajun—Beausoleil, Feufollet, Pine Leaf Boys, Les Freres Michot, Savoy Family Cajun Band. Zydeco—Clifton Chenier, Chubby Carrier, Terrance Simien, Rockin' Dopsie Jr.
GO TO: For Cajun, Mulate's the Original Cajun (Warehouse District); dba (the Marigny). For zydeco, Bruce Daigrepont's Sunday fais do do at Tipitina's (Uptown). Every Thursday Rock 'n' Bowl (Mid-City) books Cajun, zydeco, and swamp pop.
EXPERIENCE IT: at mid-June's Louisiana Cajun-Zydeco Festival (www.jazzand heritage.org/cajun-zydeco) in the French Quarter.

Above, performers at Congo Square, New Orleans, Jazz Fest.
Below, Allen Toussaint.
Top right, Dr. John.
Below right, Partners-N-Crime.

SOUL AND R&B

In the 1950s and '60s, producers like Allen Toussaint and Dave Bartholomew laid the groundwork for rock 'n' roll with funky, groove-based R&B that captured the gritty, fun-loving rhythm of New Orleans.

LISTEN TO: Professor Longhair, Fats Domino, Irma Thomas, Ernie K-Doe, Allen Toussaint, Neville Brothers, Dr. John, Guitar Lightnin' Lee, Little Freddie King.

GO SEE: Veterans like Al "Carnival Time" Johnson and Ernie Vincent still perform around town, most often at festivals, but occasionally at the Rock 'n' Bowl, dba, or neighborhood bars.

BOUNCE AND HIP-HOP

The danceable, hard-driving party rap known as bounce originated in New Orleans housing projects and neighborhood bars in the late 1980s. In the 1990s, No Limit and Cash Money Records put New Orleans hip-hop on the map.

LISTEN TO: Big Freedia, Truth Universal, Partners-N-Crime, Mystikal, Juvenile, Lil' Wayne

GO SEE: Big-name acts like Juvenile and Mystikal play at the House of Blues (the Quarter) or the Arena (CBD). Look for bounce performers and hip-hop artists at Republic (Warehouse District) and other small rock venues around town.

SECOND LINES AND JAZZ FUNERALS

Second line parade in the French Quarter.

If you encounter a marching band parading down the streets of New Orleans, chances are it's a second line, a type of parade historically associated with jazz funerals. The term second line refers specifically to the crowd that marched behind the "first line" of the brass band and family of the deceased. During the early 20th century, the New Orleans second line served an important community function; African Americans were not allowed to buy insurance, so they formed mutual-aid societies—called Social Aid and Pleasure Clubs—to help members through tough times. The tradition continues to this day; different Social Aid and Pleasure Clubs parade in all neighborhoods of the city every weekend of the year, outside of the hottest summer months. If you get wind of an authentic second line, go, but use caution. Stick to the safer-looking streets, and be prepared to make an exit if things start to get edgy. Sylvester Francis has spent the better part of a lifetime documenting second-line parades and jazz funerals; his **Backstreet Cultural Museum** (1116 St. Claude Ave., Tremé, 504/522–4806, *www.backstreetmuseum.org*) is a repository of second-line mementos and tons of photographs.

"Uncle" Lionel Batiste of the Tremé Brass Band.

JAZZ AND HERITAGE FESTIVAL

Above, crowds and performers at Jazz Fest. Opposite page, Mr. Okra vending truck.

A sprawling, rollicking celebration of Louisiana music, food, and culture, Jazz Fest is held annually the last weekend in April and the first weekend in May at the historic Fair Grounds Race Course. The grounds reverberate with rock, Cajun, zydeco, gospel, rhythm and blues, hip-hop, folk, world music, country, Latin, and, yes, traditional and modern jazz. Throw in world-class arts and crafts, exhibitions and lectures, and an astounding range of local food, and you've got a festival worthy of America's premiere party town.

Over the years, Jazz Fest lineups have come to include mainstream performers—Bruce Springsteen, Tom Petty, and Eric Clapton topped the bill in recent years—but at its heart the festival is about the hundreds of Louisiana musicians who live, work, and hone their chops in the Crescent City. Many New Orleans musicians are still recovering from the effects of Hurricane Katrina, and Jazz Fest is their chance to show a huge, international audience that the music survives.

HISTORY

Veterans of the first Jazz Fest, which took place in 1970 in what's now Armstrong Park, talk about it with the same awe and swagger of those who rolled in the mud at Woodstock in 1969. The initial lineup included such legendary performers as Mahalia Jackson, Duke Ellington, Fats Domino, The Meters, and the Olympia Brass Band, who played for a small audience of about 350 people, approximately half the number of performers and production staffers it took to put the event on. In 2006 the first post-Katrina festival drew an estimated 300,000 to 350,000 people from all over the world and showcased the talents of some 6,000 performers, artisans, and chefs. Many of the musicians who performed at the first Jazz Fest came back to play the emotional 2006 festival. In 2018 the festival welcomed more than 450,000 attendees.

Official Logo of Jazz and Heritage Festival.

MUSIC

Each of the 12 stages has its own musical bent. The Congo Square stage hosts hip-hop and world music, the Fais-Do-Do stage specializes in Cajun and zydeco performers, fans of traditional jazz head for the Economy Hall Tent, and everyone spends at least a few minutes in the Gospel Tent soaking up the exuberant testimony.

FOOD

Cooks from all over Louisiana turn out dishes both familiar (shrimp po'boys and jambalaya) and exotic (alligator sausage, anyone?). Favorites include gumbo, soft-shell-crab, cochon de lait po'boys, and Crawfish Monica, a creamy pasta dish. Beer and wine are available, but hard liquor is taboo.

CRAFTS

Craft areas at Jazz Fest include Contemporary Crafts, near the Gospel Tent, which sells wares from nationwide artists; the Louisiana Marketplace, near the Fais-Do-Do stage and Louisiana Folklife Village, which showcase area folk art; and a Native American Village, which spotlights indigenous culture. Surrounding the Congo Square stage are stands with African and African-influenced artifacts items. ■TIP➔ **Many artists have a spot for only part of the fest; ask about their schedule before putting off any purchases.**

A tent beside Economy Hall sells CDs by festival performers, as well as other New Orleans and Louisiana artists; nearby is the official merchandise, including limited-edition Jazz Fest posters, which range in price from about $70 for a numbered silkscreen to several hundred dollars for a signed and numbered remarque print. In the Books Tent, local authors sign works on Louisiana music and culture. ■TIP➔ **You don't need to bring a lot of cash. ATMs are located throughout the site.**

JAZZ FEST TIPS

■ Book hotels as early as possible.

■ Thursdays on the second weekend are the least-packed day, and a local favorite.

■ You can purchase a full program once you arrive at the festival, with detailed schedules and maps, or tear the "cubes" out of the *Gambit* weekly paper, *Offbeat* monthly, or the *Times-Picayune's* weekly Lagniappe pullout. Free iPhone apps are also available.

■ Don't stress out trying to catch all the big names; inevitably, the obscure local musicians provide the most indelible Jazz Fest memories.

■ For a break from the heat and sun (plus air-conditioned indoor restrooms), visit the Grandstand, which hosts exhibits, cooking demonstrations (often with free samples), musician interviews, and an oyster bar.

■ Longtime fest goers bring flags to let friends know where they're located. These make great markers when trying to find your friends in the crowd.

■ Cool, casual, and breathable fabrics, along with a wide-brim hat and plenty of sunscreen, are your best bets for the long day outdoors. Wear comfortable shoes, and ones that can get dirty. The grounds are a racetrack, after all, and by the end of Jazz Fest the ground is a mix of dust, straw, mud, and crawfish shells.

Hotels

Ashton's Bed & Breakfast
$$ | **B&B/INN** | Few details have been overlooked in this sumptuous 1861 mansion, where distinctively decorated guest rooms have a range of beds, including iron-frame, Shaker, and four-poster. **Pros:** sunny, spacious rooms; nice location not far from New Orleans City Park; excellent breakfast. **Cons:** if you don't have a car, you'll need to take a taxi or city bus to reach the French Quarter; more residential area might be too quiet for some; non-refundable deposit required for busy booking times. [$] *Rooms from: $190* ✉ *2023 Esplanade Ave., Mid-City* ☎ *504/942–7048* 🌐 *www.ashtonsbb.com* 🛏 *8 rooms* 🍴 *Free breakfast.*

★ Edgar Degas House
$$ | **B&B/INN** | This beautiful property was once home to French impressionist Edgar Degas, and today the 1852 mansion retains its original floor plan and colors while the spacious second-floor rooms have chandeliers suspended from 14-foot ceilings. **Pros:** meticulously maintained and expertly operated; luxe amenities and extras; on the National Register of Historic Places. **Cons:** not in the middle of the action; if you don't have a car, you'll need to catch the city bus or cab it to the Quarter; lots of tour groups and large events. [$] *Rooms from: $199* ✉ *2306 Esplanade Ave., Mid-City* ☎ *504/821–5009* 🌐 *www.degashouse.com* 🛏 *9 rooms* 🍴 *Free breakfast.*

Rathbone Mansions
$$ | **B&B/INN** | This B&B is made up of two historic 1800s mansions on Esplanade Avenue, both minutes from the French Quarter, but peaceful enough to feel much farther away. **Pros:** unique chance to stay in an Esplanade Avenue mansion; good value; nice pool and courtyard. **Cons:** standard wear-and-tear of an old house; strict cancellation policy; breakfast just okay. [$] *Rooms from: $169* ✉ *1244 Esplanade Ave., Tremé* ☎ *504/309–4479* 🌐 *www.rathbonemansions.com* 🛏 *12 rooms* 🍴 *Free breakfast.*

Jazz Funerals and Second Lines

New Orleans jazz street parades are often referred to as "second lines," a term that originated in the city's jazz funerals. Traditionally, a brass band accompanies a New Orleans funeral procession to the grave site, playing dirges along the way. On the return from the grave, however, the music becomes upbeat, celebrating the departed's passage to heaven. Behind the family, friends, and recognized mourners, a second group often gathers, taking part in the free entertainment and dancing—hence, the "second line."

Nightlife

Bullet's Sports Bar
MUSIC CLUBS | This neighborhood bar (featured on the HBO show *Treme*) crowds with locals and visitors on weekends for the lively brass band performances, plates of hot comfort food, lively DJ sets, and fan-friendly Saints games. A favorite act here is the Pinettes, an all-female brass band that plays every Friday at 9 pm. On nights when there is no live music, Bullet's is a relaxed sports bar with friendly service and cheap drinks. ✉ *2441 A P Tureaud Ave., Seventh Ward* ☎ *504/948–4003.*

Kermit's Tremé Mother-in-Law Lounge
MUSIC CLUBS | Local personality and jazz legend Kermit Ruffins now reigns at this brightly colored club that once belonged to R&B singer Ernie K-Doe. The club is a

jewel of the Tremé neighborhood, hosting the best of local talent in jazz and blues nightly. The kitchen serves popular New Orleans cuisine. Look forward to the frequent cameos from Kermit himself, who plays a set here with his band, the BBQ Swingers, most Thursday nights. The neighborhood's a bit dodgy, so take a cab. ✉ *1500 N. Claiborne Ave., Tremé* ☎ *504/975–3955* ⊕ *www.kermitslounge. com.*

Sidney's Saloon

BARS/PUBS | This is one of those hipster haunts that is just the right amount of dive bar. The drinks are cheap, the selection is big, and the beer is local. There is an event almost every night, from funk performances and karaoke to live jazz and dance parties. ✉ *1200 St. Bernard Ave., Tremé* ☎ *504/224–2672* ⊕ *www. sidneyssaloon.com.*

🎭 Performing Arts

★ Mahalia Jackson Theater of the Performing Arts

MUSIC | A $27-million post-Katrina renovation returned the lights to this fabulous stage and restored the sculpture-filled Armstrong Park grounds. With a 21st-century sound system, a digital cinema screen, enhanced lighting, a new orchestra shell, and cutting-edge ballet flooring, the 2,100-seat theater once again plays hostess to the Louisiana Philharmonic Orchestra, the New Orleans Opera Association, the New Orleans Ballet Association, the New Orleans Jazz Orchestra, Broadway shows, and much more. ✉ *Armstrong Park, 1419 Basin St., Tremé* ☎ *504/287–0350* ⊕ *www.mahaliajacksontheater.com.*

New Orleans Ballet Association

DANCE | The city's prestigious dance organization has returned to the lavishly renovated Mahalia Jackson Theater with a full schedule. Performances also take place at other venues, including Freda Lupin Memorial Hall at NOCCA. ✉ *1419 Basin St., Tremé* ☎ *504/522–0996* ⊕ *www.nobadance.com.*

Saenger Theatre

MUSIC | Built in 1927, The Saenger has impressive ceiling decorations, a chandelier that came from a château near Versailles, and Italian baroque–style flourishes. It hosts a Broadway in New Orleans series as well as national headliners. ✉ *143 N. Rampart St., Tremé* ☎ *504/525–1052* ⊕ *www.saengernola. com.*

Southern Repertory Theater

THEATER | This well-established theater company specializes in original, first-rate contemporary theater productions. It stages premiers by regional and international playwrights and hosts a variety of community workshops and classes. Performances take place in a gorgeously renovated former church, with a full bar and plenty of gothic charm. ✉ *2541 Bayou Rd., Seventh Ward* ☎ *504/522–6545* ⊕ *www.southernrep.com.*

🛍 Shopping

Domino Sound Record Shack

MUSIC STORES | This cash-only record shop is among a stretch of local and mostly black-owned businesses on Bayou Road that are well worth checking out. The shop carries new and used records and has an especially large collection of reggae and international LPs. A guest DJ often spins a set on Saturday afternoons. ✉ *2557 Bayou Rd., Seventh Ward* ☎ *504/309–0871* ⊕ *www.dominosoundrecords.com.*

La Belle Galerie & the Black Art Collection

ART GALLERIES | Global themes from Russian art to African American experiences in music, history, and culture are portrayed through limited-edition graphics, photographs, posters, paintings, furniture, ceramics, textiles, and sculpture. Call before you go as visits are by appointment only, but someone is usually around. ⊠ *1737 Esplanade Ave., Seventh Ward* ☎ *504/529–5538.*

Activities

Dashing Bicycles

SPORTING GOODS | Along with selling bikes and accessories, this community-oriented shop rents bikes for $30 a day. Bikes come with locks and safety reflectors, and part of rental proceeds go toward a nonprofit for affordable housing. Bikes are first come, first served and there are no reservations. ⊠ *1234 N. Broad St., Tremé* ☎ *504/264–3343* ⊕ *www.dashing-nola.com* ⊙ *Closed Tues.*

Chapter 7

CBD AND WAREHOUSE DISTRICT

Updated by
Cameron Quincy Todd

👁 Sights	🍴 Restaurants	🛏 Hotels	🛍 Shopping	🍸 Nightlife
★★★★☆	★★★★☆	★★★★☆	★★☆☆☆	★★☆☆☆

NEIGHBORHOOD SNAPSHOT

TOP REASONS TO GO

Warehouse District Gallery Crawl. Browse the many art galleries that line Julia Street and its surroundings.

Cutting-edge dining. Sample some of the finest in Louisiana contemporary cuisine from chefs who are quickly becoming household names.

Fascinating museums. Revisit a defining chapter of our nation's history at the National World War II Museum, or discover a new favorite artist in the airy, urban oasis of the Ogden Museum of Southern Art.

Carnival season year-round. At Blaine Kern's Mardi Gras World at Kern Studios, see floats from years past, watch video footage, observe artists working on next year's creations, and stock up on souvenirs.

GETTING HERE AND AROUND

The CBD and Warehouse District together make up a fairly small area and can be readily explored on foot; the close proximity of the Warehouse District's museums and galleries makes sightseeing especially easy. The CBD is adjacent to the French Quarter, just across Canal Street. To travel to or from Uptown or the Garden District, you can take a cab, drive, or take the St. Charles Avenue streetcar—any stop from Canal Street to Lee Circle will do. (If you have an extra 20 minutes, walking is also feasible.)

MAKING THE MOST OF YOUR TIME

Arts- and culture-loving travelers can easily spend a few days visiting the museums, auction houses, and galleries here. The area also is a great nightlife desti-nation, with some of the city's most acclaimed restaurants, music clubs, and Harrah's New Orleans.

QUICK BITES

■ **Congregation Coffee Roasters.** The house-roasted coffee here is delicious, but added takeaways are the cute alligator-themed mugs and memorabilia to take home (a "congregation" is the collective name for a group of alligators); the fresh pastries; and the hearty break-fast and lunch options, like the pickled greens and poached egg on toast. ✉ 644 Camp St., Central Business District ☎ 504/265–0194 ⊕ www.congregationcoffee. com ⊗ No dinner.

■ **Lucy's Retired Surfers Restaurant and Bar.** This bar, courtyard, and dining room are a nice spot for a margarita, fresh seafood, or a Southwestern-style snack. The menu pays homage to surfing pioneers with bios and specialty dishes. ✉ 701 Tchoupitou-las St., Warehouse District ☎ 504/523–8995 ⊕ www. lucysretiredsurfers.com ⊟ No credit cards.

■ **Willa Jean.** A quick coffee and pastry from this sunny locale is just as enjoyable as their long, decadant brunches. ✉ 611 O'Keefe Ave., Central Busi-ness District ☎ 504/509–7334 ⊕ www.willajean.com.

With a particularly welcoming atmosphere for art, design, and entertainment, the CBD (Central Business District) and Warehouse District (also known as the Arts District) are a vibrant, vital sector of downtown New Orleans that's become increasingly residential, with high-end apartments, condos, and shops taking root in once dilapidated historic buildings.

Central Business District

The CBD covers the ground between Canal and Poydras streets, with some spillover into the Warehouse District's official territory. By day the CBD hums with commerce and productivity. You'll find the National World War II Museum, the Ogden Museum of Southern Art, the Contemporary Arts Center, the Louisiana Children's Museum, and Louisiana's Civil War Museum at Confederate Memorial Hall—all within a three-square-block radius. The neighborhood also includes the Mercedes-Benz Superdome, the convention center, and Harrah's Casino. Around central Lafayette Square you'll also find historic architecture, government buildings, and office complexes. Canal Street is the CBD's main artery and the official dividing line between the business district and the French Quarter; street names change from American to French as they cross Canal into the Quarter. Served by the streetcar, the palm tree–lined Canal Street has regained some of its former elegance, particularly as it nears the river.

◉ Sights

Gallier Hall
GOVERNMENT BUILDING | This Greek Revival building, modeled on the Erechtheion of Athens, was built in 1845 by the architect James Gallier Sr. It served as City Hall in the mid-20th century and today hosts special events. It's the mayor's official perch during Carnival parades, where kings and queens of many krewes stop to be toasted by city officials and dignitaries. The grand rooms inside the hall are adorned with portraits and decorative details ordered by Gallier from Paris. ✉ 545 St. Charles Ave., Central Business District ☎ 504/658–3627 ⊕ www.nola. gov/gallier-hall.

Harrah's New Orleans
CASINO—SIGHT | Some 115,000 square feet of gaming space is divided into five areas, each with a New Orleans theme: Jazz Court, Court of Good Fortune, Smugglers Court, Mardi Gras Court,

and Court of the Mansion. There are also table games, a covered gaming courtyard for smokers, 2,100-plus slots, and live entertainment at Masquerade, which includes a lounge, video tower, and dancing show. Check the website for seasonal productions, including music, theater, and comedy. Restaurants here include the extensive Harrah's buffet, the Cafés on Canal food court, Acme Oyster House, Gordon Biersch, Grand Isle, Manning's, and Ruth's Chris Steak House. The last four are part of Harrah's Fulton Street Mall, a pedestrian promenade that attracts casual strollers, clubgoers, and diners. ⊠ *8 Canal St., Central Business District* ☎ *504/533–6000, 800/427–7247* ⊕ *www.harrahs.com.*

John Minor Wisdom United States Court of Appeals Building

GOVERNMENT BUILDING | New York architect James Gamble Rogers designed this three-story granite structure as a post office and court building in 1909. It opened in 1915, but by the 1960s, the post office had moved to larger digs, leaving it open for McDonogh No. 35 High School to find refuge after Hurricane Betsy in 1965. Today, the Italian Renaissance Revival building houses the Fifth Circuit Court of Appeals in an elaborately paneled and ornamented series of three courtrooms, one of which, the En Banc courtroom, boasts a bronze glazed ceiling. The Great Hall's plaster ceiling has been restored to its original appearance and color, a light gray. As you enter the building and pass security, turn left and continue around the corner to find the library, where you can pick up information on the courthouse. Outside, a repeating sculpture of four women stands atop each corner of the building's penthouse level: the four ladies represent History, Agriculture, Industry, and the Arts. The building is named for Judge John Minor Wisdom, the New Orleans native who was instrumental in dismantling the segregation laws of the South.

Judge Wisdom received the Presidential Medal of Freedom in 1993. ⊠ *600 Camp St., Central Business District* ☎ *504/310–7700* ⊕ *www.uscourts.gov* ⊘ *Closed weekends.*

Lafayette Square

PLAZA | Planned in 1788 as a public place for Faubourg St. Marie, this 2.5-acre park occupies one city block in between the Federal Complex and Gallier Hall. The leafy square, covered by oaks, magnolias, and maple trees, and landscaped with hydrangeas and azaleas, offers a shady spot to sit. Statues include Benjamin Franklin, Henry Clay, and the New Orleans philanthropist John McDonogh. Recently, the Square has been experiencing a renaissance brought about in large part by the Young Leadership Council's Wednesday at the Square concert series, held in the spring and early summer. ⊠ *Between Camp St., St. Charles Ave., and N. Maestri and S. Maestri Sts., Central Business District* ⊕ *www.nola.gov/parks-and-parkways.*

Mercedes-Benz Superdome

SPORTS VENUE | Home to the NFL's New Orleans Saints, the Mercedes-Benz Superdome has been the site of many Sugar Bowls, several NCAA Final Four basketball tournaments, the BCS championship game, a record seven Super Bowls, and the 1988 Republican National Convention, as well as many concerts.

The Superdome was badly damaged during Hurricane Katrina and its aftermath, when it served as a shelter of last resort for evacuees. The stadium underwent extensive renovations in the years that followed and reopened for football in September 2006, when the Saints beat the Atlanta Falcons, at the time setting a record for the largest TV audience in ESPN history.

Built in 1975, the Superdome seats 71,000 people, and has a 166,000-square-foot main arena and a roof that covers almost 10 acres at a

A ride on the streetcar is a great way to tour New Orleans in period style.

height of 27 stories. The bronze statue on the Poydras Street side of the Superdome is the Vietnam Veterans Memorial. Across from it is a large abstract sculpture called *Krewe of Poydras*. The sculptor, Ida Kohlmeyer, meant to evoke the frivolity and zany spirit of Mardi Gras. A couple of blocks down Poydras Street from the Superdome is the Bloch Cancer Survivors Monument, a block-long walkway of whimsical columns, figures, and a triumphal arch in the median of Loyola Avenue. The Smoothie King Center (formerly called the New Orleans Arena) behind the Superdome is home to the NBA's New Orleans Pelicans.

■TIP➜ **The Superdome does not offer public tours, but visitors can walk along the exterior plaza and Champions Square to get a better view. The plaza by Champions Square offers the best photo opportunity.** ✉ *1 Sugar Bowl Dr., Central Business District* ☎ *504/587–3663* ⊕ *www.superdome.com.*

The Sazerac House

MUSEUM | This state-of-the-art museum, sponsored by the Sazerac Company, is all about the city's most famous cocktail and all the people, history, and booze behind it. Exhibits are largely interactive, combining historical artifacts and technology with tastings and real-life experts. Visitors will learn about the Sazerac's origins and other boozy tales, visit Peychaud's Apothecary to see how the famous bitters are made, tour an active Sazerac Rye distillery, and spend time with lifelike, virtual bartenders in the Sophisticated Spirits room. It's best to book the complimentary tickets online; a free visit includes several tastings and an option to attend a themed tour every day at 2 pm. Upgrade your visit ($20) to attend a special tasting and cocktail-making class. Minors are free to tour the museum, but not sample (age is verified ahead of time). ✉ *101 Magazine St., Central Business District* ☎ *504/901–0100* ⊕ *www.sazerachouse. com* ⊘ *Closed Sun. and Mon.*

Spanish Plaza

PLAZA | For a place to relax with a terrific view of the river, go to Spanish Plaza behind the former World Trade Center at 365 Canal Street. This large, sunken space with beautiful inlaid tiles and a fountain was a gift from Spain in 1976; here you can enjoy occasional live music and buy tickets for riverboat cruises in the offices that face the river. If you happen to be in town for Lundi Gras (the Monday before Mardi Gras), you can watch Rex, the King of Carnival, arrive here from across the river to greet King Zulu and take symbolic control of the city for a day. ✉ *1 Poydras St., Central Business District.*

🍴 Restaurants

The CBD is as much about pleasure as work. Amid the modern condos and high-rises, you'll discover many of New Orleans's most celebrated restaurants that keep up with national trends.

★ August

$$$$ | MODERN AMERICAN | If the Gilded Age is long past, someone forgot to tell the folks at August, where the main dining room shimmers with masses of chandelier prisms, thick brocade fabrics, and glossy woods. Service is anything but stuffy, however, and the food showcases the chefs' modern techniques. **Known for:** decadent tasting menus; vegetarian options; affordable wine pairings. [$] *Average main: $38* ✉ *301 Tchoupitoulas St., Central Business District* ☎ *504/299–9777* 🌐 *www.restaurantaugust.com* 🕒 *No lunch weekends.*

Bon Ton Café

$$$ | CAJUN | Bon Ton's opening in 1953 marked the first appearance of a significant Cajun restaurant in New Orleans, and the now-famed crawfish dishes, gumbo, jambalaya, and oyster omelet continue to draw fans. The bustle in the dining room peaks at lunchtime on weekdays, when businesspeople from nearby offices come in droves for turtle soup, eggplant with a shrimp-and-crab étouffée, and warm, sugary bread pudding with whiskey sauce (it packs a serious punch). **Known for:** crawfish, gumbo, and turtle soup; rum cocktails; business lunches. [$] *Average main: $28* ✉ *401 Magazine St., Central Business District* ☎ *504/524–3386* 🌐 *www.thebontoncafe.com* 🕒 *Closed weekends.*

Borgne

$$$ | SEAFOOD | In a spacious dining room accented by nautical touches, floor-to-ceiling chalkboard panels, and local artwork, you'll find rustic Louisiana seafood dishes with a touch of city sophistication. Named after Lake Borgne in eastern Louisiana, the restaurant honors that area's many Spanish settlers with tapas and fish à la plancha along with more traditional renditions like the BBQ shrimp with cheesy jalapeño grits. **Known for:** happy hour tapas; business lunches; raw oysters. [$] *Average main: $26* ✉ *Hyatt Regency New Orleans, 601 Loyola Ave., Central Business District* ☎ *504/613–3860* 🌐 *www.borgnerestaurant.com.*

Cleo's Mediterranean Cuisine & Grocery

$ | MIDDLE EASTERN | Good things really do come in small packages, like the outstanding falafel you can order at the back of this unpretentious, pocket-size Middle Eastern convenience store outfitted with a handful of tables and chairs. Grab a drink from one of the glass cases, then order from a menu of mouthwatering options, like lamb kebabs and beef gyros. **Known for:** 24-hour kitchen; late-night falafel and tabouleh; international grocery items. [$] *Average main: $10* ✉ *940 Canal St., Central Business District* ☎ *504/522–4504.*

Compère Lapin

$$$ | FUSION | Those tired of the white-tablecloth restaurants with decades-old menus of shrimp rémoulade and redfish renditions that populate so much of the New Orleans fine dining scene will be

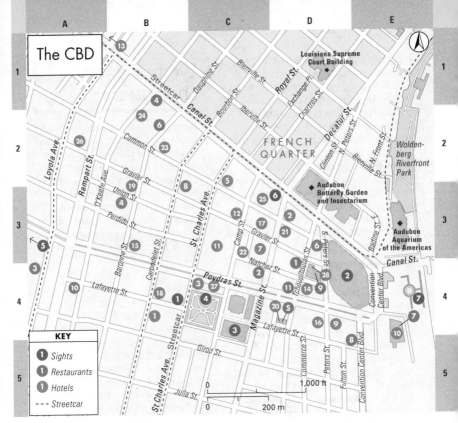

The CBD

A B C D E

1

Louisiana Supreme
Court Building

Streetcar Canal St.

FRENCH
QUARTER

Audubon
Butterfly Garden
and Insectarium

2

Wolden-
berg
Riverfront
Park

Audubon
Aquarium
of the Americas

Canal St.

3

Poydras St.

Lafayette St.

4

Convention Center Blvd

KEY

● Sights
● Restaurants
● Hotels
--- Streetcar

St Charles Ave. Streetcar

Girod St.

Julia St.

0 _____ 1,000 ft

0 _____ 200 m

5

Sights ▼

1 Gallier Hall.............. **B4**
2 Harrah's
New Orleans **D4**
3 John Minor Wisdom
United States Court of
Appeals Building.........**C4**
4 Lafayette Square **C4**
5 Mercedes-Benz
Superdome..............**A3**
6 The Sazerac House.....**D3**
7 Spanish Plaza **E4**

Restaurants ▼

1 August **D4**
2 Bon Ton Café............**C4**
3 Borgne **A4**
4 Cleo's Mediterranean
Cuisine & Grocery **B1**
5 Compère Lapin..........**D4**
6 Domenica................**B2**
7 Drago's...................**E4**
8 Grand Isle................**D5**
9 The Grill Room **D4**
10 Maypop..................**A4**
11 Mother's **D4**

Hotels ▼

1 Ace Hotel
New Orleans **B4**
2 Best Western Plus
St. Christopher
Hotel.....................**D3**
3 The Blake Hotel
New Orleans **C4**
4 Catahoula Hotel.........**B3**
5 Courtyard New Orleans
Downtown Near the
French Quarter..........**C2**
6 DoubleTree by Hilton
Hotel New Orleans **D3**
7 The Eliza Jane...........**C3**
8 Hampton Inn
Downtown...............**B3**
9 Harrah's New Orleans
Hotel.....................**D4**
10 Hilton New Orleans
Riverside.................**E4**
11 InterContinental
New Orleans **C3**
12 International House **C3**
13 The Jung Hotel
& Residences **B1**

14 Le Méridien.............. **D4**
15 Le Pavillon Hotel **B3**
16 Loews New Orleans
Hotel.....................**D4**
17 Loft 523..................**C3**
18 Maison de la Luz........**B4**
19 NOPSI Hotel.............**B3**
20 The Old No. 77 Hotel
& Chandlery.............**D4**
21 Pelham Hotel............**D3**
22 Q&C Hotelbar **C3**
23 Renaissance Pere
Marquette Hotel **B2**
24 The Roosevelt Hotel
New Orleans **B2**
25 Sheraton New Orleans
Hotel.....................**C3**
26 The Troubadour
Hotel.....................**A2**
27 The Whitney Hotel.....**C4**
28 Windsor Court Hotel....**D4**

especially pleased with Compère Lapin, a unique and distinctly contemporary ultra-fine dining experience. At the root of Chef Nina Compton's cooking are the comforting flavors and spices of St. Lucian and Italian home kitchens, but presentation and execution of her dishes are that of a top-notch professional chef. **Known for:** sweet potato gnocchi and conch croquettes; hip, minimalist decor; inventive cocktails. $ *Average main: $28* ✉ *Old No. 77 Hotel and Chandlery, 535 Tchoupitoulas St., Central Business District* ☎ *504/599–2119* ⊕ *www.comperelapin.com.*

★ Domenica

$$ | **ITALIAN** | This eatery wows diners with rustic Italian cooking, a rarity in New Orleans's culinary landscape. In the renovated Roosevelt Hotel—a 19th-century landmark—friendly and knowledgeable waiters happily help patrons with lesser-known ingredients, but it doesn't take a lengthy explanation to know that the fresh pastas and wood-fired pizzas are a must. **Known for:** wood-fired pizzas; charcuterie boards; great happy hour. $ *Average main: $20* ✉ *Roosevelt New Orleans Hotel, 123 Baronne St., Central Business District* ☎ *504/648–6020* ⊕ *www.domenicarestaurant.com.*

Drago's

$$$ | **ITALIAN** | **FAMILY** | Since 1969 the Cvitanovich family restaurant has been a fixture in Metairie, just a short drive from downtown New Orleans, so when it was revealed the family would open a second location inside the Hilton Riverside hotel, locals started salivating and the word quickly spread. The charbroiled oysters are the absolute must-order (you'll want extra bread to mop up the toothsome sauce). **Known for:** charbroiled oysters; local institution; kid-friendly food. $ *Average main: $26* ✉ *Hilton New Orleans Riverside, 2 Poydras St., Central Business District* ☎ *504/584–3911* ⊕ *www.dragosrestaurant.com.*

Wednesday at the Square 🎟

From mid-March to June, the Young Leadership Council, the Downtown Development District, and several corporate sponsors present Wednesday at the Square, a weekly event that features food, beer and soft drinks, local arts and crafts vendors, and a free evening concert in Lafayette Square. Bring a blanket and enjoy the music from 5 to 8 pm.

Grand Isle

$$ | **SOUTHERN** | The rustic interior, reminiscent of 1920s and '30s Louisiana fish camps, is the perfect backdrop for shrimp gumbo, spicy boiled shrimp, fresh Gulf fish, hearty fisherman's stew, and a lemon icebox pie that will make you fall in love with New Orleans all over again. Except for freshwater catfish and Canadian mussels, all the seafood comes from the Gulf of Mexico and often straight from the fishermen. **Known for:** fresh Gulf fish; local produce; big crowds. $ *Average main: $18* ✉ *575 Convention Center Blvd., Central Business District* ☎ *504/520–8530* ⊕ *www.grandisle restaurant.com.*

★ The Grill Room

$$$$ | **AMERICAN** | With its elegant table settings and canvases depicting the lives of British nobility, the Grill Room on the second floor of the Windsor Court has always been a beacon of class and an elegant setting for special occasions (keep your eyes peeled: celebrities in town for local film shoots often snag tables here). The creative Cajun- and Creole-influenced dinner menu allows guests to customize a three- or five-course tasting dinner, with insightful and unusual wine selections by sommelier John Mitchell, who draws from a deep cellar with an extensive Bordeaux

collection. **Known for:** elegant dining room; splurge-worthy tasting dinners; extensive wine list. $ *Average main: $36* ✉ *Windsor Court Hotel, 300 Gravier St., 2nd fl., Central Business District* ☎ *504/523–6000* ⊕ *www.grillroomne-worleans.com.*

Maypop

$$$ | **ASIAN FUSION** | After gaining notoriety for his Southeast Asian–inspired cuisine at Mopho in Mid-City, Chef Michael Gulotta moved into new territory, with a sophisticated small-bites menu for a downtown crowd. House-made pasta, cured meats, local seafood, and roti bread are accompanied by flavors like ginger, turmeric, and coconut. **Known for:** dim sum–style brunch; house-made noodles; crispy fried oysters. $ *Average main: $27* ✉ *611 O'Keefe Ave., Central Business District* ☎ *504/518–6345* ⊕ *www.maypoprestaurant.com.*

Mother's

$ | **CAFÉ** | Tourists and locals line up for solid, if unspectacular, down-home eats at this island of blue-collar sincerity amid downtown's sea of glittery hotels. Mother's dispenses baked ham and roast beef po'boys (ask for "debris" on the beef sandwich and the bread will be slathered with meat juices and shreds of meat), home-style biscuits and jambalaya, and chicken and sausage gumbo in a couple of bare-bones yet charming dining rooms. **Known for:** greasy spoon, cafeteria-style vibe; big crowds; roast beef debris po'boys. $ *Average main: $13* ✉ *401 Poydras St., Central Business District* ☎ *504/523–9656* ⊕ *www.mothersrestaurant.net.*

🛏 Hotels

★ Ace Hotel New Orleans

$$$ | **HOTEL** | This large, hip hotel is always buzzing with action. **Pros:** good entertainment and dining options on-site; excellent rooftop pool; sense of character and style. **Cons:** lobby gets loud and crowded on nights when there are shows; too sceney for some; inconsistent service. $ *Rooms from: $269* ✉ *600 Carondolet St., Central Business District* ☎ *504/900–1180* ⊕ *www.acehotel.com/neworleans* ⇆ *234 rooms* ☺ *No meals.*

Best Western Plus St. Christopher Hotel

$$ | **HOTEL** | A former office complex from the 1890s offers rooms with exposed-brick walls and basic furnishings just a block from the French Quarter. **Pros:** good location for the convention center and the French Quarter; free Wi-Fi; free continental breakfast. **Cons:** bar open Thursday to Saturday only; no gym; some rooms don't have windows. $ *Rooms from: $179* ✉ *114 Magazine St., Central Business District* ☎ *800/645–9312, 504/648–0444* ⊕ *www.stchristopherhotel.com* ⇆ *108 rooms* ☺ *Free breakfast.*

The Blake Hotel New Orleans

$$ | **HOTEL** | In season, the Blake occupies prime real estate on one of the Big Easy's best Carnival corners: the intersection of St. Charles Avenue and Poydras Street near Lafayette Square. **Pros:** convenient location on the St. Charles Avenue streetcar line; pet-friendly; free Wi-Fi. **Cons:** busy intersection; rooms lack style; some areas could use an update. $ *Rooms from: $129* ✉ *500 St. Charles Ave., Central Business District* ☎ *504/522–9000, 888/211–3447* ⊕ *www.blakehotelneworleans.com* ⇆ *124 rooms* ☺ *No meals.*

Catahoula Hotel

$$ | **HOTEL** | This charming boutique hotel is a refreshing escape from a run-of-the-mill chain stay. **Pros:** chic decor; comfortable beds; great lobby for hanging out. **Cons:** rooms are on the small side; kitchen hours are limited; bar and courtyard get noisy on popular nights. $ *Rooms from: $177* ✉ *914 Union St., Central Business District* ☎ *504/603–2442* ⊕ *www.catahoulahotel.com* ⇆ *35 rooms* ☺ *No meals.*

The Mercedes-Benz Superdome is home to the NFL's New Orleans Saints.

Courtyard New Orleans Downtown Near the French Quarter

$$ | **HOTEL** | **FAMILY** | A wraparound balcony overlooking St. Charles Avenue, a stunning six-story atrium, and some nods to period charm distinguish this family-friendly CBD hotel from other options in the neighborhood. **Pros:** central CBD location; free Wi-Fi; good breakfast. **Cons:** significant street noise at all hours; balcony rooms are in high demand during Mardi Gras; amenities are lacking. [$] *Rooms from: $219* ✉ *124 St. Charles Ave., Central Business District* ☎ *504/581–9005, 800/321–2211* 🌐 *www.marriott.com* 🛏 *140 rooms* 🍴 *No meals.*

DoubleTree by Hilton Hotel New Orleans

$$ | **HOTEL** | Many of the open, airy rooms offer views of the French Quarter, Canal Street, and the Mississippi River. **Pros:** close to the French Quarter and riverfront attractions; across the street from the Insectarium; warm chocolate-chip cookies upon arrival. **Cons:** chain-hotel vibe; attracts conferences and large parties; immediate location busy and not very charming. [$] *Rooms from: $179* ✉ *300 Canal St., Central Business District* ☎ *504/581–1300* 🌐 *www.doubletree.com* 🛏 *372 rooms* 🍴 *No meals.*

The Eliza Jane

$$ | **HOTEL** | Inspired by the printing press it once housed (and the trailblazing female publisher who ran it), this well-appointed, sleek hotel integrates thoughtful design and details into the building's original warehouse structure. **Pros:** great decor and layout, especially in the lobby area; spacious, modern rooms; good bar and restaurant. **Cons:** street outside is busy and bright; parking and traffic can be a headache; courtyard and bar area get noisy. [$] *Rooms from: $229* ✉ *315 Magazine St., Central Business District* ☎ *504/882–1234* 🌐 *www.theelizajane.com* 🛏 *196 rooms* 🍴 *No meals.*

Hampton Inn Downtown

$$ | **HOTEL** | A converted office building with large, comfortable, and pleasant rooms is an oasis in the midst of the bustling CBD. **Pros:** spacious rooms; particularly nice breakfast; free Wi-Fi. **Cons:**

rooms that face the street can be noisy; typical chain hotel; some rooms have unappealing views. $ *Rooms from: $159* ✉ *226 Carondelet St., Central Business District* ☎ *504/529–9990, 800/426–7866* ⊕ *www.neworleanshamptoninns.com* ➮ *185 rooms* �'⊙❙ *Free breakfast.*

★ Harrah's New Orleans Hotel
$$ | HOTEL | This spot is all about location, location, location—directly across the street from Harrah's New Orleans Casino, near the convention center and Riverfront attractions, close to the Warehouse District, the CBD, and the French Quarter. **Pros:** stylish rooms; convenient on-site entertainment ; nice public areas. **Cons:** the hustle and bustle of this part of town mean peace and quiet can be in short supply; casino marketing is ever-present; maze-like building layout. $ *Rooms from: $175* ✉ *228 Poydras St., at Fulton St., Central Business District* ☎ *504/533–6000, 800/427–7247* ⊕ *www.harrahsneworleans.com* ➮ *450 rooms* ❙⊙❙ *No meals.*

Hilton New Orleans Riverside
$$$ | HOTEL | FAMILY | The superb river and city views are hard to beat, and the guest rooms come with all the modern amenities, in close proximity to shops and the casino. **Pros:** well-maintained facilities; hotel runs like a well-oiled machine; two heated outdoor swimming pools. **Cons:** the city's biggest hotel; typical chain service and surroundings; extra cost for fitness facilities. $ *Rooms from: $232* ✉ *2 Poydras St., Central Business District* ☎ *504/561–0500, 855/760–0870* ⊕ *www.hiltonneworleansriverside.com* ➮ *1,696 rooms, 74 suites* ❙⊙❙ *No meals.*

InterContinental New Orleans
$$$ | HOTEL | The modern rose-granite structure overlooking St. Charles Avenue has large, well-lighted guest rooms, with contemporary, New Orleans–inspired furnishings. **Pros:** polished service; streetcar is just out front; a good spot to catch the Mardi Gras action. **Cons:** located on one of the city's busiest downtown streets; large big-box hotel; can be noisy. $ *Rooms from: $239* ✉ *444 St. Charles Ave., Central Business District* ☎ *504/525–5566* ⊕ *www.icneworleans.com* ➮ *484 rooms* ❙⊙❙ *No meals.*

International House
$$ | HOTEL | Contemporary style pairs with luxe comforts in guest rooms attractively decorated with modern New Orleans flair. **Pros:** ideal if you want sophisticated surroundings; atmospheric hotel bar; contemporary vibe with a local accent. **Cons:** no pool; hotel faces busy downtown street; rooms on the small side. $ *Rooms from: $150* ✉ *221 Camp St., Central Business District* ☎ *504/553–9550* ⊕ *www.ihhotel.com* ➮ *121 rooms* ❙⊙❙ *No meals.*

The Jung Hotel & Residences
$$ | HOTEL | This 1950s hotel was once among the limited choices for stays in the city, and its spacious rooms are now part of the J Collection, catering to conventions and extended stay visitors as well as the individual traveler looking for an affordable, convenient base. **Pros:** ample lobby and gathering spaces; spacious rooms; suites with kitchenettes and laundry available for extended stays. **Cons:** surrounding area lacks charm; one of the largest hotels in the city; some noise from the street. $ *Rooms from: $169* ✉ *1500 Canal St., Central Business District* ☎ *504/226–5864* ⊕ *www.junghotel.com* ➮ *207 rooms* ❙⊙❙ *No meals.*

Le Méridien
$$$ | HOTEL | This hip property includes a state-of-the-art fitness center, upscale contemporary decor inspired by the Crescent City, and a great restaurant. **Pros:** good location; stylish architecture and decor; free passes to several sights, including the Ogden Museum of Southern Art. **Cons:** a bit far from the Bourbon Street action; price high for experience; mixed service. $ *Rooms from: $231* ✉ *333 Poydras St., Central Business District* ☎ *504/525–9444* ⊕ *www.lemeridienneworleanshotel.com* ➮ *432 rooms* ❙⊙❙ *No meals.*

Continued on page 178

CBD and Warehouse District CENTRAL BUSINESS DISTRICT

7

DID YOU KNOW?

Crawfish is a staple in the Louisiana diet. It is found in a number of Cajun and Creole dishes, but it is most commonly boiled and served with potatoes and corn on the cob.

THE CUISINE OF NEW ORLEANS

From humble po' boy shops to white-tablecloth temples of classic Creole cuisine, food is a major reason to visit the Crescent City. People in New Orleans love to eat, and discerning local customers support a multitude of options when it comes to dining. Innovative fine dining restaurants exist alongside more modest eateries serving red beans and rice and boiled crawfish. Whatever the cost, it's hard to find a bad meal in this culinary town.

Given New Orleans's location near the mouth of the Mississippi River and the Gulf of Mexico, it was perhaps inevitable that an outstanding food culture would develop in the area. Farmers grow an abundance of produce—locally prized Creole tomato, okra, strawberries, and chayote (locally know as mirliton)—in the fertile Delta soil that surroundes the city and fishermen harvest a wealth of seafood like black drum, speckled trout, shrimp, blue crabs, oysters, and crawfish from the marshes and open waters of the Gulf of Mexico.

As a port city, New Orleans has always been something of a melting pot. The city's native Creole cuisine is a mixture of French, African, and Spanish influences; immigration from Italy and Sicily in the 19th century gave New Orleans its own version of Italian cooking. Plus, there is a lingering influence from an influx of German settlers; more recently, immigrants from Vietnam have brought their culinary traditions to New Orleans and the surrounding parishes.

Creole food is the cooking of the city, while Cajun food evolved from the rural traditions of the plains and swamps of southwest Louisiana. The Acadians, a people of French heritage, arrived in Louisiana after being expelled by the British from parts of Canada (present-day Nova Scotia and surrounding areas) in the 18th century. Like the cuisine of rural France, Cajun cooking is hearty and employs similar cooking techniques such as slow braising and the addition of a roux (a combination of flour and fat), but it features local seafood, game, and produce.

(top) A café au lait and beignets served at the renowned Café du Monde.

CLASSIC CREOLE AND CAJUN FOOD

Jambalaya

Oysters Rockefeller

BEIGNETS

Beignets are fried pillows of dough, generally served with powdered sugar (and lots of it!) and steaming cups of café au lait made with New Orleans-style chicory coffee. Beignets are typically consumed for breakfast or for dessert.

ÉTOUFFÉE

Étouffée means "smothered" in French, and the dish can be made with shrimp; chicken; and, most typically, crawfish. The dish is Cajun in origin, but there are Creole versions, as well. As with many Cajun dishes, it starts with a light roux, to which chopped onion, celery, and bell pepper (called "the trinity" in South Louisiana) is added. Some versions contain tomatoes, and the sauce is finished with stock and meat, poultry, or seafood. Crawfish étouffée is best during crawfish season (March– June), but you can find it year-round.

MUFFALETTA

The Muffaletta sandwich was invented at the Central Grocery (923 Decatur St.) by Salvatore Lupo and became popular enough that it can now be found all over town. The sandwich is served on a round loaf that's stuffed with salami, ham, pro-volone, and a local condiment called olive salad, which typically consists of olives, celery, and pickled peppers. Some restaurants heat the sandwich, but many purists consider that heresy.

OYSTERS ROCKEFELLER

Oysters Rockefeller was invented at Antoine's, the oldest continuously operated restaurant in the United States. The dish, to this day, consists of oysters baked on the half-shell with an anise-scented puree of herbs and bread crumbs. Although the recipe Antoine's uses remains a closely guarded secret, the dish typically contains parsley, chervil, tarragon, and celery leaves. This is a dish that should be ordered while oysters are at their best, between September and April.

JAMBALAYA

Jambalaya is a hearty dish that combines rice with meat, poultry, and/or seafood with a result akin to the Spanish paella. In New Orleans, the dish usually includes tomatoes, giving it a reddish hue. Ingredients can include chicken, andouille, pork, shrimp, crawfish, duck, and even alligator. The requisite "trinity" of onion, celery, and bell pepper is cooked with or

Shrimp gumbo   Pralines

without meat or seafood, and then the rice is added with stock, and the dish is covered to finish.

GUMBO

Gumbo is yet another dish that has both Cajun and Creole variations. It is a thick soup or thin stew that can include almost any meat, poultry, sausage, or seafood found in South Louisiana. Cajuns generally cook the roux for gumbo until it is very dark, giving the dish a nutty flavor, while in New Orleans a lighter roux is employed, and okra and tomatoes are often included. A common ingredient, filé powder (dried, ground sassafras leaves), used as a thickening agent and seasoning, is considered by some as a necessary ingredient for making Cajun and Creole gumbo.

BOUDIN

Boudin is a Cajun sausage that combines rice with pork or other ingredients; some of the best can be found just outside of the city at rural gas stations, where it's frequently eaten as a roadside snack. In restaurants, the stuffing is sometimes removed from its casing, formed into balls, and fried.

TASSO

Tasso is a cured and smoked pork product that is one of the treasures of Acadian charcuterie. It is a highly spiced preparation that is used as a flavor base in many local recipes such as gumbo and red beans. Though it is sometimes called tasso ham, the meat used to prepare it is from the shoulder rather than the leg.

ANDOUILLE

Andouille is a smoked sausage made with both ground and cubed pork and flavored with garlic. It is a variation of a French sausage that in the Cajun interpretation is more highly spiced and aggressively flavored. It appears as an ingredient in many South Louisiana dishes, including gumbo and jambalaya.

PRALINES

Pralines are a sweet patty-shaped Creole treats made with caramelized sugar, cream, butter, and pecans—the latter often sourced from trees that grow locally in great abundance. Modern interpretations include chocolate, peanut butter, and bourbon pralines. Be sure to pronounce it like the locals: "PRAH-line," not "PRAY-line."

Le Pavillon Hotel

$$ | **HOTEL** | One of the most regal hotels downtown offers romantic spaces, attentive service, and high-ceiling, traditionally furnished guest rooms in history-filled building dating to 1907. **Pros:** elegant French ambience; attentive staff; great bar area. **Cons:** limited restaurant hours; not a fit if you're after something contemporary; on a busy street. $ *Rooms from: $189* ⊠ *833 Poydras St., Central Business District* ☏ *504/581–3111, 800/535–9095* ⊕ *www.lepavillon.com* ⊐ *226 rooms* ⦿ *No meals.*

Loews New Orleans Hotel

$$$ | **HOTEL** | One of the friendliest large hotels in the city, this property stands out with stellar service and bright, oversized rooms. **Pros:** excellent restaurant and lounge; large rooms with great amenities; great views from all rooms. **Cons:** about a 10-minute walk to the French Quarter; mixed service; some outlets could use a revamp. $ *Rooms from: $289* ⊠ *300 Poydras St., Central Business District* ☏ *504/595–3300* ⊕ *www. loewshotels.com/en/new-orleans-hotel* ⊐ *297 rooms* ⦿ *No meals.*

Loft 523

$$ | **HOTEL** | A good option for chic, loft-style digs, it is so subtle from the outside that you may have trouble finding it among the surrounding buildings. **Pros:** sleek, hip setting; inviting lounge; top-shelf amenities. **Cons:** some guests may be put off by the trendiness of it all; the bar is only open Thursday through Saturday; gets loud with late-night revelers. $ *Rooms from: $199* ⊠ *523 Gravier St., Central Business District* ☏ *504/200– 6523* ⊕ *www.loft523.com* ⊐ *18 rooms* ⦿ *No meals.*

★ Maison de la Luz

$$$$ | **HOTEL** | A sophisticated sibling of the Ace Hotel next door, this 5-star boutique guesthouse is intimate and unique, with a playful and regal decor inspired by magical realism and the city's Caribbean, European, and Latin American influences.

Pros: access to Ace Hotel amenities next door, including pool and fitness room; extremely private and quiet; great breakfast and daily wine and cheese. **Cons:** continental breakfast costs extra; no full restaurant or other hotel amenities within the building; higher price tag than other options nearby. $ *Rooms from: $383* ⊠ *546 Carondelet St., Central Business District* ☏ *504/814–7720* ⊕ *www.maison-delaluz.com* ⊐ *67 rooms* ⦿ *No meals.*

NOPSI Hotel

$$ | **HOTEL** | This hotel repurposes the New Orleans Public Service Inc. (NOPSI) building, a grand 1920s design, where New Orleanians used to pay their utility bills. **Pros:** good on-site dining and bars, including a rooftop pool; large rooms; fun nods throughout historical significance. **Cons:** pool area has an odd dress code; mixed service; rooftop books up with private events. $ *Rooms from: $223* ⊠ *317 Baronne St., Central Business District* ☏ *844/439–1463* ⊕ *www.nopsihotel. com* ⊐ *293 rooms* ⦿ *No meals.*

The Old No. 77 Hotel & Chandlery

$ | **HOTEL** | This industrial-chic retreat opened inside a renovated 1854 warehouse which formerly housed the Ambassador Hotel in New Orleans's Central Business District, just four blocks from the buzzing French Quarter. **Pros:** central location that is near the French Quarter but not too close to the noise; stylish vibe; excellent on-site restaurant. **Cons:** some guest rooms don't have windows; lobby can get overcrowded with after-work revelers flocking to the restaurant bar; restaurant is expensive. $ *Rooms from: $107* ⊠ *535 Tchoupitoulas St., Central Business District* ☏ *504/527–5271* ⊕ *old77hotel.com* ⊐ *165 rooms* ⦿ *No meals* ▭ *No credit cards.*

Pelham Hotel

$$ | **HOTEL** | This 19th-century building with homey accommodations is close to CBD sights like the Riverwalk and the casino, and offers a less hectic alternative to

the convention hotels. **Pros:** centrally located, but far from heavily traveled tourist streets; quirky charm; fun brunch restaurant downstairs. **Cons:** rooms can be small and some lack windows; no on-site swimming pool or fitness area; noise from downtown traffic. $ *Rooms from: $179 ✉ 444 Common St., Central Business District ☎ 504/522–4444, 888/856–4486 🌐 www.thepelhamhotel.com 🛏 60 rooms 🍴 No meals.*

Q&C Hotelbar

$$ | **HOTEL** | Intimate and tasteful, this hotel three blocks outside the French Quarter is a good alternative to the megahotels that surround it. **Pros:** feels like a smaller, more intimate property; good bar; nice common areas. **Cons:** small gym; narrow hallways; main lobby gets crowded. $ *Rooms from: $143 ✉ 344 Camp St., Central Business District ☎ 504/587–9700 🌐 www.qandc.com 🛏 196 rooms 🍴 No meals.*

Renaissance Pere Marquette Hotel

$$ | **HOTEL** | On floors named after renowned jazz musicians, large, quiet rooms have soothing colors, comfortable fabrics, photography by local artists, and oversize marble bathrooms. **Pros:** good on-site bar and restaurant; excellent service; generous amenities. **Cons:** location is not especially pedestrian-friendly; showing some wear-and-tear; some rooms are small. $ *Rooms from: $209 ✉ 817 Common St., Central Business District ☎ 504/525–1111 🌐 www.renaissancehotels.com 🛏 272 rooms 🍴 No meals.*

★ The Roosevelt Hotel New Orleans

$$$ | **HOTEL** | From its glittering lobby to each beautiful, traditionally furnished guest room, this iconic New Orleans hotel offers a grand experience. **Pros:** exquisite lobby, especially when the holiday decorations are up; location near downtown and French Quarter; outstanding bar and restaurants. **Cons:** pricey fees for parking and in-room Wi-Fi; rooms aren't as exciting as other parts of the hotel; famous Sazerac Bar can get really crowded on weekends. $ *Rooms from: $269 ✉ 123 Baronne St., Central Business District ☎ 504/648–1200 🌐 www.therooseveltneworleans.com 🛏 639 rooms 🍴 No meals.*

Sheraton New Orleans Hotel

$$$ | **HOTEL** | Sheraton Club rooms come with many special amenities, but even the regular guest rooms here are spacious and well appointed, with contemporary touches and lots of extras. **Pros:** large hotel with lots of rooms; central location; rooftop pool and sundeck. **Cons:** typical corporate convention property; can be crowded during peak season; fee for Wi-Fi in guest rooms. $ *Rooms from: $244 ✉ 500 Canal St., Central Business District ☎ 504/525–2500, 800/325–3535 🌐 www.sheratonneworleans.com 🛏 1,163 rooms 🍴 No meals.*

The Troubadour Hotel

$$ | **HOTEL** | This midsize hotel has a funky, boutique vibe, a great rooftop bar, and frequent live, local music. **Pros:** modern rooms and bathrooms; rooftop bar has great views of the city; close walk to the Quarter. **Cons:** lobby is small and busy; immediate area around hotel feels remote; minimal storage space in most rooms. $ *Rooms from: $198 ✉ 1111 Gravier St., Central Business District ☎ 504/518–5800, 888/858–6652 reservations 🌐 www.thetroubadour.com 🛏 184 rooms 🍴 No meals.*

The Whitney Hotel

$$ | **HOTEL** | This stylish European-style boutique hotel, with top-notch service and comfortable rooms, is a great choice if you're looking to stay away from the Bourbon Street bustle. **Pros:** free Wi-Fi; near the convention center, the French Quarter, and the Superdome; rooms come with coffeemakers and a free bottle of artesian water. **Cons:** located at a busy downtown intersection; no restaurant on-site; decor needs updating. $ *Rooms from: $169 ✉ 610 Poydras St., Central Business District*

☎ 504/581–4222 ⊕ www.whitneyhotel.com 🛏 116 rooms ⃝ No meals.

★ Windsor Court Hotel

$$$$ | HOTEL | Located just four blocks from the French Quarter, this elegant luxury hotel has plenty of upscale amenities—think plush carpeting, marble vanities, and well-appointed dressing areas set in spacious guest rooms. **Pros:** old-world elegance; superior service; beautiful outdoor pool, spa, and gym. **Cons:** location close to casino can mean traffic outside; books up far in advance; traditional English theme doesn't scream New Orleans. $ Rooms from: $355 ✉ 300 Gravier St., Central Business District ☎ 504/523–6000, 800/262–2662 ⊕ www.windsorcourthotel.com 🛏 316 rooms ⃝ No meals.

▼ 🌙 Nightlife

The CBD is mostly quiet at night, but you can find some terrific nightspots closer to Canal Street and the French Quarter.

BARS AND LOUNGES

Bar Marilou

BARS/PUBS | An evening at this dimly-lit venue begins with an aperitif hour and ends with burlesque, a jazz trio, or other entertaiment appropriate for a place that is part intimate library and part Parisian club. The food here is fittingly European, with grazing options like almonds, olives, and anchovies; seared scallops in white miso dressing and a satisfying pub burger are among more substantial choices. If you're looking for atmosphere and romance served alongside your expertly crafted cocktails, this is your spot. ✉ Maison de La Luz, 544 Carondelet St., Central Business District ☎ 504/814–7711 ⊕ www.barmarilou.com.

Cellar Door

BARS/PUBS | Travel through the narrow doors of this cocktail bar to rooms full of wood-panelled walls and exposed brick, dimly lit chandeliers, and a general atmosphere that is a quiet, refreshing escape from the more corporate surroundings outside. Located within a historic mansion, curl up in one of the many romantic nooks and crannies for a cocktail or two; the cocktail menu favors the classics. ✉ 916 Lafayette St., Central Business District ☎ 504/265–8392 ⊕ www.cellardoornola.com.

Loa

BARS/PUBS | In voodoo tradition, loa are the divine spirits, and this bar just off the lobby of the chic International House Hotel certainly strives for an extraordinary experience with its modern, upscale decor. Well-heeled downtown professionals mingle with an international crowd gathering for the evening to sip on inventive, high-end cocktails created by the friendly bartenders here. An aperitif hour from 4 to 5 pm Thursday through Saturday includes a tasting of one of the delicious signature cocktails. ✉ International House Hotel, 221 Camp St., Central Business District ☎ 504/553–9550 ⊕ www.ihhotel.com.

Piscobar

BARS/PUBS | Hidden on a small CBD side street, this chic little bar serves both inventive and traditional cocktails crafted from the Peruvian spirit, pisco. The inner courtyard is divine for a sunset drink, and the hotel operates an equally charming rooftop bar as well. ✉ Catahoula Hotel, 914 Union St., Central Business District ☎ 504/603–2442 ⊕ www.catahoulahotel.com.

The Sazerac Bar

BARS/PUBS | One of the most famous bars in Louisiana, this art deco gem and slinger of fine libations has a pedigree that dates back to the mid-19th century. Drawn to the signature Sazerac cocktail and Ramos gin fizz, a famous and intriguing clientele has graced this hotel bar over the years, including Governor Huey P. Long, who in the 1930s built a 90-mile highway between New Orleans and the state capital, just so, many believe, he could get directly to the hotel lounge for his signature drink. ⊠ *Roosevelt Hotel, 123 Baronne St., Central Business District* ☎ *504/648–1200* ⊕ *www.theroosevelttneworleans.com.*

Victory

BARS/PUBS | Amid the city's drab business district hides another entry in the growing list of craft cocktail bars. Named for Daniel Victory, one of the city's best mixologists (and an owner), it draws a young professional crowd to its dimly lit, vaguely industrial space for drinks that push the boundaries of traditional cocktails. A cozy room in the back is available for private parties and intimate sipping. At Drink Lab (343 Barrone St.), cocktail novices can take mixology classes from Victory's experts. ⊠ *339 Baronne St., Central Business District* ☎ *504/522–8664* ⊕ *www.victorynola.com.*

CASINOS

Harrah's New Orleans Casino

CASINOS | Commanding the foot of Canal Street, where it anchors a cluster of restaurants and clubs, this beaux-arts–style casino is the largest in the South. Try your luck at one of the 3,800 slot machines, 20 poker tables, and every other game of chance that you can imagine. There's an upscale steak house and a club in the middle of the gaming floor. Valet parking is available. ⊠ *8 Canal St., Central Business District* ☎ *504/533–6000, 800/427–7247* ⊕ *www.harrahsneworleans.com.*

🎭 Performing Arts

Louisiana Philharmonic Orchestra

MUSIC | The always good, sometimes excellent LPO now holds court at the Orpheum Theater while continuing to perform at Tulane and Loyola university auditoriums and at local churches. There's also a concert series in parks around town during the spring months. ⊠ *Orpheum Theater, 129 Roosevelt Way,*

Central Business District ☎ *504/523–6530* ⊕ *www.lpomusic.com.*

🛍 Shopping

The Central Business District is filled with large hotels, national chain stores, and a few high-end and locally owned boutiques that cater to a loyal clientele.

SHOPPING CENTERS AND MARKETS

The Shops at Canal Place

SHOPPING CENTERS/MALLS | This high-end shopping center focuses on national chains, including Saks Fifth Avenue, Michael Kors, Anthropologie, Banana Republic, J.Crew, Lululemon, and BCBG Max Azria. But the mall also includes quality local shops. A highlight is the Mignon Faget jewelry store, which carries the renowned local designer's full line of upscale, Louisiana-inspired creations. ⊠ *333 Canal St., Central Business District* ☎ *504/522–9200* ⊕ *www.canalplacestyle.com.*

CLOTHING

Friend

CLOTHING | A boutique in the lobby of the Ace Hotel features local and small designers of hip, unique menswear. Small gifts and accessories from other local shops are also available. Next door, the Marfa-born Freda boutique sells women's clothes. ⊠ *Ace Hotel New Orleans, 600 Carondolet St., Suite 120, Central Business District* ☎ *504/342–2162* ⊕ *www.friendneworleans.com.*

★ Rubensteins

CLOTHING | One of the city's premier men's stores has been selling high-end suits, tuxedos, casual wear, and made-to-measure apparel since 1924. Brands range from Brioni and Zegna to Ralph Lauren, Prada, and Hugo Boss. ⊠ *102 St. Charles Ave., Central Business District* ☎ *504/581–6666* ⊕ *www.rubensteinsneworleans.com.*

JEWELRY AND ACCESSORIES

Adler's

JEWELRY/ACCESSORIES | This century-old, locally owned jewelry store carries upscale watches, engagement rings, gemstone jewelry, wedding gifts, top-of-the-line china, silver, crystal, and more. ⊠ *722 Canal St., Central Business District* ☎ *504/523–5292, 800/925–7912* ⊕ *www.adlersjewelry.com.*

Clock and Watch Shop

JEWELRY/ACCESSORIES | Master clockmaker Josef Hirzinger repairs and restores all types of new, vintage, and antique watches and clocks at his two-story shop. He also sells many brands of new watches and clocks, ranging from miniature and mantel styles to large grandfather clocks. ⊠ *824 Gravier St., Central Business District* ☎ *504/525–3961* ⊕ *www.theclockwatchshop.com.*

Meyer the Hatter

JEWELRY/ACCESSORIES | One of the South's largest hat stores has been in operation for more than a hundred years and is currently run by the fourth generation of the Meyer family. A favorite of locals and out-of-towners, the shop carries a large selection of fedoras, tweed caps, Kangols, cowboy hats, and just about any type of topper you can put on your head. ⊠ *120 St. Charles Ave., Central Business District* ☎ *504/525–1048, 800/882–4287* ⊕ *www.meyerthehatter.com.*

Warehouse District

Bordered by the river, St. Charles Avenue, Poydras Street, and the Pontchartrain Expressway, and filled with former factories and cotton warehouses, the Warehouse District began its renaissance when the city hosted the World's Fair here in 1984. Structures that housed the international pavilions during the fair now make up the New Orleans Morial Convention Center and a number of hotels, restaurants, bars, and music venues.

Today the Warehouse District is one of the trendiest residential and arts-and-nightlife areas of the city, dotted with modern renovations of historic buildings and upscale lofts. Galleries, auction houses, and artist studios line Julia Street, a main thoroughfare, and you can try your hand at glassmaking and printmaking in some of the workshops. By night you'll find excellent restaurants, bustling live-music venues old and new, and numerous neighborhood and hotel bars ranging from casual to the very chic. Inside, scores of young professionals mix with tourists and longtime residents.

◉ Sights

★ Arthur Roger Gallery

MUSEUM | One of the most respected local galleries has compiled a must-see collection of contemporary artwork by Lin Emery, Jacqueline Bishop, and Willie Birch, as well as national names such as glass artist Dale Chihuly and the film director and photographer John Waters. ⊠ *432–434 Julia St., Warehouse District* ☎ *504/522–1999* ⊕ *www.arthurrogergallery.com* ⊗ *Closed Sun. and Mon.*

★ Blaine Kern's Mardi Gras World at Kern Studios

MUSEUM | FAMILY | If you're not in town for the real thing, here's a fun (and family-friendly) backstage look at the history and artistry of Carnival. The massive 400,000-square-foot complex, just upriver from the New Orleans Morial Convention Center, features an enhanced guided tour through a maze of video presentations, decorative sculptures, and favorite megafloats from Mardi Gras parades such as Bacchus, Rex, and Endymion. A gift shop sells masks, beads, and Mardi Gras posters, as well as tickets for the tour, during which participants can sample king cake and coffee, pose for pictures in front of parade floats, and see artists at work, sculpting with papier-mâché and fiberglass. For special events, visitors enter through a plantation alley that is part Cajun swamp-shack village, part antebellum Disneyworld (Kern was a friend of, and inspired by, Walt Disney). ⊠ *1380 Port of New Orleans Pl., Warehouse District* ☏ *504/361–7821* ⊕ *www.mardigrasworld.com* 🖅 *$22.*

Callan Contemporary

MUSEUM | This sleek gallery specializes in contemporary sculpture and paintings from both local and internationally renowned artists, including Pablo Atchugarry, Eva Hild, Raine Bedsole, Key-Sook Geum, Adrian Deckbar, and Sibylle Peretti. ⊠ *518 Julia St., Warehouse District* ☏ *504/525–0518* ⊕ *www.callancontemporary.com* ☼ *Closed Sun. and Mon.*

★ Contemporary Arts Center

ARTS VENUE | Take in cutting-edge exhibits, featuring both local artists and the work of national and international talent, at this cornerstone of the vibrant Warehouse District. Two theaters present jazz, film, dance, plays, lectures, and experimental and conventional concerts, including a New Orleans music series. Check the website for details. ⊠ *900 Camp St., Warehouse District* ☏ *504/528–3805, 504/528–3800 tickets* ⊕ *www.cacno.org* 🖅 *$10* ☼ *Closed Tues.*

Crescent City Farmers Market

MARKET | This year-round Saturday market offers an array of locally grown produce, baked goods, cut flowers, non-farmed Louisiana seafood, fresh dairy, locally farm-raised meat, and prepared foods from regional vendors. Special events and holidays mean cooking demonstrations and appearances by local musicians. Meet and greet the local farmers, chefs, and fishers who make this city's amazing food culture possible. The market also makes an appearance Uptown on Tuesday morning, in the French Quarter on Wednesday afternoon, and in Mid-City on Thursday evening. ⊠ *750 Carondolet St., Warehouse District* ☏ *504/861–4488* ⊕ *www.crescentcityfarmersmarket.org.*

George Schmidt Gallery

MUSEUM | History—and New Orleans's rich past in particular—is the passion of artist George Schmidt. His gallery displays and sells paintings and narrative art, from small-scale monotypes to mural-size depictions of historic moments. He also sells signed and numbered prints of his work. ⊠ *626 Julia St., Warehouse District* ☏ *504/592–0206* ⊕ *www.georgeschmidt.com* ☼ *Closed Sun. and Mon.*

Jonathan Ferrara Gallery

MUSEUM | Cutting-edge art with a message is the focus of this gallery's monthly exhibits. Contemporary paintings, photography, mixed-media artworks, sculpture, glass, and metalwork by local and international artists are displayed. ⊠ *400A Julia St., Warehouse District* ☏ *504/522–5471* ⊕ *www.jonathanferraragallery.com* ☼ *Closed Sun.*

Julia Street

NEIGHBORHOOD | Contemporary art dealers have adopted this strip in the Warehouse District as their own. The street is lined with galleries and specialty shops, with the greatest concentration stretching from South Peters Street to St. Charles Avenue. On the first Saturday evening of each month, gallery owners throw open their doors to show off new exhibits to the accompaniment of wine, music, and general merriment. During White Linen Night in August and Art for Art's Sake in October, the galleries welcome visitors with artist receptions and live entertainment. ⊠ *Warehouse District.*

Lee Circle

NEIGHBORHOOD | In a traffic circle at the northern edge of the Warehouse District, an 1884 bronze statue of Civil War General Robert E. Lee, by sculptor Alexander Doyle, stood high above the city on a white marble column—until spring 2017, that is, when Mayor Landrieu responded to local protests and nationwide attention

The Warehouse District

KEY
- ① Sights
- ① Restaurants
- ① Hotels
- --- Streetcar

0 — 1,000ft
0 — 200m

Sights ▼

1 Arthur Roger Gallery **C2**
2 Blaine Kern's
   Mardi Gras World
   at Kern Studios........... **E5**
3 Callan Contemporary.... **C2**
4 Contemporary
   Arts Center **C2**
5 Crescent City
   Farmers Market......... **B1**
6 George Schmidt
   Gallery **C2**
7 Jonathan Ferrara
   Gallery **C2**
8 Julia Street **B2**
9 Lee Circle **B3**
10 LeMieux Gallery **D2**
11 Louisiana's Civil War
   Museum at Confederate
   Memorial Hall **B3**
12 National World War II
   Museum **C3**
13 Octavia Art Gallery **C2**
14 New Orleans
   Glassworks &
   Printmaking Studio **C2**
15 Ogden Museum of
   Southern Art............. **C2**
16 Soren Christensen....... **D2**
17 St. Patrick's Church...... **C1**

Restaurants ▼

1 Carmo **C2**
2 Cochon.................. **D3**
3 Cochon Butcher **D3**
4 Emeril's.................. **D2**
5 Gianna **C2**
6 Herbsaint **B1**
7 La Boca **D2**
8 Marcello's **B1**
9 Pêche Seafood Grill **C2**
10 Tommy's Cuisine **D2**

Hotels ▼

1 Embassy Suites
   New Orleans-
   Convention Center
   and Lofts
   Club Tower **D2**
2 Hampton Inn and
   Suites–Convention
   Center.................... **D4**
3 The Higgins Hotel
   & Conference Center.... **C3**
4 Renaissance Arts
   Hotel...................... **D2**

to remove glorified Confederate monuments. Plans are underway to redevelop (and rename) the circle as a public space that unites the city, rather than divides it. ✉ *Warehouse District.*

LeMieux Gallery

MUSEUM | Gulf Coast artists from Louisiana to Florida display art and high-end crafts here, alongside work by the late New Orleans abstract artist Paul Ninas. ✉ *332 Julia St., Warehouse District* ☎ *504/522–5988* ⊕ *www.lemieuxgalleries.com* ⊙ *Closed Sun.*

Louisiana's Civil War Museum at Confederate Memorial Hall

MUSEUM | Established in 1891, this ponderous stone building is the oldest museum in Louisiana and features heavy trusses, gleaming cypress paneling, and elaborate Richardsonian Romanesque architecture. It houses a collection of artifacts from the Civil War, including uniforms, flags, soldiers' personal effects, and a rudimentary hand grenade. ✉ *929 Camp St., Warehouse District* ☎ *504/523–4522* ⊕ *www.confederatemuseum.com* ⊠ *$10* ⊙ *Closed Sun. and Mon.*

★ National World War II Museum

MUSEUM | This vast and still-expanding museum is a moving and well-executed examination of World War II events and its aftermath. Seminal moments are re-created through vintage propaganda from the period, including posters, radio, and film clips; more than 7,500 oral histories of the military personnel involved; a number of short documentary films; and collections of weapons, personal items, and other artifacts from the war. Highlights of the museum include "Final Mission: The USS *Tang* Experience," which re-creates the experience of being in a submarine, and the 4-D theater experience (across the street from the main exhibits) called "Beyond All Boundaries," produced and narrated by Tom Hanks. Other popular exhibits are the replicas

Gallery Hopping ◉ the Warehouse District

In the vibrant Warehouse District, museums and art galleries abound, showcasing works from local, regional, and nationally known artists. Julia Street in particular is a destination for art lovers—it's packed with galleries, many of them owned by artists. NOLA.com publishes detailed listings of exhibition openings. The events are generally accompanied by wine and hors d'oeuvres and sometimes live music. The galleries' days of operation can vary, so it's best to confirm gallery hours; many owners are happy to set up appointments.

of the Higgins boat troop landing craft, which was invented and manufactured in New Orleans by Andrew Jackson Higgins during WWII, and the U.S. Freedom Pavilion: The Boeing Center, which honors all service branches and includes a restored Boeing B-17. Galleries dedicated to the European and Pacific theaters, as well as the Homefront's role in the war, are among the museum's comprehensive permanent exhibits. The Stage Door Canteen features WWII-era entertainment and an adjoining restaurant serves a "Victory Garden-to-table" menu. Check the website for updates on the museum's ongoing expansion and for current offerings. ✉ *945 Magazine St., main entrance on Andrew Higgins Dr., Warehouse District* ☎ *504/528–1944* ⊕ *www.nationalww2museum.org* ⊠ *$28.50; Beyond All Boundaries and Final Mission presentations $7 each.*

New Orleans Glassworks & Printmaking Studio

MUSEUM | FAMILY | See free demonstrations of printmaking, glassmaking and design, and silver alchemy in this restored, 1800s-era brick warehouse (with a whopping 25,000-square-foot interior). The studio offers group and individual classes. Call in advance to make reservations for hands-on instruction. A shop and gallery display and sell the finished products. ⊠ *727 Magazine St., Warehouse District* ☎ *504/529–7279* ⊕ *www.neworleansglassworks.com* ⊘ *Closed Sun.*

Octavia Art Gallery

MUSEUM | This gallery space features a number of established, mid-career, and emerging local and international artists who work in a variety of media. The gallery also shows works by 20th-century masters such as Andy Warhol, Keith Haring, and Alex Katz. ⊠ *700 Magazine St., Suite 103, Warehouse District* ☎ *504/309–4249* ⊕ *www.octaviaartgallery.com* ⊘ *Closed Sun. and Mon.*

★ Ogden Museum of Southern Art

MUSEUM | FAMILY | Art by Southern artists, made in the South, about the South, and exploring Southern themes fills this elegant five-story building. The basis of the museum's permanent collection are 1,200 works collected by local developer Roger Ogden since the 1960s. It has now grown to more than 4,000 pieces, including paintings, ceramics, drawings, sculptures, photographs, and designs. These pieces, along with special exhibitions, showcase artists from Washington, D.C., and 15 Southern states spanning the 18th through 21st century. A central stair atrium filters natural light through the series of galleries, and a rooftop patio serves as a sculpture garden with lovely views of the surrounding area. The gift shop sells crafts and jewelry by Southern artists and books and movies celebrating the South. Thursday night (6–8 pm)

comes alive with Ogden After Hours, featuring live music, artist interviews, refreshments, children's activities, and special gallery exhibitions. ⊠ *925 Camp St., Warehouse District* ☎ *504/539–9650* ⊕ *www.ogdenmuseum.org* ☑ *$13.50.*

St. Patrick's Church

RELIGIOUS SITE | A stark exterior gives way to a far more ornate interior in the first church built in the American sector of New Orleans, intended to provide the city's Irish Catholics with a place of worship as distinguished as the French St. Louis Cathedral. The vaulted interior was completed in 1840 by local architect James Gallier, who moved here from Ireland in 1834. High stained-glass windows and huge murals, painted in 1841, enrich the interior. ⊠ *724 Camp St., Warehouse District* ☎ *504/525–4413* ⊕ *www.oldstpatricks.org.*

Søren Christensen

MUSEUM | More than 30 local, national, and international artists working in a diverse range of media and aesthetics showcase their talents at this gallery. Popular artists include Gretchen Weller Howard, Steven Seinberg, Karen Scharer, and Audra Kohout. ⊠ *400 Julia St., Warehouse District* ☎ *504/569–9501* ⊕ *www.sorengallery.com* ⊘ *Closed Sun. and Mon.*

🍴 Restaurants

In the sprawling Warehouse District, gallery hoppers and condo dwellers fuel up at trendy bistros and stylish casual eateries.

Carmo

$ | CARIBBEAN | Vegan, vegetarian, and gluten-free options abound at this self-proclaimed "tropical café," which playfully references the cuisines of Latin America, Southeast Asia, and the Caribbean. Fresh, local, and organic produce are used to create dishes like *acarajé*, a black-eyed-pea fritter stuffed with *vatapá* (a cashew, peanut, and coconut paste) or the Rico sandwich, a breadless creation of grilled plantains, melted cheese, vegan meat, avocado, salsa fresca, and a tangy secret sauce. **Known for:** vegan options; excellent ceviche; fresh juice from exotic fruits. $ *Average main: $14* ⊠ *527 Julia St., Warehouse District* ☎ *504/875–4132* ⊕ *www.cafecarmo.com* ⊗ *Closed Sun.*

★ Cochon

$$$ | **CAJUN** | Chef-owned restaurants are common in New Orleans, but this one builds on owner Donald Link's family heritage as he, working with co-owner Stephen Stryjewski (who received a James Beard Award for his work here), prepares Cajun dishes he learned to cook at his grandfather's knee. The interior may be a bit too hip and noisy for some patrons, but the food makes up for it. **Known for:** cochon de lait; rabbit and dumplings; fried boudin with pickled peppers. $ *Average main: $26* ⊠ *930 Tchoupitoulas St., Warehouse District* ☎ *504/588–2123* ⊕ *www.cochonrestaurant.com.*

★ Cochon Butcher

$ | **SOUTHERN** | Around the corner from its big brother Cochon, Butcher packs its own Cajun punch with an upscale sandwich menu that dials up the flavor on local classics. With house-cured meats and olive salad, the muffuletta reveals exactly how delicious Italian-Creole can be, though the pork-belly sandwich, with refreshing mint and cucumber, also brings customers back. **Known for:** pork-belly sandwich; to-go treats; delicious cocktails. $ *Average main: $10* ⊠ *930 Tchoupitoulas St., Warehouse District* ☎ *504/588–7675* ⊕ *www.cochonbutcher.com* ⊗ *No dinner Sun.*

Emeril's

$$$ | **AMERICAN** | Celebrity-chef Emeril Lagasse's urban-chic flagship restaurant is always jammed, so it's fortunate that the basket weave–pattern wood ceiling muffles much of the clatter and chatter. The ambitious menu gives equal emphasis to Creole and modern American cooking—try the andouille-crusted drum fish or the barbecue shrimp (one of the darkest, richest versions of that local specialty). **Known for:** barbecue shrimp; decadent desserts; long wine list. $ *Average main: $30* ⊠ *800 Tchoupitoulas St., Warehouse District* ☎ *504/528–9393* ⊕ *www.emerilsrestaurants.com* ⊗ *No lunch Sun.*

Gianna

$$$ | **ITALIAN** | An evening at this corner restaurant combines a sophisticated night out with nourishing, down-to-earth food. Chef Rebecca Wilcomb, the former James Beard Award–winning Chef de Cuisine at Herbsaint, named the restaurant after her nonna, who is also responsible for the menu's tortellini en brodo recipe, a hearty-yet-light favorite from Northern Italy. **Known for:** seasonal, local ingredients; fresh pasta; group meal menus. $ *Average main: $26* ⊠ *700 Magazine St., Warehouse District* ☎ *504/399–0816* ⊕ *www.giannarestaurant.com.*

★ Herbsaint

$$$ | **SOUTHERN** | Chef Donald Link (also of Cochon, Cochon Butcher, and Pêche Seafood Grill) turns out food that sparkles with robust flavors and top-grade ingredients at this casually upscale restaurant. Small plates and starters such as a daily gumbo, charcuterie, and homemade pastas are mainstays. **Known for:** homemade pasta; Muscovy duck leg confit with dirty rice and citrus gastrique; convivial crowds. $ *Average main: $27* ⊠ *701 St. Charles Ave., Warehouse District* ☎ *504/524–4114* ⊕ *www.herbsaint.com* ⊗ *Closed Sun. No lunch Sat.*

La Boca

$$$ | **LATIN AMERICAN** | Need a break from the bounties of the sea prevalent in New Orleans restaurants? Book a table at this classic Argentine steak house, where wine and meat are simple but satisfying priorities. **Known for:** malbec-heavy

Food Glossary

Barbecue shrimp. Shrimp baked in the shell in a blend of olive oil and butter, and seasoned with garlic and other herbs and spices.

Béarnaise. A sauce of egg yolk and butter with shallots, wine, and vinegar, used on meat and fish.

Boudin (pronounced boo- *dan*). A soft Cajun sausage, often spicy, made of pork, rice, and a bit of liver for seasoning.

Bouillabaisse (pronounced *booey-yah*-base). A stew of various fish and shellfish in a broth seasoned with saffron and other spices.

Boulette (pronounced *boo*-let). Minced, chopped, or puréed meat or fish shaped into balls and fried.

Café brûlot (pronounced broo- *loh*). Cinnamon, lemon, clove, orange, and sugar, steeped with strong coffee, then flambéed with brandy and served in special pedestaled cups.

Chicory coffee. The ground and roasted root of a European variety of chicory is added to ground coffee in varying proportions.

Crème brûlée. Literally meaning "burned cream," a custard with a brittle crust of browned sugar.

Dirty rice. In this cousin of jambalaya, bits of meat, such as giblets or sausage, and seasonings are added to white rice before cooking.

Dressed. A po'boy "dressed" contains lettuce, tomato, pickles, and mayonnaise or mustard.

Meunière (pronounced muhn- *yehr*). This method of preparing fish or soft-shell crab entails dusting it with seasoned flour, sautéing it in brown butter, and using the butter with lemon juice as a sauce.

Mirliton (pronounced merl-i- *tawn*). A pale-green member of the squash family, usually identified as a vegetable pear or chayote.

Oysters Bienville (pronounced byen- *veel*). Oysters lightly baked in the shell and topped with a cream sauce flavored with bits of shrimp, mushroom, and green seasonings.

Oysters en brochette (pronounced awn-bro- *shet*). Whole oysters and bits of bacon dusted with seasoned flour, skewered, and deep-fried; traditionally served on toast with lemon and brown butter.

Panéed veal (pronounced pan- *aid*). Breaded veal cutlets sautéed in butter.

Po'boy. A hefty sandwich made with local French bread and any number of fillings: roast beef, fried shrimp, oysters, ham, meatballs in tomato sauce, and cheese are common.

Ravigote (pronounced rah-vee- *gote*). In Creole usage, this is a piquant mayonnaise—usually made with capers—used to moisten crabmeat.

Rémoulade (pronounced ray-moo- *lahd*). A mixture of olive oil, mustard, scallions, cayenne, lemon, paprika, and parsley, served on cold peeled shrimp or lumps of back-fin crabmeat.

Souffléed potatoes. Thin, hollow puffs of deep-fried potato, produced by two fryings at different temperatures.

Sno-balls. Shaved ice topped with flavored syrup.

Tasso. Smokey cured pork often diced fine and added to dishes as a flavoring.

wine list; flank steak; grilled provolone as a side. $ *Average main: $27* ✉ *870 Tchoupitoulas St., Warehouse District* ☎ *504/525–8205* ⊕ *www.labocasteaks.com* ⊘ *Closed Sun. No lunch.*

Marcello's

$$ | **SOUTHERN ITALIAN** | There are two very good reasons to visit Marcello's: comforting Sicilian-American dishes at a reasonable price, and the well-stocked wine store (and cellar) next door, where diners choose from a wide selection of Italian wines to accompany their meal (markups are slightly below regular restaurant prices). Southern Italian food might not scream New Orleans, but the convivial bistro atmosphere, made more picturesque by the passing St. Charles streetcar, will make you feel part of the neighborhood crowd. **Known for:** great wine cellar; grilled artichokes; pork marsala. $ *Average main: $21* ✉ *715 St. Charles Ave., Warehouse District* ☎ *504/518–6333* ⊕ *www.marcelloscafe.com* ⊘ *No lunch weekends.*

Pêche Seafood Grill

$$$ | **SEAFOOD** | The name implies fish, and that's what you'll find at this modern temple to seafood, the brainchild of nearby Cochon proprietors Donald Link and Stephen Stryjewski. In addition to an airy, modern space enhanced by exposed beams and a wood-burning grill, the dining room has a fascinating history: the building was a former mortuary that claims to have embalmed Confederate president Jefferson Davis. **Known for:** seafood small plates; raw bar of Gulf oysters; big crowds. $ *Average main: $28* ✉ *800 Magazine St., Warehouse District* ☎ *504/522–1744* ⊕ *www.pecherestaurant.com* ⊘ *Closed Sun.*

Tommy's Cuisine

$$ | **ITALIAN** | The upscale dining rooms here are clubby and festive, the crowd is always interesting, and the menu seamlessly blends Creole and Italian. There are several types of oyster appetizers

to choose from, including the signature Oysters Tommy with Romano cheese, pancetta, and roasted red pepper. **Known for:** baked oysters; formal service; lively crowd. $ *Average main: $22* ✉ *746 Tchoupitoulas St., Warehouse District* ☎ *504/581–1103* ⊕ *www.tommyscuisine.com.*

🛏 Hotels

Embassy Suites New Orleans–Convention Center and Lofts Club Tower

$$ | **HOTEL** | **FAMILY** | If your primary destination is the convention center (three blocks away) or the restaurants, galleries, and museums in the Warehouse District, these suites with bedrooms and separate parlors are a great choice. **Pros:** evening reception with cocktails and snacks; breakfast included with all rooms; outdoor heated lap pool. **Cons:** a significant distance from the French Quarter; attracts big business groups for conventions; some noise and construction. $ *Rooms from: $199* ✉ *315 Julia St., Warehouse District* ☎ *504/525–1993, 800/362–2779* ⊕ *www.embassyneworleans.com* ⇆ *370 rooms* ❏ *Free breakfast.*

Hampton Inn and Suites–Convention Center

$$ | **HOTEL** | Convention center lodgings with character can be hard to come by, but here, two century-old warehouses have been converted into a French colonial–style hotel with large, airy rooms that are comfortable, architecturally distinctive, and moderately priced. **Pros:** architecturally stunning; minutes from convention center; free Wi-Fi. **Cons:** extremely busy area; can be daunting to both pedestrians and drivers; no restaurant on-site. $ *Rooms from: $169* ✉ *1201 Convention Center Blvd., Warehouse District* ☎ *504/566–9990, 800/292–0653* ⊕ *www.neworleanshamptoninns.com* ⇆ *288 rooms* ❏ *Free breakfast.*

New Orleans Music with Kids

Bourbon Street's entertainment options are largely off-limits to children, but younger music fans need not feel excluded. Dozens of options exist outside of barrooms and traditional clubs, and several of the most prestigious clubs offer all-ages shows.

Preservation Hall and **Palm Court Jazz Café**, both legendary jazz venues, welcome underage patrons. **Tipitina's** and **Howlin' Wolf** occasionally host all-ages shows as well. Around **Jackson Square**, talented street musicians perform most days of the week, and the **French Market** hosts a regular series of concerts as well as a separate busking stage for local and visiting performers to play for tips. The **Louisiana Music Factory**, an excellent New Orleans music store, regularly hosts in-store performances. And kids are always welcome at the free shows staged by the National Park Service's **New Orleans Jazz Historical Park**, both at the park's visitor center and at the shows Tuesday through Saturday afternoon in the French Market.

The Higgins Hotel & Conference Center
$$ | **HOTEL** | **FAMILY** | Unique in its position as a hotel owned and operated by a museum (in partnership with Hilton), the Higgins is both an extension of the WWII Museum and a convenient, modern stay full of art deco touches and museum-quality photographs and art. **Pros:** unique concept; modern amenities and custom decor; great bar and restaurant outlets. **Cons:** WWII theme isn't for everyone; area outside gets easily congested; long walk to French Quarter. [$] *Rooms from: $182* ✉ *1000 Magazine St., Warehouse District* ☎ *504/528–1941* 🌐 *www.higginshotelnola.com* 🛏 *230 rooms* 🍴 *No meals.*

Renaissance Arts Hotel
$$ | **HOTEL** | Art lovers looking to stay close to downtown should check out this circa-1910 warehouse-turned-hotel, where huge windows now make for great views from comfortable, spacious, well-designed rooms furnished with a minimalist bent. **Pros:** modern, well-appointed facilities; beautiful artwork; hotel "navigators" serve as personal guides to the city. **Cons:** not suitable for those who want a traditional New Orleans hotel; not convenient to the French Quarter; inconsistent service. [$] *Rooms from: $189* ✉ *700 Tchoupitoulas St., Warehouse District* ☎ *504/613–2330* 🌐 *renaissance-hotels.marriott.com* 🛏 *217 rooms* 🍴 *No meals.*

🍸 Nightlife

With its many apartment buildings converted from 19th-century warehouses and cotton mills as backdrop, the Warehouse District has become a real draw for locals and visitors alike with numerous bars, restaurants, and clubs that cater to hip professionals. It's also home to the contemporary-arts scene, with dozens of galleries arranged throughout the district that host their own series of parties and celebrations.

BARS AND LOUNGES

Ernst Cafe
BARS/PUBS | Ernst has been operating as a bar since the first years of the 20th century, and the classic interior and upstairs balcony provide a welcome respite for conventioneers, lawyers from nearby

firms, and service-industry folks winding down from shifts at area hotels. The classic menu includes local bar-food staples like fried green tomatoes, po'boys, wraps, and burgers. ✉ *600 S. Peters St., Warehouse District* ☎ *504/525–8544* ⊕ *www.ernstcafe.com.*

Rusty Nail

MUSIC CLUBS | Nestled in between the overhead highway and a series of converted 18th-century warehouses, this discreet neighborhood bar can be difficult to find. With lively DJs and football crowds, a great selection of scotches, a gorgeous renovated patio, frequent visits by food trucks, and even the occasional play reading, it's worth the trek to get here. ✉ *1100 Constance St., Warehouse District* ☎ *504/525–5515* ⊕ *www. rustynailnola.com.*

MUSIC CLUBS
Circle Bar

MUSIC CLUBS | Like something out of a Tim Burton film, this teetering old Victorian house that straddles the concrete jungles of downtown and the Warehouse District hides one of the coolest indie-rock clubs in the city. Scenesters descend around 10 pm, but earlier in the evening this is a laid-back neighborhood haunt. Pull on your skinny jeans, so that you can squeeze into the room that holds what might be the world's tiniest stage. ✉ *1032 St. Charles Ave., Warehouse District* ☎ *504/588–2616* ⊕ *www.circlebarneworleans.com.*

Howlin' Wolf

MUSIC CLUBS | This New Orleans favorite has long been a premier venue and anchor of the Warehouse District club and music scene. With a great corner location in a converted warehouse, they host larger rock, funk, blues, Latin, and hip-hop shows nearly every night on the main stage. Meanwhile, a side bar called The Den books intimate events and popular weekly parties like Brass Band Sundays. ✉ *907 S. Peters St., Warehouse* District ☎ *504/529–5844* ⊕ *www.the-howlinwolf.com.*

Mulate's

MUSIC CLUBS | Across the street from the convention center, this large venue seats 400, and the dance floor quickly fills with couples twirling and two-stepping to authentic Cajun bands from the countryside. Regulars love to drag first-timers to the floor for impromptu lessons. The home-style Cajun cuisine is acceptable, but what matters is the nightly music. ✉ *201 Julia St., Warehouse District* ☎ *504/522–1492* ⊕ *www.mulates.com.*

Republic

MUSIC CLUBS | Part of the new generation of music venues in the Warehouse District, this rock club retains the rough-timbered feel of the cotton-and-grain warehouse it used to be. The club books touring hip-hop stars and rock bands as well as local acts, and DJs take over the sound system late at night for popular dance parties. ✉ *828 S. Peters St., Warehouse District* ☎ *504/528–8282* ⊕ *www.republicnola.com.*

🛍 Shopping

SHOPPING CENTERS AND MARKETS
The Outlet Collection at Riverwalk Marketplace

SHOPPING CENTERS/MALLS | Built in what was once the International Pavilion for the 1984 World's Fair, the Outlet Collection at Riverwalk is an upscale outlet mall with shops such as Neiman Marcus Last Call, Johnston & Murphy Factory Store, and outlets for Coach, Forever 21, Carter's Babies and Kids, Chico's, and Steve Madden. Outside the mall is Spanish Plaza, the scene of frequent outdoor concerts and special events. ✉ *500 Port of New Orleans Pl., Warehouse District* ☎ *504/522–1555* ⊕ *www.riverwalkneworleans.com.*

ARTWORK
Ariodante

ART GALLERIES | Mostly local and Gulf Coast artists are represented in this gallery, featuring high-end and reasonably priced contemporary crafts and fine art, including jewelry, blown glass, sculpture, furniture, photography, paintings, ceramics, and decorative accessories. ⊠ *535 Julia St., Warehouse District* ☎ *504/524–3233* ⊕ *www.ariodantegallery.com.*

★ Center for Southern Craft and Design Store

ART GALLERIES | You don't have to pay admission to enter this part of the Ogden Museum of Southern Art, where you can buy ceramics, glasswork, decorative pieces, books, scarves, and jewelry by Southern artists. The museum itself is filled with contemporary and folk paintings, mixed-media artworks, photography, and sculpture. ■TIP→ **Live music and after-hours events are held on Thursday.** ⊠ *925 Camp St., Warehouse District* ☎ *504/539–9650* ⊕ *www.ogdenmuseum. org.*

FOOD, WINE, AND SPIRITS
Simplee Gourmet

FOOD/CANDY | FAMILY | You'll find every culinary gadget imaginable at this packed neighborhood kitchen boutique, along with cookbooks, ceramics and servingware, pre-made snacks and mixes, and specialty Louisiana goods. Check the calendar for themed cooking classes, held in the store's kitchen about twice a month. ⊠ *1000 Girod St., Ste. B-5, Warehouse District* ☎ *504/962–9162* ⊕ *www. simpleegourmet.com.*

Wine Institute of New Orleans

WINE/SPIRITS | This hybrid institute, best known as "WINO," is part wine school, part wine store, and part high-tech wine-tasting experience. Walk around with a glass and sample this shop's more than 120 wines, available to taste for a fee by the ounce, half glass, or full glass using Enomatic serving systems (the machines resemble a soda fountain or beer taps). Buy the wines you like by the bottle, or just continue to taste to your heart's content—just make sure you keep tabs on your credit card tally, as it's easy to get carried away. Charcuterie, artisanal cheese, and other small plates are also on offer. The Thursday-evening wine-tasting classes fill up quickly, so plan ahead if you are interested. ⊠ *610 Tchoupitoulas St., Warehouse District* ☎ *504/324–8000* ⊕ *www.winoschool.com.*

Chapter 8

THE GARDEN DISTRICT

8

Updated by
Katie Fernelius

⊙ Sights	🍴 Restaurants	🛏 Hotels	🛍 Shopping	🍸 Nightlife
★★★☆☆	★★☆☆☆	★★☆☆☆	★★★★☆	★☆☆☆☆

NEIGHBORHOOD SNAPSHOT

TOP REASONS TO GO

Architecture. View antebellum homes built during New Orleans's most prosperous era by renowned architects, including Henry Howard, Lewis E. Reynolds, William Freret, and Samuel Jamison.

Magazine Street dining. Rubbing shoulders with vintage boutiques and dive bars, the eateries along this stretch serve a mélange of cuisines—you'll find everything from po'boys to French crêpes to crawfish-stuffed sushi rolls.

Local art. Peruse both fine and funky jewelry, paintings, pottery, and other locally made artwork at the galleries on Magazine Street. Or visit the community art centers on OC Haley Boulevard.

History. View the aboveground tombs at Lafayette Cemetery No. 1, in continual use since 1833 and one of the most beautiful burial grounds in the city.

GETTING HERE AND AROUND

The Garden District is easily accessible by car, streetcar, and city bus, or on foot from the CBD or Uptown. It's easy and free to park your car on any side street, but you have to pay to park along the busier stretches of Magazine Street and Prytania Street.

The streetcar runs about every 30 minutes (more frequently during rush hour), 24 hours a day, and makes several stops along St. Charles Avenue. Because the tracks are undergoing maintenance, segments of the line are periodically out of commission, and in those instances a shuttle service is available. You may have to wait longer than 30 minutes for the streetcar to arrive at night, but it's generally a safe, if leisurely, mode of transportation. It takes about 20 minutes on the streetcar to get to Jackson Avenue in the lower Garden District from Canal Street. The No. 11 bus runs up Magazine Street, making stops at all major intersections every 20 minutes. The ride from Canal Street to Jackson Avenue takes about 10 minutes depending on traffic.

QUICK BITES

■ **French Truck Roastery and Espresso Bar.** You'll find some of the best locally roasted coffee and espresso drinks in this bright, pint-sized space. ✉ *1200 Magazine St., Lower Garden District* ☎ *504/298–1115* ⊕ *www.frenchtruckcoffee. com* ⊗ *No dinner.*

■ **Stein's Market and Deli.** This Jewish and Italian deli serves the "Muphuletta," a Philly take on a New Orleans muffuletta with sopressata, ham, provolone, and olive salad on ciabatta. ✉ *2207 Magazine St., Garden District* ☎ *504/527–0771* ⊕ *www.steinsdeli.com* ▭ *No credit cards* ⊗ *Closed Mon. No dinner.*

MAKING THE MOST OF YOUR TIME

■ Plan at least a day to see the Garden District's gorgeous mansions, to shop Magazine Street, and to visit **Lafayette Cemetery No. 1**, the oldest municipal cemetery in the city. Historic New Orleans Tours runs quality tours of the Garden District that includes the former house of Anne Rice and the cemetery.

Boasting some of the most stunning homes in the city, the Garden District has acquired fame for its antebellum mansions and manicured gardens. Residents take great pride in their gorgeous properties, and the neighborhood is in bloom year-round. Although most homes are closed to the public (except for tours on special occasions), the views from outside the intricate cast-iron fences are still impressive. A stroll through the neighborhood is a peaceful break from more touristy areas of New Orleans.

Originally part of the Livaudais plantation, the Garden District was laid out in the late 1820s and remained part of the city of Lafayette until incorporated into New Orleans in 1852. The neighborhood attracted "new-moneyed" Americans who, snubbed by the Creole residents of the French Quarter, constructed grand houses with large English-style gardens featuring lush azaleas, magnolias, and camellias. Three architectural styles were favored: the three-bay Greek Revival, center-hall Greek Revival, and raised cottage. Renovations and expansions to these designs through the years allowed owners to host bigger and more ostentatious parties, particularly during the social season between Christmas and Carnival. Today many of the proud residents represent fourth- or fifth-generation New Orleanians.

The lower Garden District (along Magazine Street east of Jackson Avenue) boasts offbeat boutiques selling original art, antiques, vintage clothing, and jewelry, catering to the young professional and student crowds in particular. A "green light district" of eco-friendly shops has taken root in its 2000–2100 blocks. Coliseum Square, in the center of the neighborhood, features a fountain and walking trails that wind around looming oak trees, and the mansions flanking the park display a distinctly faded beauty. The neighborhood quiets down considerably in the evening, though there are a few nighttime hangouts and restaurants, especially near the triangular intersection at St. Mary Street and Sophie Wright Place.

A morning walk in the upper Garden District (west of Jackson Avenue) provides a peaceful break from the more touristy areas of New Orleans. Besides beautiful mansions with wrought-iron fences that wrap around vibrant, manicured gardens, this part of the neighborhood is where you'll find Lafayette Cemetery No. 1, one of the city's oldest and most beautiful cemeteries. Return to the present day by visiting the stretch of Magazine Street that runs alongside the upper Garden District, which boasts an eclectic mix of restaurants and chichi boutiques.

👁 Sights

Brevard House

HOUSE | Though Anne Rice moved out of her elegant Garden District home in 2004, the famous novelist's fans still flock to see the house that inspired the Mayfair Manor in her series *Lives of the Mayfair Witches*. The house is a three-bay Greek Revival, extended over a luxurious, lemon tree–lined side yard and surrounded by a fence of cast-iron rosettes that earned the estate its historical name, Rosegate. ⊠ *1239 First St., Garden District.*

Briggs-Staub House

HOUSE | The only Gothic Revival house in the district was built in 1849. Garden District Americans shunned the Gothic Revival style, deeming it a little too close to Creole-Catholic tradition, but Londoner Charles Briggs ignored decorum and had James Gallier Sr. design this anomaly, touted as a "Gothic cottage." The interior departs from a strict Gothic layout to make it better suited for entertaining. A miniature replica of the structure stands next door; it once housed Briggs's servants, who were reputedly free men of color. ⊠ *2605 Prytania St., Garden District.*

Buckner Mansion

HOUSE | This 1856 home was built by cotton king Henry S. Buckner in overt competition with the famous Stanton Hall in Natchez, built by Buckner's former partner. Among the luxurious details are its 48 fluted cypress columns and a rare honeysuckle-design cast-iron fence. Now privately owned, the house served as the campus of Soulé College from 1923 to 1975 and appeared in *American Horror Story*. ⊠ *1410 Jackson Ave., Garden District.*

Christ Church Cathedral

RELIGIOUS SITE | The present-day English Gothic church, completed in 1887, has pitched gables, an architectural detail that prefigured the New Orleans Victorian style. Its congregation was actually established in 1805, however, making it the first non–Roman Catholic church in the Louisiana Purchase territory. ⊠ *2919 St. Charles Ave., Garden District* ⊕ *www. cccnola.org.*

Coliseum Square Park

CITY PARK | Established in the mid-19th century, this lush green space is the centerpiece of the lower Garden District. With cycling and walking trails as well as a beautiful fountain, the wedge-shape park is a great spot to stop and relax after a walk through the neighborhood. Although the area bordered by Race and Melpomene streets can be bustling with activity during the day, it's best not to wander around alone at night. ⊠ *1700 Coliseum St., Garden District.*

Colonel Short's Villa

HOUSE | Built in 1859, this house's stylistic influence was due to the two-story galleries of its dining room wing, which had railings made of cast iron. The fence features a pattern of morning glories and cornstalks and is the most famous work of cast iron in the Garden District. Colonel Robert Short, a cotton merchant from Kentucky, purchased the fence for his wife, who was homesick for her native

Iowa. The house was occupied by Union governor Michael Hahn and by governor Nathaniel Banks during the Civil War, but after the war ended, it was returned to Colonel Short. ✉ *1448 Fourth St., Garden District.*

Eiffel Society

BUILDING | Thirty years ago, engineers in Paris discovered hairline fractures in the Eiffel Tower supports. To lighten the load, they removed the restaurant on the second platform. New Orleans auto dealer McDonald Stephens bought that restaurant, which was disassembled into 11,062 pieces for shipping. Stephens hired New Orleans architect Steven Bingler to build a "jewel box" out of the pieces for his four beloved daughters. Bingler's vision, assembled on St. Charles Avenue in 1986, incorporated scattered pieces from the original restaurant into a structure meant to resemble the Eiffel Tower. The building has gone through many incarnations; today it is a lounge and event space. ✉ *2040 St. Charles Ave., Garden District* ☎ *504/525–2951* ⊕ *www.eiffelsociety.com.*

Goodrich-Stanley House

BUILDING | This restored Creole cottage was a modest prototype for much of the far more elaborate architecture of the surrounding Garden District. The scale, derived from the climate-conscious design prevalent in the West Indies, made this style easily adaptable to the higher pretensions of the Greek Revival look, as well as the slightly more reserved Colonial Revival. Built in 1837, the house has had one famous occupant: Henry Morton Stanley, renowned explorer of Africa and founder of the Congo Free States who most famously uttered the phrase "Dr. Livingstone, I presume" upon encountering the long-lost Scottish missionary. ✉ *1729 Coliseum St., Garden District.*

House of Broel's Victorian Mansion and Dollhouse Museum

MUSEUM | This restored antebellum home was built in two periods: its present-day second floor was actually constructed first, in 1850, and in 1884 the house was elevated and a new first floor added. The extensive dollhouse collection includes 60 historically accurate, scale-model miniatures of Victorian, Tudor, and plantation-style houses and covers more than 3,000 square feet on the mansion's second floor. All were created by owner Bonnie Broel over a 15-year period. Visitors can only view the property on tours, which can fill up, so it's best to call ahead. ✉ *2220 St. Charles Ave., Garden District* ☎ *504/522–2220, 504/494–2220 tour info and reservations* ⊕ *www. houseofbroel.com* ✉ *Tour $15.*

★ Lafayette Cemetery No. 1

CEMETERY | New Orleans found itself amid a large influx of Italian, German, Irish, and American immigrants from the North when this magnolia-shaded cemetery opened in 1833. Many who fought or played a role in the Civil War have plots here, indicated by plaques and headstones that detail the site of their death. Several tombs also reflect the toll taken by the yellow fever epidemic, which affected mostly children and newcomers to New Orleans; 2,000 yellow fever victims were buried here in 1852. Movies such as *Interview with the Vampire* and *Double Jeopardy* have used this walled cemetery for its eerie beauty. Save Our Cemeteries, a nonprofit, offers hour-long, volunteer-led tours daily at 7:00 am. All proceeds benefit the organization's cemetery restoration and advocacy efforts. ✉ *1400 block of Washington Ave., Garden District* ☎ *504/658–3781* ⊕ *www. saveourcemeteries.org.*

Lonsdale House

HOUSE | As a 16-year-old immigrant working in the New Orleans shipyards, Henry Lonsdale noticed how many damaged

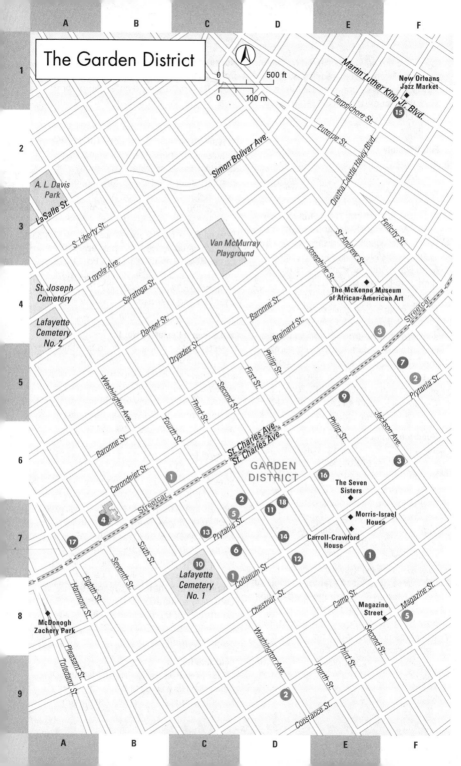

The Garden District

A. L. Davis Park

LaSalle St.

S. Liberty St.

Loyola Ave.

St. Joseph Cemetery

Lafayette Cemetery No. 2

Saratoga St.

Daneel St.

Dryades St.

Washington Ave.

Baronne St.

Carondelet St.

Sixth St.

Seventh St.

Eighth St.

Harmony St.

Pleasant St.

Toledano St.

McDonogh Zachery Park

Simon Bolivar Ave.

Van McMurray Playground

Baronne St.

First St.

Second St.

Third St.

Fourth St.

Philip St.

Brainard St.

Josephine St.

St. Andrew St.

Felicity St.

Oretha Castle Haley Blvd.

Euterpe St.

Terpsichore St.

Martin Luther King Jr. Blvd.

New Orleans Jazz Market
15

The McKenna Museum of African-American Art

Streetcar

3

7

2

Prytania St.

Jackson Ave.

St. Charles Ave.

St. Charles Ave.

GARDEN DISTRICT

9

Philip St.

3

16

The Seven Sisters

Morris-Israel House

Carroll-Crawford House

1

2

18

11

5

14

12

13

Prytania St.

6

10

1

Lafayette Cemetery No. 1

Coliseum St.

Chestnut St.

Washington Ave.

Camp St.

Magazine Street
1

Second St.

Third St.

Fourth St.

Constance St.

Magazine St.

5

2

17

4

Streetcar

0   500 ft
0   100 m

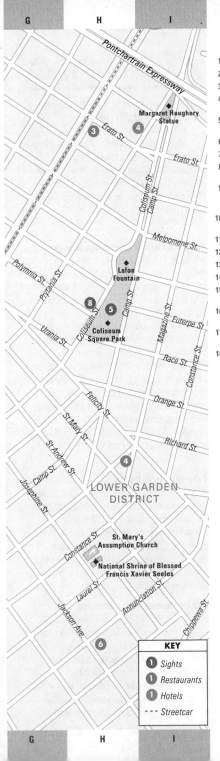

Sights ▼

1 Brevard House **E7**
2 Briggs-Staub House **D6**
3 Buckner Mansion **F6**
4 Christ Church
 Cathedral **B7**
5 Coliseum Square
 Park **H4**
6 Colonel Short's Villa **C7**
7 Eiffel Society **F5**
8 Goodrich-Stanley
 House **H4**
9 House of Broel's Victorian
 Mansion and
 Dollhouse Museum **E5**
10 Lafayette Cemetery
 No. 1 .... **C7**
11 Lonsdale House **D7**
12 Musson House **D7**
13 The Rink **C7**
14 Robinson House **D7**
15 Southern Food and
 Beverage Museum **F1**
16 Toby-Westfeldt
 House **E6**
17 Van Benthuysen-
 Elms Marision **A7**
18 Women's Guild of
 the New Orleans Opera
 Association House **D7**

Restaurants ▼

1 Commander's Palace **C7**
2 Coquette **D9**
3 Emeril's Delmonico **H2**
4 Gris-Gris **H6**
5 Molly's Rise
 and Shine **F8**
6 Turkey and the Wolf **H8**

Hotels ▼

1 Grand Victorian
 Bed & Breakfast **C6**
2 Henry Howard Hotel **F5**
3 Pontchartrain Hotel **E4**
4 The Quisby **I2**
5 Sully Mansion **C7**

goods were arriving from upriver. Spotting a need for more-protective shipping materials, he developed the burlap sack and made a fortune, only to lose it all in the 1837 depression. Lonsdale turned to coffee importing, and in order to stretch his supply, he thought to cut the coffee grounds with chicory, a bitter root—and New Orleanians have been drinking the blend ever since. This house includes intricate cast-iron work and a carved marble entrance hall. The statue of Our Mother of Perpetual Help in the front yard is a remnant of the house's more than 70 years as an active Catholic chapel. ⊠ *2521–2523 Prytania St., Garden District.*

Musson House

HOUSE | This Italianate house was built by impressionist Edgar Degas's maternal uncle, Michel Musson—a rare Creole inhabitant of the predominantly American Garden District. Musson had moved to his Esplanade Street residence before Degas visited New Orleans, so it's unlikely the artist ever stayed at this address. A subsequent owner added the famous "lace" iron galleries. ⊠ *1331 Third St., Garden District.*

The Rink

STORE/MALL | This collection of shops was once the location of the South's first roller-skating rink. Locals browse the **Garden District Book Shop,** which stocks regional and antiquarian books, along with an assortment of autographed first editions by regional writers. Another favorite is **Judy at the Rink,** an upscale gifts and housewares boutique. ⊠ *2727 Prytania St., Garden District.*

Robinson House

HOUSE | Built in 1859 and styled after an Italian villa, this home is one of the largest in the district. Doric and Corinthian columns support its rounded galleries. It is believed to be the first house in New Orleans with "waterworks," as indoor plumbing was called then. ⊠ *1415 Third St., Garden District.*

Speak Big Easy 👁

The "muse streets" that transverse the lower Garden District are not pronounced like the Greek goddess names you may recall. New Orleanians have their own way of speaking: Calliope isn't "kal-eye-oh-pee"—it's "kal-ee-ope," Melpomene is pronounced "mel-puh-meen," and Terpsichore is "terp-sih-core."

Southern Food and Beverage Museum

MUSEUM | This 30,000-square-foot museum was designed to educate visitors on the vast amount of knowledge and art that has accrued around two near-obsessions in the South: eating and drinking. Exhibits feature information on fishermen, farmers, and chefs as well as the many cultures that contribute to this region's tradition of cocktails and cuisine. There's a food gift shop and a tasting room with chef demonstrations; call ahead for updates, current exhibitions, and programs. ⊠ *1504 OC Haley Blvd., Garden District* ☎ *504/569–0405* ⊕ *www. southernfood.org* ⊠ *$10.50* ⊗ *Closed Tues.*

Toby-Westfeldt House

HOUSE | Dating to the 1830s, this Greek Revival cottage sits amid a plantationlike garden, surrounded by a copy of the original white-picket fence. Businessman Thomas Toby moved to New Orleans and had the house raised aboveground to protect it from flooding. ⊠ *2340 Prytania St., Garden District.*

Van Benthuysen-Elms Mansion

HOUSE | Built in 1869, this stately Italianate mansion served as the German consulate in the early 20th century, until the start of World War II. The house has been meticulously maintained and furnished with period pieces, and is now mainly a venue for private receptions and special events. Highlights include

Lafayette Cemetery No. 1 has been an important part of New Orleans history since 1833.

a carved-oak staircase and mantelpiece and 24-karat gilt moldings and sconces. ✉ *3029 St. Charles Ave., Garden District* ☎ *504/895–9200* 🌐 *www.elmsmansion.com.*

Women's Guild of the New Orleans Opera Association House

HOUSE | This Greek Revival house, built in 1865, has an octagonal turret added in the late 19th century. The last private owner, Nettie Seebold, willed the estate to the Women's Guild in 1965. It's still furnished today with 18th- and 19th-century European and American pieces. Tours are available Monday through Wednesday, given on an ad hoc basis with no advance reservations required. In addition, walking tour companies will schedule a visit here as part of their tours. ✉ *2504 Prytania St., Garden District* ☎ *504/267–9539* 🌐 *neworleansopera.org/womens-guild* 🎫 *$15* 🕒 *No public tours Memorial Day–Labor Day.*

🍴 Restaurants

Although a stroll through this quiet enclave of stately antebellum mansions is an essential part of a New Orleans trip, the dining options here are limited, since most of the area is residential. The handful of recommended restaurants, however, are some of the city's most talked about.

★ Commander's Palace

$$$$ | **CREOLE** | No restaurant captures New Orleans's gastronomic heritage and celebratory spirit as well as this grande dame of New Orleans fine dining. The menu's classics include a spicy and meaty turtle soup; shrimp and tasso Henican (shrimp stuffed with ham, with pickled okra); and a wonderful pecan-crusted Gulf fish. **Known for:** historic gem; one of the best jazz brunches in the city; strict dress code (no shorts, T-shirts, or ripped jeans allowed). [$] *Average main: $38* ✉ *1403 Washington Ave., Garden District* ☎ *504/899–8221* 🌐 *www.commanderspalace.com.*

Take a Peek

The Women's Guild of the New Orleans Opera Association House conducts interior tours. It's one of the few houses in the Garden District open to the public.

WALK-IN TOURS
MONDAYS 10-12 AND 1-4

THIS PROPERTY
IS LISTED ON THE
NATIONAL REGISTER OF HISTORIC PLACES

The Greek Revival design by
architect William A. Freret
was built for Edward A. Davis in 1859.
Dr. and Mrs. Herman de Bachelle Seebold
purchased the home in 1944 and
donated the mansion, furnishings and art
in 1965 to the
Women's Guild
of the
New Orleans Opera Association.

★ Coquette

$$$ | **AMERICAN** | Every neighborhood needs a hangout, and the dwellers of the Garden District's elegant mansions tend to spend their time at this fabulous corner bistro, enhanced by elaborate chandeliers and a gleaming white-tile floor. The relentlessly creative chef changes the menu almost nightly, making every meal here a new adventure. **Known for:** creative menus focusing on stellar fresh seafood; warm vibe; nice views over Magazine Street. [$] *Average main: $26* ✉ *2800 Magazine St., Garden District* ☎ *504/265–0421* 🌐 *www.coquettenola.com* 🕒 *Closed Mon. No lunch.*

★ Emeril's Delmonico

$$$$ | **CREOLE** | Chef Emeril Lagasse bought the century-old Delmonico restaurant in 1998 and converted it into a large, extravagant restaurant serving some of the most ambitious reinterpretations of classic Creole dishes in town. Prime dry-aged steaks with traditional sauces have emerged as a specialty in recent years, but the menu gets more ambitious by the month. **Known for:** house-cured charcuterie; inventive Creole plates; lavish dining room. [$] *Average main: $35* ✉ *1300 St. Charles Ave., Garden District* ☎ *504/525–4937* 🌐 *www.emerilsrestaurants.com* 🕒 *No lunch Mon.–Thurs.*

★ Gris-Gris

$$$ | **SOUTHERN** | If you're looking for an opportunity to converse with a top New Orleans chef, then Gris-Gris is your best bet. The first level of this Magazine Street restaurant is a wrap-around chef's table where you can watch all the action in the kitchen while enjoying homey and refined classics like shrimp and gris-gris grits and chicken gizzards served with grit cakes, carmelized peppers and onions, and gravy. **Known for:** engaging atmosphere; classy comfort food; great cocktails. [$] *Average main: $25* ✉ *1800 Magazine St., Garden District* ☎ *504/272–0241* 🌐 *www.grisgrisnola.com.*

Molly's Rise and Shine

$ | **AMERICAN** | **FAMILY** | In this second restaurant from Turkey and the Wolf chef Mason Hereford, attention is turned to the classics of breakfast food. Decorated with '80s and '90s pop culture memorabilia, Molly's Rise and Shine feels like a trip down memory lane, and so do its riffs on McMuffins and bagel bites. **Known for:** nostalgic charm; greasy breakfast classics; running out of the most popular dishes, so coming early is smart. [$] *Average main: $10* ✉ *2368 Magazine St., Garden District* ☎ *504/302–1896* 🌐 *www.mollysriseandshine.com* 🕒 *Closed Tues. No dinner.*

Turkey and the Wolf

$ | **AMERICAN** | **FAMILY** | A young, energetic team adds gourmet touches (all meat is cured in-house) to over-the-top comfort foods at Turkey and the Wolf: towering fried bologna sandwiches, deviled eggs with crispy chicken skins, and cheesy melts with peppered dressing. The vibe is pleasantly divey, a cross between grandma's kitchen and a hipster's haven. **Known for:** huge sandwiches; long lines; energetic crowd. [$] *Average main: $8* ✉ *739 Jackson Ave., Garden District* ☎ *504/218–7428* 🌐 *www.turkeyandthewolf.com* 🕒 *Closed Tues. No dinner.*

Hotels

★ Grand Victorian Bed & Breakfast

$$ | **B&B/INN** | This escape from the New Orleans hoopla more than lives up to its lofty name with well-appointed rooms that evoke old Louisiana through period antiques and distinctive private baths. **Pros:** elegant atmosphere; on the St. Charles Avenue streetcar line and close to key Garden District dining; free Wi-Fi throughout the house and guest rooms. **Cons:** limited parking; not within easy walking distance of the French Quarter or CBD; usually requires a three-night minimum stay. [$] *Rooms from: $208*

✉ *2727 St. Charles Ave., Garden District* ☎ *504/895–1104, 800/977–0008* ⊕ *www.gvbb.com* ⇥ *8 rooms* ¶⊙¶ *Free breakfast.*

★ Henry Howard Hotel

$$$ | **HOTEL** | A historic mansion reinvented as a chic boutique hotel, rooms have high ceilings, four-poster beds, and modern amenities. **Pros:** large, quiet rooms; close to Magazine Street; a good mix of history and style. **Cons:** no on-site restaurant; lacking amenities like gym or pool; residential street might be too quiet for some. ⓢ *Rooms from: $229* ✉ *2041 Prytania St., Garden District* ☎ *504/313–1577* ⊕ *henryhowardhotel.com* ⇥ *19 rooms* ¶⊙¶ *No meals.*

Pontchartrain Hotel

$$$ | **HOTEL** | A team of local experts restored this 1930s hotel to its former glory with inventive decor and excellent dining options. **Pros:** excellent bars and restaurants on-site; lots of style; convenient but quieter part of town. **Cons:** not as much in the immediate walking area as other parts of town; comings and goings of bar patrons makes for a noisy lobby; atmosphere might be too lively for some guests. ⓢ *Rooms from: $249* ✉ *2031 St. Charles Ave., Garden District* ☎ *504/206–3114* ⊕ *www.thepontchartrainhotel.com* ⇥ *106 rooms* ¶⊙¶ *No meals.*

★ The Quisby

$ | **HOTEL** | This spacious European-style hostel is a great budget-friendly option, especially during Mardi Gras, when parades roll right past your window. **Pros:** fun lobby bar; much more than you would expect from a hostel; very affordable. **Cons:** shared rooms and bathrooms; single beds; common·spaces are quite active. ⓢ *Rooms from: $55* ✉ *1225 St. Charles Ave., Garden District* ☎ *504/208–4881* ⊕ *www.thequisby.com* ⇥ *30 rooms* ¶⊙¶ *Free breakfast.*

Sully Mansion

$$ | **B&B/INN** | Famous 19th-century architect Thomas Sully built this handsome, rambling Queen Anne–style house in 1890. **Pros:** old-world charm; individualized attention to guests; great breakfasts. **Cons:** a mile or so from the French Quarter; most rooms are only accessible by stairs; parking is free, but it's street parking. ⓢ *Rooms from: $158* ✉ *2631 Prytania St., Garden District* ☎ *504/891–0457* ⊕ *www.sullymansion.com* ⇥ *10 rooms* ¶⊙¶ *Free breakfast.*

🍸 Nightlife

Near downtown and right on the streetcar line, the Garden District is relatively easy to reach and offers numerous options for dining and going out, especially along St. Charles Avenue, the main thoroughfare. Running parallel, just a few blocks toward the river, Magazine Street is another corridor rich with restaurants, bars, and nightspots. St. Charles Avenue tends to offer a more upscale and elegant version of nightlife, with historic venues and a touch of haute couture, while Magazine Street caters to a younger crowd of students and young professionals looking for vibrant neighborhood hangouts, beer gardens, and sidewalk cafés.

BARS AND LOUNGES

The Avenue Pub

BARS/PUBS | Beer lovers from around the globe make a beeline to this 24-hour neighborhood joint with pressed-tin ceilings. Boasting the best beer selection in New Orleans, the bar hosts a regular schedule of tastings and special events. The whiskey selection also ranks among the top in town. Sip your pint on the wraparound balcony upstairs, where you can watch streetcars roll past on St. Charles Avenue. ✉ *1732 St. Charles Ave., Garden District* ☎ *504/586–9243* ⊕ *www.theavenuepub.com.*

Barrel Proof

BARS/PUBS | This dimly lit whiskey bar is popular with the local service industry crowd. The bar boasts more than 250 types of the spirit, and the kitchen serves a menu of meat and cheese dishes that pair well with whiskey sipping. ⊠ *1201 Magazine St., Garden District* ☎ *504/299–1888* ⊕ *www.barrelproofnola. com.*

The Bulldog

BARS/PUBS | The postcollege set claims most of the seats on the beautiful brick patio here, with its views of the Magazine Street bustle and a fountain made from dozens of beer taps. The dog-friendly venue bills itself as "Uptown's International Beer Tavern," and it backs up that boast with 50 different brews on tap and more than 100 bottles. Solid bar food keeps patrons well fueled, but during crawfish season, boiled mudbugs from the seafood market across the street are the preferred fare. ⊠ *3236 Magazine St., Garden District* ☎ *504/891–1516* ⊕ *bulldog.draftfreak.com.*

Garden District Pub

BARS/PUBS | Just down the block from some of Magazine Street's finest boutiques, you'll find this neighborhood haunt that exudes the ambience of a 19th-century pub. Its exposed-brick walls and copper-top bar are completed with Sazeracs and absinthe on the terrific drinks menu. It's a great place to end a day of exploring or to get the evening started, while mingling among neighborhood denizens. ⊠ *1916 Magazine St., Garden District* ☎ *504/267–3392* ⊕ *www. gardendistrictpub1916.com.*

★ Hot Tin

BARS/PUBS | The view from this hip penthouse bar is unbeatable, but if you can't get a seat outside, curl up in a plush booth under the plated tin ceiling and enjoy the Tennessee Williams-inspired memorabilia filling the walls. Even the cocktails are served in antique glassware.

⊠ *The Pontchartrain Hotel, 2031 St. Charles Ave., Garden District* ☎ *504/323–1500* ⊕ *www.hottinbar.com.*

Parasol's Restaurant & Bar

BARS/PUBS | Roast beef po'boy devotees genuflect at the mention of this friendly hole-in-the-wall, which for more than 60 years has served the sloppy sandwiches along with Guinness on tap. The annual St. Patrick's Day block party at Parasol's spills out into the surrounding lower Garden District neighborhood; it's grown so large that police have had to erect barricades to keep traffic out—or to keep the revelers in. ⊠ *2533 Constance St., Garden District* ☎ *504/302–1543.*

Tracey's

BARS/PUBS | This cavernous sports bar and neighborhood pub comes with a backstory. The owners used to manage Parasol's, a nearby dive famous for its roast beef po'boys. When new owners at Parasol's forced them out, they took their recipe and most of their regulars around the corner to this larger location on Magazine Street. And, well, now the neighborhood has two great bars with stellar roast beef po'boys. ⊠ *2604 Magazine St., Garden District* ☎ *504/897–5403* ⊕ *www.traceysnola.com.*

🎭 Performing Arts

New Orleans Shakespeare Festival at Tulane

THEATER | Tulane's Shakespeare Festival, at the university's Dixon Concert Hall, interprets the Bard's work in a series of three to four imaginative, high-quality productions each season. ⊠ *Tulane University, Garden District* ☎ *504/865–5106* ⊕ *www.neworleansshakespeare.org.*

★ Trinity Artist Series

MUSIC | Gratifying concerts of all types—solo, choral, orchestral, and chamber—fill the vaulted interior of Trinity Episcopal Church most Sunday evenings. Organized by local organist Albinas Prizgintas, the series features both local and regional artists, though the occasional star passes through. Admission is free, and a relaxed, enjoyable evening is assured. And if you're fortunate enough to be in town the right weekend in late March or early April, don't miss "Bach Around the Clock," a 29-hour performance marathon that features everything from the eponymous composer's fugues and variations to classic rock hits arranged for organ. ✉ *1329 Jackson Ave., Garden District* ☎ *504/522–0276* ⊕ *www.trinityartistseries.com.*

🛍 Shopping

A winding, 6-mile strip of kitsch, commerce, funk, and fashion, Magazine Street is a shopper's mecca, a browser's paradise, and a perch for prime people-watching. It meanders from Uptown through the Garden District to downtown. Young professionals, college students, and hipsters flock to the area's funky vintage shops, cafés, boutiques, restaurants, and casual bars. Clothing stores here run from on-trend casual wear to vintage and consignment goods to high-end designer apparel. The street houses mostly locally owned stores, but there are also a few chains. Antiques and home furnishing shops also are scattered throughout.

City buses provide transportation to and along Magazine Street, and streetcars travel St. Charles Avenue, which is a short walk away. Walking the 6-mile length of Magazine is possible, but some blocks have more stores than others, and you're better off making a plan and deciding your focus beforehand. If you're looking for a clothing-driven shopping experience, for example, try the blocks farther west, between Nashville and Jefferson avenues, where there are a number of stores carrying designer labels. Between Jackson Avenue and Felicity Street, to the east, you'll find a stretch of shops selling eco-friendly attire and accessories, menswear, and home decor. The blocks between Louisiana and Washington avenues are filled with popular restaurants, bars, and boutiques. Detailed maps are available from the Magazine Street Merchants Association.

Magazine Street Merchants Association
SHOPPING NEIGHBORHOODS | The Magazine Street Merchants Association publishes a free brochure with maps and descriptions of the myriad stores, galleries, restaurants, and shops that line the city's boutique strip; it's available in hotels and stores, or you can request or download one from the association's website. ✉ *New Orleans* ☎ *504/342–4435* ⊕ *www.magazinestreet.com.*

ANTIQUES AND COLLECTIBLES
As You Like It Silver Shop
ANTIQUES/COLLECTIBLES | Everything you'd want in silver is available here, with a bounty of discontinued, hard-to-find, and obsolete American sterling-silver tea services, trays, and flatware. Victorian pieces, art nouveau and art deco items, and engraved pillboxes round out the selection. The store also offers monogramming, repair, and sterling-silver pattern identification. ✉ *3033 Magazine St., Garden District* ☎ *800/897–6915* ⊕ *www.asyoulikeitsilvershop.com.*

La Belle Nouvelle Orleans
ANTIQUES/COLLECTIBLES | In this eclectic shop, industrial lighting and reclaimed building materials mix with European antique furniture, artwork, porcelain, sculpture, and oddities from the 18th to 20th centuries. An open-air patio outfitted with garden benches, fountains, and other outdoor decor is linked to the main showroom by a warehouse-type gallery stacked almost floor to ceiling with furniture, salvaged doors, and other architectural items. ✉ *2112 Magazine St., Garden District* ☎ *504/581–3733* ⊕ *www.labellenouvelle.com.*

Magazine Antique Mall

ANTIQUES/COLLECTIBLES | If you are easily overwhelmed, you should take a deep breath before you walk into this expansive shop, where every possible inch of counter and shelf space is filled with antiques and vintage goods. You will find an array of costume and fine jewelry, vintage photographs, antique clocks, home decor, glassware, clothing, silver, furniture, china and ceramics, and a variety of other collectibles from a number of vendors. ⊠ *3017 Magazine St., Garden District* ☎ *504/896–9994.*

ARTWORK

Derby Pottery

MUSEUM | Fragments of wrought ironwork and other architectural details form the inspiration for many of Mark Derby's beautiful pottery pieces, from mugs and vases to handmade Victorian reproduction tiles. His clocks and plaques, fashioned from reproductions of New Orleans's historic art deco water-meter covers, have earned cult popularity, and his reproductions of letter tiles found on Crescent City street corners can be spotted all over town. ⊠ *2029 Magazine St., Garden District* ☎ *504/586–9003* ⊕ *www.derbypottery.com.*

RHINO Contemporary Crafts Co.

ART GALLERIES | The name of this shop stands for Right Here In New Orleans, which is where most of the artists involved in this upscale co-op live and work. You'll find original paintings in a variety of styles, metalwork, sculpture, ceramics, glass, functional art, jewelry, fashion accessories, and artwork made from found objects. The gallery also holds art classes for children and adults. ⊠ *2028 Magazine St., Garden District* ☎ *504/523–7945* ⊕ *www.rhinocrafts.com.*

Thomas Mann Gallery I/O

ART GALLERIES | Handmade jewelry by local artist Thomas Mann, known for his "technoromantic" pins, earrings, bracelets, and necklaces (often featuring industrial-style hearts), is showcased here, alongside work by a changing slate of other artists. The result is an eclectic mix of contemporary jewelry, housewares, sculpture, and unique gifts—the "I/O" stands for "Insight-full Objects." ⊠ *1810 Magazine St., Garden District* ☎ *504/581–2113, 800/875–2113* ⊕ *www.thomasmann.com.*

BEAUTY

★ Aidan Gill for Men

GIFTS/SOUVENIRS | Merging the attentiveness of a spa with the old-world charm of a barbershop, this high-end men's salon caters to guys who prefer getting a hot-towel shave and a haircut while enjoying a whiskey. The front of the store is devoted to manly diversions, with shaving sets, contemporary and New Orleans–theme cuff links, pocket knives, wallets, bow ties (a specialty), grooming products for face and hair, and gifts. ⊠ *2026 Magazine St., Garden District* ☎ *504/587–9090* ⊕ *www.aidangillformen.com.*

BOOKS

Garden District Book Shop

BOOKS/STATIONERY | This small store at the Rink boutique shopping center is packed with works of history, fiction, and cookbooks by local, regional, and national authors; it was the first stop on novelist Anne Rice's book tours when she lived in New Orleans. Autographed copies and limited editions of her titles are usually in stock, and the store hosts frequent author events. ⊠ *The Rink, 2727 Prytania St., Garden District* ☎ *504/895–2266* ⊕ *www.gardendistrictbookshop.com.*

CLOTHING

Defend New Orleans

CLOTHING | The stylish, minimalist designs on the T-shirts, sweatshirts, tanks, and baseball caps at this shop focus on a love for the city and its spirit. Many proceeds go to nonprofits and community organizations. An additional store can be found at the Ace Hotel New Orleans (*600 Carondolet St.*) in the Warehouse District. ⊠ *1101 First St., Garden District* ☎ *504/941–7010* ⊕ *www.defendneworleans.com.*

Funky Monkey
CLOTHING | Popular with local college students, this clothing exchange mixes new, used, and vintage apparel for men and women with hipster T-shirts, handmade costumes, and lots of quirky accessories—all at affordable prices. ⊠ *3127 Magazine St., Garden District* ☎ *504/899–5587* ⊕ *www.funkymonkeynola.com.*

Tchoup Industries
JEWELRY/ACCESSORIES | This shop represents a new movement in local, ethically sourced products with a distinct New Orleans stamp imprinted on them. Handmade shoulder bags, backpacks, fanny packs, and dopp kits are fashioned from locally grown or repurposed durable and waterproof materials. ⊠ *115 Saint Mary St., Garden District* ☎ *504/872–0726* ⊕ *www.tchoupindustries.com.*

FOOD
★ Southern Food and Beverage Museum Gift Shop
FOOD/CANDY | The Southern Food and Beverage Museum documents and celebrates Southern culinary heritage, so its gift shop, of course, carries some of the best cookbooks from the South. It also has food-related and New Orleans–centric gifts, cooking utensils, and vintage and modern cocktail tools and manuals. ⊠ *1504 OC Haley Blvd., Uptown* ☎ *504/569–0405* ⊕ *www.southernfood.org.*

HOUSEWARES
★ perch
HOUSEHOLD ITEMS/FURNITURE | Eclectic, feminine, and contemporary, this store's home furnishings are the sort you'd find in a high-end architectural magazine. If you love the look but don't have the

Looking for Lagniappe 👁

A *lagniappe* (pronounced LAN-yap), a little something extra, is a tradition in New Orleans, whether it's getting a free taste of fudge at the candy store, free whipped cream on your latte, or an unexpected balloon animal from the clowns who entertain visitors on Jackson Square.

8

The Garden District

decorating gene, the staff provide interior design services. ⊠ *2844 Magazine St., Garden District* ☎ *504/899–2122* ⊕ *www.perch-home.com.*

Spruce Eco-Studio
HOUSEHOLD ITEMS/FURNITURE | Even if you aren't looking for environmentally friendly furniture and accessories, this chic home-decor store is worth a visit for its carefully chosen collection of Jonathan Adler ceramics and lamps, John Robshaw bedding, and Greenform outdoor items. The owner has a sharp eye for design, and an environmental consciousness that makes going green seem smart and easy. Note that you can visit by appointment only. ⊠ *2043 Magazine St., Garden District* ☎ *504/265–0946* ⊕ *www.sprucenola.com.*

JEWELRY
Gogo Jewelry
JEWELRY/ACCESSORIES | You'll find yourself in a good mood after spending just a few minutes in this store surrounded by Gogo Borgerding's brightly colored jewelry designs. Her vibrant cuff bracelets, made of sterling silver and anodized aluminum, are the store's signature pieces. The boutique also carries her sterling-silver necklaces, rings, and other items, as well as works by a few other artists. A quirky blend of kitsch and high-end, the shop also features offbeat items like

paint-by-number sets and taxidermy. ✉ *2036 Magazine St., Suite A, Garden District* ☎ *504/529–8868* ⊕ *www. ilovegogojewelry.com.*

MUSIC

Peaches Records

MUSIC STORES | This locally owned music shop specializes in vinyl as well as CDs, with a focus on New Orleans rap, hip-hop, and bounce. You'll also find jazz, gospel, classic soul, and a few music accessories, along with the record store's signature apparel. ✉ *4318 Magazine St., Garden District* ☎ *504/282–3322* ⊕ *www. peachesrecordsandtapes.com.*

NOVELTIES AND GIFTS

Lionheart Prints

GIFTS/SOUVENIRS | Local designer Liz Maute Cooke is known for her witty and whimsical hand-printed greeting cards, sold in this shop alongside her signature apparel, paper goods, and other curated small gifts. The shop also holds workshops on letterpress printing and other crafts. ✉ *3312 Magazine St., Garden District* ☎ *504/267–5299* ⊕ *www. lionheartprints.com.*

Chapter 9

UPTOWN AND CARROLLTON-RIVERBEND

Updated by
Katie Fernelius

👁 Sights
★★☆☆☆

🍴 Restaurants
★★★☆☆

🛏 Hotels
★☆☆☆☆

🛍 Shopping
★★★★☆

🍸 Nightlife
★★★☆☆

RIDING THE STREETCAR

View the beautiful mansions and experience the fun local vibe of Uptown via the St. Charles Avenue streetcar, which runs the length of the avenue, from Canal Street right outside of the French Quarter to Carrollton-Riverbend. The relaxing ride takes about an hour and costs $1.25 one-way.

If you're coming from the French Quarter, board at Canal and Carondelet. Jump off at Jackson Avenue (a 20-minute ride) and follow our Garden District Walking Tour (⇨ see Chapter 2). Reboard at Louisiana Avenue, which forms the boundary between the Garden District and Uptown. As you approach Louisiana Avenue, the huge white mansion on your left at the intersection was formerly the **Bultman Funeral Home,** whose interiors inspired Tennessee Williams when he was writing his play Suddenly Last Summer. It's now a Fresh Market grocery store. Note that unless you have an unlimited day pass ($3) for the streetcar, you'll need to ask for a 25¢ transfer when you pay—otherwise you'll have to pay the full $1.25 (exact change) each time you board.

STREETCAR HISTORY

In the 1900s, streetcars were the most prominent mode of public transit in New Orleans, and by the early 20th century, the city had almost 200 miles of streetcar lines; a ride cost just 5¢. In the 1920s, buses started to overtake the old-fashioned system. Four lines operate today, with plans for expansion under way.

The St. Charles streetcar line runs through Uptown (above) and the CBD (right page, top).

The **Columns Hotel,** built in 1883 as a private home, is on the right after Peniston Street. It's a great place for a cocktail on the grand veranda or for a casual brunch on Sunday. Next, you'll pass the Gothic-style **Rayne Memorial Methodist Church,** built in 1875, one block past the hotel on the left. The 1887 Queen Anne–style **Grant House** up the block was designed by local architect Thomas Sully, with a decorative porch and balcony balustrades.

As you continue, the large avenue at the next stop is Napoleon. The spectacular **Academy of the Sacred Heart,** a private girls' school, is on the right in the next block, past Jena Street. Across the street, the Mediterranean **Smith House** claims one of the most picturesque settings on the avenue. It was built in 1906 for William Smith, president of the New Orleans Cotton Exchange. The **Anthemion,** at 4631 St. Charles Avenue, designed by architect Frank P. Gravely, is an early example of Colonial Revival architecture. The **Brown House,** on the right before Bordeaux Street, is one of the largest mansions on St. Charles Avenue.

Several houses in the next block are turn-of-the-20th-century buildings that emulate an antebellum style. On the left, at No. 4920, is the Colonial Revival **Rosenberg House,** built in 1911. At No. 5120 is the **Milton H. Latter Memorial**

Library, inside a beaux-arts mansion. It's one of the few mansions along St. Charles open to the public.

Several blocks ahead, the **Benjamin House,** between Octavia and Joseph streets, is a stunning mansion (circa 1916) with a stone facade designed by the architect Emile Weil. On the next block, past Joseph Street on the right, is the **McCarthy House,** a 1903 Colonial Revival home with ornate columns and flattop doors and windows. The plantation home used in the film *Gone With the Wind* was a set, but it served as inspiration for the columned New Orleans **Tara,** built in 1941, at the corner of Arabella.

As you cross Nashville Avenue, the **Wedding Cake House,** an elaborate Victorian mansion built circa 1896, is on the right. Its most notable feature is the beveled leaded glass in its front door, one of the most beautiful entryways in the city. As you enter the university district, dominating the next block on the left is the neo-Gothic **St. Charles Avenue Presbyterian Church.**

Castles House, on the left after State Street, is in the Colonial Revival style, as is the **St. Charles Avenue Christian Church,** two blocks up on the left. On the right, across from the church, is **Temple Sinai,** the first Reform Jewish congregation in New Orleans. This

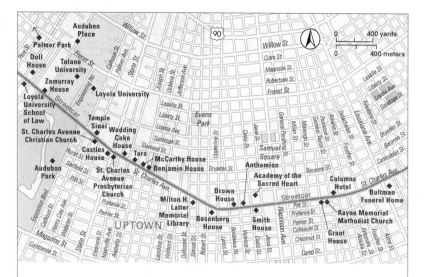

building dates from 1928; the annex on the corner was built in 1970.

Just beyond Calhoun Street, **Loyola University,** on the right, takes up the block after Temple Sinai. **Tulane University,** founded in 1834, is directly beside Loyola. Campuses for both universities extend several blocks off the avenue. On the left, across the avenue from the two universities, is **Audubon Park.**

Back on the streetcar, the heavy stone archway on the right just after Tulane University is the guarded entrance to **Audubon Place.** The private drive has some of the most elegant mansions in the city. **Zemurray House,** the columned white home facing the archway, was built in 1908 by the cotton broker William T. Jay, who sold it to Samuel Zemurray, head of the United Fruit Company. It is now the official residence of Tulane's president. The **Doll House,** a miniature house in the corner yard on the right at Broadway, is said to be the smallest house in New Orleans with its own postal address.

At Broadway, to the left, is the **Loyola University School of Law,** an Italianate building that housed the Dominican Sisters and the college they operated until the 1980s. The street continues several more stops past Broadway along St. Charles until it turns at the Riverbend onto Carrollton Avenue, once the entrance to a former resort town.

You'll travel through the Carrollton-Riverbend neighborhood before reaching the end of the line at **Palmer Park,** where an arts market is held the last Saturday of every month. Reboard the streetcar headed downtown at South Carrolton Avenue and Claiborne Avenue, where the St. Charles Avenue line both begins and ends.

NEIGHBORHOOD SNAPSHOT

TOP REASONS TO GO

The streetcar. Take a scenic and leisurely streetcar ride from Canal Street to Audubon Park, ogling the stately mansions that stretch along St. Charles Avenue.

Audubon Park and Zoo. Considered one of the best in the nation, Audubon Zoo offers a wide range of interesting exhibits for visitors of all ages. The adjoining park has beautiful walking trails lined with 100-year-old oaks.

Carrollton-Riverbend. This bustling neighborhood along Oak Street, Maple Street, and South Carrollton Avenue has restaurants, shops, and popular hangouts for college students and locals.

Shopping. Magazine Street is the city's premier shopping destination.

GETTING HERE AND AROUND

Uptown and Carrollton-Riverbend are easily walkable neighborhoods. The **St. Charles Avenue streetcar** is a reliable and picturesque mode of transportation. It runs approximately every 10 minutes, 24 hours a day (less frequently nights and weekends), from Canal Street at the edge of the French Quarter to South Claiborne Avenue. It stops at all main intersections across St. Charles Avenue, leaving you within walking distance of Audubon Park and Zoo. Expect the entire ride, from Canal Street to Carrollton-Riverbend, to take about an hour (longer during rush hour or on holidays or weekends). Visit the RTA's website (⊕ www.norta.com) for updates. The **No. 11 bus** runs the length of Magazine Street up to Audubon Park from Canal Street. It runs every 20 minutes, making stops at five major intersections. The fare is $1.25 for both the streetcar and the bus.

MAKING THE MOST OF YOUR TIME

You could easily spend two days in this neighborhood: a full day visiting the **Audubon Zoo** and enjoying the park that surrounds it, and another day exploring the boutiques, galleries, and restaurants along **Magazine Street.**

QUICK BITES

■ **Audubon Clubhouse Café.** Eat in an airy dining room overlooking Audubon Park golf course, or relax with a drink on the veranda. ⊠ *6500 Magazine St., Uptown* ✛ *Turn onto Golf Club Dr.* ☎ *504/212–5285* ⊕ *www.auduboninstitute. org* ⊟ *No credit cards* ☾ *No dinner.*

■ **Refuel Café.** This modern café serves fresh salads and sandwiches. At brunch, try the hand-whisked grits. ⊠ *8124 Hampson St., Carrollton-Riverbend* ☎ *504/872–0187* ⊕ *www. refuelcafe.com* ⊟ *No credit cards* ☾ *No dinner.*

SAFETY

■ Most of Uptown and Carrollton-Riverbend is safe to walk around during the day and evening. However, take extra care when walking at night in the area between Magazine Street and the river up to Jefferson. Also avoid the area close to the river west of Audubon Park and dark side streets when out late at night.

Discover the more residential face of New Orleans in the sprawling Uptown and Carrollton-Riverbend neighborhoods. Just a 30-minute streetcar ride from Canal Street, you'll find blocks of shops on bustling Magazine Street, stunning homes along oak-lined streets, and the first-class Audubon Park and Zoo. Head farther into Uptown and spend a couple of hours walking the length of the levee in Riverbend for stunning views of the Mississippi.

Uptown

Uptown encompasses the area upriver from Louisiana Avenue between Tchoupitoulas Street and South Claiborne Avenue, on the west side of the Garden District. Stately mansions line the length of St. Charles Avenue, where you'll likely see colorful Mardi Gras beads hanging from tree limbs throughout the year. Traveling along the avenue from downtown to Uptown provides something of a historical narrative: the city's development unfolded upriver, and the houses grow more modern the farther up you go. Smaller shotgun and Victorian-style homes on side streets display old-world charm, and this family-oriented neighborhood is home to Loyola and Tulane universities. Magazine Street bustles with

6 miles of shops, bars, and restaurants, all the way from the CBD up to Audubon Park.

◉ Sights

Academy of the Sacred Heart
BUILDING | This Colonial Revival building, housing a Catholic girls' school, was built in 1900 and features wide, wraparound balconies (or galleries) and colonnades facing a large garden. The academy is exceptionally beautiful during the December holiday season, when the galleries are decked with wreaths and garlands. ✉ *4521 St. Charles Ave., Uptown.*

Anthemion
BUILDING | The emergence of Colonial Revival architecture in the late 19th century was expressive of local weariness with the excesses of the Greek Revival

craze that had dominated the mid-century. Anthemion is an excellent example of this return to simplicity. Built in 1896 for the druggist Christian Keppler, it served as the headquarters of the Japanese consulate from 1938 to 1941. ✉ *4631 St. Charles Ave., Uptown.*

★ Audubon Park

CITY PARK | FAMILY | Formerly the plantation of Etienne de Boré, the father of the granulated-sugar industry in Louisiana, this large, lush patch of greenery stretches from St. Charles Avenue across Magazine Street to the river. Designed by John Charles Olmsted, nephew of Frederick Law Olmsted (who laid out New York City's Central Park and Asheville's Biltmore Estate), it contains the world-class **Audubon Zoo;** a 1.8-mile track for running, walking, or biking; picnic and play areas; Audubon Park Golf Course; tennis courts; a swimming pool; horse stables; and a river view. Calm lagoons wind through the park, harboring egrets and other indigenous species. The park and zoo were named for the famous ornithologist and painter John James Audubon, who spent many years working in and around New Orleans. ✉ *6500 Magazine St., Uptown* ☎ *504/581–4629* ⊕ *www. auduboninstitute.org* 💵 *Free.*

Audubon Zoo

ZOO | FAMILY | Consistently ranked as one of the top zoos in the nation, the Audubon Zoo presents a wide array of animals in exhibits that mimic their natural habitats, including giraffes, lions, and elephants. The Louisiana Swamp exhibit re-creates the natural habitat of alligators, including a rare white alligator (technically a leucistic gator), nutrias (large swamp rodents), and catfish; feeding time is always well attended. Among other highlights are the Reptile Encounter, the Komodo dragon exhibit, and gorilla and flamingo exhibits. Several attractions are available for additional fees, including a train tour that departs every 30 minutes from the swamp exhibit. Cool Zoo, a splash park featuring a 28-foot white-alligator slide, bubbling fountains, and splash zones, has one area set aside for toddlers and young children. Gator Run is a lazy river with sand beaches, water cannons, and jumping jets. (Cool Zoo is open weekends in May, then opens daily until mid-August, when it returns to weekends only until Labor Day; separate admission to both the Cool Zoo and Gator Run attractions is $12 for nonmembers.) ✉ *6500 Magazine St., Uptown* ⊕ *www.auduboninstitute.org* 💵 *$29.95* ⊘ *Closed Mon.*

Brown House

BUILDING | This mansion, completed in 1904 for cotton magnate William Perry Brown, is one of the largest houses on St. Charles Avenue. Its solid monumental look, Syrian arches, and steep gables make it a choice example of Romanesque Revival style. ✉ *4717 St. Charles Ave., Uptown.*

Carol Robinson Gallery

MUSEUM | This two-story Uptown house features contemporary paintings and sculpture by U.S. artists, with a special nod to those from the South, including Jere Allen, David Goodman, Nell C. Tilton, and Jean Geraci. ✉ *840 Napoleon Ave., at Magazine St., Uptown* ☎ *504/895–6130* ⊕ *carolrobinsongallery.net* ⊘ *Closed Sun., Mon., and Wed.*

Castles House

HOUSE | The renowned local architect Thomas Sully designed this 1896 Colonial Revival house after the Longfellow House in Cambridge, Massachusetts. The interior has often appeared in the pages of design magazines. It was built for John Castles, president of Hibernia National Bank. ✉ *6000 St. Charles Ave., Uptown.*

Cole Pratt Gallery

MUSEUM | Contemporary paintings and sculptures by more than 40 Southern artists are displayed in this modern space. Opening receptions are held the

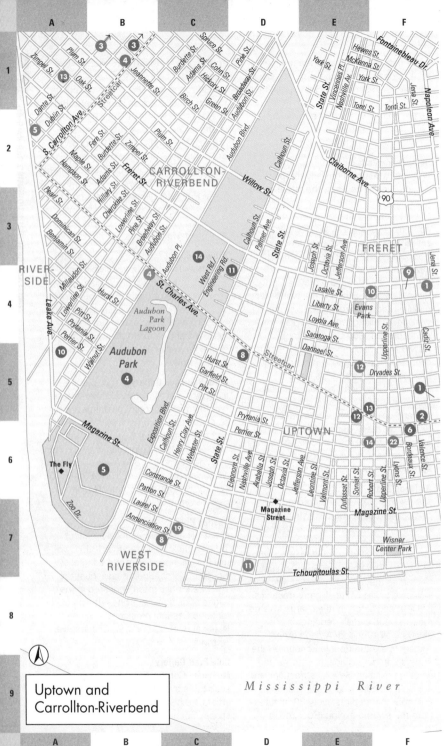

Uptown and
Carrollton-Riverbend

Mississippi River

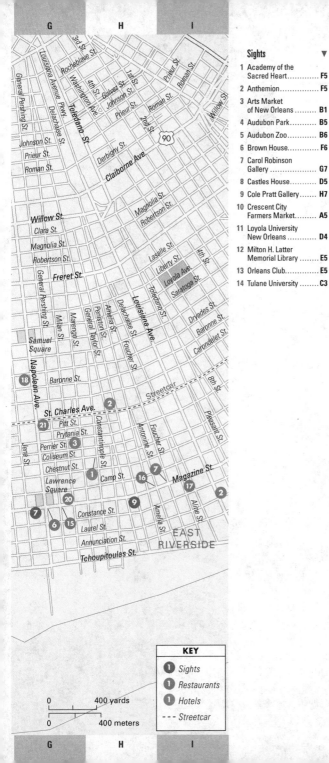

Sights ▼

1 Academy of the
  Sacred Heart............. **F5**
2 Anthemion................. **F5**
3 Arts Market
  of New Orleans......... **B1**
4 Audubon Park........... **B5**
5 Audubon Zoo............ **B6**
6 Brown House............. **F6**
7 Carol Robinson
  Gallery **G7**
8 Castles House........... **D5**
9 Cole Pratt Gallery....... **H7**
10 Crescent City
  Farmers Market......... **A5**
11 Loyola University
  New Orleans **D4**
12 Milton H. Latter
  Memorial Library **E5**
13 Orleans Club............. **E5**
14 Tulane University **C3**

Restaurants ▼

1 Ancora **F4**
2 Atchafalaya **I6**
3 Bellegarde Bakery...... **B1**
4 Boucherie **B1**
5 Brigtsen's **A2**
6 Casamento's............. **G7**
7 Cavan **I6**
8 Clancy's.................. **C7**
9 Company Burger......... **F4**
10 Dat Dog **F4**
11 Frankie & Johnny's **D7**
12 Gautreau's............... **E5**
13 Jacques-Imo's Cafe **A1**
14 La Crêpe Nanou.......... **E6**
15 La Petite Grocery **G7**
16 Lilette.................... **H6**
17 Mahony's Po-Boy
  Shop...................... **I6**
18 Pascal's Manale **G5**
19 Patois **C7**
20 Shaya ,.................... **G6**
21 Superior Seafood....... **G6**
22 Upperline **F6**

Hotels ▼

1 Chimes Bed
  and Breakfast........... **H6**
2 Columns Hotel........... **H5**
3 Maison Perrier
  Bed & Breakfast........ **G6**
4 Park View
  Guest House............. **B4**

Did You Know

The Audubon Zoo has several exhibits showcasing different natural habitats, including an African savannah where kids can get up-close-and-personal with the trees.

first Saturday of every month. ✉ *3800 Magazine St., Uptown* ☎ *504/891–6789* ⊕ *www.coleprattgallery.com* ⊗ *Closed Sun. and Mon.*

Loyola University New Orleans

COLLEGE | Chartered by the Jesuits in 1912, Loyola University is a local landmark. Its communications, music, and law programs are world-renowned. The Gothic- and Tudor-style Marquette Hall, facing St. Charles Avenue and Audubon Park, provides the backdrop for a quintessential New Orleans photo opportunity. The fourth floor of the neo-Gothic J. Edgar and Louise S. Monroe Library houses the university's Collins C. Diboll Art Gallery, open to the public seven days a week (Monday–Saturday 10 am–6 pm, Sunday noon–6 pm). ✉ *6363 St. Charles Ave., Uptown* ⊕ *www.loyno.edu.*

Milton H. Latter Memorial Library

LIBRARY | This former private house serves as the most elegant public library in New Orleans. Built in 1907, the Italianate beaux-arts mansion was once the home of the silent-movie star Marguerite Clark. The Latter family bought it and donated it to the city as a library in 1948 in memory of their son, who was killed in World War II. An extensive renovation restored the home to its former grandeur. ✉ *5120 St. Charles Ave., Uptown* ☎ *504/596–2625* ⊕ *www.neworleanspubliclibrary.org.*

Orleans Club

BUILDING | This sumptuous mansion was built in 1868 as a wedding gift from Colonel William Lewis Wynn to his daughter. The side building, on the Uptown side of the main building, is an auditorium added in the 1950s. The house is closed to the public, but serves as headquarters to a ladies' social club and hosts many debutante teas and wedding receptions. ✉ *5005 St. Charles Ave., Uptown.*

Tulane University

COLLEGE | Next to Loyola on St. Charles Avenue, Tulane University's three original

buildings face the avenue: **Tilton Hall** (1902) on the right, **Gibson Hall** (1894) in the middle, and **Dinwiddie Hall** (1923) on the left. The Romanesque style, with its massive stone composition and arches, is repeated in several buildings around the quad. More modern campus buildings extend another three blocks to the north, including Newcomb Art Museum, a 3,600-square-foot exhibition facility offering contemporary and historical exhibits (free; closed Sunday and Monday). Tulane offers undergraduate, graduate, and professional degrees in liberal arts, science and engineering, architecture, business, law, social work, medicine, public health, and tropical medicine.

The **Middle American Research Institute and Gallery** (✉ *504/865–5110;* ⊕ *mari.tulane.edu*), located on the third floor of Tulane's Dinwiddie Hall, includes the world's largest documented Guatemalan textile collection and replicas of classic Mayan sculpture. Established in 1924, the institute's collection also includes rare artifacts like poison-dart arrows from Venezuela and shrunken heads from the Brazilian rain forest. On view at the gallery is "Faces of the Maya." The pre-Columbian artifacts are complemented by a collection of books on Latin American culture housed in Tulane's main library (free; closed weekends, appointment recommended). ✉ *6823 St. Charles Ave., Uptown* ⊕ *www.tulane.edu.*

🍴 Restaurants

The homes in this residential zone range from brightly colored shotguns to imposing historic mansions. The restaurants also run the gamut: there are corner po'boy shops and seafood joints, as well as ambitious bistros. Along Magazine Street, you'll discover everything from bakeries and sno-ball stands to family eateries and nationally recognized dining destinations.

Ancora

$ | **ITALIAN** | **FAMILY** | Every dish on the short menu here shows an obsessive attention to detail. The main attraction are the pizzas, which follow Neapolitan rules and use only flour, water, yeast, and salt for their dough; they enter an 800°F oven—imported from Naples—and emerge a minute later charred and fragrant. **Known for:** authentic Italian pizza; casual neighborhood vibe; house-cured meats. [$] *Average main: $15* ✉ *4508 Freret St., Uptown* ☎ *504/324–1636* 🌐 *www.ancorapizza.com.*

Atchafalaya

$$ | **CREOLE** | Even with reservations, expect to wait for weekend brunch at this Uptown institution, but your taste buds will thank you later. Locals tend to linger over sultry Creole creations like étouffée omelets and house-made sausage, a DIY Bloody Mary bar, and jumping live jazz on Saturday and Sunday. **Known for:** Bloody Mary bar; jazz brunch; excellent shrimp and grits. [$] *Average main: $20* ✉ *901 Louisiana Ave., Uptown* ☎ *504/891–9626* 🌐 *www.atchafalayarestaurant.com* 🕒 *No lunch Tues. and Wed.*

Casamento's

$ | **SEAFOOD** | **FAMILY** | This eatery has been a haven for Uptown seafood lovers since 1919. Family members still wait tables and staff the immaculate kitchen in back, while a reliable handful of oyster shuckers ensure that plenty of cold ones are available for the standing room–only oyster bar. **Known for:** neighborhood vibe; fresh oysters; fried seafood and popular oyster loaf sandwich. [$] *Average main: $8* ✉ *4330 Magazine St., Uptown* ☎ *504/895–9761* 🌐 *www.casamentosrestaurant.com* 💳 *No credit cards* 🕒 *Closed Mon.–Wed. No lunch Sun.*

Cavan

$$ | **SOUTHERN** | Set back from Magazine Street in a gorgeous converted town house (eating on the large veranda on warm evenings is especially a treat), the sophisticated menu showcases (mostly) local seafood, as well as the best East and West Coast oysters. The whole roasted fish and anything from the raw section of the menu are always good choices. **Known for:** whole fish; fresh oysters; charming setting. [$] *Average main: $23* ✉ *3607 Magazine St., Uptown* ☎ *504/509–7655* 🌐 *www.cavannola.com* 🕒 *No lunch Mon.–Thurs.*

Clancy's

$$$ | **CREOLE** | Understatement characterizes the mood at locally beloved Clancy's, and the classy but neutral decor reflects this, though the scene can get lively. Most of the dishes are imaginative treatments of New Orleans favorites. **Known for:** local favorite; extensive wine list; exceptional veal dishes. [$] *Average main: $30* ✉ *6100 Annunciation St., Uptown* ☎ *504/895–1111* 🌐 *www.clancysneworleans.com* 🕒 *Closed Sun. No lunch Mon.–Wed. and Sat.*

★ **Company Burger**

$ | **AMERICAN** | **FAMILY** | At the Company Burger, your order is simple: the amazing signature burger comes with two fresh-ground patties, bread-and-butter pickles, American cheese, and red onions on a freshly baked bun. No lettuce and no tomatoes, but you can load it up with homemade condiments like basil or roasted-garlic mayonnaise and Creole honey mustard. **Known for:** quality burgers; affordable prices; no-frills local favorite. [$] *Average main: $8* ✉ *4600 Freret St., Uptown* ☎ *504/267–0320* 🌐 *www.thecompanyburger.com.*

★ **Dat Dog**

$ | **AMERICAN** | **FAMILY** | At Dat Dog, the sprawling stand is painted in primary hues, as if the work had been outsourced to a talented kindergarten class, and the Hawaiian shirt–clad staff bustle about with the enthusiasm of amateur actors staging a musical. The menu is all about hot dogs, and frank options range from standard German wieners to Louisiana alligator sausages. **Known for:** creative hot dogs; rowdy crowds; local draft beers. $ *Average main: $8* ✉ *5030 Freret St., Uptown* ☎ *504/899–6883* ⊕ *www. datdog.com.*

Frankie & Johnny's

$ | SEAFOOD | If you're trying to find the quintessential New Orleans neighborhood restaurant, look no further: team pennants and posers vie for space on the paneled walls of the low-ceiling bar and dining room, while a jukebox blares beneath them. From the kitchen's steaming cauldrons come boiled shrimp, crabs, and crawfish, piled high and ready to be washed down with ice-cold beer. **Known for:** fresh boiled seafood, including a classic fried-shrimp po'boy; local clientele; cold beers. $ *Average main: $11* ✉ *321 Arabella St., Uptown* ☎ *504/243–1234* ⊕ *www.frankieandjohnnys.net.*

★ Gautreau's

$$$ | MODERN AMERICAN | This vine-covered neighborhood bistro doesn't have a sign, but that hasn't stopped the national food media from finding it. Lauded chefs cook with elegant confidence in a classic French style, but with surprising bursts of understated creativity, which can be seen in dishes like seared scallops with parsnip purée and pickled chanterelles. **Known for:** well-heeled locals; hidden gem with hard-to-get reservations; caramelized banana split for dessert. $ *Average main: $30* ✉ *1728 Soniat St., Uptown* ☎ *504/899–7397* ⊕ *www.gautreausrestaurant.com* ☾ *Closed Sun. No lunch.*

La Crêpe Nanou

$$ | FRENCH | French chic for the budget-minded is the style at this welcoming neighborhood bistro, where during peak hours there might be a half-hour wait for a table. Woven café chairs on the sidewalk and awnings that resemble metro-station architecture evoke the Left Bank of Paris, and the Gallic focus is also evident in dishes like the filet mignon, served with a choice of several classic French sauces. **Known for:** tasty crepes and moules-frites; intimate, slightly crowded setting; classic French vibes.

$ *Average main: $22* ✉ *1410 Robert St., Uptown* ☎ *504/899–2670* ⊕ *www.lacrepenanou.com* ☾ *No lunch Mon.–Sat.*

La Petite Grocery

$$$ | SOUTHERN | Flower shops sometimes bloom into intimate fine-dining establishments in New Orleans, and this one, with just-bright-enough lighting and a sturdy mahogany bar, has caught on in a big way with the locals. In the kitchen, chef-owner Justin Devillier draws on contemporary American tastes, using Louisiana raw materials whenever he can. **Known for:** blue-crab beignets; neighborhood bistro vibes; nice cocktail menu. $ *Average main: $27* ✉ *4238 Magazine St., Uptown* ☎ *504/891–3377* ⊕ *www. lapetitegrocery.com* ☾ *No lunch Mon.*

Lilette

$$$ | MODERN AMERICAN | Proprietor-chef John Harris uses French and Italian culinary traditions as springboards for Lilette's inspired dishes. Look for Italian wedding soup, roasted Muscovy duck breast, and fresh crudos. **Known for:** curated wine list; intimate setting; outstanding appetizers. $ *Average main: $29* ✉ *3637 Magazine St., Uptown* ☎ *504/895–1636* ⊕ *www.lilletterestaurant.com* ☾ *Closed Sun. No lunch Mon.*

Mahony's Po-Boy Shop

$ | DELI | FAMILY | What happens when a fine-dining chef opens a po'boy joint? You get delicious local shrimp, hand-cut french fries, and nontraditional menu items like chicken livers with coleslaw or fried oysters "dressed" with rémoulade sauce. **Known for:** roast beef and fried oyster po'boys; local brews; long waits at peak meal times. $ *Average main: $10* ✉ *3454 Magazine St., Uptown* ☎ *504/899–3374* ⊕ *www.mahonyspoboys.com* 🚫 *No credit cards.*

Pascal's Manale

$$$ | ITALIAN | Barbecue shrimp is an addictive regional specialty that involves neither a barbecue nor barbecue sauce, and Pascal's is considered the dish's birthplace. The original recipe, introduced a half century ago, remains unchanged: jumbo shrimp, still in the shell, are cooked in a buttery pool enhanced with just the right amount of Creole spice and pepper. **Known for:** entertaining oyster shuckers; old-school vibes; city's original barbecue shrimp. [$] *Average main: $30* ✉ *1838 Napoleon Ave., Uptown* ☎ *504/895–4877* 🌐 *www.pascalsmanale.com* 🕒 *Closed Sun. No lunch Sat.*

★ Patois

$$$ | FRENCH | Hidden on a quiet residential corner, this bustling bistro could have been transported directly from Provence. The menu continues the French theme, but with a Louisiana attitude. **Known for:** romantic date night; local produce; French delicacies. [$] *Average main: $26* ✉ *6078 Laurel St., Uptown* ☎ *504/895–9441* 🌐 *www.patoisnola.com* 💳 *No credit cards* 🕒 *Closed Mon. and Tues. No dinner Sun. No lunch Sat., Wed., and Thurs.*

★ Shaya

$$ | ISRAELI | You may think you've been transported to sexy Tel Aviv in this softly lighted but thoroughly modern dining room set on a hopping stretch of Magazine Street. Here, the inventive Israeli cooking shines: picture copper trays bedecked with small plates of classic Israeli foods, like hummus with soft-cooked eggs, red onions, pickles, and harissa; avocado toast with smoked whitefish and pink peppercorns; and grape leaves stuffed with rice and shiitake mushrooms (plus there's puffy, made-to-order pita from Shaya's signature wood-burning oven). **Known for:** lamb ragu hummus; pita bread from the wood-burning oven; wine and spirits list with Israeli options. [$] *Average main: $18* ✉ *4213 Magazine St., Uptown* ☎ *504/891–4213* 🌐 *www.shayarestaurant.com.*

Superior Seafood

$$ | CREOLE | FAMILY | The menu at this Uptown seafood specialist reads like a greatest hits collection from the New Orleans culinary canon: from po'boys and fried green tomatoes on the casual end to stuffed catfish and shrimp andouille brochettes on the fancier side. The cavernous space mimics a Parisian bistro, with a tad too much polish to feel authentic. **Known for:** premium Mardi Gras and streetcar watching; seafood staples; high-spirited crowd, especially at brunch. [$] *Average main: $18* ✉ *4338 St. Charles Ave., Uptown* ☎ *504/293–3474* 🌐 *www.superiorseafoodnola.com.*

★ Upperline

$$$ | CREOLE | For more than 25 years, this gaily colored cottage filled with a museum's worth of regional art has defined New Orleans Creole bistro fare, combining traditional items like dark gumbo or étouffée with enough elegance to be worthy of white tablecloths. Boisterous regulars know their orders before the cocktails even arrive: perhaps fried green tomatoes with shrimp rémoulade, spicy local shrimp with jalapeño corn bread, or duck with ginger-peach sauce. **Known for:** fried green tomatoes with shrimp; historic gem; "Taste of New Orleans" sampler menu. [$] *Average main: $29* ✉ *1413 Upperline St., Uptown* ☎ *504/891–9822* 🌐 *www.upperline.com* 🕒 *Closed Mon. and Tues. No lunch.*

🛏 Hotels

★ Chimes Bed and Breakfast

$$ | B&B/INN | Charming, homey guest rooms all open onto the courtyard and have private entrances in this well-appointed B&B. **Pros:** just three blocks from the streetcar and Magazine Street; lovely courtyard for cocktails; Wi-Fi and parking included with room rate. **Cons:** noise carries easily from room to room; 3 miles from the French Quarter, which might be too far for some; books up fast. [$] *Rooms from: $158* ✉ *1146 Constantinople St., Uptown* ☎ *504/899–2621* 🌐 *www.chimesneworleans.com* 🛏 *5 rooms* 🍴 *Free breakfast.*

Columns Hotel

$$ | HOTEL | This white-column 1883 Victorian hotel drips with local charm and is listed on the National Register of Historic Places—guests especially enjoy the lovely, wide veranda. **Pros:** exquisite architecture; perfect veranda for watching the St. Charles Avenue parades during Mardi Gras; live jazz in the ballroom. **Cons:** rooms are large but need updating; transportation necessary to French Quarter and CBD; rooms don't get a lot of sunlight. $ *Rooms from: $144* ⊠ *3811 St. Charles Ave., Uptown* ☎ *504/899–9308* ⊕ *www.thecolumns.com* ⟿ *20 rooms* |❍| *Free breakfast.*

Maison Perrier Bed & Breakfast

$$ | B&B/INN | Redolent of Southern hospitality and historic elegance, this 1890s Victorian mansion is filled with antiques, local art, and many extra comforts. **Pros:** personalized service; lovely residential setting; free Wi-Fi. **Cons:** not well located if you prefer to spend most of your time in the French Quarter; no elevator; books up quickly. $ *Rooms from: $190* ⊠ *4117 Perrier St., Uptown* ☎ *504/897–1807* ⊕ *www.maisonperrier.com* ⟿ *9 rooms* |❍| *Free breakfast.*

Park View Guest House

$$ | B&B/INN | This Victorian guesthouse, steps from the streetcar and Audubon Park, adds to the delightful selection of smaller Uptown lodgings. **Pros:** great park views; good restaurants nearby; historic ambience. **Cons:** not walkable to downtown or the French Quarter; rooms can feel dated; some rooms are much smaller than others. $ *Rooms from: $179* ⊠ *7004 St. Charles Ave., Uptown* ☎ *504/861–7564* ⊕ *www.parkview-guesthouse.com* ⟿ *22 rooms* |❍| *Free breakfast.*

 # Nightlife

Uptown is rich in clubs, although they are far less concentrated here than downtown. They tend to be tucked down residential side streets or scattered along one of the main drags, and they mostly cater to the large populations of college students and young professionals who dwell in this part of town. Many are local institutions and ever-popular destinations for music lovers drawn to the beats of funk, brass, blues, and rock.

BARS AND LOUNGES

Bar Frances

BARS/PUBS | This bar's casual elegance is readily apparent during its popular happy hour, when Francophiles can enjoy pork rillette, chicken liver mousse, and Chartreuse cocktails. A small patio of bistro tables looks out onto Freret Street. ⊠ *4525 Freret St., Uptown* ☎ *504/371–5043* ⊕ *www.barfrances.com.*

★ Columns Hotel's Victorian Lounge Bar

BARS/PUBS | One of New Orleans's most traditional drinking experiences, enjoy an old-fashioned or a Sazerac here on the expansive front porch, shaded by centuries-old oak trees and overlooking the St. Charles Avenue streetcar route. Built in 1883 as a private home, the Columns has been the scene of TV ads, movies, and plenty of weddings. The interior scenes of Louis Malle's *Pretty Baby* were filmed here. The Victorian Lounge, with its restored period decor and a fireplace, has a decaying elegance marred only by the television above the bar. There's a great happy hour, too, with live jazz combos playing Monday through Friday. ⊠ *3811 St. Charles Ave., Uptown* ☎ *504/899–9308* ⊕ *www.thecolumns.com.*

Cooter Brown's

BARS/PUBS | This rambling tavern across from the Mississippi River levee boasts 400 different bottled beers and 45 on tap. That, along with the excellent cheese fries and an oyster bar, makes it a favorite haunt of students from nearby Tulane and Loyola universities, along with nostalgic alums. ⊠ *509 S. Carrollton Ave., Uptown* ☎ *504/866–9104* ⊕ *www.cooterbrowns. com.*

Cure

BARS/PUBS | This pioneer of the revitalized Freret Corridor and one of the city's first serious cocktail bars adds a touch of urban chic to a historic neighborhood. A doorman welcomes guests into a converted fire station with 20-foot ceilings and a lovely patio. Knowledgeable bartenders use a breathtaking arsenal of liquor to push the boundaries of what a drink can be. Take note that even in August, men must wear long pants on Thursday, Friday, and Saturday, and baseball caps are not allowed at any time. ⊠ 4905 Freret St., Uptown ☎ 504/302–2357 ⊕ www.curenola.com.

★ Delachaise

BARS/PUBS | A long, slender room with plush banquettes in a charming sliver of a building on a busy stretch of St. Charles Avenue looks as if it were air-dropped straight from Paris. Offering a carefully chosen (and reasonably priced) selection of beer, spirits, and wines by the glass, the menu also includes upscale small plates, such as frog legs, frites fried in goose fat, and house-made paté. ⊠ 3442 St. Charles Ave., Uptown ☎ 504/895–0858 ⊕ www.thedelachaise.com.

F&M Patio Bar

BARS/PUBS | For college kids and grown-ups reliving their youth, an all-nighter in New Orleans isn't complete until you've danced on top of a pool table at this classic hangout. There's a loud jukebox, a popular photo booth, and a late-night kitchen (it fires up around 7 pm and keeps serving until early morning). The party really gets going around 1 am, but the tropical-themed patio can actually be peaceful at times. You'll need to get here by car or taxi. ⊠ 4841 Tchoupitoulas St., Uptown ☎ 504/895–6784 ⊕ www.fandmpatiobar.com.

The Kingpin

BARS/PUBS | Deep-red walls and a velvet Elvis lend this Uptown spot a touch of kitsch, but the friendly atmosphere, jukebox stocked with vintage soul and modern rock, and young, fun crowd keep people coming back nightly. It's a frequent destination for food trucks and a favorite place to cheer on the city's beloved Saints. ⊠ 1307 Lyons St., Uptown ☎ 504/891–2373.

St. Joe's

BARS/PUBS | A young, Uptown professional crowd packs this narrow bar known for its blueberry mojitos and religious-themed decor. The narrow front bar has more crosses than a Catholic church; the back patio, strung with Chinese lanterns and decorated with statues of Asian deities, is a "Caribbean Zen temple," in the owner's words. ⊠ 5535 Magazine St., Uptown ☎ 504/899–3744 ⊕ stjoesbar.com.

Sovereign Pub

BARS/PUBS | No need to book a ticket to the United Kingdom when this cozy bar so faithfully re-creates a British pub. Even the daily newspapers come from the other side of the pond. Accordingly, you can count on a well-poured pint and warm company. ⊠ 1517 Aline St., Uptown ☎ 504/899–4116.

MUSIC CLUBS

Dos Jefes Uptown Cigar Bar

MUSIC CLUBS | A 20-minute cab ride from downtown, this popular Tchoupitoulas Street hangout for grown-ups is a lively den of blue smoke. The selection of scotches, brandies, ports, and bourbons is outstanding. The nightly live music runs the gamut of New Orleans styles. A full calendar of performances is available online. The low-key patio offers a quiet retreat from the haze. ⊠ 5535 Tchoupitoulas St., Uptown ☎ 504/891–8500 ⊕ www.dosjefes.com.

Le Bon Temps Roulé

MUSIC CLUBS | Local acts from a wide range of genres—including the Soul Rebels with their standing Thursday-night gig—shake the walls of this ramshackle Magazine Street nightspot. The music normally gets started after 10 pm. Pool tables and a limited bar-food menu keep the crowd, including plenty of students from nearby Tulane and Loyola universities, occupied until the show starts. ⊠ *4801 Magazine St., Uptown* ☎ *504/895–8117.*

Neutral Ground Coffeehouse

CAFES—NIGHTLIFE | This 1960s-style coffeehouse attracts an artsy crowd, including adventurous local high schoolers who want to hear live music, but can't get into the bars yet. Sofas, chessboards, laid-back counter service, and a bulletin board encourage an intimacy unmatched in most other cafés. On Sunday night there's an open mike for aspiring musicians. On other nights, a string of singer-songwriters and contemporary or traditional folk artists perform. It's a 20-minute cab ride from downtown and opens every night at 7 pm. ⊠ *5110 Danneel St., Uptown* ☎ *504/891–3381* ⊕ *www.neutralgroundcoffeehouse.com.*

★ Tipitina's

MUSIC CLUBS | Rub the bust of legendary New Orleans pianist Professor Longhair (aka "Fess") inside this Uptown landmark named for one of the late musician's popular songs. The old concert posters on the walls read like an honor roll of musical legends, both local and national. The midsize venue boasts an eclectic and well-curated calendar, particularly during the weeks of Jazz Fest. The long-running Sunday afternoon Cajun dance party still packs the floor. Although the neighborhood isn't dangerous, it's far enough out of the way to require a cab trip. ⊠ *501 Napoleon Ave., Uptown* ☎ *504/895–8477* ⊕ *www.tipitinas.com.*

🔊 Performing Arts

CLASSICAL MUSIC

Friends of Music

MUSIC | This organization brings superior performers from all over the world to Tulane University's Dixon Hall. Concerts take place approximately once a month,

and tickets usually cost $30 to $35. ⊠ *Willow St. entrance, Tulane University, Uptown* ☎ *504/895–0690* ⊕ *www.friendsofmusic.org.*

Roussel Performance Hall at Loyola University

DANCE | The excellent Loyola music department hosts regular performances at its Roussel Performance Hall, including guest appearances by internationally known performers and the occasional opera. The Montage Fine and Performing Arts Series spotlights students in everything from jazz to ballet. ⊠ *6363 St. Charles Ave., Uptown* ☎ *504/865–2074* ⊕ *cmfa.loyno.edu.*

FILM

Prytania Theatre

FILM | A visit to the city's last single-screen movie house, hidden in an Uptown residential area, is a reminder of the days when neighborhood movie theaters offered entertainment as well as air-conditioned relief from the summer heat. The Prytania shows first-run crowd-pleasers and the occasional independent feature. The Grindhouse Cafe sells coffee and snacks out front. ⊠ *5339 Prytania St., Uptown* ☎ *504/891–2787* ⊕ *www.prytaniatheatreneworleans.com.*

Zeitgeist Multidisciplinary Arts Center

FILM | Working with volunteer staff and a shoestring budget, Zeitgeist founder and filmmaker Rene Broussard established this funky and eclectic space as a venue for experimental theater. It later developed into the city's center for alternative cinema, though it continues to stage live performances as well. ⊠ *1618 OC Haley Blvd., Uptown* ☎ *504/352–1150* ⊕ *www. zeitgeistnola.org.*

THEATER

New Orleans Shakespeare Festival at Tulane

THEATER | Tulane's Shakespeare Festival, at the university's Dixon Concert Hall, interprets the Bard's work in a series of three to four imaginative, high-quality productions each season. ⊠ *Tulane University, Uptown* ☎ *504/865–5106* ⊕ *www.neworleansshakespeare.org.*

Summer Lyric Theatre

THEATER | This theater produces three crowd-pleasing musicals every summer at Tulane's Dixon Hall. Tickets run from $5 to $35 and tend to sell out fast. ⊠ *Tulane University, Uptown* ☎ *504/865–5269* ⊕ *www.summerlyric.tulane.edu.*

🛍 Shopping

Clothing boutiques, home-decor stores, contemporary art galleries, and trendy restaurants, many housed in turn-of-the-20th-century cottages, are scattered throughout the area near Tulane and Loyola universities. Reflecting the neighborhood's family-friendly vibe, you'll find something for every age: toys and novelties, locally made jewelry, books, artwork, and Crescent City–centric T-shirts. The Uptown end of Magazine Street, a popular haunt for college students and young professionals, is a main shopping drag. On Maple Street, boutiques cover about six blocks, from Carrollton Avenue to Cherokee Street, and in the Riverbend, they dot the streets behind a shopping center on Carrollton Avenue. Oak Street, a burgeoning boutique corridor and one of the city's up-and-coming dining destinations, has several of the city's newest cafés and restaurants, serving everything from barbecue to sushi.

ANTIQUES AND COLLECTIBLES

Kevin Stone Antiques & Interiors

ANTIQUES/COLLECTIBLES | Unusual European antiques, most from the 17th, 18th, and early 19th centuries, fill this shotgun house; the collection includes many large, very ornate pieces from the Louis XIV and XV eras. The inventory ranges from small decorative bowls and sconces to grand pianos and armoires. ⊠ *3420 Magazine St., Uptown* ☎ *504/891–8282, 504/458–7043* ⊕ *www.kevinstoneantiques.com.*

ARTWORK

Nuance/Louisiana Artisans Gallery

ART GALLERIES | Local and regional blown-glass artists are represented in this Riverbend neighborhood studio, which also carries an eclectic mix of jewelry, pewter, ceramics, lamps, T-shirts, and more. ⊠ *728 Dublin St., Uptown* ☎ *504/865–8463* ⊕ *www.nuanceglass.com* ۞ *Closed Sun.*

BEAUTY

Belladonna Day Spa

SPA/BEAUTY | This haven of relaxation offers the usual day-spa services—pedicures, manicures, massages, facials, etc.—while the gift shop area, called "retail therapy," features decorative housewares, pajamas, and high-end bath and body products. ⊠ *2900 Magazine St., Uptown* ☎ *504/891–4393* ⊕ *www.belladonnadayspa.com.*

BOOKS

Octavia Books

BOOKS/STATIONERY | The building's contemporary architecture stands out, and the attractive layout inside invites customers to leisurely browse a selection with an emphasis on architecture, art, and fiction as well as books of local interest. The store hosts frequent book signings. ⊠ *513 Octavia St., Uptown* ☎ *504/899–7323* ⊕ *www.octaviabooks.com.*

CLOTHING

Jean Therapy

CLOTHING | Popular for its diverse range of denim brands—the store carries more than 100 styles of jeans for men and women—this busy shop also offers a small collection of tops, jackets, and accessories, as well as T-shirts emblazoned with New Orleans slogans and local lingo. There's another branch at 2022 Magazine Street. ⊠ *5505 Magazine St., Uptown* ☎ *504/897–5535* ⊕ *www.jeantherapy.com.*

Perlis

CLOTHING | The first floor of this venerable New Orleans retail institution is devoted to outfitting men with classic suits (white linen and seersucker are very popular), sportswear, shoes, ties, and accessories, as well as the store's signature crawfish-logo polo shirts. The second floor is filled with dressy, casual, and formal wear for women. ⊠ *6070 Magazine St., Uptown* ☎ *504/895–8661* ⊕ *www.perlis. com* ☾ *Closed Sun.*

FOOD AND WINE
St. James Cheese Company
FOOD/CANDY | Inspired by cheese shops in Europe, the stock here includes massive wheels and wedges of Gruyère, Brie, cheddar, blue, and exotic cheeses from around the globe. Owners Danielle and Richard Sutton pride themselves on the select inventory, which also includes specialty meats and a variety of great foodie gifts, such as cutting boards, preserves, pastas, cutlery, crackers, and more. Sandwiches and salads are served daily, making this a popular, and crowded, spot at lunchtime. ⊠ *5004 Prytania St., Uptown* ☎ *504/899–4737* ⊕ *www. stjamescheese.com.*

JEWELRY AND ACCESSORIES
Fleur D'Orleans
JEWELRY/ACCESSORIES | Silver jewelry adorned with the fleur-de-lis is the main attraction here, but you'll also find items that carry other New Orleans icons such as crowns, masks, hearts, and architectural details. In addition to jewelry, the store sells handbags, handmade paper, glassware, wood and ceramic boxes, batik scarves, ironwork, and more. Another location is at 818 Chartres Street, in the French Quarter. ⊠ *3701-A Magazine St., Uptown* ☎ *504/899–5585* ⊕ *www. fleurdorleans.com.*

★ Mignon Faget
JEWELRY/ACCESSORIES | Mignon Faget is the most famous jewelry designer in New Orleans, and her upscale sterling-silver and 14k-gold collections reflect her love and fascination with botany, nature, architecture, and the city's culture. Elements of bamboo, fleurs-de-lis, honey bees, red beans, and iron balconies have all been inspirations. Faget studied sculpture at Newcomb College at Tulane University and started out as a fashion designer in 1969, but she quickly gave up clothing to focus exclusively on jewelry. Her work has been featured in museums and shops around the world, but her biggest fan club remains right here in New Orleans, where her pieces are instantly recognized. In addition to her boutique on Magazine Street, she has a gallery at the Shops at Canal Place. ⊠ *3801 Magazine St., Uptown* ☎ *504/891–2005* ⊕ *www. mignonfaget.com.*

LINGERIE
Basics Underneath
CLOTHING | The ladies here are focused on ridding the world of sagging bra straps and overflowing cups. With a sharp eye for measurement, the staff specialize in finding the right fit, whether it's something for work or for a more romantic occasion. The store also carries sleepwear and gifts. Next door, at 5515 Magazine Street, is Basics Swim and Gym, a fitness and swimwear boutique from the same owners. ⊠ *5513 Magazine St., Uptown* ☎ *504/894–1000* ⊕ *www. basicsunderneath.com.*

NOVELTIES AND GIFTS
Aux Belles Choses
GIFTS/SOUVENIRS | This dreamy cottage of French and English delights has richly scented soaps, vintage and new linens, antique enamelware, collectible plates, and decorative accessories. ⊠ *3912 Magazine St., Uptown* ☎ *504/891–1009* ⊕ *www.abcneworleans.com.*

Canine Connection & Canine Culture
GIFTS/SOUVENIRS | This dog boarding facility has a retail shop that stocks an array of gourmet pet food and treats, designer bowls, toys, health products, canine fashions, and doggie-themed home decor. ⊠ *4920 Tchoupitoulas St., Uptown* ☎ *504/218–4098* ⊕ *www.canineconnectionnola.com.*

Dirty Coast

CLOTHING | T-shirts and bumper stickers with the phrase "Be a New Orleanian. Wherever you are" deeply resonated with displaced residents after Hurricane Katrina. Since then, locals leave it to this shop's shirts, stickers, and hats to both satirize ("New Orleans: So far behind, we're ahead") and celebrate local culture in a clever way. The store has a second location at 713 Royal Street, in the French Quarter. ✉ *5631 Magazine St., Uptown* ☎ *504/324–3745* ⊕ *www.dirtycoast.com.*

Hazelnut

GIFTS/SOUVENIRS | Founded by stage and television actor Bryan Batt (he played Salvatore Romano on *Mad Men*) and his partner, Tom Cianfichi, this jewel box of a shop carries gorgeous home accessories and gifts, including New Orleans–themed toile frames, decorative items, stemware, tableware, accent furniture, frames, and more. ✉ *5515 Magazine St., Uptown* ☎ *504/891–2424* ⊕ *www.hazelnutneworleans.com* ☽ *Closed Sun.*

Orient Expressed Imports

GIFTS/SOUVENIRS | Imported porcelain, vases, ceramics, jewelry, and the store's own line of smocked children's clothing are popular gift items. The shop also has a showroom of home furnishings, including accent furniture, lamps, and antique accessories. ✉ *3905 Magazine St., Uptown* ☎ *504/899–3060* ⊕ *www.orientexpressed.com.*

Scriptura

GIFTS/SOUVENIRS | The Italian-leather address books, fancy journals, hand-decorated photo albums, specialty papers, custom stationery, handmade invitations, and high-quality fountain pens sold here are fitting tributes to the art of handwriting. The store also creates gorgeous stationery with New Orleans themes. ✉ *5423 Magazine St., Uptown* ☎ *504/897–1555* ⊕ *www.scriptura.com.*

SHOES

Victoria's Shoes

SHOES/LUGGAGE/LEATHER GOODS | Jimmy Choo, Giuseppe Zanotti, Hoss Intropia, and Marni are just a few of the high-end brands available here. The boutique also carries handbags and jewelry. ✉ *4858 Magazine St., Uptown* ☎ *504/265–8010.*

TOYS

Magic Box

TOYS | **FAMILY** | This toy shop, beloved by both children and adults, sells the kind of items you won't find in big-box stores. While they do carry popular toys by LEGO and Playskool, the emphasis is on independent brands. You'll find everything from baby toys to play items for older children to party games for adults. The staff go above and beyond with customer service, and can help with shipping and assembly. ✉ *5508 Magazine St., Uptown* ☎ *504/899–0117* ⊕ *www.magicboxneworleans.com.*

Carrollton-Riverbend

Before becoming part of New Orleans in 1874, this area was a resort town, providing a relaxing getaway with riverfront views. Now the neighborhood is mostly composed of smaller one- and two-story family homes, shady oak-lined streets, and plenty of small restaurants and cafés. With the success of local events, such as the annual Oak Street Po'Boy Festival in October (⊕ *www.poboyfest.com*), the retail strip on Oak Street has blossomed with shops, clothing boutiques, restaurants, and popular bars such as the Maple Leaf, where the Rebirth Brass Band plays every Tuesday night. Nearby Maple Street is a great shopping destination in its own right, attracting the college crowd with an array of bars and cafés.

Sights

Arts Market of New Orleans

MARKET | Spend a morning perusing the craftsmanship of 100 or more artists from all over the region in this open-air market held the last Saturday of each month in beautiful Palmer Park. Vendors include jewelry artists, painters, textile designers, soap makers, and potters. Musicians, a kids' tent, and food stands round out the event. ✉ *Palmer Park, corner of S. Carrollton and S. Claiborne Aves., Carrollton-Riverbend* 🌐 *www.artsneworleans.org* 🎟 *Free.*

Crescent City Farmers Market

MARKET | Rub shoulders with New Orleans chefs as they rush to pick up fresh vegetables, fish, and meat before their restaurants open every Tuesday. The market caters to both home cooks and professionals who embrace the concept of showcasing local and seasonal ingredients. A new chef is featured each month to prepare delicious lunches. Visitors can indulge in tasty treats like homemade popsicles, fresh-squeezed juice, and hot-from-the-oven bread, as well as sample the local produce. ✉ *200 Broadway St., between Leake Ave. and Broadway, Carrollton-Riverbend* 🌐 *www.crescentcityfarmersmarket.org* 🎟 *Free* 🕒 *Closed Wed.–Mon.*

Restaurants

With Tulane and Loyola universities nearby, it's fitting that the Carrollton-Riverbend neighborhood is filled with casual, affordable, and on-trend eateries, particularly on busy Maple Street.

Bellegarde Bakery

$ | BAKERY | At Bellegarde Bakery, far from the popular tourist sites, Graison Gill and his team freshly mill all of their flour on-site, producing bread and baked goods for some of the top restaurants in New Orleans. A commitment to local and single-origin ingredients embodies the ethos of the whole operation. **Known for:** sourdough bread; quality ingredients; baking classes. [$] *Average main: $5* ✉ *8300 Apple St., Carrollton-Riverbend* ☎ *504/827–0008* 🌐 *bellegardebakery.com* 🕒 *Closed Sun. and Mon. No dinner.*

★ Boucherie

$$ | SOUTHERN | Nathanial Zimet's gutsy, down-home cooking, a unique blend of Louisiana and contemporary Southern styles, fits right in at its cozy location in a converted Uptown home. The menu here is updated monthly, but it always kicks off with small plates, including every imaginable iteration of grits: as fries, cakes, and even crackers. **Known for:** boudin balls; grits of all kinds; Krispy Kreme bread pudding for dessert. [$] *Average main: $21* ✉ *8115 Jeannette St., Carrollton-Riverbend* ☎ *504/862–5514* 🌐 *www.boucherie-nola.com* 🕒 *Closed Mon. and Tues.*

Brigtsen's

$$$ | CREOLE | Chef Frank Brigtsen's fusion of Creole refinement and Acadian earthiness reflects his years as a Paul Prudhomme protégé, and his dishes here represent some of the best south Louisiana cooking you'll find anywhere. Everything is fresh and filled with deep, complex flavors, and the menu changes daily. **Known for:** creative seafood platters; whimsical dining room; excellent butternut shrimp bisque. [$] *Average main: $29* ✉ *723 Dante St., Carrollton-Riverbend* ☎ *504/861–7610* 🌐 *www.brigtsens.com* 🕒 *Closed Sun. and Mon. No lunch.*

★ Jacques-Imo's Cafe

$$ | CREOLE | Oak Street might look like any other sleepy urban thoroughfare by day, but once the sun sets, the half-block stretch containing Jacques-Imo's Cafe feels like the center of the universe. Prepare for lengthy waits (two hours at times) in the festive bar for a table in the boisterous, swamp-theme dining rooms (fortunately, the bartenders are fast), but most agree the wait for the modest-looking but innovative food is worth it: deep-fried roast-beef po'boys, shrimp-and-alligator-sausage cheesecake, Cajun bouillabaisse, and fried rabbit tenderloin with Creole mustard sauce are among the only-at-Jacques-Imo's specialties. **Known for:** long lines and required reservations for groups over five people; entertaining crowds; shrimp-and-alligator-sausage cheesecake. $ *Average main: $18* ⊠ *8324 Oak St., Carrollton-Riverbend* ☎ *504/861–0886* ⊕ *www.jacques-imos.com* ⊗ *Closed Sun. No lunch.*

🍸 Nightlife

The Carrollton-Riverbend area is a favorite among students at Loyola and Tulane universities and is home to citywide favorites like the famous Maple Leaf club, which hosts live music every night of the week. Around the corner, Carrollton Station is a more laid-back option, with bands on weekends and some weeknights.

BARS AND LOUNGES
Oak Wine Bar and Bistro
BARS/PUBS | The dark windows give no hint of the sleek, modern lounge inside. This sophisticated spot for grown-ups to mingle over glasses of wine and gourmet nibbles draws professionals from Uptown and the nearby suburbs. Jazz and folk musicians perform Friday and Saturday. ⊠ *8118 Oak St., Carrollton-Riverbend* ☎ *504/302–1485* ⊕ *www. oaknola.com.*

MUSIC CLUBS
Carrollton Station
MUSIC CLUBS | This cozy neighborhood bar keeps unfolding the farther back you go—from the front bar to the stage to the backyard. The regular schedule of live music emphasizes local roots, rock, and acoustic acts. It's two blocks off the Carrollton streetcar line and close to the Oak Street commercial district. ⊠ *8140 Willow St., Carrollton-Riverbend* ☎ *504/865–9190* ⊕ *www.carrolltonstation.com.*

★ **Maple Leaf**
MUSIC CLUBS | The phrase "New Orleans institution" gets thrown around a lot, but this place deserves the title. It's wonderfully atmospheric, with pressed-tin walls and a lush tropical-themed patio, and it's also one of the city's best venues for blues, New Orleans–style R&B, funk, zydeco, and jazz. On Sunday afternoons, the bar hosts the South's longest-running poetry reading. Rebirth Brass Band's standing Tuesday gig is a show everyone should see, and Joe Krown starts his set around 10:30 pm. It's a long haul from the French Quarter, but worth the trip, especially if combined with a visit to one of the restaurants clustered near this commercial stretch of Oak Street. ⊠ *8316 Oak St., Carrollton-Riverbend* ☎ *504/866–9359* ⊕ *www.mapleleafbar. com.*

🛍 Shopping

BOOKS
Blue Cypress Books
BOOKS/STATIONERY | At this shop, college students, locals, and visitors alike sift through the crowded shelves and tables of used and rare books in all genres, including children's. The shop also sells postcards and small locally themed gifts by the register. ⊠ *8126 Oak St., Carrollton-Riverbend* ☎ *504/352–0096* ⊕ *www. bluecypressbooks.com.*

CLOTHING
Angelique
CLOTHING | This upscale women's clothing store provides on-trend apparel, shoes, and accessories from contemporary labels such as Diane von Furstenburg, Halston Heritage, Vince, Red Valentino, and Alice & Olivia. ⊠ *7725 Maple St., Carrollton-Riverbend* ☎ *504/866–1092.*

C. Collection
CLOTHING | Geared toward fashion-forward college students, this store resembles a sorority-house closet jammed with hip, flirty, affordable clothes, shoes,

handbags, and accessories, ranging from casual to dressy, by brands such as Kensie and Tulle. ⊠ *8141 Maple St., Carrollton-Riverbend* ☎ *504/861–5002* ⊕ *www.ccollectionnola.com* ⊘ *Closed Sun.*

Encore Shop

CLOTHING | This high-end resale shop supports the local symphony orchestra by selling previously owned designer clothes, from casual to formal wear, as well as shoes, handbags, and jewelry. The shop also sells consignment items. ⊠ *7814 Maple St., Carrollton-Riverbend* ☎ *504/861–9028* ⊕ *www.lpovolunteers. org/encore-shop.*

Gae-Tana's

CLOTHING | Racks are filled with a mix of natural fabrics and stylish but comfortable clothing that stay on trend. The combination makes this shop a favorite stop for fashion-conscious mature women as well as college students looking for skirts, jeans, shorts, dresses, blouses, casual shoes, handbags, and jewelry. ⊠ *7732 Maple St., Carrollton-Riverbend* ☎ *504/865–9625* ⊕ *www.gaetanas.com.*

Swap

CLOTHING | You're as likely to find designer duds by Diane von Furstenberg and Dolce & Gabbana as Ann Taylor and J.Crew on the racks of this upscale consignment store. New consignors come in every day, adding fresh inventory. A second women's store is at 5530 Magazine Street. ⊠ *7716 Maple St., Carrollton-Riverbend* ☎ *504/304–6025* ⊕ *www.swapboutique.com.*

Yvonne LaFleur

CLOTHING | Although the clothes may be stylish and contemporary, this beloved local boutique's approach is decidedly old-world elegance. Owner Yvonne LaFleur custom designs hats for all occasions, and her store is always infused with the soft scent of her signature perfume line. The romantic fashions here run the gamut from casual dresses and flirty skirts to lingerie, ball gowns, and a whole room filled with bridal dresses in a variety of styles. ⊠ *8131 Hampson St., Carrollton-Riverbend* ☎ *504/866–9666* ⊕ *www.yvonnelafleur.com.*

JEWELRY

Symmetry Jewelers

JEWELRY/ACCESSORIES | Designer Tom Mathis creates custom wedding and engagement rings and other in-house designs and also repairs jewelry. The shop also stocks a variety of contemporary designs by local, national, and international jewelry artists. ⊠ *8138 Hampson St., Carrollton-Riverbend* ☎ *504/861–9925, 800/628–3711* ⊕ *www. symmetryjewelers.com.*

Chapter 10

MID-CITY AND BAYOU ST. JOHN

Updated by
Katie Fernelius

👁 Sights   🍴 Restaurants   🛏 Hotels   🛍 Shopping   🍸 Nightlife
★★☆☆☆   ★☆☆☆☆   ★☆☆☆☆   ★☆☆☆☆   ★☆☆☆☆

NEIGHBORHOOD SNAPSHOT

TOP REASONS TO GO

City Park. This gorgeous and sprawling park is home to dozens of attractions, including a museum, sculpture garden, and amusement park.

Cemetery tours. Mid-City has some of the largest, safest, and best-kept cemeteries in New Orleans.

Walking along Bayou St. John. The grassy banks offer biking and walking trails and splendid views of some of the most historic and lovely homes and landmarks in the city.

GETTING HERE AND AROUND

From downtown there are two easy ways to get into Mid-City: Canal Street or Esplanade Avenue, both of which border the French Quarter. There are two streetcar lines that run down Canal Street. One will take you straight down Canal to Metairie Cemetery, and the other will turn down Carrollton Avenue and deposit you right in front of City Park. The No. 91 Jackson-Esplanade bus, which you can catch anywhere along Rampart Street in the French Quarter, turns onto Esplanade Avenue, stops near the Degas House, and also takes you right by City Park. The streetcar ride from downtown takes approximately 30 minutes. Allow about 15 minutes for the bus ride down Esplanade. The Lafitte Greenway connects Mid-City to the French Quarter via a paved biking and walking path with pleasant city views. The Greenway begins at Basin Street in the French Quarter and ends at the entrance to City Park

MAKING THE MOST OF YOUR TIME

City Park and the Mid-City cemeteries are generally open during daylight hours, but the outdoor patios of Esplanade Avenue restaurants and cafés stay open well into the night. Allow yourself at least half a day and start in the afternoon, so you can enjoy both activities. City Park is one of the largest urban parks in the nation, and you could easily spend much of your time exploring its art collections, hiking trails, vintage carousel, botanical gardens, and gondola rides.

QUICK BITES

■ **Fair Grinds Coffeehouse.** Just off Esplanade Avenue, Fair Grinds Coffeehouse is the neighborhood spot for fair-trade coffee, tea, and snacks—including vegan treats. There's an upstairs balcony for alfresco dining, and live music at least twice a week. ✉ *3133 Ponce de Leon St., Bayou St. John* ☎ *504/913–9072* ⊕ *www.fairgrinds.com* ⊟ *No credit cards.*

■ **Finn McCool's Irish Pub.** This convivial spot is more than just your average corner bar: it streams European soccer games (opening as early as 7 am to do so) and hosts a popular trivia night on Monday. The kitchen serves sophisticated pub food. ✉ *3701 Banks St., Mid-City* ☎ *504/486–9080* ⊕ *www. finnmccools.com* ⊟ *No credit cards.*

With their tree-lined streets and avenues, gathering places, and landmarks, the Mid-City and Bayou St. John neighborhoods are decidedly more tranquil than their downtown counterparts. You're not likely to find "Huge-Ass Beers to Go" or music blaring out of every doorway here.

Instead, you'll find a quieter charm in the gardens, galleries, and lagoons of City Park, in the cemeteries with their elaborately constructed tombs, and on the tree-shaded patios and decks of restaurants and cafés, where you can listen to the church bells keep time as you relax with a cold drink.

Above the French Quarter and below the lakefront, neither Uptown nor quite downtown, Mid-City embraces everything from massive, lush City Park to storefronts along gritty Broad Street. Much of this primarily working-class neighborhood was low-lying swamplands until the late 1800s, and you can still see where the "high ground" was, along the Esplanade Ridge (now Esplanade Avenue). These are the stretches with many of the neighborhood's largest historic houses, churches, and landmarks. Along Carrollton Avenue you can find everything from an old-school Italian ice-cream parlor to strips of inexpensive Central American restaurants. The neighborhood hosts more than a dozen festivals and celebrations a year, from block parties like the Bayou Boogaloo to grand-scale mega-events like the Voodoo Experience. It's easy to figure out which festival is approaching by the bright flags that spring up on people's porches.

Mid-City

◉ Sights

★ City Park
CITY PARK | FAMILY | Founded in 1854, this 1,300-acre expanse of moss-draped oaks and 11 miles of gentle lagoons is just 2 miles from the French Quarter, but feels like it could be a world apart. With the largest collection of live oaks in the world, including old grove trees that are more than 600 years old, City Park offers a certain natural majesty that's difficult to find in most other urban areas. The art deco benches, fountains, bridges, and ironwork are remnants of a 1930s Works Progress Administration (WPA) refurbishment and add to the dreamy scenery that visitors enjoy boating and biking through. Within the park are the **New Orleans Museum of Art,** the **Louisiana Children's Museum ,** the **Sydney and Walda Besthoff Sculpture Garden,** the **New Orleans Botanical Garden,** the kid-friendly **Carousel Gardens Amusement Park,** a golf course, equestrian stable, sports facilities, and picnic areas. Check the park's website for seasonal activities and special events, such as music festivals, the annual Easter egg hunt, and the eye-popping

wonderland that is Celebration in the Oaks between Thanksgiving and New Year's Day. The Café du Monde coffee stand, behind the Sculpture Garden, serves hot beignets and café au lait 24/7. Most of the park's offerings are free, but several of the venues inside City Park charge separate admission fees.

Open seasonally, the 17-ride **Carousel Gardens Amusement Park** (✉ 504/483–9402; 🖳 $5 admission, rides $4 each) has a New Orleans treasure as its centerpiece: a 1906 carousel (one of only 100 antique wooden carousels left in the country) listed on the National Register of Historic Places. In addition to the cherished "flying horses," the park has rides like the Musik Express, Rockin' Tug, Coney Tower, Ferris Wheel, Bumper Cars, Monkey Jump, Red Baron miniplane, Scrambler, and Tilt-a-Whirl. The rides here are mostly geared to children, not hard-core thrill seekers, but adults and kids alike enjoy the miniature train that takes passengers on a gentle sightseeing tour through City Park. There are also two 18-hole miniature golf courses, one with a New Orleans theme and one with a Louisiana theme.

The **New Orleans Botanical Garden** (✉ 504/483–9386; $8), opened in 1936 as a Depression-era project of the WPA, is one of the few remaining examples of public garden design from the art-deco period. The garden's collections contain more than 2,000 varieties of plants from all over the world, complemented by sites such as the Conservatory, the Pavilion of the Two Sisters, and the Yakumo Nihon Teien Japanese Garden, as well as theme gardens containing aquatics, roses, native plants, ornamental trees, and shrubs and perennials. The garden showcases three notable talents: New Orleans architect Richard Koch, landscape architect William Wiedorn, and artist Enrique Alférez. Adding a touch of fun, the Historic Train Garden, open on weekends, offers visitors the chance to enjoy baguette-size cars rolling through a miniature version of New Orleans.

Featuring figures and settings from classic children's literature, the whimsical **Storyland** (✉ 504/483–9402; 🖳 $5), adjacent to the amusement park, has been a favorite romping ground for generations of New Orleans kids. Youngsters can climb aboard Captain Hook's pirate ship, visit the old lady who lived in a shoe, and journey with Pinocchio into the mouth of a whale. There are more than 25 larger-than-life storybook exhibits in all. ✉ Bordered by City Park Ave., Robert E. Lee Blvd., Marconi Dr., and Bayou St. John, Mid-City ☎ 504/482–4888 ⊕ www. neworleanscitypark.com.

Cypress Grove Cemetery

CEMETERY | This expansive and still-used cemetery was founded by the Fireman's Charitable and Benevolent Association in 1840. Over time, as the cemetery expanded, other societies and individuals joined the volunteer firemen in building impressive monuments. Leading architects and craftsmen were called upon to design and build tombs commemorating the lives of many of New Orleans's most prominent citizens. Crafted in marble, granite, and cast iron, tombs at Cypress Grove are among the nation's leading examples of memorial architecture. Of particular note is the Chinese Soon On Tong Association's tomb, which features a grate in front so that visitors can burn prayers written on paper in it. Admission is free and visitors are encouraged to explore on their own, although outside companies do offer tours. ✉ 120 City Park Ave., Mid-City.

Lake Lawn Metairie Cemetery

CEMETERY | The largest cemetery in the metropolitan area, known to locals simply as Metairie Cemetery, is the final resting place of nine Louisiana governors, seven New Orleans mayors, and musician Louis Prima. Many of New Orleans's prominent families are also interred here in elaborate monuments ranging from Gothic

City Park is one of the most serene places in all of New Orleans.

crypts to Romanesque mausoleums to Egyptian pyramids. The arrangement of tombs reflects the cemetery's former life as a horse-racing track, with the tombs arranged around the perimeter and interior. Cemetery staff are happy to offer a map to anyone who asks. ✉ *5100 Pontchartrain Blvd., Mid-City* ⊕ *www.lakelawnmetairie.com.*

Longue Vue House and Gardens

HOUSE | While technically in the Lakewood neighborhood, this beautiful destination is within easy walking distance of the Mid-City streetcar. Fourteen separate gardens are arranged throughout the 8 acres of the beautifully maintained property, embellished with fountains, architectural flourishes, and gorgeous pathways of hand-laid Mexican pebbles and rough-cut marble. This city estate, now a National Historic Landmark, was fashioned in the 1940s after the great country houses of England, and the villa-style mansion is decorated with its original furnishings of English and American antiques, priceless tapestries, modern art, and porcelain.

Longue Vue is open Tuesday through Sunday, and guests can visit the house by guided tour or explore the gardens at their own leisure. Themed gardens include the formal Spanish court, modeled after a 14th-century Spanish garden, as well as a Discovery Garden, which introduces kids to the intricacies and wonders of horticulture. ■**TIP**➔ **While the verdant gardens are open year round, March and April see the amarillos, daffodils, azaleas, spring snowdrops, tulips, and poppies in full bloom.** ✉ *7 Bamboo Rd., Lakewood* 🖷 *504/488–5488* ⊕ *www.longuevue.com* 🖃 *House and garden guided tour $18, self-guided tour $8* ⊙ *Closed Mon.*

Louisiana Children's Museum

MUSEUM | FAMILY | This top-notch children's museum covers 8½ acres of educational fun and exploration within City Park. Favorite indoor exhibits include a hands-on history of New Orleans and its architecture as well as an interactive exploration through food for the young mind, from growing it to shopping and cooking. On the second floor, children

Mid-City's Cemeteries

One of Mid-City's biggest attractions is its many cemeteries, which have a haunting beauty. These "cities of the dead" are the final resting places of famous musicians, Storyville madams, voodoo practitioners, politicians, and pirates.

You'll find few if any burials here, though; the dead are in aboveground tombs instead. New Orleans, most of which lies below sea level, has a high water table, which caused (and continues to cause, in some circumstances) buried coffins to pop out of the ground during a heavy rain. Raised graves and vaulted tombs were also an old tradition among the French and Spanish.

Most vaults or plots are adorned with symbols, revealing a secret language between the living and dead. An anchor stands for hope, a broken column represents a life cut short, and a broken flower symbolizes a life terminated. Sculpted ivy is a symbol of enduring friendship. Clasped hands stand for unity and love, even after death.

Mid-City cemeteries are some of the safest and most-trafficked in the city. One of the area's most popular is **St. Louis Cemetery No. 3**, but **Cypress Grove Cemetery** and **Lake Lawn Metairie Cemetery** are good alternatives. It all depends on what's most convenient.

Located in a less-visited cemetery across from Lake Lawn Metairie, visitors can take a somber pause to remember victims at the Hurricane Katrina Memorial.

Save our Cemeteries (⊕ *www.saveourcemeteries.org*) is a great source for historical knowledge, safety info, and tours.

---

can splash through the mighty Mississippi with a 100-foot water table. The best part of the museum's new location in City Park is perhaps its acres of outdoor fun, with tunnels, slides, and educational exhibits on Louisiana flora and fauna, right in the city's best urban backyard. ✉ *City Park, 15 Henry Thomas Dr., Mid-City* ☎ *504/523–1357* ⊕ *www.lcm.org* 🎟 *$14* ⊗ *Closed Mon.*

★ **New Orleans Museum of Art (NOMA)**
MUSEUM | FAMILY | Gracing the main entrance to City Park since 1911, this traditional fine-arts museum draws from classic Greek architecture, with several modern wings that bring additional light and space to the grand old building. NOMA now has 46 galleries housing an outstanding permanent collection. Made up of nearly 40,000 objects, the installations and exhibits represent historical periods from the Italian Renaissance to the best of the contemporary world. A wealth of American and European art—French, in particular—makes up much of the collection, with works by Monet, Renoir, Picasso, Cornell, and Pollock. Louisiana artists are also well represented, and the museum boasts photography, ceramics, and glassworks from cultures around the globe, plus outstanding holdings in African, pre-Columbian, and Asian art. In addition, the museum offers a year-round schedule of traveling and special exhibitions, events, tours, and public programs.

Henry Moore's handsome *Reclining Mother and Child* greets visitors at the entrance of the **Sydney and Walda Besthoff Sculpture Garden.** Most of the garden's 60-some sculptures, representing some of the biggest names in modern art, were donated by avid local collector Sydney Besthoff. Meandering trails and bridges carry visitors over bayou lagoons and past a fascinating combination of famed traditional sculpture and contemporary works, including major pieces by Jacques Lipchitz, Barbara Hepworth, and Joel Shapiro. The garden is open daily from 10am to 5pm; admission is free. ✉ *City Park, 1 Collins Diboll Circle, Mid-City* ☎ *504/658–4100* 🌐 *www.noma.org* 🎟 *$15* 🕒 *Closed Mon.*

🍴 Restaurants

Most visitors make their way to Mid-City for Jazz Fest but there's lots happening any time of year. The surrounding dining options include both hip, unpretentious newcomers as well as neighborhood establishments that have been feeding locals affordably for generations.

Angelo Brocato's

$ | **CAFÉ** | **FAMILY** | Traditional Sicilian gelato, spumoni, cannoli, pastries, and candies are the attractions at this quaint little sweetshop, now over a century old. The crisp biscotti, traditional Sicilian desserts, and the lemon and strawberry ices haven't lost their status as local favorites. **Known for:** city's best tiramisu; authentic gelato; local clientele and long lines. [$] *Average main: $4* ✉ *214 N. Carrollton Ave., Mid-City* ☎ *504/486–1465* 🌐 *www.angelobrocatoicecream.com* 🕒 *Closed Mon.*

Blue Oak BBQ

$ | **BARBECUE** | Originally a popular pop-up at music venue Chickie Wah Wah's, Blue Oak BBQ has finally got its own storefront, and with pitmasters Ronnie Evans and Philip Moseley at the helm, it consistently ranks as some of the best BBQ in the city. The beef brisket and pulled pork are both crowd favorites. **Known for:** excellent pulled pork sandwich; sports-friendly neighborhood crowd; location near City Park. [$] *Average main: $13* ✉ *900 N Carrollton Ave., Mid-City* ☎ *504/822–2583* 🌐 *www.blueoakbbq.com* 🕒 *Closed Mon.*

Mandina's

$$ | **CREOLE** | **FAMILY** | Also known as "the pink house," Mandina's has been a neighborhood favorite for locals since 1932. Although this Canal Street fixture has expanded over the years, nothing has diminished the full flavors of the shrimp rémoulade, the crawfish cakes, the turtle soup, or (on Monday) tender red beans with Italian sausage. **Known for:** delicious turtle soup; large plates of classic Southern-Creole cuisine; Sunday football viewings. [$] *Average main: $16* ✉ *3800 Canal St., Mid-City* ☎ *504/482–9179* 🌐 *www.mandinasrestaurant.com.*

Mopho

$ | **VIETNAMESE** | In general, you'll find the best Vietnamese food in New Orleans at authentic hole-in-the-walls on the city's outskirts, but Mopho is an exception to the rule. At this minimalist, modern space just minutes from City Park, Chef Micheal Gulotta creates elevated dishes based on Vietnamese flavors and locally sourced ingredients. **Known for:** ginger-glazed chicken wings; crispy brussels sprouts; charming inner courtyard seating. [$] *Average main: $13* ✉ *514 City Park Ave., Mid-City* ☎ *504/482–6845* 🌐 *www.mophonola.com* 🕒 *Closed Mon.*

Ralph's on the Park

$$$ | **CREOLE** | **FAMILY** | Seasoned restaurateur Ralph Brennan has matched this beautifully renovated historic building with a menu that features innovative twists on contemporary Creole standbys. The culinary staff excel with full-flavored seafood dishes like the Parmesan-fried oysters and a variety of fresh fish. **Known for:** scenic location overlooking City Park; old-school service; three-course lunches. [$] *Average main: $27* ✉ *900 City Park Ave., Mid-City* ☎ *504/488–1000* 🌐 *www.ralphsonthepark.com* 🕒 *No lunch Mon.*

Toups' Meatery

$$ | **CAJUN** | As the restaurant's name might hint, on the menu here you'll find meat, meat, and more meat, from foie gras and charcuterie to a lamb neck with

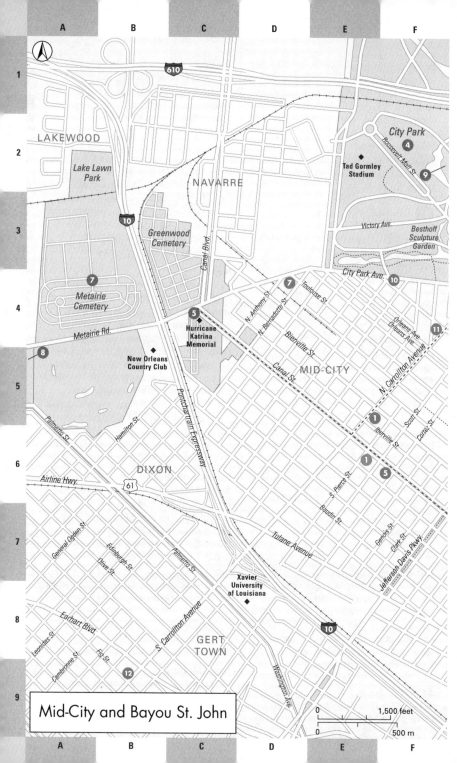

Mid-City and Bayou St. John

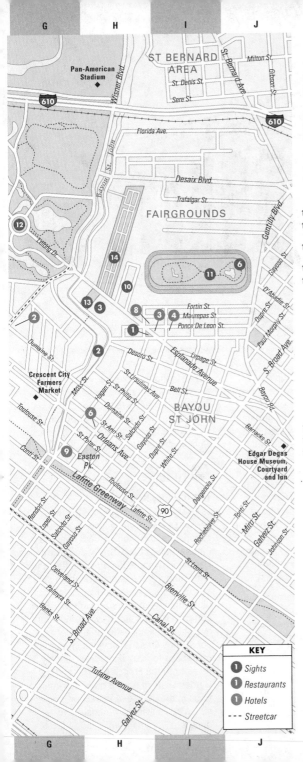

Sights ▼

1 Alcée Fortier Park **H4**
2 Bayou St. John..................... **H5**
3 Cabrini High School
   and Mother Cabrini Shrine **H4**
4 City Park **F2**
5 Cypress Grove Cemetery **C4**
6 Fair Grounds Race Course
   and Slots............................ **J4**
7 Lake Lawn Metairie
   Cemetery **A4**
8 Longue Vue House
   and Gardens...................... **A5**
9 Louisiana Children's Museum..... **F2**
10 Luling Mansion.................... **H4**
11 New Orleans Jazz
   and Heritage Festival.............. **I4**
12 New Orleans Museum of Art
   (NOMA)............................. **G3**
13 Pitot House **H4**
14 St. Louis Cemetery No. 3.......... **H3**

Restaurants ▼

1 Angelo Brocato's **E5**
2 Blue Oak BBQ..................... **G4**
3 Café Degas **I4**
4 Liuzza's by the Track............... **I4**
5 Mandina's **F6**
6 Mayhew Bakery **H6**
7 Mopho **D4**
8 1000 Figs **H4**
9 Parkway Bakery & Tavern........ **G6**
10 Ralph's on the Park **F4**
11 Toups' Meatery **F4**
12 Ye Olde College Inn............... **B9**

Hotels ▼

1 1896 O'Malley House.............. **E6**

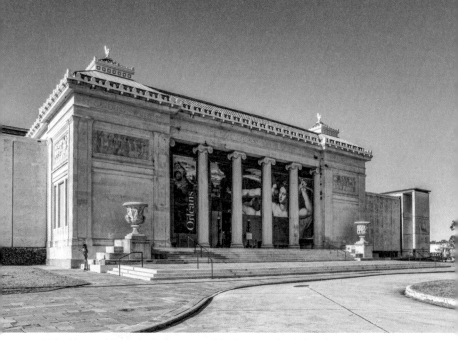

A bike ride around City Park will take you to acclaimed museums like the New Orleans Museum of Art.

black-eyed-pea salad and tri-tip steak with Bordelaise sauce (even the grilled veggies come with a bacon vinaigrette). Chef Isaac Toups, a *Top Chef* contestant and crowd favorite, is hardly the only young American chef obsessed with animal flesh, but at this intimate spot with DIY elegance, he adds a Louisiana edge with items like boudin, cracklings, or sides of dirty rice. **Known for:** fantastic charcuterie plates; must-try bone marrow; housemade pickles. $ *Average main: $22 ⊠ 845 N. Carrollton Ave., Mid-City ☎ 504/252–4999 ⊕ www.toupsmeatery.com ⊗ Closed Sun. and Mon.*

Ye Olde College Inn

$$ | CREOLE | FAMILY | A stalwart neighborhood joint, the age-old College Inn now occupies a newer building after decades in an older, now-razed structure next door. The flat, greasy burgers are still popular, particularly when ordered with french fries and a cold Abita, but the diner fare has been joined by more sophisticated plates. **Known for:** local produce from restaurant's own urban gardens;

family-friendly ambience; veal cutlet that has been on the menu since the 1930s. $ *Average main: $18 ⊠ 3000 S. Carrollton Ave., Mid-City ☎ 504/866–3683 ⊕ www.collegeinn1933.com ⊗ Closed Sun. and Mon. No lunch.*

🛏 Hotels

1896 O'Malley House

$$ | B&B/INN | Best suited for those seeking a less touristy New Orleans experience, this elegant B&B near the intersection of Canal Street and North Carrollton Avenue offers rooms furnished with antiques and equipped with heavy cypress doors, hardwood floors, and plush drapery at oversize windows. **Pros:** complimentary snacks, wine, and beer available; an iPad loaded with information about New Orleans provided in rooms; good base for Jazz Fest. **Cons:** roughly 3 miles from the French Quarter and the Garden District; not for guests wanting to be in the middle of the action; most suites can only accommodate two guests. $ *Rooms from: $155 ⊠ 120 S.*

Pierce St., Mid-City ☎ 504/488–5896 ⊕ www.1896omalleyhouse.com ⌁ 8 rooms ⦿ Free breakfast.

▽ Nightlife

A quick streetcar ride up Canal from downtown, this mostly residential area around City Park is almost like a small town. Its neighborhood joints are unknown to most tourists, but the area has lots to offer if you know where to look. Venues are spread out, so a car or taxi is recommended at night.

BARS AND LOUNGES

Finn McCool's Irish Pub

BARS/PUBS | Created by devoted soccer fans from Belfast, this popular and expansive neighborhood bar beams in European games via satellite. Pool and darts tournaments are a regular feature as well, and the kitchen serves tasty pub fare. On Monday night, there's popular and competitive trivia. If you happen to be in town for St. Patrick's Day, don't miss their rollicking daylong festival. ⊠ 3701 Banks St., Mid-City ☎ 504/486–9080 ⊕ www.finnmccools.com.

Haifa Cuisine & Hookah Bar

CAFES—NIGHTLIFE | Bordering St. Patrick Cemetery, this Canal Street lounge provides a perfect respite from a long day of being a tourist. It offers not only a variety of hookah options, but also an assortment of Mediterranean specialties like stuffed grape leaves and falafel. It's a humming, large space where you can wind down your day before an evening of fun or mingle and talk late into the night. ⊠ 4740 Canal St., Mid-City ☎ 504/309–7719.

Twelve Mile Limit

BARS/PUBS | This neighborhood joint might be off the beaten path, but it's worth the trip for its unlikely combination of an innovative cocktail menu and barbecue. This place compares favorably to swanky wine and cocktail bars like Cure or the Delachaise, yet it offers a decidedly down-home vibe with its pulled pork and brisket, its run-down exterior (a contrast with the nicely done interior), and reasonable prices. ⊠ 500 Telemachus St., Mid-City ☎ 504/488–8114 ⊕ www.twelvemilelimit.com.

MUSIC CLUBS

Banks Street Bar and Grill

MUSIC CLUBS | This comfortable Mid-City nightspot has become one of the city's most reliable venues for local music, with live shows—sometimes several a night—every day of the week. The bill of fare leans toward blues and funk. There is no cover charge for music. ⊠ 4401 Banks St., Mid-City ☎ 504/486–0258 ⊕ www.banksstreetbarnola.com.

Chickie Wah Wah

MUSIC CLUBS | Right on the Canal Street streetcar line, this neighborhood music club is unassuming from the outside but hosts some of the city's most popular acts. With happy hour and early evening sets and a covered patio, this destination is a favorite among low-key New Orleanians who aren't into late nights. ⊠ 2828 Canal St., Mid-City ☎ 504/304–4714 ⊕ www.chickiewahwah.com.

Rock'n'Bowl

MUSIC CLUBS | FAMILY | Down-home Louisiana music, rockabilly, R&B, and New Orleans swing in a bowling alley? Go ahead: try not to have fun. This iconic venue has a terrific lineup of music Wednesday through Saturday. Thursday is Cajun, Zydeco, and Swamp Pop Night, when some of the best musicians from rural Louisiana take the stage. The Front Porch Grill serves burgers made from grass-fed Louisiana beef. ⊠ 3000 S. Carrollton Ave., Mid-City ☎ 504/861–1700 ⊕ www.rocknbowl.com.

⬤ Shopping

This neighborhood isn't known as a shopping destination. However, the store inside the New Orleans Museum of Art (NOMA) is worth a stop for anyone interested in art-related gifts or souvenirs. Small wine shops in the area also provide perfect companions for picnics in City Park or along Bayou St. John.

FOOD, WINE AND SPIRITS
Pearl Wine Co.

WINE/SPIRITS | This wine-and-spirits shop is connected to Pearl Bar next door, and you can grab a bottle here and enjoy it at the bar. Besides wine, the store also has a well-stocked spirits selection with a wide array of Scotches, bourbons, vodkas, and tequilas. The shop also offers tastings and frequent wine classes that take participants on virtual wine tours around the world. ✉ *American Can Company, 3700 Orleans Ave., Suite C, Mid-City* ☎ *504/483–6314* ⊕ *www. pearlwineco.com.*

Swirl

WINE/SPIRITS | This shop specializes in inexpensive, everyday wines. The cozy neighborhood spot also has a wine bar that's a comfortable place to sip and learn about different vintages. Organized with colorful signs describing the bottles, including a "Cheap and Tasty" designation, the store has a small selection of cheeses and gifts too. ✉ *3143 Ponce de Leon St., Mid-City* ☎ *504/304–0635* ⊕ *www.swirlnola.com* ☽ *Closed Sun.*

NOVELTIES AND GIFTS
The GOOD Shop

GIFTS/SOUVENIRS | This unassuming storefront within a coffee shop is a great stop for gifts with a socially conscious spin: every purchase of a handcrafted candle, soap, jewelry item, or T-shirt sold here goes toward a specific charity or relief effort. The boutique also sells goods from beloved local brands like Tchoup Industries bags, Smoke Perfume, and Zeko jewelry. ✉ *4201 Canal St., Mid-City* ☎ *504/264–2478.*

New Orleans Museum of Art Gift Shop

GIFTS/SOUVENIRS | Stocked with art and photography books, children's items, puzzles, jewelry, and locally made crafts, this gift shop is well worth a visit, even if you're not browsing the museum's exhibits. The shop has its own cookbook, as well as items created exclusively for it by local favorite jewelry designer Mignon Faget. You don't have to pay museum admission to enter the shop; just say you are shopping at the front desk, and you will receive a special pass. ✉ *1 Collins Diboll Circle, Mid-City* ☎ *504/658–4116* ⊕ *www.noma.org* ☽ *Closed Mon.*

Bayou St. John

Just up Esplanade Avenue from the French Quarter, the Bayou St. John neighborhood is known for its beautiful shady lanes, gorgeous homes, and laid-back vibe. Great restaurants, cafés, and bars dot the landscape, with sidewalk seating and relaxed patios. It's also home to the New Orleans Fairgrounds Race Course and Slots, one of the nation's major horse-racing venues, and the world-famous New Orleans Jazz and Heritage Festival. St. Louis Cemetery No. 3 opens its gates onto Esplanade Avenue, inviting visitors to explore rows of aboveground tombs and mausoleums. At the end of the avenue you'll discover Bayou St. John, the scenic waterway that begins in Mid-City, meanders through Faubourg St. John, and ends at the lakefront. You'll find all sorts of people out enjoying the wide grassy banks—biking, fishing, or just strolling along and admiring the reflection of a sunset on the smooth water.

◉ Sights

Alcée Fortier Park

CITY PARK | FAMILY | Situated at Esplanade Avenue and Mystery Street, this tiny sliver of a park was named for the philanthropist and professor Alcée Fortier, who owned much of the surrounding area in the late 19th century and who founded a public school. A neighborhood favorite, the park is almost completely maintained by the efforts of local volunteers who tend the lush landscaping, which includes palms, caladiums, and azaleas, keep up the collection of whimsical sculptures and art, and make sure the concrete chess tables are ready for game time (complete with baskets of chess pieces). A focal point of the Bayou St. John neighborhood, Alcée Fortier Park is surrounded by a concentration of hip restaurants and neighborhood grocers. ⊠ *Esplanade Ave. at Mystery St., Bayou St. John.*

Bayou St. John

BODY OF WATER | A bayou is a natural inlet, usually a slow-moving, narrow waterway that emerges from the swamp at one end and joins a larger body of water at the other, and this bayou—the only one remaining in New Orleans—borders City Park on the east and extends about 7 miles from Lake Pontchartrain to just past Orleans Avenue. It is named for John the Baptist. June 23 (St. John's Eve, and therefore the day before his feast day) was the most important day in the year for voodoo practitioners, and it was notoriously celebrated on the bayou's banks in the 1800s. The first European settlers in the area, most likely trappers, coexisted with Native Americans here beginning in 1704. Today, the bayou is still a popular destination among New Orleanians, whether for tradition's sake— as is the case for the famed Mardi Gras Indians, who gather here for their annual celebrations—for a festival such as the Bayou Boogaloo in May, or simply for a relaxing afternoon of fishing, canoeing, or picnicking along the grassy banks. Scenic biking and walking trails run alongside the waterway all the way to the lake, where you all can watch the graceful old homes of picturesque Moss Street morph into the dazzling waterfront mansions of Bancroft Drive. ⊠ *From the foot of Jefferson Davis Pkwy. to Lakeshore Dr., Bayou St. John.*

Cabrini High School and Mother Cabrini Shrine

COLLEGE | Mother Frances Cabrini, the first American citizen to become a saint (canonized in 1946), purchased the land between Esplanade Avenue and Bayou St. John near City Park in 1905 and built the Sacred Heart Orphan Asylum here. She stayed in the Pitot House, which was on her property until she gave it to the city during construction of the orphanage. In 1959, the institution was converted to a girls' high school in Mother Cabrini's name. Her bedroom here, preserved as it was in her time, is filled with personal effects and maintained as a shrine. Tours of her room and Sacred Heart Chapel are available by appointment. ⊠ *1400 Moss St., Bayou St. John* ☎ *504/483–8690* ⊕ *www.cabrinihigh. com.*

Fair Grounds Race Course and Slots

SPORTS VENUE | The third-oldest racetrack in the country sits just off Esplanade Avenue, among the houses of Bayou St. John. The popular Starlight Racing series, held Friday nights, features live music, DJs, food trucks, a beer garden, and go-go dancers dressed as jockeys. The grounds are also home to the New Orleans Jazz and Heritage Festival. For the clubhouse, be sure to make reservations and be aware that proper attire is required—in this case that means collared shirts, closed shoes, and no shorts. ⊠ *1751 Gentilly Blvd., Bayou St. John* ☎ *504/943–2200 box and restaurant reservations, 504/944–5515 general info* ⊕ *www.fairgroundsracecourse. com* 🎟 *Grandstand free, clubhouse $10* 🕐 *Closed May–Oct.*

Luling Mansion

HOUSE | Also called the "Jockey's Mansion," this massive, three-story Italianate mansion is a neighborhood landmark (and now a popular setting for Hollywood film crews). Designed by the prominent New Orleans architect James Gallier Jr., it was built in 1865 for Florence A.

Luling, whose family had made a fortune selling turpentine to Union soldiers when they occupied New Orleans during the Civil War. When the Louisiana Jockey Club took over the Creole Race Course (now the Fair Grounds) in 1871, they purchased the mansion and used it as a clubhouse for the next 20-odd years. It is not open to the public. ✉ *1436–1438 Leda St., Bayou St. John.*

New Orleans Jazz and Heritage Festival

FESTIVAL | Don't let the four-letter word at the center of its name intimidate you—one need not be a jazz fanatic to love the New Orleans Jazz and Heritage Festival. "Jazz Fest," as it's more commonly known, is a sprawling, rollicking celebration of Louisiana music, food, and culture held the last weekend in April and the first weekend in May. It takes place at the city's historic Fair Grounds Race Course, which reverberates with the sounds of rock, Cajun, zydeco, gospel, rhythm and blues, hip-hop, folk, world music, country, Latin, and, yes, traditional and modern jazz. Throw in world-class arts and crafts, exhibitions and lectures, and an astounding range of Louisiana-made food—alone reason enough for many Jazz Fest fans to make the trek—and you've got a festival worthy of America's premier party town. Over the years, Jazz Fest lineups have come to include internationally known performers, but at its heart the festival is about the hundreds of Louisiana musicians who live, work, and cut their chops in the Crescent City. The festival is an important showcase for local musicians, introducing them to fans around the world. For a peek at the schedule of featured artists, visit the festival website. ✉ *Bayou St. John* ☎ *504/410–4100* ⊕ *www.nojazzfest. com.*

Pitot House

HOUSE | One of the few surviving houses that lined the bayou in the late 1700s, and the only Creole colonial–style country house in the city open to the public,

Pitot House is named for James Pitot, who bought the property in 1810 as a country home for his family. In addition to being one of the city's most prosperous merchants, Pitot served as New Orleans mayor from 1804 to 1805, the city's first after the Louisiana Purchase, and later as parish court judge. The Pitot House was restored and moved 200 feet to its current location in the 1960s to make way for the expansion of Cabrini High School. It is noteworthy for its stuccoed brick-and-post construction, an example of which is exposed on the second floor. The house is typical of the West Indies style brought to Louisiana by early colonists, with galleries around the house that protect the interior from both rain and sunshine. There aren't any interior halls to stifle ventilation, and the doors are lined up with one another to encourage a cross breeze. The house is furnished with period antiques from the United States, including special pieces from Louisiana. ✉ *1440 Moss St., Bayou St. John* ☎ *504/482–0312* ⊕ *www. louisianalandmarks.org* 🎫 *$10* ⊗ *Closed Sat.–Tues.*

St. Louis Cemetery No. 3

CEMETERY | One block from the entrance to City Park, at the end of Esplanade Avenue, stands this cemetery, on an area of high ground along Bayou St. John. It opened in 1854 on the site of an old leper colony. Governor Galvez had exiled the lepers here during the yellow fever outbreak of 1853, but they were later removed to make room for the dead. The remains of Storyville photographer E. J. Bellocq are here, and the cemetery is notable for its neat rows of elaborate aboveground crypts, mausoleums, and carved stone angels. Many tour companies, including Save Our Cemeteries, offer tours that include St. Louis No. 3, but it's perfectly safe to walk through and explore on your own. ✉ *3428 Esplanade Ave., Bayou St. John* ⊕ *www.saveourcemeteries.org.*

🍴 Restaurants

Café Degas

$$ | FRENCH | Dining at Café Degas is like being at a sidewalk café in Paris, even though the restaurant is completely covered: there's a tree growing through the center of the dining room, and the front windows overlook picturesque Esplanade Avenue. The fare here is a mixture of French-bistro cooking and what you might find at a countryside inn—homemade pâtés, onion soup, steamed mussels, steaks, and crème brûlée. **Known for:** romantic setting; authentic French food; great pâté and charcuterie. *[$] Average main: $20 ✉ 3127 Esplanade Ave., Mid-City ☎ 504/945–5635 🌐 www.cafedegas.com ⏲ Closed Mon. and Tues.*

Liuzza's by the Track

$ | CREOLE | Fried-oyster po'boys drenched in garlic butter, bowls of sweet-corn-and-crawfish bisque, and grilled Reuben sandwiches with succulent corned beef are some of the reasons you might decide to tolerate the poor ventilation in this barroom near the racetrack and Jazz Fest grounds. The pièce de résistance here is a barbecue-shrimp po'boy, for which the shrimp are cooked in a bracing lemon-pepper butter with enough garlic to cure a cold. **Known for:** one of the city's best barbecue-shrimp po'boys; great people-watching; early kitchen closing at 7 pm. *[$] Average main: $10 ✉ 1518 N. Lopez St., Mid-City ☎ 504/218–7888 🌐 www.liuzzasnola.com ⏲ Closed Sun.*

Mayhew Bakery

$ | BAKERY | This bakery is the first brick-and-mortar venture for chef Kelly Mayhew, who previously sold his tasty baked goods at farmers' markets around the city. Previously the sous chef of Brennan's, Mayhew has become famous for his cranberry-orange scones, chocolate tarts, and sourdough bread. **Known for:** freshly baked bread; lemon cookies; local clientele. *[$] Average main: $5 ✉ 3201 Orleans Ave., Bayou St. John ☎ 504/702–8078 ⏲ Closed Mon. and Tues. No dinner.*

1000 Figs

$ | MEDITERRANEAN | Young chef-owner couple Theresa Galli and Gavin Cady, creators of the popular Fat Falafel food truck, now serve slightly more sophisticated and hearty versions of their food truck favorites, from overstuffed falafel sandwiches with beet and carrot slaw to shareable mezze plates. Don't skip the house-made french fries and *toum* (Middle Eastern creamy garlic sauce). **Known for:** fantastic falafel and mezze plates; sidewalk seating in nice weather; cozy neighborhood vibe. *[$] Average main: $11 ✉ 3141 Ponce de Leon St., Bayou St. John ☎ 504/301–0848 🌐 www.1000figs.com ⏲ Closed Sun.*

Parkway Bakery & Tavern

$ | CAFÉ | FAMILY | Former contractor Jay Nix resurrected more than just a dilapidated building when he reopened Parkway: he also brought back to life a dormant community spirit. You can find neighbors and regulars from other parts of the city sinking their teeth into Parkway's roast beef and grilled ham po'boys; some simply wander in for a hot dog and beer at the bar, and to take in the New Orleans nostalgia decorating the walls (President Barack Obama was just one of many famous guests). **Known for:** classic New Orleans local scene; long lines; roast beef and fried seafood po'boys (famous oyster po'boy on Monday and Wednesday only). *[$] Average main: $9 ✉ 538 Hagan Ave., Mid-City ☎ 504/482–3047 🌐 www.parkwaypoorboys.com ⏲ Closed Tues.*

🍸 Nightlife

A few solid bars offer entertainment and cheap cocktails, but if you want to really do like the locals, get a go cup and sit along the water.

BARS AND LOUNGES

Bayou Beer and Wine Garden

BARS/PUBS | Claim a seat on the sprawling multilevel outdoor patio at this low-key neighborhood pub and sip a pint from the great selection of beers. Multiple TVs show the big game, and the bar occasionally hosts live music. Next door, and sharing an adjoining courtyard, a slightly more sophisticated sister property has opened as a wine garden. The wine garden offers gourmet meat and cheese boards and popular wines on tap. ⊠ *326 N. Jefferson Davis Pkwy., Mid-City* ☎ *504/302–9357* ⊕ *bayoubeergarden. com.*

Pal's

BARS/PUBS | Tucked away in a quiet residential neighborhood, this hipster hangout updated a neighborhood bar with the kind of carefully designed run-down vibe that might make Tom Waits smile. All the details are there, down to the soft-core porn on the restroom walls. The bar regularly hosts beloved pop-up restaurants serving Thai, Mexican, and Cajun food. ⊠ *949 N. Rendon St., Bayou St. John* ☎ *504/488–7257* ⊕ *www. palslounge.com.*

SIDE TRIPS FROM NEW ORLEANS

11

Updated by
Matt Haines

👁 Sights	🍴 Restaurants	🛏 Hotels	⬤ Shopping	🍸 Nightlife
★★★★★	★★★★★	★★★★★	★★★★★	★★★★★

WELCOME TO SIDE TRIPS FROM NEW ORLEANS

TOP REASONS TO GO

★ **Take a swamp tour:** Get to know the wetlands surrounding New Orleans on a boat ride. The area is home to alligators, snakes, nutria, and more.

★ **Visit quirky Abita Springs:** Head to the home of the Abita brewery for an afternoon trip, and check out the Abita Mystery House museum.

★ **Jam to Cajun and zydeco music:** Ensembles of fiddles, accordions, and guitars produce eminently danceable folk music, with songs sung in a mélange of English and Cajun French. Zydeco, closely related to Cajun music, adds washboard and drums to the mix to create an R&B-infused, jumping rhythm.

★ **Confront America's complicated history at Whitney Plantation:** The region surrounding New Orleans is dotted with a multitude of historic plantation homes. Only one former plantation in Louisiana, Whitney Plantation, has been turned into a museum dedicated to the history of slavery, focusing entirely on the experiences of the slaves that lived there.

1 Abita Springs. This quirky town is an easy day trip from New Orleans. Part of the drive is on a 23.8-mile causeway over Lake Pontchartrain, the world's longest bridge built entirely over water.

2 Plantation Country. Within an hour's drive of New Orleans are dozens of plantation homes in various states of repair scattered along either side of the Mississippi. These palatial antebellum estates are certainly beautiful, but their legacies, built on the enslavement of human beings, are important to awknowledge. Many of these homes still struggle to adequately reflect this history, but more plantations are working to put the stories and experiences of slaves at the forefront of visits and tours.

3 Baton Rouge. The state capital is a worthwhile stop for history and food enthusiasts.

4 St. Francisville. Take a day trip here to explore the historic downtown, shop for antiques, or visit the nearby plantation homes.

5 Lafayette. Experience the traditional Cajun way of life in one of two simulated villages.

6 Grand Coteau. This village is listed on the National Register of Historic Places.

7 Opelousas. One of the oldest towns in Louisiana, Opelousas is known for its history and zydeco music.

8 Eunice. Spend a Saturday here jamming to Cajun music and catching theater performances.

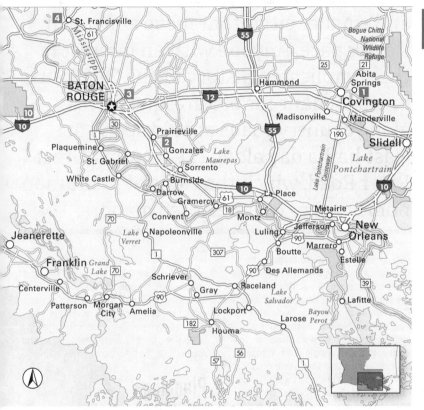

9 Breaux Bridge.
Crawfish and antiques
shops take center stage in
this small Cajun town.

10 Atchafalaya Basin.
Nature enthusiasts flock
to this swamp basin for
bird watching, boating,
and photography.

11 St. Martinville. A quiet
and historic town, St.
Martinville was a refuge
for Acadians and French
royalists.

12 New Iberia. This arts
and cultural hub has a
walkable downtown filled
with galleries and shops.

13 Avery Island. The
birthplace of Tabasco
sauce is also home to a bird
sanctuary and a 170-acre
garden.

14 Jefferson Island. Visit
this salt dome for the Rip
Van Winkle Gardens.

15 Erath. This small town
is a classic Cajun village.

16 Abbeville. Historic
buildings and village
squares make this small
town perfect for walking
around.

17 Maurice. Nestled
between Lafayette and
Abbeville, this small town
has a well-known butcher
shop and flea market.

New Orleans has never been a typical Southern city. But look away to the west of town, and you'll still find towns and smaller cities that move at a much slower pace. Anyone with an interest in the complicated history of the Old South or a penchant for picturesque drives along country roads should spend at least half a day along the winding Great River Road, which the ruins of plantation homes share with restored manors.

Popular day trips include tours of the swamps and brackish, slow-moving bayous that surround New Orleans—once the highways of the Choctaw, Chickasaw, Chitimacha, and Houma. Two centuries ago Jean Lafitte and his freebooters easily hid in murky reaches of swamp, covered with thick canopies of subtropical vegetation; it's said that pirate gold is still buried here. The state has a wild alligator population of about 2 million, and most of them laze around in these meandering tributaries and secluded backwaters of south Louisiana.

A variety of tour companies take groups to swampy sites a half hour to two hours away from the city center. Guides steer you by boat through still waters, past ancient gnarled cypresses with gray shawls of Spanish moss, explaining the state's flora and fauna and the swamp traditions of the trappers who settled here.

South Louisiana, the center of the Cajun population, is decidedly French in flavor.

In small communities along the coast and in the upland prairie, Cajun French is still spoken, though just about everyone also speaks English. After a hard day's work fishing or working crawfish ponds, rural residents of Cajun Country often live up to the motto *"Laissez les bons temps rouler!,"* or "Let the good times roll!"

Planning

When To Go

Any Saturday is a great day to explore the uniqueness of Cajun Country. Spring and fall are especially full of small-town, family-friendly festivals celebrating local food and culture. Cooler temperatures make late September and October a good time to learn the history of plantation homes and to take swamp tours as well, but it's also the tail end of hurricane season. In December, seasonal bonfires glow along the river.

Getting Here and Around

AIR

Baton Rouge Metropolitan Airport, 7 miles north of downtown, is served by American, Delta, and United. Louis Armstrong New Orleans International Airport is off Interstate 10, 20 minutes from Destrehan Plantation.

AIRPORT INFORMATION Baton Rouge Metropolitan Airport. (*BTR*) ✉ *9430 Jackie Cochran Dr., Baton Rouge* ☎ *225/355–0333* ⊕ *www.flybtr.com.*

BUS

Greyhound Southeast Lines has frequent daily service from New Orleans to Baton Rouge and Lafayette, and limited service to surrounding areas.

BUS INFORMATION Greyhound Southeast Lines. ☎ *800/231–2222* ⊕ *www.greyhound.com.*

CAR

From New Orleans the fastest route to the River Road plantations is Interstate 10 west to Interstate 310 to Exit 6 (River Road). Alternatives to the Great River Road are to continue on either Interstate 10 or U.S. 61 west; both have signs marking exits for various plantations. Route 18 runs along the west bank of the river, Route 44 on the east.

Interstate 10 and U.S. 190 run east–west through Baton Rouge. Interstate 12 heads east, connecting with north–south Interstate 55 and Interstate 59. U.S. 61 leads from New Orleans to Baton Rouge and north. The easiest way to cross the river is by bridge, and most bridges between the two cities are free. Route 1 travels along False River, which is a blue "oxbow lake" created ages ago when the Mississippi changed its course and cut off this section. The drive along Interstate 10 will take about 80 minutes from New Orleans to Baton Rouge. Expect the drive to take two hours if you take either Route 18 or 44, which wind with the river.

Restaurants

Part of the considerable charm of the region west of New Orleans is the Cajun food, popularized across America in the 1970s and early 1980s by Cajun chef Paul Prudhomme, a native of Opelousas. This is jambalaya, crawfish pie, and filé gumbo country, and nowhere else on Earth is Cajun food done better than where it originated. Cajun food is often described as the robust, hot-peppery country kin of Creole cuisine. It's a cuisine built upon economy—heavy on the rice and the sauces, lighter on the meats—and strongly influenced by African and French cooking traditions. Indigenous sea creatures turn up in étouffées, bisques, and pies, and you can find jambalaya, gumbo, and blackened fish on almost every Acadian menu. Alligator meat is a great favorite, as are sausages like andouille and boudin (stuffed with a spicy pork-and-rice dressing). Cajun food is very rich, and portions tend to be ample. Biscuits and grits are breakfast staples, and many an evening meal ends with bread pudding.

Cajun cuisine extends beyond Cajun Country itself and into many of the restaurants along River Road. North of Baton Rouge, however, in St. Francisville, more typical Southern fare prevails. Here you will still find po'boys and sometimes gumbo, but barbecue is more common than boudin.

Hotels

Some of the handsome antebellum mansions along River Road are also bed-and-breakfasts, allowing visitors to roam the stately rooms during the day and then live out the fantasy of spending the night there in a big four-poster or canopied bed. The greatest concentration of accommodations in Cajun Country is in Lafayette, which has an abundance of chain properties as well as some bed-and-breakfasts. Charming B&Bs are also abundant in other nearby towns, including St. Francisville, which is considered one of the best B&B towns in the South.

Restaurant and hotel reviews have been shortened. For full information, visit Fodors.com. Restaurant prices are the average cost of a main course at dinner or, if dinner is not served, at lunch. Hotel prices are the lowest cost of a standard double room in high season.

What it Costs			
$	$$	$$$	$$$$
RESTAURANTS			
under $16	$16–$22	$23–$30	over $30
HOTELS			
under $90	$90–$120	$121–$150	over $150

Tours

Cajun Encounters Tour Co.
GUIDED TOURS | This tour company will pick you up at 15 locations in New Orleans and bring you to guided tours of Whitney, Oak Alley, and Laura Plantations, as well as to personal tours of Honey Island Swamp—there's even one that's at night. ☎ 866/928–6877 ⊕ www.cajunencounters.com.

Visitor Information

CONTACTS Baton Rouge Area Convention and Visitors Bureau. ⊠ 359 Third St., Baton Rouge ☎ 225/383–1825, 800/527–6843 ⊕ www.visitbatonrouge.com. **Louisiana Tourism Baton Rouge Welcome Center.** ⊠ 900 North Third St., Baton Rouge ☎ 225/342–7317 ⊕ www.crt.state.la.us. **West Feliciana Parish Tourist Commission.** ⊠ 11757 Ferdinand St., St. Francisville ☎ 225/635–4224, 800/789–4221 ⊕ www.stfrancisville.us.

Abita Springs

45 miles north of New Orleans.

Tiny Abita Springs, north of Lake Pontchartrain, is notable for three things: artesian spring water, Abita beer, and an oddball institution known as the Abita Mystery House. It's a fun day trip from New Orleans.

◉ Sights

★ **Abita Brewing Company**
WINERY/DISTILLERY | Head out to Abita Springs to see where this popular beer is made—the area has long been known for its artesian spring water, which is used in brewing. Half-hour guided tours ($8) are on Wednesday and Thursday at 2 and 4 pm, and on the hour Friday 1–4 pm, Saturday 11 am–4 pm, and Sunday noon–3 pm. Tours include four 4-ounce brew samplings. Note that closed-toe shoes need to be worn on all tours. The Tap Room on premises features 30 taps, including Abita mainstays and beer only available on-site. ⊠ 21084 Hwy 36, Covington ✛ On the line between Abita Springs and Covington ☎ 985/893–3143 ⊕ www.abita.com.

Abita Mystery House
MUSEUM | Artist John Preble's strange vision—sort of a Louisiana version of the Watts Towers of Los Angeles—is an obsessive collection of found objects (combs, old musical instruments, paint-by-number art, and taxidermy experiments gone horribly awry) set in a series of ramshackle buildings, including one covered in mosaic tiles. This museum is odd and entertaining, but not for clutter-phobes. If he's there, ask Preble if you can see his studio, where he creates paintings of green-eyed Creole beauties. ⊠ 22275 Hwy. 36, at Grover St. ☎ 985/892–2624 ⊕ www.abitamysteryhouse.com ☑ $4.

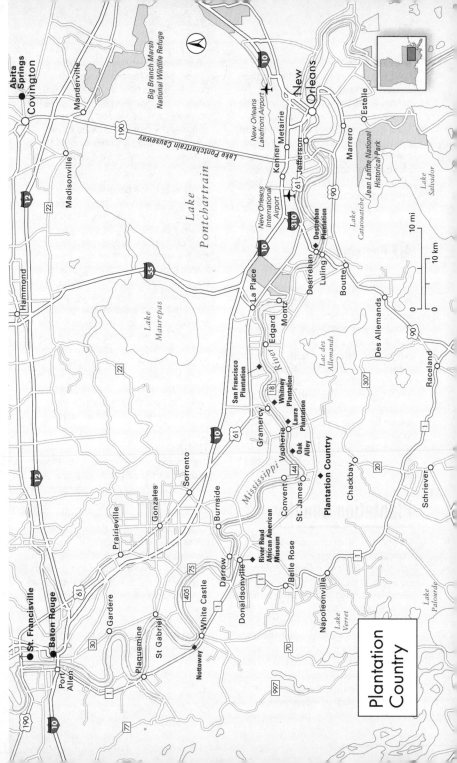

Tammany Trace

TRAIL | Abita Springs is located on this 31-mile hiking and biking trail that connects the town to Covington in the west and Mandeville, Fontainebleau State Park, and Slidell to the east. Walk a stretch of the peaceful corridor from the Abita Brew Pub or rent a bicycle and hop between towns and/or a number of the nearby breweries. The trail is flat, safe, and mostly covered by a canopy of trees. ⊠ 22049 Main St. ☎ 985/892–0711 ⊕ www.tammanytrace.org.

🍴 Restaurants

Abita Brew Pub

$$ | AMERICAN | This was the site of Abita's original brewery until 1994, when the company found a much needed larger space up the road. Today, the Abita Brew Pub is a lovely setting for indoor and outdoor meals chosen from a surprisingly lengthy menu of traditional comfort food and regional favorites including pasta, salads, burgers, and entrées like jambalaya, barbecue ribs, and pecan-crusted catfish. **Known for:** Abita brews on tap; hearty pub fare; Southern flavors. $ Average main: $18 ⊠ 72011 Holly St. ☎ 985/892–5837 ⊕ www.abitabrewpub.com ⊗ Closed Mon.

Plantation Country

Nowhere is America's complicated, violent past more apparent than in Louisiana's Plantation Country, where a parade of plantations unfolds along the Great River Road leading west from New Orleans, and another group of fine old houses dots the landscape around the town of St. Francisville. Louisiana plantation homes range from the grandiose Nottoway on River Road to the humbler, owner-occupied Butler Greenwood near St. Francisville. Some sit upon an acre or two; others, such as Rosedown, are surrounded by extensive, gorgeous grounds.

All of these River Road plantations are closely tied to New Orleans's culture and society: It was here that many of the city's most prominent families made their fortunes generations ago. It's also where some of the most unspeakable crimes against humanity occured as all of these fortunes were built on the backs of slave labor.

Looking at these palatial homes and their lush, landscaped grounds filled with cypress trees and hanging moss, it can be easy to spend a visit simply admiring their unique beauty and marveling at the power and wealth of their former owners. But it's important to awknowledge the brutality, dehumanization, and violence of the slavery that occured here. This is a truth that was ignored or glossed over for many years by the plantations themselves, but more organizations are working to put the experience of slaves on the forefront of plantation visits. Whichever plantation you visit or type of tour you take, it's important to be willing to hear the full story of American history with all its heartbreaking contrasts.

TIMING

Don't try to visit every plantation listed here—your trip will turn into a blur of columns and history. Each plantation has a different focus, and each prioritizes different information, so you'll want to read through our listings to determine which experiences best match your interests. Oak Alley, Laura, and Whitney are just a few miles from each other and provide major contrasts in architectural styles and historical approaches. If you're visiting from New Orleans and are pressed for time, then Destrehan, one of the state's oldest plantations, might fit the bill; it's 23 miles from the city.

⊙ Sights

Destrehan Plantation

HOUSE | The closest intact plantation to New Orleans is also the oldest intact plantation in the entire lower Mississippi Valley. It's a simple West Indies–style house, built in 1787–90 by an enslaved builder of mixed race for the Destrehan family; it's typical of the homes built by the earliest planters in the region. It is notable for the hand-hewn cypress timbers used in its construction and for the insulation in its walls, made of *bousillage,* a mixture of horsehair, Spanish moss, oyster shells, and mud. A costumed guide leads a 45-minute tour through the house furnished with period antiques, starting every half-hour. "The Unheard Voices of the German Coast Tour" is a special two-hour tour offered on Fridays and Saturdays at 10:15 am and 1:15 pm, focusing on the marginalized people of the region—especially enslaved Africans. The grounds also hold exhibits showcasing documents signed by former Presidents, a history of the extraordinary 1811 Slave Revolt, and original slave cabins from a nearby plantation. Demonstrations of crafts such as weaving, barrel-making, or open-hearth cooking occur regularly, and an annual fall festival with music, crafts, and food is held the second weekend in November. ✉ *13034 River Rd., Destrehan* ✛ *23 miles west (upriver) of New Orleans* ☎ *985/764–9315* ⊕ *www. destrehanplantation.org* 🎫 *$22.*

Laura Plantation

HOUSE | Telling the story of four generations of free and enslaved Creole women, this is a more intimate and better-documented presentation of Creole plantation life than most properties on River Road. The narrative of the guides is built on first-person accounts, estate records, and original artifacts from the Locoul family, who built the simple, Creole-style house in 1805. Laura Locoul, whose great-grandparents founded the estate, wrote a detailed memoir of plantation life, family fights, and the management of slaves. The information from Laura's memoir and the original slave cabins and other outbuildings (workers on the plantation grounds lived in the cabins into the 1980s) provide rare insights into slavery in south Louisiana. The plantation gift shop stocks a large selection of literature by and about slaves and slavery in south Louisiana and the United States. Senegalese slaves at Laura are believed to have first told folklorist Alcée Fortier the tales of Br'er Rabbit; his friend, Joel Chandler Harris, used the stories in his Uncle Remus tales. Tours take place approximately every 40 minutes. ✉ *2247 Hwy. 18, Vacherie* ✛ *57 miles west of New Orleans* ☎ *225/265–7690, 888/799–7690* ⊕ *www.lauraplantation. com* 🎫 *$23.*

Nottoway

HOUSE | Touring the South's largest existing antebellum mansion will give you an appreciation of the grandeur of the area's plantation homes, but it is lacking in the information it provides about slavery's central role in the construction and maintenance of the estate. Built in 1859, Nottoway's mansion is Italianate in style, with 64 rooms, 22 columns, and 200 windows. The crowning achievement of architect Henry Howard, it was saved from destruction during the Civil War by a Northern officer (a former guest of the owners, Mr. and Mrs. John Randolph). An idiosyncratic, somewhat rambling layout reflects the individual tastes of the original owners and includes a grand ballroom, famed in these parts for its crystal chandeliers and hand-carved columns. As an alternative to the 45-minute guided tour, visitors also can opt for a self-guided and self-paced audio tour. You can stay at Nottoway overnight, and a formal restaurant serves breakfast, lunch, and dinner daily. The plantation is 2 miles north of its namesake, the town of White Castle (you'll understand how the town got its name when you see this vast, white mansion, which looks like a castle). ✉ *31025 Hwy. 1, White Castle* ⊹ *75 miles west of New Orleans* ☎ *225/545–2730, 866/527–6884* ⊕ *www. nottoway.com* 🍴 *$20.*

Oak Alley

HOUSE | The most famous of all the antebellum homes in Louisiana is a darling of Hollywood, having appeared in major movies and television productions. Built between 1837 and 1839 by Jacques T. Roman, a French Creole sugar planter from New Orleans, Oak Alley is an outstanding example of Greek Revival architecture and is now owned and operated by the Oak Alley Foundation. The 28 stately oak trees that line the drive and give the columned plantation its name were planted in the early 1700s by an earlier settler. A guided tour introduces you to the grand interior of the manor, but be aware that you're unable to book specific times for your tour, so you may want to arrive early in the day to avoid lengthy lines. Leave time to explore the expansive grounds and visit an excellent slavery exhibit where regularly scheduled conversations with staff members tell the lives of those owned and kept on the plantation, as well as their lives after emancipation. Other exhibits cover the history of sugarcane in the region, the Civil War, and much more. A number of late-19th-century cottages behind the main house provide simple overnight accommodations, and a restaurant is open daily from 8:30 am to 3 pm. ✉ *3645 Hwy. 18, Vacherie* ⊹ *3 miles west of Laura Plantation, 60 miles west of New Orleans* ☎ *225/265–2151, 800/442–5539* ⊕ *www.oakalleyplantation.com* 🍴 *$25.*

River Road African American Museum

MUSEUM | The contributions of African Americans in Louisiana's rural Mississippi River communities come to light through exhibits that explore the slave trade, African American cuisine, the Underground Railroad, free people of color, Reconstruction, the rural roots of jazz, and more. ✉ *406 Charles St.,* *Donaldsonville* ☎ *225/474–5553* ⊕ *www. africanamericanmuseum.org* 🍴 *$10* ☽ *Closed Sun.–Tues.*

San Francisco Plantation

HOUSE | An intriguing variation on the standard plantation style, with galleries resembling the decks of a ship, the San Francisco Plantation seems to have inspired a new architectural term: "Steamboat Gothic." The house, completed in 1856, was once called "St. Frusquin," a pun on a French slang term, *sans fruscins,* which means "without a penny in my pocket"—the condition its owner, Valsin Marmillion, found himself in after paying exorbitant construction costs. Valsin's father, Edmond Bozonier Marmillion, had begun the project, and according to lore, his design for the house was inspired by the steamboats he enjoyed watching along the Mississippi. Upon his father's death, Valsin and his German bride, Louise von Seybold, found themselves with a plantation on their hands. Unable to return to Germany, Louise brought German influence to south Louisiana instead. The result was an opulence rarely encountered in these parts: ceilings painted in trompe-l'oeil, hand-painted toilets with primitive flushing systems, and cypress painstakingly rendered as marble and English oak. Tour guides impart the full fascinating story on the 45-minute tour through the main house and attempt to tell the parallel story of the enslaved population forced to labor in the house and throughout the plantation. An authentic one-room schoolhouse and a slave cabin have been installed on the grounds, which you can tour at your leisure. ✉ *2646 Hwy. 44, Garyville* ⊹ *18 miles west of Destrehan Plantation, 35 miles west of New Orleans* ☎ *985/535–2341* ⊕ *www. sanfranciscoplantation.org* 🍴 *$20.*

★ Whitney Plantation

MUSEUM | The only plantation museum in the area focused exclusively on slavery, the goal of Whitney Plantation is to convince visitors that a plantation tour isn't about a house, but rather about the cruel and unfair system of human bondage that took place on these grounds in the 18th and 19th centuries. Ninety-minute guided tours are offered multiple times each day, leading visitors into and around 16 original structures, including the Big House and slave cabins. The plantation also features several memorials to enslaved African Americans forced to live and work across Louisiana. Before or after the tour, there's are exhibits focused on topics such as the slave trade, and a gift shop with an impressive collection of indigenous crafts and topical books. The house might not be the grandest, and the plantation's subject matter is harrowing, but that's the point: it's impossible to get an accurate picture of the region without confronting the atrocities Whitney Plantation is determined to ensure we understand. Tours are extremely popular and online reservations are strongly recommended. ✉ *5099 LA-18, Edgard* ☎ *225/265–3300* 🌐 *www.whitneyplantation.org* 🎟 *$25.*

🍴 Restaurants

B&C Seafood

$ | **CAJUN** | This small shop and restaurant serves some of the tastiest seafood gumbo around River Road (and there's plenty of competition). Try a dash of hot sauce and a sprinkle of filé, or sample the alligator burgers; finish with a scoop of rich, dense bread pudding. **Known for:** exotic meats; seafood to-go; bread pudding. [$] *Average main: $12* ✉ *2155 Rte. 18, beside Laura Plantation, Vacherie* ☎ *225/265–8356* 🕓 *Closed weekends. No dinner.*

★ Spuddy's Cajun Foods

$ | **CAJUN** | Midway between Laura and Oak Alley plantations, downtown Vacherie is short on sights but long on flavor, thanks in no small part to this downhome lunchroom. Photos and murals on the walls tell tales of local history, while po'boys, jambalaya, and fried catfish fill the tables. **Known for:** rotating lunch specials; homemade sausages; unforgettable owner. [$] *Average main: $10* ✉ *2644 Hwy. 20, Vacherie* ☎ *225/265–4013* 🕓 *Closed weekends. No dinner.*

Wayne Jacob's Smokehouse Restaurant

$ | **CAJUN** | LaPlace is known as the andouille capital of the world, and the spicy, smoky, Cajun-style sausage is deservedly popular here. In this butcher shop that doubles as a functional, straightforward restaurant for weekday lunches, you can get andouille in burgers, in gumbo, made into chips for dipping, or worked into white beans and rice. **Known for:** rotating sausage of the month; Sunday jazz brunch; country store shopping. [$] *Average main: $13* ✉ *769 W. Fifth St., Laplace* ☎ *985/652–9990* 🌐 *www.wjsmokehouse.com* 🕓 *Closed Sat. No dinner.*

Baton Rouge

80 miles northwest of New Orleans via I–10.

Hemmed in as it is by endless industrial plants, Baton Rouge may not look like much from the road. Yet government-history enthusiasts will want to stop here on their way through the south Louisiana countryside, and foodies will be impressed by the city's rising culinary scene. The state capital has several interesting and readily accessible sights, including the attractive capitol grounds and an educational planetarium. This is the city from which the colorful, cunning, and often corrupt Huey P. Long ruled the state; it is also the site of his assassination. Even today, more than 80 years after Long's death, legends about the controversial governor and U.S. senator abound.

The parishes to the north of Baton Rouge are quiet and bucolic, with gently rolling hills, high bluffs, and historic districts.

John James Audubon lived in West Feliciana Parish in 1821, tutoring local children and painting 80 of his famous bird studies. In both terrain and trait, this region is more akin to north Louisiana than to south Louisiana—which is to say, the area is very Southern.

⊙ Sights

Louisiana Arts & Science Museum and Irene W. Pennington Planetarium

MUSEUM | FAMILY | Housed in a 1925 Illinois Central railroad station near the Old State Capitol, this idiosyncratic but high-quality collection brings together a contemporary art gallery, an Egyptian tomb exhibit featuring a mummy from 300 BC, a children's museum, and a kid-friendly planetarium. The planetarium presents shows regularly, as does the ExxonMobil Space Theater. The museum hosts traveling exhibits, and houses the nation's second-largest collection of sculptures by 20th-century Croatian artist Ivan Meštrović, many of which adorn the entrance hall. ⊠ 100 River Road South ☎ 225/344–5272 ⊕ www.lasm. org ➦ $12, including planetarium show ⊗ Closed Mon.

Louisiana State Museum–Capital Park Museum

MUSEUM | The Capitol Park Museum showcases the history of Louisiana through two permanent exhibits. "Grounds for Greatness: Louisiana and the Nation" situates Louisiana events in U.S. and world history, from the Louisiana Purchase to World War II. "Experiencing Louisiana: Discovering the Soul of America" takes the visitor on a road trip–like exhibit that courses through the different regions of the state. Rotating exhibits in the museum's gallery explore the arts, culture, and history of the region. ⊠ 660 N. 4th St. ☎ 225/342–5428 ⊕ www.louisianastatemuseum.org ➦ $7 ⊗ Closed Mon.

Old Governor's Mansion

HOUSE | This Georgian-style house was built for Governor Huey P. Long in 1930, and eight other governors lived here thereafter until 1962. The story goes that Long instructed the architect to design his home to resemble the White House, representing Long's unrealized ambition to live in the real one. Notable features on the guided tour include Long's bedroom and a secret staircase. This historic house museum also serves as the Preserve Louisiana headquarters and functions as a venue for special events. ⊠ 502 North Blvd. ☎ 225/387–2464 ⊕ www.preserve-louisiana.org ➦ $10 ⊗ Closed Sat.–Mon.

Old State Capitol

GOVERNMENT BUILDING | When this turreted Gothic Victorian castle was constructed between 1847 and 1852, it was declared by some a masterpiece, by others a monstrosity. No one can deny that the restored building is colorful and dramatic. In the entrance hall a stunning cast-iron spiral staircase with gold leafing winds toward a stained-glass atrium. The building is now an education and research facility with audiovisual exhibits including the "assassination room," which covers the legendary Huey Long's final moments and is a major draw. The Ghost of the Castle Exhibit is a 12-minute 4D presentation that tells the history of the building, as narrated by an actress playing Sarah Morgan, whose father sold the land on which the building was built. ⊠ 100 North Blvd. ☎ 225/342–0500, 800/488–2968 ⊕ www.louisianaoldstate-capitol.org ➦ Free ⊗ Closed Sun. and Mon.

Rural Life Museum and Windrush Gardens

MUSEUM | Run by Louisiana State University, this outdoor teaching and research facility aims to represent the rural life of early Louisianans. Three major areas—the Barn, the Working Plantation, and Folk Architecture—contain more than 32 rustic 19th-century structures spread over 25 acres. A visitor center adjoins the Barn, which holds a collection that includes old farm tools, quilts, 19th-century horse-drawn carriages, items once belonging to slaves, and much more. The plantation section's buildings include a gristmill, a smithy, and several outbuildings. The gardens were created by the late landscape designer Steele Burden. ✉ *4560 Essen La.* ☎ *225/765–2437* ⊕ *www.lsu.edu/rurallife* ✍ *$10.*

Shaw Center for the Arts
ARTS VENUE | This arts facility houses the Louisiana State University (LSU) Museum of Art, the LSU Museum Store, the Manship Theatre, Hartley/Vey Studio and Workshop Theatres, LSU School of Art Glassell Gallery, two sculpture gardens, and a rooftop terrace with great views of the Mississippi River. On-site restaurants include Tsunami Sushi, Capital City Grill, PJ's Coffee, and Stroubes Chophouse. ✉ *100 Lafayette St.* ☎ *225/346–5001* ⊕ *www.shawcenter.org* ✍ *Museum of Art $5.*

State Capitol Building
GOVERNMENT BUILDING | This building has housed the offices of the governor and the Legislature since 1932. It is a testament to the personal influence of legendary Governor Huey P. Long that funding for such a massive building was approved during the Great Depression, and that the building itself was completed in a mere 14 months. You can tour the first floor, richly decorated with murals and mosaics, and peer into the halls of the Louisiana Legislature. Long's colorful personality—and autocratic ways—eventually caught up with him: he was assassinated in 1935, and the spot where he was shot (near the rear elevators) is marked with a plaque. At 34 stories, this is America's tallest state capitol; an observation deck on the 27th floor affords an expansive view of the Mississippi River, the city, and the industrial outskirts. ✉ *900 N. 3rd St.* ☎ *225/342–7317* ⊕ *www.crt.state.la.us* ✍ *Free.*

Huey's "Deduct Box" ◉

One of the biggest mysteries about Huey P. Long is what happened to his "deduct box." The deduct box was where Long kept his political contributions—cash—from individuals and corporations. State employees, no matter how high or low, also gave a portion of their salary to Long. The box had a number of homes, and the best known was at the Roosevelt Hotel in New Orleans. But when Long was assassinated in 1935, the location of the deduct box went to the grave with him. Many still think it's within the walls of the hotel.

USS *Kidd* Veterans Museum
NAUTICAL SITE | This World War II ship has been restored to its V-J Day configuration. A self-guided tour covers more than 50 inner spaces of the ship and the separate **Nautical Center** museum. Among the museum's exhibits are articles from the United States' 175 Fletcher-class destroyers, a collection of ship models, and a restored P-40 fighter plane hanging from the ceiling. The Louisiana Memorial Plaza lists more than 7,000 Louisiana citizens killed during combat, including the 127 citizens killed in the Iraq and Afghanistan wars. An A-7E Corsair plane pays tribute to the veterans of the Vietnam War. ✉ *305 S. River Rd.* ☎ *225/342–1942* ⊕ *www.usskidd.com* ✍ *$12.53.*

🍴 Restaurants

Juban's
$$$$ | SOUTHERN | This upscale bistro with a lush courtyard and walls adorned with art is about three miles from the Louisiana State University campus. Tempting main courses, including seafood, beef,

The Louisiana State Capitol Building is considered "Huey Long's monument" thanks to the role the governor played getting it built during the Great Depression.

and pork dishes, as well as roasted duck and quail, highlight the menu. **Known for:** softshell "Halleluhah" crab stuffed with seafood and topped with "creoloaise" sauce; beautiful skylit atrium bar; elevated Creole cuisine. [$] *Average main: $32* ✉ *Acadian Perkins Shopping Center, 3739 Perkins Rd.* ☎ *225/346–8422* 🌐 *www.jubans.com* 🕓 *No lunch Mon. and Sat. and no dinner Sun.*

★ Mike Anderson's

$$$ | **SEAFOOD** | Locals praise the seafood at this busy spot, and rightly so: the food is consistently good, fresh, and served in large portions. The fried seafood platter—shrimp, oysters, crawfish tails, catfish, and stuffed crab served with onion rings, hush puppies, and a choice of salad or various coleslaws—is your best bet. **Known for:** seafood platters; mahi-mahi topped with Gulf shrimp and Louisiana crawfish; several types of oysters. [$] *Average main: $24* ✉ *1031 W. Lee Dr.* ☎ *225/766–7823* 🌐 *www.mikeandersons.com.*

Ruffino's

$$$ | **ITALIAN** | A broad, clubby dining room invites lingering over some of the best Italian cuisine in town. Local ingredients find their way into hearty Italian dishes, such as eggplant Parmesan and cedar plank redfish. **Known for:** local seafood; romantic ambience; savory crab meat cheesecake. [$] *Average main: $23* ✉ *18811 Highland Rd.* ☎ *225/753–3458* 🌐 *www.ruffinosrestaurant.com* 🕓 *No lunch Mon.–Thurs. and Sat.*

Tsunami

$ | **JAPANESE** | On the roof of the Shaw Center for the Arts, the sleek, modern dining room of this Japanese restaurant commands one of the best views in town, with tables overlooking the busy Mississippi River (an open-air patio is available, too). In addition to the usual sushi-bar fare, the chefs here prepare creative Louisiana-style variations: try the panko-crusted alligator roll or the soft shell crab, for instance. **Known for:** fun atmosphere; locally themed sushi rolls; sunset views over the Mississippi River.

$ Average main: $15 ⊠ Shaw Center for the Arts, 100 Lafayette St., 6th fl. ☎ 225/346–5100 ⊕ www.servingsushi. com ⊗ Closed Sun. and Mon.

 Hotels

Embassy Suites

$$ | HOTEL | This centrally located property has two-room suites with mahogany furniture and a wet-bar area with a micro-wave, coffeemaker, and mini-refrigerator. **Pros:** great location if you're going to an LSU football game; comfortable rooms; lots of services. **Cons:** downtown sights are not within walking distance; occa-sionally packed with conventioneers—or high-spirited LSU fans; more business hotel than charming vacation retreat. $ Rooms from: $129 ⊠ 4914 Constitution Ave. ☎ 225/924–6566, 800/362–2779 ⊕ www.embassysuites.com ⊟ No credit cards ⇌ 223 suites ⦿ Free breakfast.

Hilton Baton Rouge Capitol Center

$$ | HOTEL | A fitness center and many other amenities make this historic riverside landmark a popular choice for business people and conventioneers. **Pros:** spectacular view of the river; near all the downtown sites; next to Shaw Performing Arts Center, access to great arts and restaurants. **Cons:** generic businesslike surroundings; can get crowded during conventions; must pay $28/night for valet parking if you bring a car. $ Rooms from: $140 ⊠ 201 Lafayette St. ☎ 225/344–5866 ⊕ www.hiltoncapi-tolcenter.com ⊟ No credit cards ⇌ 299 rooms ⦿ No meals.

Marriott Baton Rouge

$$ | HOTEL | This high-rise hotel has somewhat formal rooms and public spaces with traditional furnishings, and rooms on the top four floors come with such perks as continental breakfast and afternoon hors d'oeuvres and cocktails. **Pros:** accommodating to large groups; full-service hotel; lots of comforts. **Cons:** not that close to downtown sights; no

microwaves in the rooms; chain hotel means less of a unique, local experience. $ Rooms from: $179 ⊠ 5500 Hilton Ave. ☎ 225/924–5000, 800/627–7468 ⊕ www. marriott.com ⊟ No credit cards ⇌ 299 rooms ⦿ No meals.

★ The Stockade B&B

$$ | B&B/INN | It may be named for the Civil War–era military prison that once occupied the site, but you definitely won't feel like a prisoner in this pleasant, tile-roofed, contemporary brick house on winding, oak-lined Highland Road. **Pros:** Southern hospitality and country ele-gance; tasty breakfast; property is on the National Register of Historic Places. **Cons:** downtown sights can feel far away; small property means you should book far in advance; less food and beverage options available than other accommodations. $ Rooms from: $159 ⊠ 8860 Highland Rd. ☎ 225/769–7358, 888/900–5430 ⊕ www.thestockade.com ⇌ 6 rooms ⦿ Free breakfast.

St. Francisville

25 miles north of Baton Rouge on U.S. 61.

A cluster of plantation homes all within a half-hour drive, a lovely, walkable historic district, renowned antiques shopping, and a wealth of comfortable B&Bs draw visitors and locals from New Orleans to overnight stays in St. Francisville. The town is just a two-hour drive from New Orleans, so it's also possible to make this a day trip.

St. Francisville's historic district, particu-larly along Royal Street, is dotted with markers identifying basic histories of various structures, most of them dating to the late 18th or early 19th century. The region's Anglo-Protestant edge, in contrast to the staunchly French-Catholic tenor of the River Road plantations, is evident in the prominent **Grace Episcopal Church,** on a hill in the center of town and surrounded by a peaceful, Spanish moss–shaded cemetery. A smaller (and older) Catholic cemetery is directly across a small fence from the Episcopal complex.

Sights

Angola Museum

JAIL | The 18,000 acres that make up the notorious Angola prison are a half-hour drive from St. Francisville, at the dead end of Highway 66. With a prison population of about 6,000 inmates, this is one of the largest prisons in the United States. Nicknamed "The Farm," Angola was once a working plantation, with prisoners for field hands. Now it produces 4 million pounds of vegetables each year, which feed 11,000 inmates across the state. The prison has been immortalized in countless songs and several films and documentaries, including *Dead Man Walking* and *The Wildest Show in the South: The Angola Prison Rodeo*. The latter film is based on the prison's biannual rodeo in April and October, which offers visitors a rare look inside the grounds of the prison. Inmates set up stands where they sell their arts and crafts during the rodeo. A small, year-round museum outside the prison's front gate houses a fascinating, eerie, and often moving collection of photographs documenting the people and events that have been a part of Angola. Items such as makeshift prisoner weapons and the electric chair used for executions until 1991 are also on display. ⊠ *17544 Tunica Trace* ☎ *225/655–2592* ⊕ *www.angolamuseum.org* ✉ *Free* ☽ *Closed Sun.*

Audubon State Historic Site and Oakley Plantation House

HISTORIC SITE | John James Audubon did a major portion of his *Birds of America* studies in this 100-acre park, and the three-story Oakley Plantation House is where Audubon tutored the young Eliza Pirrie, daughter of Mr. and Mrs.

James Pirrie, who owned the house. The simple—even spartan—interior contrasts sharply with the extravagances of many of the River Road plantations and demonstrates the Puritan influence in this region. The grounds, too, recall the English penchant for a blending of order and wilderness in their gardens. You must follow a short, peaceful walking path to reach the house from the parking lot. A state-run museum at the start of the path provides an informative look at plantation life as it was lived in this region 200 years ago. A permanent exhibit tells the story of the slaves who lived on this site—including many of their names—and the grounds include a pair of authentic slave cabins brought here from another plantation. ⊠ *11788 LA Hwy. 965* ✚ *2 miles south of St. Francisville off U.S. 61* ☎ *225/635–3739, 888/677–2838* ⊕ *www. crt.state.la.us* ✉ *Park and plantation tour $10* ☽ *Closed Mon. and Tues.*

Rosedown Plantation and Gardens

HOUSE | The opulent, beautifully restored house at Rosedown dates from 1835. The original owners, Martha and Daniel Turnbull, spent their honeymoon in Europe; Mrs. Turnbull fell in love with the gardens she saw there and had the land at Rosedown laid out even as the house was under construction. She spent the rest of her life lovingly maintaining some 28 acres of exquisite formal gardens. The State of Louisiana owns Rosedown, and the beauty of the restored manor, including the furniture (90% of which is original), can be appreciated on an hour-long tour led by park rangers that—while thorough in some respects—mostly glosses over the lives of the slaves who lived on the property. Be sure to allow ample time for roaming the grounds after the tour. ⊠ *12501 Hwy. 10* ☎ *225/635–3332, 888/376–1867* ⊕ *www.crt.state. la.us* ✉ *$12.*

🍴 Restaurants

★ Magnolia Café

$$ | **AMERICAN** | This low-key and unassuming restaurant turns into a St. Francisville hot spot on Friday and Saturday nights. During the day, locals and tourists flock to "the Mag" for sandwiches, pizza, steaks, and Southern and Mexican dishes. **Known for:** live music on weekend nights; nice cocktails; blend of local and Mexican flavors. [$] *Average main: $17* ✉ *5689 Commerce St.* ☎ *225/635–6528* 🌐 *www.themagnoliacafe.net* 🕒 *No dinner Sun.–Wed.*

🛏 Hotels

Barrow House Inn

$$ | **B&B/INN** | Fittingly located on St. Francisville's historic Royal Street, these two old houses hold some of the most comfortable bed-and-breakfast accommodations in the area, with antique furnishings in most of the rooms. **Pros:** good location in downtown St. Francisville; comfortable atmosphere; friendly staff. **Cons:** if you don't like antiques, you may feel as if you're in a museum or your grandmother's home; small property means inn can sometimes be full during busy times; complimentary breakfast is sparse but you can pay extra for additional items. [$] *Rooms from: $150* ✉ *9779 Royal St.* ☎ *225/635–4791* 🌐 *www.topteninn.com* 🔑 *7 rooms* 🍽 *Free breakfast.*

Lafayette

136 miles west of New Orleans.

Lafayette (pronounced lah-fay- *ette*), with a population of more than 125,000 (the largest city in Cajun Country), is a major center of Cajun life and lore. It's an interesting and enjoyable city, with some worthwhile historical and artistic sights. The simulated Cajun villages at **Vermilionville** and **Acadian Village** provide evocative introductions to the traditional Cajun way of life. Excellent restaurants and B&Bs make Lafayette a good jumping-off point for exploring the region. In recent years the city has had an infusion of new restaurants and nightclubs—particularly downtown.

Murals

There are several outdoor murals by the local artist Robert Dafford in the center of Lafayette, including a 100-foot-wide Louisiana swamp scene titled *'Til All That's Left is a Postcard*, across from Dwyer's Café. Another work, titled *Ex-Garage* and full of splashy cars and TVs with vignettes of Cajun life, is on the Jefferson Tower Building. The reflections in the bumpers of the cars reveal area musicians and traditions.

👁 Sights

Acadiana Center for the Arts

ARTS VENUE | This multicultural arts center hosts art exhibits, musical performances, lectures, workshops, and children's programs. Film screenings are occasionally held at the in-house movie theater. ✉ *101 W. Vermilion St.* ☎ *337/233–7060* 🌐 *www.acadianacenterforthearts.org* 🕒 *Closed Sun.*

Acadian Cultural Center

MUSEUM | A unit of the National Park Service, the center traces the history of the area through numerous audiovisual exhibits on food, music, and folklore. Be sure to watch the introductory film, which is a dramatization of the Expulsion of the Acadians (1755–1764), when the British deported the descendants of French settlers in the maritime provinces of Canada to the 13 colonies. Clips from the 1929 silent movie *Evangeline* (a fictional account based on the Longfellow poem about an Acadian girl's search

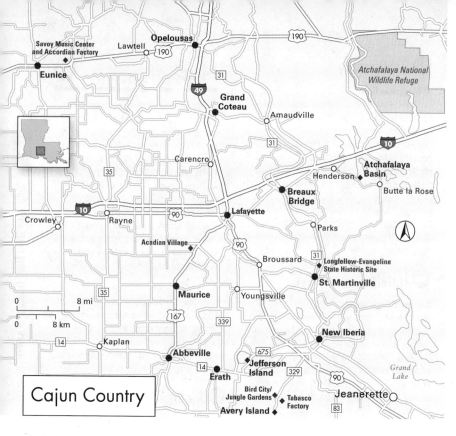

Cajun Country

for her lost love) are incorporated into the presentation—film buffs will love it. Ranger-guided boat tours of Bayou Vermilion take place March through June and September through November in a traditional Cajun boat, but require two weeks' advance registration to book. Ranger talks on local history and culture take place every Tuesday at 10 am. ⊠ 501 Fisher Rd. ☎ 337/232–0789 ⊕ www. nps.gov/jela ✉ Free, boat tours from $8 ⏾ Closed Sun. and Mon.

Acadiana Park Nature Station
NATIONAL/STATE PARK | FAMILY | Naturalists are on hand in the interpretive center at this three-story cypress structure, which overlooks 150 acres of easy, peaceful nature trails and natural forest. The northern section includes a managed butterfly habitat. The focus here is on environmental education. Free weekend nature talks begin at 1 pm on the first Saturday of each month, and free guided tours are offered on the first Saturday and Sunday of every month by request. A guided evening hike on the last Saturday of the month is available by reservation ($2.17 per person). ⊠ 1205 E. Alexander St. ☎ 337/291–8448 ⊕ www.naturesta-tion.org ✉ Free.

Acadian Village
MUSEUM VILLAGE | Most of the structures at this re-creation of an early-19th-century bayou settlement were moved here to construct a representative "village." They actually represent a broad range of Acadian architectural styles, and the rustic general store, smithy, and chapel are replicas. The park is on 10 wooded acres, with a meandering bayou crisscrossed by wooden footbridges. Each house is decorated with antique furnishings. The

weeks before Christmas bring "Noel Acadien au Village," with evening-only hours, musicians, food, and buildings covered in festive lights. ⊠ *200 Greenleaf Dr.* ☎ *337/981–2364, 800/962–9133* ⊕ *www. acadianvillage.org* ⊠ *$10* ⊙ *Closed Sun.*

Alexandre Mouton House and Lafayette Museum

MUSEUM | Built in 1800 as the *maison dimanche,* or "Sunday house" (a town house used when attending church services) of town founder Jean Mouton, this galleried town house with a mid-19th-century addition now preserves local history. It was later home to Alexandre Mouton (1804–1885), the first Democratic governor of Louisiana. The older section is an excellent example of early Acadian architecture and contains artifacts used by settlers. The main museum features Civil War–era furnishings and memorabilia and an exhibit on Mardi Gras. ⊠ *1122 Lafayette St.* ☎ *337/234–2208* ⊕ *www.lafayettemuseum.com* ⊠ *$5* ⊙ *Closed Sun. and Mon.*

Cathedral of St. John the Evangelist

RELIGIOUS SITE | This Dutch Romanesque structure with Byzantine touches was completed in 1916 (construction began in 1912). In the cemetery behind the church are aboveground tombs that date back to 1820; interred here are town founder Jean Mouton, Civil War General Alfred Mouton, General Alfred Gardiner, and Cidalese Arceneaux. Next to the cathedral is a nearly 500-year-old St. John Oak, one of the charter members of the silent but leafy Louisiana Live Oak Society. Docent-guided tours are available on most Mondays, Wednesdays, and Fridays at 10 am, though calling ahead is recommended. Booklets are also available for self-guided tours. ⊠ *914 St. John Street* ☎ *337/232–1322* ⊕ *www.saintjohncathedral.org* ⊠ *Free; $5 suggested donation.*

Children's Museum of Acadiana

MUSEUM | FAMILY | Good on a rainy day or to burn off extra energy in the kids, this museum is basically a large indoor playground, with educational games and interactive exhibits such as a grocery store, a kid-size TV news studio, a bubble exhibit, and a health exhibit. ⊠ *201 E. Congress St.* ☎ *337/232–8500* ⊕ *www. childrensmuseumofacadiana.com* ⊠ *$7* ⊙ *Closed Mon.*

Lafayette Courthouse

GOVERNMENT BUILDING | The courthouse contains an impressive collection of more than 2,000 historical photographs of life in the Lafayette area. There are images of famous politicians such as Dudley LeBlanc and Huey Long working the stump, and scenes from the Great Mississippi Flood of 1927. ⊠ *800 S. Buchanan St.* ☎ *337/232–8211* ⊙ *Closed weekends.*

Lafayette Science Museum

MUSEUM | FAMILY | This sparkling natural-history museum includes changing exhibitions and lots of fun hands-on science for kids. The most popular permanent attraction is the planetarium, outfitted with high-definition digital equipment. ⊠ *433 Jefferson St.* ☎ *337/291–5544* ⊕ *www.lafayettesciencemuseum. org* ⊠ *$5* ⊙ *Closed Mon.*

Paul and Lulu Hilliard University Art Museum

MUSEUM | Inside a gleaming glass box, this museum on the campus of the University of Louisiana at Lafayette features world-class works, including 150 paintings and collages by Henry Botkin and a Louisiana collection including artists Elemore Morgan Jr., George Rodrigue, and Hunt Slonem. ⊠ *710 E. St. Mary Blvd.* ☎ *337/482–2278* ⊕ *hilliardmuseum. org* ⊠ *$5* ⊙ *Closed Sun. and Mon.*

★ Vermilionville Historic Village

MUSEUM | FAMILY | Directly behind the Acadian Cultural Center, this living-history village—serene and set beautifully along a bayou—re-creates the early life of the region's Creoles, Cajuns, and Native Americans, focusing on the late 1700s to 1890. On select days, visitors can see a blacksmith demonstration or watch weavers at work. There are exhibits in 19 Acadian-style structures, including a music hall where live Cajun or zydeco music is played on weekend afternoons, often luring dancers onto the floor. A large, rustic restaurant serves Cajun classics. Check ahead for live demonstrations from the on-site cooking school. ✉ *300 Fisher Rd.* ☎ *337/233–4077, 866/992–2968* 🌐 *www.vermilionville.org* 🎟 *$10* ⏲ *Closed Mon.*

🍴 Restaurants

★ Café Vermilionville

$$$$ | CAJUN | This 19th-century inn with crisp white linens and old brick fireplaces serves French and Cajun dishes to a well-dressed crowd. Among the specialties are Gulf fish Acadian and grilled duck breast. **Known for:** historic setting; old-fashioned service; fine dining. [$] *Average main: $34* ✉ *1304 W. Pinhook Rd.* ☎ *337/237–0100* 🌐 *www.cafev.com* ⏲ *Closed Sun. No lunch Sat.*

Dwyer's Café

$ | SOUTHERN | People jam into this diner as early as 6 am for hot biscuits and grits. Dwyer's also serves red beans and rice, jambalaya, pot roast, burgers, and omelets. **Known for:** rotating plate lunch specials; great gumbo; classic Southern breakfast. [$] *Average main: $8* ✉ *323 Jefferson St.* ☎ *337/235–9364* ⏲ *No dinner.*

★ Johnson's Boucaniere

$ | SOUTHERN | This outstanding *boucaniere* (Cajun French for smokehouse) is run by the next generation of the family that once operated the iconic Johnson's Grocery in Eunice, Louisiana. Music from young local bands plays over the sound system and is available for purchase; customers sit on the covered porch and dig into boudin sausages, sandwiches, and the heartily recommended barbecue—smoked in-house and rubbed with Cajun-style seasonings. **Known for:** boudin sausages; Cajun-style barbecue; laid-back vibe. [$] *Average main: $8* ✉ *1111 St. John St.* ☎ *337/269–8878* 🌐 *www.johnsons-boucaniere.com* ⏲ *Closed Sun. and Mon. No dinner.*

Louisiana Crawfish Time

$$ | CAJUN | From roughly December through June, when Louisiana crawfish are in season, local families pack in to partake in the outrageous abundance. Order from the menu—including crawfish, oysters, and a few sides like sausage links and boiled potatoes, plus cold beer—in the simple, stripped-down dining room filled with big tables. **Known for:** classic Louisiana crawfish; boiled shrimp; drive-thru window for take-away seafood. [$] *Average main: $18* ✉ *2019 Verot School Rd.* ☎ *337/988–2645* 🌐 *www.lacrawfishtime.com* 💳 *No credit cards* ⏲ *Closed June–Nov. No lunch.*

★ Pamplona Tapas Bar

$$$$ | SPANISH | An authentic interior (one wall is covered with bullfighting posters) creates just the right mood for chef Kris Allen's wide array of sophisticated small plates and one of the best wine lists in the area. The bacon-wrapped dates, the lamb sliders, and the foie gras are especially delicious. **Known for:** traditional and inventive tapas; energetic atmosphere; great paella. [$] *Average main: $32* ✉ *631 Jefferson St.* ☎ *337/232–0070* 🌐 *www.pamplonatapas.com* ⏲ *Closed Sun. and Mon. No lunch Sat.*

Prejean's

$$ | CAJUN | In this cypress house decorated with swamp trees and a large stuffed alligator at the entrance, people gather over red-and-white-check tablecloths to chow down on some local classics: crawfish and alligator sausage cheesecake, Cajun duckling, or any of the kitchen's four distinctive gumbos. Grilled seafood provides some lighter options. **Known for:** crawfish étouffée; boudin sausage; live music. [$] *Average main: $21* ✉ *3480 N.E. Evangeline Throughway* ☎ *337/896–3247* 🌐 *www.prejeans.com.*

T-Coon's Café

$ | **CAJUN** | This often-busy diner serves a hearty Cajun breakfast and lunch, which feature daily specials such as smothered rabbit, catfish court boulion, or crawfish omelets. The Southern fare also includes fried chicken and seafood dishes. **Known for:** Cajun flavors; comfort food; country breakfast. [$] *Average main: $10* ✉ *1900 W. Pinhook Rd.* ☎ *337/233–0422* 🌐 *www.tcoons.com* 🕒 *No dinner.*

Tsunami

$$ | **JAPANESE** | A stylish contemporary restaurant as chic as the crowd it attracts delivers fresh and innovative sushi and Japanese cuisine. Entrées include a sumo rib eye, Chilean sea bass, and various tempura dishes. **Known for:** lively atmosphere; locally themed sushi rolls; fun cocktails. [$] *Average main: $20* ✉ *412 Jefferson St.* ☎ *337/234–3474* 🌐 *www.servingsushi.com* 🕒 *Closed Sun. and Mon.*

Creole vs. Cajun Food

Cajun cuisine relies on locally available ingredients, including pork, seafood, smoked meats, yams, and rice. Creole cuisine is more cosmopolitan, incorporating French, Spanish, Italian, African, and French Caribbean influences. Most Cajun and Creole dishes include the "holy trinity" of sautéed celery, bell pepper, and garlic or onion as a base, but Creole dishes, like their French counterparts, are defined by their sauces. Examples include shrimp Creole, crawfish bisque, and oysters Rockefeller.

Hotels

Buchanan Lofts

$$ | **B&B/INN** | These five rooms inside a refurbished building that once was the first department store in Lafayette are like seriously stylish apartments—each has a different layout, but they're all quite spacious, with floor-to-ceiling windows, lots of exposed brick, and streamlined, minimalist furnishings. **Pros:** close to everything downtown; huge rooms filled with stylish furnishings; kitchen included. **Cons:** not much local character; often sold out; can be loud because of proximity to downtown. [$] *Rooms from: $200* ✉ *403 S. Buchanan St.* ☎ *337/534–4922* 🌐 *www.buchananlofts.com* 🛏 *5 rooms* 🍴 *No meals.*

Doubletree by Hilton Hotel Lafayette

$ | **HOTEL** | In this large high-rise quite close to Interstate 10 and near the business district, traditional furnishings outfit the standard accommodations, and the riverside rooms overlook the Bayou Vermilion. **Pros:** typical Hilton amenities; location is convenient for sightseeing; comfy beds. **Cons:** reservations are hard to come by if there's a wedding or event; halls can be loud when the hotel is full; lacks local charm. [$] *Rooms from: $103* ✉ *1521 W. Pinhook Rd.* ☎ *337/235–6111, 800/445–8667* 🌐 *www.hilton.com* 🛏 *327 rooms* 🍴 *No meals.*

T'Frere's House

$$ | **B&B/INN** | Built circa 1890 of native cypress and handmade bricks, some rooms in the Acadian-style "Little Brother's House" are furnished with French and Louisiana antiques while others are more modern. **Pros:** charming decor; owners like to feed their guests well; some decent bars and restaurants nearby. **Cons:** fifteen-minute drive from downtown; food options not great for those with dietary restrictions; somewhat busy intersection could be problematic for the lightest of sleepers. [$] *Rooms from: $130* ✉ *1905 Verot School Rd.* ☎ *337/984–9347, 800/984–9347* 🌐 *www.tfrereshouse.com* 🛏 *9 rooms* 🍴 *Free breakfast.*

ⓨ Nightlife

Pick up a copy of the *Times of Acadiana* to find listings for *fais-do-dos*, zydeco dances, and other events. The free weekly is available online and in hotels, restaurants, and shops.

Artmosphere

MUSIC CLUBS | Between hosting local and touring Cajun and zydeco acts and a healthy weekly showing of karaoke, this lively neighborhood bistro has music seven nights a week. Combine that with an art gallery, a wide-ranging food menu, beers, and imaginative cocktails, and Artmosphere can make any night out in Lafayette an enjoyable one. ⊠ *902 Johnston St.* ☎ *337/233–3331* ⊕ *www.artmosphere.vpweb.com.*

★ Blue Moon Saloon

MUSIC CLUBS | This cottage doesn't look like much from the street, but after you pay your cover at the garden gate, you'll soon find yourself on a large covered deck packed with a young crowd dancing to the hottest local Cajun, zydeco, and roots music acts. Check their calendar online for upcoming shows. ⊠ *215 E. Convent St.* ☎ *337/234–2422* ⊕ *www.bluemoonpresents.com.*

El Sido's Zydeco & Blues Club

MUSIC CLUBS | This family-run zydeco club hosts music on Friday and Saturday nights. Sid Williams manages the club, and his brother's band, Nathan and the Zydeco Cha-Chas, perform frequently— as does Nathan's son's band, Lil Nathan and the Zydeco Big Timers. ⊠ *1523 N. St. Antoine St.* ☎ *337/235–0647.*

Randol's

MUSIC CLUBS | This good Cajun restaurant is also a *salle de danse*, with music and dancing seven nights a week. ⊠ *2320 Kaliste Saloom Rd.* ☎ *337/981–7080, 800/962–2586* ⊕ *www.randols.com.*

The Wurst Biergarten & Public Market

BREWPUBS/BEER GARDENS | Stop by the Wurst if you're looking for comedy, live music, dancing, a market, and—of course—beer. The outdoor German-style beer garden has it all, and it's a popular downtown spot for Lafayette's trendy crowd to gather and be entertained. Space heaters keep it comfortable in the winter. ⊠ *537 Jefferson St.* ☎ *337/534–4612.*

🎭 Performing Arts

FESTIVALS

ArtWalks

ART GALLERIES—ARTS | Downtown galleries are open and the streets are hopping during this popular event, held on the second Saturday of each month. ⊠ *Lafayette* ☎ *337/291–5566* ⊕ *www.downtownlafayette.org.*

Downtown Alive!

GATHERING PLACES | For nearly 40 years, on Friday evenings from mid-March through June and from September through November, dancing crowds converge on downtown Lafayette, where bands play an open-air stage. A happy hour starts at 5 pm, there are local food vendors throughout the evening, and there's even a Kids Zone full of family-friendly activities. ⊠ *Jefferson St. at Main St.* ☎ *337/291–5566* ⊕ *www.downtownlafayette.org.*

Festivals Acadiens et Creoles

MUSIC CLUBS | This huge music-and-food fest—which kicks off with the official "Cutting of the Boudin"—is held mid-October in Girard Park. Admission's free and the food's outstanding, but the music is the best thing about it all. ⊠ *Girard Park, Girard Park Dr.* ☎ *337/232–3737, 800/346–1958* ⊕ *www.festivalsacadiens.com.*

Festival International de Louisiane

MUSIC CLUBS | Taking place on the last weekend of April, this free multi-day Lafayette music festival is a worthy alternative to the New Orleans Jazz and Heritage Festival. A regional favorite, it fills the streets with some of the best entertainers, artisans, and chefs from French-speaking nations and communities. ⊠ *Lafayette* ☎ *337–232–8086* ⊕ *festivalinternational.org.*

Mardi Gras

GATHERING PLACES | The biggest bash in this neck of the woods is in February or March (depending on when Lent occurs). About a dozen parades take to the streets over a couple of weeks, culminating on "Fat Tuesday," and a festive atmosphere fills the city. ⊠ *Lafayette* ⊕ *www.lafayettetravel.com.*

 Shopping

ANTIQUES

Sans Souci Fine Crafts Gallery

ANTIQUES/COLLECTIBLES | If you are looking for authentic Louisiana crafts, you've come to the right place. Pottery, furniture, items made out of gourds, metal, and wood, and corn-husk dolls and jewelry are all created by members of the Louisiana Crafts Guild, headquartered here. ⊠ *219 E. Vermilion St.* ☎ *337/266–7999* ⊕ *www.louisianacrafts.org* ☉ *Closed Mon.*

FOOD

⭐ **Don's Specialty Meats & Grocery**

FOOD/CANDY | Stuff your face with Cajun favorites on-site or fill your cooler with boudin, cracklins, stuffed pork chops, quail, and a variety of sausages. There's another location at 104 Highway 726 in Carencro, also just outside Lafayette. ⊠ *730 I–10 S. Frontage Rd., Scott* ☎ *337/234–2528, 337/896–6370 Carencro* ⊕ *www.donsspecialtymeats.com.*

Poupart Bakery

FOOD/CANDY | The fresh French bread and pastries made here are outstanding. The shop also sells specialty sauces and preserves, as well as king cakes, available during the Carnival season. ⊠ *1902 W. Pinhook Rd.* ☎ *337/232–7921* ⊕ *www.poupartsbakery.com* ☉ *Closed Mon.*

Grand Coteau

15 miles north of Lafayette.

The tiny village of Grand Coteau ("Big Hill") may be the most serene place in south Louisiana. Nestled against a sweeping ridge that formed a natural levee of the Mississippi River centuries ago, the town is oriented around a core of grand and beautiful religious institutions. Covering the hill itself is a peaceful cemetery, behind the stately St. Charles College, a Jesuit seminary. When the Mississippi overflowed its banks during the cataclysmic flood of 1927, the water stopped at the base of Grand Coteau's ridge, and the town was preserved. Today the entire town center is listed on the National Register of Historic Places, with dozens of historical structures including Creole cottages, early Acadian-style homes, and the grand Academy and Convent of the Sacred Heart. Antiques and gift stores line Martin Luther King Drive (Route 93), the main thoroughfare.

◉ Sights

Academy and Convent of the Sacred Heart

RELIGIOUS SITE | A magnificent avenue of pines and moss-laden oaks leads to the entrance of the first international branch of Sacred Heart schools (founded in 1821) and the site of the only Vatican-certified miracle to occur in the United States. The miracle occurred when nuns at the convent said novenas to St. John Berchmans, a 15th-century Jesuit priest, on behalf of Mary Wilson, a very ill novice. St. John Berchmans subsequently appeared to Mary twice, and she was suddenly and unexpectedly cured. St. John Berchmans was canonized in 1888. Make an appointment to enter a shrine on the exact site of the miracle, as well as to tour the museum with artifacts dating from the school's occupation by Union troops during the Civil War. ⊠ *1821 Academy Rd., end of Church St.* ☎ *337/662–5275* ⊕ *www.sshcoteau.org.*

Cajun and Zydeco Music

It's 9 am on a typical Saturday morning in the Cajun prairie town of Mamou, and Fred's Lounge is already so full that people are spilling out the door. Inside, Cajun singer Donald Thibodeaux gets a nod from the radio announcer, squeezes his accordion, and launches into the "Pine Grove Blues." Oblivious to the posted warning that reads "This is not a dance hall," the packed bar begins to roll. Fred's Lounge may not be a "formal" dance hall, but plenty of dancing is done here; it gets especially lively during Mamou's Mardi Gras and July 4 celebrations. And every Saturday morning for more than 40 years, live Cajun radio shows have been broadcast from the late Fred Tate's lounge. Things get revved up at 8 am and keep going till 1 pm, and the show is aired on Ville Platte's KVPI radio (1050 AM).

Music has been an integral expression of Cajun culture since early Acadian immigrants unpacked stringed instruments and gathered in homes for singing and socializing. "*Fais-do-do*" (pronounced *fay*-doh-doh) is what mothers would murmur to put their babies to sleep as the fiddlers tuned up before one of these house parties. With the growth of towns, most of the fais-do-dos were supplanted by dance halls, but the name stuck. Accordions, steel guitars, and drums were added and amplified to be heard over the noise of crowded barrooms.

Cajun music went through some lean years in the 1940s and '50s, when the state attempted to eradicate the use of the Cajun-French language, but today Cajun music is enjoyed at street festivals and restaurants such as Randol's and Prejean's, which serve equal portions of seafood and song. These places not only keep the music and dance tradition alive, but also serve as magnets for Cajun dance enthusiasts from around the world.

Zydeco, the dance music of rural African Americans of south Louisiana, is closely related to Cajun music, but with a slightly harder, rock-influenced edge. The best place to find the music is in one of the roadside dance halls on weekends. Modern zydeco and Cajun music both feature the accordion, but zydeco tends to be faster and uses heavy percussion and electric instruments; electric guitars and washboards (called a *frottoir*), largely absent from Cajun music, are staples. Zydeco bands often play soul- and R&B-inflected tunes sung in Creole French.

Dance is the universal language of Cajun Country, but don't worry if you're not fluent—there's always someone happy to lead you around the floor and leave you feeling like a local.

🍴 Restaurants

Chicory's Coffee & Cafe

$ | CAFÉ | Come here during the morning or afternoon and you're likely to find the people of Grand Coteau and nearby towns chatting over a smoothie or cup of coffee. Whether you're looking for local favorites or healthier fare, this is a no-brainer stop during your Grand Coteau excursion. **Known for:** coffee and smoothies; boudin, egg, and cheese biscuit; white chocolate bread pudding. $ *Average main: $8* ⊠ *219 E. MLK Dr.* ☎ *337/886–5770* ⊘ *Closed Mon. No dinner.*

Dropping in on a jam session is a must-do in Cajun country.

☐ Nightlife

★ Bayou Teche Brewing

WINERY/DISTILLERY | A lot of Cajun Country is about the food. Back in 2009, the three brothers who founded this brewery wanted to create beers that would complement their favorite regional eats. Bayou Teche Brewing is eight miles from Grand Coteau and has an outdoor space you'll want to hang out all day in. You can find a few of this popular brewery's flagship beers in all of Louisiana's major cities, but visitors come here to try as many as 15 brews—most of which can only be tasted at this location. There are movies screened on Thursday nights, live music on Fridays, Saturdays, and Sundays, and wood-fired pizza every day the taproom's open. ☒ 1094 Bushville Hwy ☎ 337/754–5122 ⊕ www.bayoutechebrewing.com ☉ Closed Mon. and Tues.

☐ Shopping

The Kitchen Shop

FOOD/CANDY | One of Grand Coteau's historic cottages houses a collection of regional cookbooks and cooking supplies, in addition to gifts and other merchandise, including prints, books, and greeting cards by famed local photographer John Slaughter. In the tea room, scones, cookies, and a specialty pecan torte called *gateau-na-na* are served. ☒ 296 E. MLK Dr. ☎ 337/662–3500 ☉ Closed Mon.

Opelousas

15 miles north of Grand Coteau.

In the heart of St. Landry Parish, Opelousas is the third-oldest town in the state—Poste de Opelousas was founded in 1720 by the French as a trading post with the Opelousas Indians. It's a sleepy spot with a historic central square and a provincial museum, and it hosts an annual zydeco festival. Look for two murals located in a pocket park–parking lot adjacent to the St. Landry Bank & Trust Co. building. One depicts the history of the area and historical monuments in St. Landry Parish, and the other illustrates the legend of the Seven Brothers Oak, which is located south of Washington, a charming nearby town. While it currently feels like a town past its prime, there are still ample opportunities to learn about its past as well as to experience zydeco music.

Sights

Louisiana Orphan Train Museum
MUSEUM | Between 1854 and 1929, more than 2,000 orphans from New York were transplanted via train to Louisiana. The museum, housed in an old depot building, has more than 200 photos and articles of clothing from the orphans who made the journey. ✉ *233 S. Academy St.* ☎ *337/948–9922* 🌐 *www.laorphantrain-museum.com* 🎟 *$5* 🕒 *Closed Sun. and Mon.*

Opelousas Museum and Interpretive Center
MUSEUM | This museum traces the history of Opelousas from prehistoric times to the present. There's an exhibit on the town's brief stint as state capital during the Civil War, and a collection of more than 400 dolls; exhibits of artists' works rotate every three months. The museum is also home to the Louisiana Video Library and the Southwest Louisiana Zydeco Festival archives. ✉ *315 N. Main St.* ☎ *337/948–2589* 🎟 *Free* 🕒 *Closed weekends.*

Opelousas Tourist Information Center
INFO CENTER | At the intersection of Interstate 49 and U.S. 190, look for the Opelousas Tourist Information Center, where you can get plenty of information, arrange for tours of historic homes, and see memorabilia pertaining to Jim Bowie, the Alamo hero who spent his early years in Opelousas. ✉ *828 E. Landry St.* ☎ *337/948–6263* 🌐 *www.cityofopelousas.com* 🕒 *Closed Sun.*

Weekend Antiques Hunting

Antiques lovers will want to stop in **Washington**, a short 2-mile detour from the main route if you're traveling from Opelousas to Ville Platte. Settled in 1720, Washington has many buildings on its main street that are on the National Register of Historic Places. About half a dozen antiques stores cluster within walking distance of one another. Most of these stores are open Friday to Sunday only.

Restaurants

Billy's Boudin & Cracklin
$ | **CAJUN** | You're probably not going to go to Billy's for your fanciest occasions (or if you're trying to eat healthy), but if you're looking for some amazing Cajun snacks with no frills, then this is the place for you. Go inside and order at the counter to see what they've serving that day or swing through the drive-thru if you're in a rush. **Known for:** pepperjack boudin balls; classic boudin; cracklins. [$] *Average main: $5* ✉ *904 Short Vine St.* ☎ *337/942–9150* 🌐 *www.billysboudin.com* 🕒 *No dinner Sun.*

Nightlife

The roads surrounding Opelousas are the best place in Cajun Country to catch authentic, sweaty zydeco music.

Arpeggios Lounge & Event Center
MUSIC CLUBS | If you're heading to Opelousas for music, give this downtown restaurant a visit. They serve breakfast and lunch on weekdays, but they also host live bands several Sunday nights each month. Just check with them before showing up to make sure they've got a performance scheduled

when you're there. ⊠ *204 N. Main St.*
☎ *337/407–5188.*

Evangeline Downs

MUSIC CLUBS | This racetrack and casino
also has two performance venues inside
its large, entertainment facility: Fast &
Lucy's Pub and the Event Center. The
latter is used for bigger, ticketed shows
while the former has live, no-cover gigs
happening just about every weekend.
It's an unexpected but exciting place to
get your zydeco fix. ⊠ *2235 Creswell Ln.*
☎ *866/472–2466* ⊕ *www.evangeline-*
downs.com.

St. Landry Parish Visitor Center

GATHERING PLACES | This award-winning
visitor center is worth a look, especially at 1 pm on the second and third
Saturdays of every month when it hosts
a zydeco jam session. Stop in to see how
this structure was built to tell the story of
St. Landry Parish, then hang out to enjoy
some of the region's most talented musicians. ⊠ *978 Kennerson Rd.* ☎ *337/984–*
8004 ⊕ *www.cajuntravel.com.*

Toby's Lounge & Reception Center

MUSIC CLUBS | It may be a 10-minute drive
outside of downtown, but Toby's Lounge
is packed with excited music-lovers of all
ages, making it worth the trip. Very few
Friday or Saturday nights go by that you
won't find a crowd jamming to live jazz,
zydeco, or Cajun music. Give them a call
to confirm who's playing and at what
time, and then get ready to hit the dance
floor—or at least to watch others dance
while you sip on your beverage of choice.
⊠ *132 Toby's Ln.* ☎ *337/948–3800.*

Eunice

20 miles southwest of Opelousas.

As home to some of Cajun music's most
prominent proponents and establishments, tiny Eunice lays claim to some
heft within the Cajun music world.
Saturday is the best time to visit: spend

the morning at a jam at the Savoy Music
Center; at midday move on for dancing
at Fred's Lounge; end the day at the
Rendez-Vous des Cajuns variety show, in
Eunice's Liberty Theater.

◉ Sights

Eunice Depot Museum

MUSEUM | This museum, in a former rail-
road depot, contains modest exhibits on
Cajun culture, including music and Mardi
Gras celebrations. ⊠ *220 S. CC Duson St.*
☎ *337/457–6540, 337/457–2565* ⊕ *www.*
eunice-la.com/historical-sites ⊠ *Free*
𝄢 *Closed Sun. and Mon.*

Prairie Acadian Cultural Center

MUSEUM | Part of the Jean Lafitte National
Historical Park, this impressive center
has well-executed exhibits tracing
the history and culture of the Prairie
Acadians, whose lore and customs
differ from those of the Bayou Acadians
south of Lafayette. Food, crafts, music,
dancing, cooking demonstrations,
language classes, and ranger talks are
held on Saturdays. ⊠ *250 W. Park Ave.*
☎ *337/457–7700* ⊕ *www.nps.gov/jela/*
prairie-acadian-cultural-center-eunice.htm
⊠ *Free* 𝄢 *Closed Sun.–Tues.*

★ Savoy Music Center and Accordion Factory

STORE/MALL | Part music store and part
Cajun accordion workshop, proprietor
Marc Savoy's factory turns out about five
specialty accordions a month for people
around the world. On Saturday mornings,
from 9 am until noon, accordionists and
other instrumentalists head here for a
Cajun jam session that has been attracting musicians from across the region for
40 years. Chairs are set up as well for
those who just want to stop by and enjoy
the music. ⊠ *4413 U.S. 190* ⊹ *3 miles*
east of town ☎ *337/457–9563* ⊕ *www.*
savoymusiccenter.com ⊠ *Free* 𝄢 *Closed*
Sun. and Mon.

Did You Know?

Plant life in the Louisiana swamps includes Spanish moss, cypresses, water oaks, and water hyacinths (members of the lily family).

Alligators Up Close: Swamp Tours

If you want to add unique wildlife sightings to your Cajun Country excursion, the bayous, swamps, and rivers of south Louisiana's wetlands present a tantalizingly unfamiliar landscape to many visitors, and the best way to get acquainted is by boat. Most tour operators use airboats or pontoon boats, but—depending on the size of the group—a bass boat might be used. Anticipate one to two hours on the water, with prices generally around $20 per person. Expect to see nutria, members of the rodent family that resemble beavers in appearance and size; egrets, white, long-necked herons with flowing feathers; turtles; and the occasional snake. During the warmer months, alligator sightings are common. Many of the guides use either chicken or marshmallows to attract them. In the summer months be prepared for the heat and humidity—and don't forget insect repellent and a hat.

Cajun Country Swamp Tours Tours are frequently led by guide Walter "Butch" Guchereau, who was born, raised, and still lives on the banks of Bayou Teche in Breaux Bridge. An experienced outdoorsman with a degree in zoology and biology, Guchereau uses Cajun crawfish skiffs for his tours to make them environmentally unobtrusive. His son Shawn also leads tours. ⌧ 1209 Rookery Rd., Breaux Bridge ☎ 337/319–0010 ⊕ www.cajuncountryswamptours.com ⏎ $20.

McGee's Louisiana Swamp & Airboat Tours Boats take passengers out daily for 90-minute tours of the Atchafalaya Basin. Tour times are contingent upon the presence of at least four passengers. McGee's is a 25-minute drive east of Lafayette. The company also organizes canoe and airboat trips, sunset tours, and photography excursions. ⌧ 1337 Henderson Levee Rd., Henderson ⊹ From I–10, Exit 115 at Henderson, turn left on Rte. 352 (1 block south of the highway) and follow it more than 2 miles east over Bayou Amy; turn right atop the levee onto Levee Rd. ☎ 337/228–2384 ⊕ www.mcgeesswamptours.com ⏎ From $30.

ⓨ Nightlife

BARS
★ Fred's Lounge
MUSIC | This bar is a Cajun Country institution, and is hopping on Saturday from about 9 am until about 2 pm—or for as long as the Cajun band jams and dancers crowd the tiny dance floor. A regular radio broadcast (on KVPI 1050 AM) captures the event. Drive north from Eunice on Route 13 to reach the tiny town of Mamou. ⌧ 420 6th St., Mamou ☎ 337/468–5411.

Rendez-Vous des Cajuns
CABARET | In addition to showcasing the best Cajun and zydeco bands, this two-hour variety program presents local comedians and storytellers and even a "Living Recipe Corner." The show, mostly in French, has been dubbed the "Cajun Grand Ole Opry"; it's held every Saturday at 6 pm in a 1924 movie house and is broadcast on local radio and TV. ⌧ Liberty Theater, 200 Park Ave. ☎ 337/457–7389 ⏎ $5.

EVENTS
Courir de Mardi Gras
FESTIVAL | The area surrounding Eunice is the major stomping ground for an annual

event, Courir de Mardi Gras, French for "Fat Tuesday Run," which takes place on Mardi Gras Day. Costumed horseback riders dash through the countryside, stopping at farmhouses along the way to shout, "*Voulez-vous recevoir cette bande de Mardi Gras?*" ("Do you wish to receive the Mardi Gras krewe?") The answer is always yes, and the group enlarges and continues, gathering food for the street festivals that wind things up. ✉ *Eunice.*

Southwest Louisiana Zydeco Music Festival
FESTIVALS | The town of Plaisance, on the outskirts of Opelousas, holds this event in a bean field on the Saturday before Labor Day. A parade, accordion contest, and zydeco breakfast are all part of the festivities. ✉ *Yambilee Festival Grounds, 1939 W. Landry St., Opelousas* ☎ *337/290–6048* 🌐 *www.zydeco.org* 🎫 *$15.*

Breaux Bridge

10 miles northeast of Lafayette, 20 miles southeast of Grand Coteau.

During the first full weekend in May, the Crawfish Festival draws more than 100,000 visitors to this little dyed-in-the-wool Cajun town on Bayou Teche. The town has attracted a small arts community and has traded its honky-tonks for B&Bs, antiques shops, and restaurants.

VISITOR INFORMATION

CONTACTS Chamber of Commerce. ✉ *314 E. Bridge St.* ☎ *337/332–5406* 🌐 *www.breauxbridgeacc.com.*

🍴 Restaurants

★ Buck & Johnny's
$$ | **CAJUN** | With its exposed brick interior and exterior, this Breaux Bridge eatery puts a spicy, Cajun twist on rich Italian classics. It's their world-famous Saturday morning zydeco brunch, however, that really brings in the visitors: locals and tourists swing by as early as 8 am to fill up on breakfast favorites and bottomless cocktails, and to dance to live local bands before making the rounds to other Cajun Country parties. **Known for:** live music Thursday through Saturday; crawfish enchiladas; Saturday morning dancing with bottomless cocktails. [$] *Average main: $21* ✉ *100 Berard St.* ☎ *337/442–6630* 🌐 *www.buckandjohnnys.com* 🕒 *No dinner Sun. and Mon.*

Poche's
$ | **CAJUN** | Order your authentic Cajun cooking at the counter of this butcher shop and lunchroom, then eat in or take away. The daily specials will always stick to your ribs. **Known for:** cracklings; Cajun sweet dough pies; stuffed chicken. [$] *Average main: $8* ✉ *3015 Main Hwy.* ☎ *337/332–2108* 🌐 *www.poches.com.*

🛏 Hotels

Bayou Cabins
$ | **B&B/INN** | These cozy one- and two-bedroom cabins are right on a main drag, but with their homey decor and shade from the property's many trees—and with some featuring porches facing Bayou Teche—they feel rustic and have personality galore. **Pros:** socializing with guests and locals in the café; good proximity to Breaux Bridge and Lake Martin; tasty breakfast included. **Cons:** you can hear the busy road nearby; cabins might be a little too rustic for some; a little far if trying to go out in Lafayette. [$] *Rooms from: $80* ✉ *100 W. Mills Ave.* ☎ *337/332–6158* 🌐 *www.bayoucabins.com* 🕒 *Café closed Mon. and Tues.* 🛏 *14 cabins* 🍽 *Free breakfast.*

Maison des Amis
$$ | **B&B/INN** | In this 19th-century house on the bank of Bayou Teche, rooms have either queen- or full-size beds covered with luxurious linens and pillows and

The charming waters of the Atchafalaya Basin are best seen via a boat tour.

private bathrooms with claw-foot tubs. **Pros:** bayou views; steps from downtown Breaux Bridge; local charm. **Cons:** breakfast is provided at a nearby restaurant, where you may have to wait; small property so call in advance to ensure a room; some private bathrooms are outside the rooms at the end of the hall. [$] *Rooms from: $135* ✉ *111 Washington St.* ☎ *337/507–3399* 🌐 *www.maisondes-amis.com* 🛏 *4 rooms* 🍴 *Free breakfast.*

🍸 Nightlife

★ La Poussière

BARS/PUBS | This ancient Cajun honky-tonk has live music on Saturday nights and Sunday afternoons. The bar is open with beers, wine, and cocktails, and the dance floor is always full. ✉ *1215 Grand Point Ave.* ☎ *337/332–1721* 🌐 *www.lapous-siere.com.*

Atchafalaya Basin

5 miles northeast of Breaux Bridge, 12 miles east of Lafayette.

The Atchafalaya Basin is an eerily beautiful 800,000-plus-acre swamp wilderness, the storybook version of mystical south Louisiana wetlands. Boating enthusiasts, bird-watchers, photographers, and nature lovers are drawn by vast expanses of still water, cypresses rising out of the marsh and dripping with Spanish moss, and blue herons taking flight. The basin is best viewed from one of the tour boats on its waters, but it's also possible to explore around its edges on the seven miles of Henderson Levee Road (aka Route 5; Exit 115 off Interstate 10), which provides several opportunities to cross the levee and access swamp tours, bars, and restaurants on the other side.

🍴 Restaurants

★ Pat's Fisherman's Wharf Restaurant
$$$ | CAJUN | Overlooking Bayou Amy, Pat's is the real deal, with heaping platters of seafood. On a cool night, get a table on the porch overlooking the bayou and go for the shrimp dinner, which presents the local favorite no fewer than eight different ways. **Known for:** great seafood platters; crab dinners; serene views. [$] *Average main: $24* ✉ *1008 Henderson Levee Rd., Breaux Bridge* ☎ *337/228–7512* 🌐 *www.patsfishermanswharf.com* 💳 *No credit cards.*

St. Martinville

15 miles south of Breaux Bridge.

St. Martinville, along winding Bayou Teche, is the heart of Evangeline country. It was founded in 1761 and became a refuge for Acadians expelled from Nova Scotia as well as royalists who escaped the guillotine during the French Revolution. Known as Petit Paris, this little town was once the scene of lavish balls and operas, and you can still see the original old opera house on the central square. St. Martinville is tucked away from the state's major highways and misses much of the tourist traffic. It's a tranquil and historically interesting stop, although neighboring towns are better for dining and nightlife. The St. Martinville Tourist Information Center is across the street from the Acadian Memorial and the African American Museum.

👁 Sights

Acadian Memorial
MUSEUM | A video introduction, a wall of names of Acadian Louisiana refugees, an audio tour, and a huge mural relate the odyssey of the Acadians. Behind the small heritage center containing these memorials, an eternal flame and the coats of arms of Acadian families pay tribute to their cultural and physical stamina. ✉ *121 S. New Market St.* ☎ *337/394–2258* 🌐 *www.acadianmemorial.org* 🎟 *$3, includes admission to African American Museum* 🕒 *Closed Sun. and Mon.*

★ African American Museum
MUSEUM | This museum traces the African and African American experience in south Louisiana. Videos, artifacts, and text panels combine to create a vivid, disturbing, and inspiring portrait of a people. It is an ambitious and refreshing counterpoint to the sometimes sidelined references to slavery and its legacy. ✉ *125 S. New Market St.* ☎ *337/394–2233* 🎟 *$3, includes admission to Acadian Memorial* 🕒 *Closed Sun. and Mon.*

Longfellow-Evangeline State Historic Site
HISTORIC SITE | Shaded by giant live oaks draped with Spanish moss, this 157-acre park has picnic tables and pavilions and early Acadian structures. The on-site museum traces the history of the Acadians and their settlement along the Bayou Teche in the early 1800s. The modest house was built in 1815 of handmade bricks, and it contains Louisiana antiques. An hour-long tour includes many interesting details about life on the plantation. ✉ *1200 N. Main St.* ☎ *337/394–3754, 888/677–2900* 🌐 *www.crt.state.la.us/louisiana-state-parks/historic-sites/longfellow-evangeline-state-historic-site* 🎟 *$4* 🕒 *Closed Mon. and Tues.*

St. Martin de Tours
RELIGIOUS SITE | The mother church of the Acadians and one of the country's oldest Catholic churches, this 1840 building was erected on the site of an earlier church. Inside is a replica of the Lourdes grotto and a baptismal font said to have been a gift from Louis XVI. Emmeline Labiche, who may have inspired Henry Wadsworth Longfellow's poem "Evangeline," is buried in the small cemetery behind the church. ✉ *133 S. Main St.* ☎ *337/394–6021* 🌐 *www.saintmartindetours.org.*

Hotels

Old Castillo Bed and Breakfast

$$ | B&B/INN | Comfortable rooms with hardwood floors and the odd early Louisiana antique occupy a two-story redbrick building that in the early 1800s was an inn for steamboat passengers and a gathering place for French royalists. **Pros:** right by a number of attractions; friendly staff; delicious breakfast. **Cons:** downstairs rooms are a bit noisy; decor is a little dated; 25-minute drive from Lafayette if that's your destination. *$ Rooms from: $180 ⊠ 220 Evangeline Blvd. ☎ 337/394–4010 ⊕ www.oldcastillo.com ⇗ 7 rooms ⦿| Free breakfast.*

New Iberia

10 miles south of St. Martinville.

The hub of lower Cajun Country is second only to Lafayette as an arts-and-culture draw. Grand homes of sugarcane planters dominate the residential section of Main Street, just off Bayou Teche, pointing to a glorious past as the center of a booming sugar industry. Park downtown or stay in one of the numerous B&Bs and you can easily walk to the bayou, restaurants, art galleries, and shops in the historic business district. Downtown stretches eight blocks east and west on Main Street (Route 182) from the intersection of Center Street (Route 14). The Shadows-on-the-Teche plantation home is at this intersection and is a good place to park.

◉ Sights

Bayou Teche Museum

MUSEUM | The story of New Iberia's Spanish colonial roots and the role of Bayou Teche in helping nurture Cajun culture are on display in this small, well-organized museum, housed in a historic building that was once a grocery. Interactive exhibits cover the area's history, its colorful characters, and its culture. The museum's interior layout is based on the snakelike curves of Bayou Teche itself. ⊠ 131 E. Main St. ☎ 337/606–5977 ⊕ www.bayoutechemuseum.org ⊠ $5 ⊙ Closed Sun.–Wed.

Conrad Rice Mill

FACTORY | The country's oldest rice mill that's still in operation, dating from 1912, produces distinctive wild pecan rice. Tours are conducted on the hour between 10 am and 3 pm. The adjacent **Konriko Company Store** sells Cajun crafts and foods. ⊠ 307 Ann St. ☎ 337/364–7242, 800/551–3245 ⊕ www.conradrice.com ⊠ Tour $4.

Shadows-on-the-Teche

HOUSE | One of the South's best-known plantation homes was built on the bank of Bayou Teche using slave labor for the wealthy sugar planter David Weeks in 1834. In 1917 his descendant William Weeks Hall conducted one of the first historically conscious restorations of a plantation home, also preserving truckloads of documents that helped explain day-to-day life here for the Weeks family, as well as for many of the people they enslaved. The result is one of the most fascinating tours in Louisiana, taking place hourly, every day except Sundays. Weeks Hall willed the property to the National Trust for Historic Preservation in 1958, and each year the trust selects a different historical topic to emphasize. Surrounded by 2½ acres of lush gardens and moss-draped oaks, the two-story rose-hue house has white columns, exterior staircases sheltered in cabinet-like enclosures, and a pitched roof pierced by dormer windows. The furnishings are 85% original to the house. ⊠ 317 E. Main St. ☎ 337/369–6446, 877/200–4920 ⊕ www.shadowsontheteche.org ⊠ $10.50 house and gardens; $8.50 gardens only ⊙ Closed Sun.

Avery Island

9 miles southwest of New Iberia.

The Louisiana coastline is dotted with "hills" or "domes" that sit atop salt mines, and Avery Island is one of these. They are covered with lush vegetation, and because they rise above the surface of the flatlands, they are referred to as islands. Avery Island is also the birthplace of Tabasco sauce, which pleases the Cajun palate and flavors many a Bloody Mary.

Sights

Bird City

NATURE PRESERVE | The bird sanctuary on the southeast edge of Jungle Gardens is sometimes so thick with egrets that it appears to be blanketed with snow. The largest egret colony in the world (20,000) begins nesting here in February or March, and offspring remain until the following winter. Herons and other birds find refuge here as well. ⌧ *Hwy. 329* ☎ *337/369–6243* ⊕ *www.junglegardens. org* ✉ *$8, $12.50 with Tabasco Visitors Center.*

Jungle Gardens

GARDEN | **FAMILY** | This 170-acre garden has trails through stands of wisteria, palms, lilies, irises, and ferns, and offers a lovely perspective on south Louisiana wilderness. Birdlife includes white egrets and Louisiana herons, and there's also a 900-year-old statue of Buddha. These gardens belonged to Edward Avery McIlhenny, the son of the Tabasco company's founder, who brought back plants from his travels: lotus and papyrus from Egypt, bamboo from China. You can park your car at the beginning of the trails and strike out on foot, or drive through the gardens and stop at will. ⌧ *Hwy. 329* ☎ *337/369–6243* ⊕ *www.junglegardens. org* ✉ *$8, $12.50 with Tabasco Visitors Center.*

Tabasco Factory

FACTORY | Tabasco was invented by Edmund McIlhenny in the mid-1800s, and the factory is still presided over by the McIlhenny family. Tabasco is sold all over the world, but it is aged, distilled, and bottled only here, on Avery Island (these days the peppers themselves are mostly grown in Central and South America). You can take a self-guided factory tour that lasts about an hour and a half and highlights the production process along with conservation efforts on the island. You can also grab a meal at the on-site Tabasco Restaurant 1868, which includes a Bloody Mary bar and a boatload of Cajun classics—all infused with your favorite varieties of Tabasco sauce, of course. The Jungle Gardens and Bird City are adjacent. ⌧ *32 Wisteria Rd.* ☎ *337/373–6129, 800/634–9599* ⊕ *www.tabasco.com* ✉ *$5.50, $12.50 with Jungle Gardens.*

Jefferson Island

4 miles from Avery Island, 9 miles from New Iberia.

Like Avery Island, Jefferson Island is actually a salt dome.

Sights

Rip Van Winkle Gardens

GARDEN | The highlight of a visit here is the magnificent 20-acre garden filled with semitropical vegetation and the sort of vistas that only a salt dome can offer in south Louisiana. A café looks over Lake Peigneur and provides a restful and picturesque spot for refreshments after exploring the gardens. Be on the lookout for the peacocks—if you're lucky, one of the males will open his feathers for you. Also on the grounds is the **Joseph Jefferson Home,** a highly idiosyncratic mansion that combines Steamboat Gothic, Moorish, and French-plantation styles. It was built as a country home for stage actor Joseph Jefferson in the mid-19th century and is open for 40-minute tours. There is also a bed-and-breakfast on the grounds. ✉ *5505 Rip Van Winkle Rd.* ☎ *337/359–8525* ⊕ *www.ripvanwinklegardens.com* 🎫 *$12 for house and garden tour.*

Erath

9 miles west of Jefferson Island.

The little town of Erath is a quintessential tiny Cajun village.

◉ Sights

Acadian Museum
MUSEUM | The Acadian Museum is filled to the rafters with memorabilia donated by local folks—antique radios, butter churns, patchwork quilts, and yellowed newspaper clippings are all part of the mix. ✉ *203 S. Broadway St.* ☎ *337/456–7729, 337/233–5832* ⊕ *www.acadianmuseum.com* 🎫 *Free (suggested donation)* ⊗ *Closed weekends.*

🍴 Restaurants

T-Bob's Seafood
$$ | SEAFOOD | If you want a truly authentic Cajun experience, eat at T-Bob's. It's like dining in someone's home—one that's filled with Cajun memorabilia. **Known for:** crawfish cooked to order; local vibe; boiled shrimp year-round. 💲 *Average main: $18* ✉ *109 E. Lastie St.* ☎ *337/937–4573* ⊗ *No lunch.*

Nightlife

Smiley's Bon Ami
DANCE CLUBS | Wilbert "Smiley" Menard operates this popular 1950s-style dance hall. On Sunday afternoons from 2 to 6 pm, an older crowd fills the dance floor, gliding to a live band in the way that only the elder generation of Cajun dancers

seems to have mastered. ✉ *2206 Veterans Memorial Dr.* ☎ *337/937–4591.*

Abbeville

15 miles south of Lafayette.

Abbeville has a number of historic buildings and three pretty village squares anchoring the center of downtown. It's a good stop for pleasant walks and for oysters on the half shell, a local obsession. The town sponsors the annual Giant Omelet Festival each November, and some 5,000 eggs go into the concoction. Abbeville is also the base for Steen's Cane Syrup.

Sights

St. Mary Magdalen Catholic Church
RELIGIOUS SITE | This fine Romanesque Revival building built in 1920 has stunning stained-glass windows. ✉ *300 Père Megret St.* ☎ *337/893–0244* ⊕ *www.stmarymagdalenparish.org.*

Vermilion Parish Tourist Commission
INFO CENTER | You can pick up information about the town of Abbeville and the entire parish at the Vermillion Parish Tourist Commission. Many buildings in Abbeville's 20-block Main Street district are on the National Register of Historic Places. ✉ *200 N. Magdalen Sq.* ☎ *337/898–6600* ⊕ *www.mostcajun.com* ⊗ *Closed Sun.*

🍴 Restaurants

Dupuy's
$$ | SEAFOOD | This small and simply furnished restaurant has been serving oysters in the same location since 1869. Seafood platters feature seasonal catches. **Known for:** fresh Gulf oysters; po'boys; seafood platters. 💲 *Average main: $20* ✉ *108 S. Main St.* ☎ *337/893–2336* ⊕ *www.dupuysoystershop.com* ⊗ *Closed Sun. and Mon. No lunch Sat.*

Richard's Seafood Patio
$$ | **CAJUN** | Cross the Vermilion River on a vintage drawbridge and continue down a winding country road to find this classic Cajun "seafood patio," a no-frills dining room serving immense quantities of boiled crawfish, shrimp, and crabs. There's a full menu of fried and grilled items—and cold beer. **Known for:** low-key setting; fresh shellfish; long waits. [$] *Average main: $18* ✉ *1516 S. Henry St.* ☎ *337/893–1693* ⏲ *Closed Sun. No lunch.*

Maurice

10 miles north of Abbeville, almost 11 miles south of Lafayette.

Maurice is considered the gateway to Vermilion Parish and lies between Lafayette and Abbeville. Many overlook this small town, but it's worth the stop for Hebert's Specialty Meats' world-famous turducken and the Maurice Flea Market.

🍴 Restaurants

Hebert's Specialty Meats
$ | **CAJUN** | A visit to Cajun country is not complete without a stop at Hebert's. This butcher shop is one of several contenders claiming credit for inventing turducken—a turkey stuffed with a duck that's stuffed with a chicken. **Known for:** original turducken; andouille sausage; great boudin. [$] *Average main: $14* ✉ *8212 Maurice Ave. (Rte. 167)* ☎ *337/893–5062* 🌐 *www.hebertsmaurice.com* ⏲ *No dinner Sun.*

👜 Shopping

Maurice Flea Market
ANTIQUES/COLLECTIBLES | From fine antiques to slightly rusted kitchen utensils, this is a treasure hunter's paradise. Be prepared to spend more than an hour at this unique store. ✉ *9004 Maurice Ave. (Rte. 167)* ☎ *337/898–2282* ⏲ *Closed Sun.–Tues.*

Index

Photo Credits

Front Cover: f11photo/Shutterstock [Description: Streetcar in downtown New Orleans, USA at twilight]. **Back cover, from left to right:** Sean Pavone/istockphoto, Mike Flippo/Shutterstock, Dudarev Sean Pavone/Shutterstock. **Spine:** Lori Monahan Borden/Shutterstock. **Interior, from left to right:** Rainer Puster/iStockphoto (1). Kruck20/iStockphoto (2). Pogs, Yayie and Me Street Dancing @ Mardi Gras, New Orleans 2011 by Dahon (5). **Chapter 1: Experience New Orleans:** f11photo/iStockphoto (6-7). Paul Broussard (8). Paul Broussard (9, Top Right). f11photo/Shutterstock (9). Wangkun Jia/Shutterstock (10). Michael Smith/Jonathan Ferrara Gallery (10). Ljoy25/Dreamstime (10). Allard1/Dreamstime (10). JAMES LANGE/Alamy (11). Walleyelj/Dreamstime (11). pisaphotography/Shutterstock (12). Audubon Nature Institute (12). Bacchanal Wine (12). Courtesy of MardiGrasNewOrleans.com (12). The National WWII Museum (13). Paul Broussard/New Orleans Convention and Visitors Bureau (14). Dbvirago | Dreamstime.com (14). Zack Smith Photography/New Orleans Convention and Visitors Bureau (14). Daniellenhassett/Dreamstime (14). Picturecorrect/Dreamstime (15). Andriy Blokhin | Shutterstock (15). Ezume Images/Shutterstock (20). DeliriumTrigger/Shutterstock (20). Cochonbutcher (20). Katie's Restaurant and Bar (21). NJKen/iStockphoto (21). Urban South Brewery (22). Brent Hofacker/Shutterstock (23). Meyer The Hatter (24). Giovanni Gagliardi/Dreamstime (24). Garden District Book Shop (24). PALACE MARKET (25). Courtesy of Jason Kruppa (25). Christian Ouellet/Dreamstime (26). Everett Historical/Shutterstock (26). Museum of Death (26). Andriy Blokhin/Shutterstock (27). J.Stephen Young/Bourbon Orleans Hotel (27). Alexandr Junek Imaging/Shutterstock (28). AllWays lounge & Cabaret (28). Nola Beer (28). Instagram Capture (28). Infrogmation (29). Crystal Shelton Photography (29). The Howling Wolf (29). Mid-City Lanes Rock'n'Bowl (29). **Chapter 3: The French Quarter:** Micha Weber (63). GTS Productions/Shutterstock (70). SeanPavonePhoto (72). Luis Castaneda / age fotostock (76). Pogs, Yayie and Me Street Dancing @ Mardi Gras, New Orleans 2011 by Dahon/Flickr, [CC BY 2.0] (77). Alvaro Leiva / age fotostock (78). Public domain (79). howieluvzus/Howie Luvzus/Flickr, [CC BY 2.0] (80). MGD07JaxSquareLBKitty by Infrogmation of New Orleans/Flickr, [CC BY 2.0] (82). Costumes by Mark Gstohl (82). Mardi Gras Indian (82). WWOZ 30th Birthday Parade Esplanade Avenue Royal Strutters 3 by Infrogmation of New Orleans/Flickr, [CC BY 2.0] (83). C P Orange Indian by Infrogmation of New Orleans/Flickr, [CC BY 2.0] (83). Paul Wood / Alamy (83). Molly Moker (84). Giuseppe Masci / age fotostock (97). Adalberto Ros Lanz / age fotostock (100). Travel Division Images / Alamy (114). **Chapter 4: Faubourg Marigny:** Heeb Christian / age fotostock (117). Marigny Mardi Gras 05 by Team at Carnaval.com Studios/Flickr, [CC BY 2.0] (121). **Chapter 5: The Bywater, St. Claude, and the Lower Ninth Ward:** Bernard Spragg. NZ/Flickr, [CC BY 2.0] (129). Page Light Studios/iStockphoto (132). Tulane Public Relations/Wikimedia (139). **Chapter 6: Tremé/Lafitte and the Seventh Ward:** Nazar Skladanyi (141). Molly Moker (146). Ruben Martinez Barricarte (148). Meinzahn | Dreamstime. com (150). Franz Marc Frei / age fotostock (152). jazz fest 2011 020 by djnaquin67 (153). Backstreet Cultural Museum in New Orleans by Ted Drake/Flickr, [CC BY 2.0] (153). Wikimedia Commons (153). Ellis Marsalis by Tulane Public Relations (153). Jim West / age fotostock (153). Herman Hiller/Library of Congress Prints & Photographs Division (154). Fritzel's European Jazz Pub by Ishwar (154). Wikimedia Commons (154). Soul Rebel @ Le Bon Temps Roule by Stephen Kennedy (155) Curley Taylor and Zydeco Trouble at the Dance Depot by Janet Spinas Dancer/Flickr, [CC BY 2.0] (155). ???/Kermit Ruffins and the Barbecue Swingers by Robbie Mendelson/Flickr, [CC BY 2.0] (156). Allen Toussaint by rickh710/Flickr, [CC BY 2.0] (156). Zjbrewer/Wikimedia Commons (156). DSC_0580.JPG by Linda Marie (156). Lionel Batiste Bass Drum by Infrogmation of New Orleans/Flickr, [CC BY 2.0] (157). Franz Marc Frei / age fotostock (157). jazz fest 2011 150 by djnaquin67 (158). AcuraStageCrowds by Infrogmation of New Orleans/Flickr, [CC BY 2.0] (158). New Orleans Jazz Fest 2009 by Ray Devlin/Flickr, [CC BY 2.0] (158). Jazzfest2010ThursMrOkraTruck by Infrogmation of New Orleans/Flickr, [CC BY 2.0] (159). **Chapter 7: CBD and Warehouse District:** Mardi Gras World New Orleans Jimi Hendrix/Flickr (163). New Orleans RTA Streetcar No. 2021 by vxla/Flickr, [CC BY 2.0] (167). SuperStock (172). easyFotostock / age fotostock (174). Café au l ait and beignets by Leo/Flickr, [CC BY 2.0] (175). Cathy Yeulet/Hemera/Thinkstock (176). marika (176). K Chelette/Shutterstock (177). Jupiterimages/Comstock Images/Thinkstock (177). **Chapter 8: The Garden District:** krblokhin/iStockphoto (193). Meinzahn (201). Women's Opera Guild House by Chris Waits/Flickr, [CC BY 2.0] (202-203). **Chapter 9: Uptown and Carrollton-Riverbend:** zimmytws/iStockphoto (211). Carl Purcell /New Orleans Convention and Visitors Bureau (212). St. Charle's street car by Chris Waits/Flickr, [CC BY 2.0] (213). St. Charles Avenue Streetcar, New Orleans, Louisiana by Ken Lund/Flickr, [CC BY 2.0] (213). Digital Roux Photography LLC/Audubon Nature Institute (220-221). **Chapter 10: Mid-City and Bayou St. John:** SnippyHolloW/Flickr, [CC BY-SA 2.0] (235). City Park Bayou Bridge by Infrogmation of New Orleans/Flickr, [CC BY 2.0] (239). Rmbarricarte | Dreamstime.com (244). **Chapter 11: Side Trips from New Orleans:** SeanPavonePhoto (251). Sean Pavone/Shutterstock (264). FRILET Patrick / age fotostock (275). Kathryn8/iStockphoto (278). Anton Foltin/Shutterstock (281). **About our writers:** All photos are courtesy of the writers except for the following: Cameron Quincy Todd, courtesy of Sara Todd.

Every effort has been made to trace the copyright holders, and we apologize in advance for any accidental errors. We would be happy to apply the corrections in the following edition of this publication.

Notes

Notes

Notes

Notes

Notes

Notes

Notes